Tibetan Civilization

Tibetan Civilization

R. A. STEIN

Professeur
Collège de France

translated by
J. E. Stapleton Driver

with original drawings by
Lobsang Tendzin

STANFORD UNIVERSITY PRESS
Stanford, California

Stanford University Press
Stanford, California
This translation © Faber and Faber Ltd, 1972
First published in the U.S.A. by Stanford University
Press in 1972
Printed in the United States of America
Cloth ISBN 0-8047-0806-1
Paper ISBN 0-8047-0901-7
Last figure below indicates year of this printing:
84 83 82 81 80 79 78 77 76 75

Consider ye the seed from which ye sprang;
Ye were not made to live like unto brutes,
But for pursuit of virtue and of knowledge.

Ulysses to his comrades
Dante, *Inferno,* Canto **XXVI**

Contents

9

CONTENTS

Illustrations

---❀---

PLATES

11

ILLUSTRATIONS

FIGURES

12

ILLUSTRATIONS

MAPS

13

Preface

Writing a book on Tibetan civilization might be thought an ambitious undertaking at this point in time, in fact rather a gamble. To start with, our knowledge is still highly incomplete. Tibetan studies as such are scarcely a hundred years old, and the number of scholars who have devoted themselves to the field is tiny. Most of them have never been able to visit Tibet, while the literary sources they might have consulted have always been scarce, often even unobtainable. Moreover, Tibetan civilization itself has naturally changed over the centuries—it dates back more than a millennium— and its aspect varies with differing regions and social *milieux*. On the other hand, a 'civilization' is a whole. Its distinctive character derives from the sum of its component parts. In other words, one needs to deal with everything—as much with diet as religion, with housing as the feudal system, with dress as with festivals. Not that any such comprehensive treatment could have been attempted in these pages. Our space is limited. But in any case, a systematic recital of all the facts with their historical and regional transformations would have resulted in something like a dictionary or textbook: no doubt very useful, but also somewhat indigestible, a dry and rather boring tale.

Nor was there any question of making a new book by summarizing nine or ten earlier books and repeating yet again what can be read anywhere. I have thought it more useful to draw upon Tibetan and Chinese writings as far as possible without at the same time neglecting the basic facts already reported by travellers or of course the admirable labours of learning that have already contributed so much to our knowledge of Tibet. The choice of subject-matter, documentation and facts has been made with the aim of giving an overall view of what strikes me as significant. And a guiding principle

15

has been the hope that this book may serve the needs of both the non-specialist educated reader and those wishing to make a closer study of the material.

Ideally, each period and region should have been treated separately; and eventually specialist works will concern themselves with achieving this. However that day has not yet arrived. It is seldom that we can draw up a full inventory for each period or trace a given element of civilization down through the ages. The approach I have adopted, therefore, combines the diachronic and synchronic points of view, allowing our attention to move freely from one period to another. And though my choice here has doubtless been dictated by the state of our information, I have felt it to be the right one because of my impression that, for all its changes, this civilization displays enough individuality and homogeneity to be contemplated in a single sweep. I consider, too, that such an overall view is what the non-specialist reader is looking for and needs at present. In addition, I have particularly tried to show how the Tibetans themselves look upon the different aspects of their civilization, wherever this has been possible.

It has been my exceptional good fortune to be able to ask a Tibetan, Lobsang Tendzin, to illustrate the book in his own way. His drawings strike me as both charming and interesting; for as well as providing accurate evidence on various subjects they convey a good idea of the traditional style. I am glad to express my gratitude for this collaboration, and I must also thank all those who have been good enough to supply photographs of Tibet and the Tibetan friends whose unpublished information has often filled gaps in our knowledge.

I have long hesitated over the need to find an adequate method of transcribing Tibetan names. The ideal solution would have been a letter-for-letter representation of the Tibetan spelling. But in most cases a transliteration of this kind reduces the general reader to despair and makes the names hard for him to remember. It is not possible, either, to give easy rules for its pronunciation; for this differs considerably from the orthography. So the course I have adopted is to give the names of people and places, and a few common words, in a simplified transcription that more or less corresponds to present-day *pronunciation*. It is only a makeshift to be sure but it approximates to that taken by maps and newspapers which have popularized a certain number of geographical names. These transcriptions are in roman type. A slight effort will still be required of the reader since some letters in this system are used with their English values and others with their German and Italian ones. The rules to remember are as follows:

> *a, e, i, o,* and *u* are pronounced as in Italian (final *e* is never silent: both 'Ode' and 'Guge' are words of two syllables. I use *ê* to distinguish a long, broader 'e' sound, as in English 'where'.
>
> *ö* and *ü* as in German.
>
> *j, ch* and *sh* have their usual English values.
>
> *g* is always hard (as in German), even before *e* and *i*. Thus 'Derge' does *not* rhyme with English 'merge', but sounds rather like 'dare gay'.
>
> *ph* is not an *f*, but *p* followed by a puff of breath or aspiration, as *p* often is in English.
>
> *th* is similarly a strongly aspirated *t* (and not like *th* in English *thin* or *this*).
>
> *kh* is likewise a strongly aspirated *k*.
>
> *p, t* and *k* are never aspirated (unlike their English equivalents), and this sometimes makes them sound like *b, d* and *g* to English ears.

All other transcriptions of Tibetan words, including the titles of books, appear in italics (as do Sanskrit terms): they represent a strict transliterated form and will be readily understood by specialists. To facilitate identification by the latter class of readers, the simplified spellings used are listed alphabetically in the table of proper names at the end of the book (pages 293–303) with an exact transliteration of the Tibetan orthography against each entry. It is for the benefit of specialist readers, too, that I have added footnotes supplying references to the Tibetan and Chinese sources, or occasionally to modern works in which they are quoted. The numbers in the footnotes correspond to entries in the Bibliography on pages 305–316: thus '150, ff. 189*b*–190*a*' means: 'Consult item No. 150 in the Bibliography, referring to folios 189 (*verso*) and 190 (*recto*) of the work listed there'. In the case of works by modern authors, I have generally refrained from giving chapter and verse at every turn from a wish to avoid the needless proliferation of notes. I have confined myself to listing them in the Bibliography. Similarly I have added to this list a certain number of works that may be recommended to the reader seeking further information. In the Tibetan-language section of the Bibliography, which will scarcely be intelligible to non-specialists anyway, the 'simplified' phonetic spellings are not used at all.

Preface to English Edition

Nine years have gone by since this book was first written. As in every field of study, new documents have of course become available during that period and new research work has been done by scholars in various countries. The book could therefore have been expanded and made more bulky. But as I said in my original preface, my aim in writing it was to give an overall view of Tibetan civilization and not to produce a complete manual of Tibetan studies. A number of necessary adjustments have been made, new information has been made use of, and two paragraphs have been added to the historical survey to bring it up to the present. Otherwise, I believe the book remains up to date as far as our knowledge of Tibet goes.

R. A. Stein

September 1971

1

Habitat and Inhabitants

The area occupied by the Tibetans as representatives of a well-defined culture falls within the following bounds. To the south, the line of the Himalayas curves down from west to east (taking in Nepal, Sikkim and Bhutan on its way) till it reaches the point where Assam (India), upper Burma and Yünnan (China) meet. To the west, this same curve continues into Kashmir and Baltistan and from there, northwards, to Gilgit and the Karakorum mountains. Of Tibet's westernmost province, Ladakh, the greater part belongs politically to India. To the north, the Karakorum and Kunlun ranges mark off the Tibetan area from Chinese Turkestan, a desert region with large, populous oases. Whilst to the east, Tibet extends as far as the Kansu corridor (which links China proper with Chinese Turkestan), incorporating the Koko Nor region and, further south, overlapping the mountainous part of western China, the Sino-Tibetan borderland—an area largely peopled by aboriginals whose languages are allied to Tibetan. All this eastern part has been treated as two Chinese provinces (Tsinghai and Sikang) for many years. But for many years, too, the whole of Tibet has effectively been incorporated into China from the political point of view, though until recently it has retained internal self-government under a Tibetan administration.

REGIONS AND LOCALITIES

The central part of the country—the region to which Tibetans give the name *Bod* (pronounced Pö) from which our word 'Tibet' is derived—lies on either side of an axis formed by the Tsangpo. This great river rises near Mt Kailāśa (the Indian name; Tise in Tibetan) and Lake Manasarowar (Tibetan Mapham) in the west of the

19

region. After flowing to the east, it leaves Tibet with a great sweep southwards into Assam, where its name changes to Brahmaputra. The two most important provinces are found along this river: Tsang, the more westerly, on both sides of the stream, with its great towns of Shigatse and Gyantse; and its neighbour Ü where, north of the Tsangpo, in the broad, fertile valley of its tributary the Kyichu, stands the Tibetan capital, Lhasa. Further eastward, near the Tsangpo's great bend, there are three districts, Dakpo, Kongpo and Nyang, which the Tibetans customarily mark off from the rest by naming them as a group. Like two other districts to the south of the Tsangpo, Yarlung and Lhotrak—which witnessed the first emergence of a Tibetan state—these three are especially suitable for cultivation and rich in forest-land. They border on the tribal fringes of Assam, upper Burma and Yünnan.

The source of the Tsangpo lies quite close to those of two other major rivers flowing in the opposite direction, from east to west, and then turning south, the Indus and the Sutlej. They cross 'Lesser Tibet', the area comprising Ngari Korsum (the 'three districts of Ngari' *viz.* Guge, Mar-yül and Purang) and Ladakh. The latter in turn communicates with Kashmir and, through Baltistan, with Gilgit.

The north of the country consists entirely of the great 'Northern Plain' (Changthang), a huge elevated plateau criss-crossed with mountain ranges and liberally scattered with salt lakes, particularly in the west. While a great deal of it is desert, it does contain grazing lands of vast extent though generally rather poor quality. On the north-east, it adjoins the wide grassy salt-fen of Tsaidam and, further round, Amdo. Amdo occupies the whole of north-eastern Tibet, including the great lake of Koko Nor and the entire upper course of the Yellow River (Chinese Hwang ho; Tibetan Machu), and is enclosed to the south by the Bayan Kara range. South of these mountains, again, stretches Kham, covering all eastern Tibet and marching with the Chinese provinces of Szechwan and Yünnan. Here are the mighty rivers of the Far East, almost parallel as they flow from north to south with high mountain ranges to keep them apart, their upper, middle and lower reaches bearing different Tibetan and Chinese names—the Salween, the Mekong, the Kinsha kiang (which becomes the Yangtze) and the latter's great tributary, the Yalung kiang. This land is divided into numerous districts some of which used to have the status of self-governing principalities.

REGIONS AND LOCALITIES

Special note should be made of Derge, a great cultural centre, and the still almost unknown area of Poyül or Powo, covered with virgin forest, which borders on Kongpo.

The Sino-Tibetan border country of eastern Kham is inhabited by a vast collection of aboriginal peoples most of whom are related, in language at least, to the Tibetans: the Ch'iang (K'iang), Jyarung, Lolo and Nakhi (or Moso), to name only the more important groups.

All this adds up to a tremendous amount of space. With its one and a half million square miles, the region covers over fifteen times the area of Great Britain; but its population is a scant three and a half or four million. It is common knowledge that Tibet is the world's highest country, with its settlements often as much as 10,000 feet above sea-level, its roads crossing 15,000-foot passes, and its highest mountains towering to 25,000 feet and more. We usually picture it, also, as a very cold, wild, inhospitable country. However, this impression must be corrected at once. Tibet's latitude is the latitude of Algeria, and it is far from true that the whole region is a mere wilderness of snow. This reputation results from the accounts of explorers who had to follow routes far removed from the inhabited areas in order to make survey-maps of unknown territory, or because they were not authorized to enter Tibet. True, we have the largely desert Changthang region in the north. And the habitable area is considerably reduced by huge mountain ranges which force caravan-routes to cross gruelling passes. Some like the Nyenchen Thanglha range run from west to east, north of the Tsangpo or north-east of Lhasa. Some stretch from north to south, in eastern Tibet. But in most plains and valleys, of whatever size, there are fields, hillside pastures or woodlands. There must have been a time when these last were more widespread, covering places where erosion has left only bare, rounded summits. What remain are copses and patches of woodland, as at Reting, north of Lhasa. South-east Tibet (especially Poyül) contains true virgin forests of great age where the trees reach gigantic proportions.

Up in the mountains the winter is long and hard, but it is made very tolerable in the valleys and plains by the extraordinary amount of daily sunshine. Rainfall is sparse, save in the eastern valleys whose alignment lays them open to the monsoon coming up from the south by way of Assam and Yünnan, and some of the southern

21

valleys where the monsoon bursts through gaps in the Himalayas. For agricultural needs any deficiency in the water-supply is made up from the thawing snows and from glacier streams. The spring winds indeed threaten the land with swift impoverishment, sweeping away the fine, fertile particles of arable soil. For this the farmer prepares in autumn by watering his fields, which has a binding effect on the moistened earth, especially after frost. Then again, hailstorms threaten the crops. But the village sorcerer is there to ward them off.

In short, there can be no generalizing. The lie of the valleys and the folds of the mountain ranges, as well as the particular latitude and altitude of a place, give rise to a host of micro-climates with a vast diversity of local conditions. And this is evident not only in the natural surroundings but also in the activities of the communities that live in them. 'Every ten "li" (i.e. every three miles) heaven is different,' according to the maxim reported by an eighteenth-century Chinese traveller; and 'each district has its way of speaking, each Lama his way of teaching,' rejoins a current proverb. Significantly it is the word for 'valley' (*lung-pa*) which is used in this proverb, as in folklore and the spoken language, to express the idea of a 'country' or 'district'.

Everywhere one finds the juxtaposition of different environments that gives Tibetan society one of its most important characteristics, a two-fold structure governing the separate groupings within the society and their way of life. If we set out to define major natural sub-regions of the area as a whole, meaningful for the people living there, about the only real contrast to emerge is that of two types: the inhabited regions, and the uninhabitable, comprising deserts and mountain peaks. Possibly we might go on to distinguish the east-west strip of predominantly pastoral and nomadic land that runs across the north of the country, at the edge of the desert plateau and in Amdo. It is interesting to note, however, that the inhabitants here are either non-Tibetans (Mongols mostly) or Tibetans of still discernible foreign origin (e.g. the Hor people). But everywhere else there is the same dual morphology of contrasted yet complementary natural environments which we may sum up in the opposing terms mountain pasture and sown field, grazing and agriculture. Often one and the same group will alternate between these two environments according to the season. Sometimes the two are inhabited by groups differing from one another not only in their way of life but even in ethnic type. We shall return to this point later.

Having briefly taken our bearings, let us next study some of the most typical regions and localities.

First, and distinct from the remainder of inhabited Tibet, there are the great stretches of grassland where herdsmen with their tent-dwellings range over a given area. In the north and north-east, particularly, there are no trees, just grass and, in the way of animal life, the wild yak and hemione or wild ass (*equus kiang*). Domesticated animals comprise the yak, yak-and-cow hybrids, goats, sheep and Mongolian ponies. From the region north of Saka in the west as far as Koko Nor or Amdo in the east such conditions are the general rule. Another great stretch of the type occurs around Riwoche and Lhari. The only vegetable foodstuff man finds on these grassy plains is the silverweed (*gro-ma*), a species of *potentilla* or cinquefoil with a kind of floury root that marmots hoard in their holes. To hunt the marmots, to live on them and their potentilla, this—the epics have much to say on the matter—is to lead the wretched life of an exile.

Against this type, there are a few regions where there is no sign of grazing or stock-breeding, only cultivation: the Gyamda district of Kongpo, the Kyichu plain, and indeed such other plains as there are.

Nearly everywhere else, inhabited places extend down valleys in zones corresponding to the altitude, with pastures (*'brog*, pronounced drok) on the upper slopes and fields chiefly along the valley bed (*rong*). Often there are trees growing between the two levels and there men live as fruit-gatherers.

Reading how a ninth-century official, sent to Amdo (district of Dzorge and the T'ao ho) to collect taxes, seized a fief for himself instead, we are also told of the ten virtues of this land. There are two virtues in its grass, one good for meadows near home, the other for more distant pasture; two virtues in its soil, earth to build houses and good earth for the fields; two virtues in its water, for drinking and irrigation; two virtues in its stones, good for building and for mill-stones; two virtues in its wood, timber for building and firewood: a land ideal for agriculture, and at the same time good for pasturing flocks[1]. Much later, in 1582, when the Tibetan chieftain of Dzorge presented himself to the Emperor of China (Wan li) for investiture,

[1] 150, ff. 189b–190a.

he was given authority over the forest-dwelling (*nags-pa*) 'savages', i.e. aboriginals, of the district.[1]

In the chronicles and in epic literature, the region of Amdo is described as the home of 'mountain-dwellers' (*ri-pa*) and 'dwellers in the plain' (thang-pa),[2] while a little farther north Minyak is inhabited by 'grass-men' (*rtsa-mi*) and woodsmen (*shing-mi*).[3]

These 'grass-men' and all Amdo have long been famous for their splendid horses. Another strain of fine horses is reported in Poyül (Powo) and Kongpo. With horse-breeding, in these south-eastern provinces, goes the rearing of the celebrated small pigs[4] that are also one of the products for which Dakpo is famous. There are no pigs in the north and the country folk of Amdo loathe pork. But in the south, large herds are raised in the wooded lands of Dakpo. The earliest annals known to us tell of sixth-century conspirators against the king hiding by day in the hollow trees of Swine Wood (*phag-tshal*) near the royal castle of Chingkar, in Yarlung.[5] And in the oath taken by the king and his minister, they swear never to separate, like pigs and fowl (hens of a small breed are reared at Riwoche, Ngemda and Lhasa, and in Poyül, always in the company of pigs; whereas Amdoan folk have no hens and never eat eggs). The Tibetan deity of hearth and home has a pig's head: not an image to be attributed to the herders of larger beasts, in the grassy northern plains. Yet the antiquity of this feature is proven. Ancient Chinese texts affirm that the Tibetans, and their neighbours and kinsmen the Ch'iang, reared pigs. It is interesting too that the staple cereal of the Tibetans, barley—which in the expression used by the texts has ears 'with six points' (six-rowed barley)—originated in the same region of south-eastern and eastern Tibet.[6]

Barley is particularly suited to Tibetan conditions because it will grow at altitudes as high as 15,000 feet, which means that it can be cultivated almost anywhere. But there are plenty of other crops too, wheat, buckwheat, oats, peas, mustard and an assortment of vegetables. There is even a second harvest in some regions: barley with

[1] *Ibid.*, f. 193*b*.
[2] 142, *PA*, f. 107.
[3] *Ibid.*, *JA*, ff. 22*b*, 65*b*.
[4] *Ibid.*, *PA*, ff. 127*b*–128*a* for the pigs; personal informants and 99, p. 497, for the horses.
[5] 6, p. 104.
[6] 59, p. 208, n. 117.

rye or wheat at Kyirong (south-west of Trashilhünpo); barley with millet in the Rechu and Raga Tsangpo valleys; and rice with barley in Kongpo.[1] And delicacies are available that suggest at once a wide diversity of climate and environment.

In the eighteenth century, white grapes were grown at Batang (along with pomegranates, peaches, plums and nectarines), at Draya and Ngemda (where nuts were also to be had), and south of Lhasa at Chunggye (in addition to nuts and bamboos).[2] The Jesuit missionaries who settled in Lhasa at the beginning of the eighteenth century used Dakpo grapes to make their sacramental wine. As early as 1374 the (?) Chaori district of Kham boasted 350 families whose long established profession was the production of wine from grapes.[3] Tibetans nowadays only use the grape in raisin form, as a sweetmeat, their customary alcoholic drink being barley-beer (*chang*). But for the Bonpo ritual described in ancient manuscripts (ninth or tenth century), a fermentation of wheat was used, with another of grapes, a third of rice and a fourth of honey.[4] The treasury of the eighth-century king Trhisong Detsen contained, according to a fairly old chronicle,[5] an alcoholic beverage made of rice from the land of Mon (Himalayas) and another made of grapes from Tshawa(-rong). A comparable pattern prevails at the western end of the Tibetan world today, with barley-beer in Ladakh, rice 'beer' or spirit in Lahul, and grape 'beer' or liquor in Kunawar.

Honey belongs to the woodlands of the south-east. It is found in Poyül (Powo), Kongpo and the area between Ngemda and Chödzong. In Kongpo in the fifteenth century, the sage Thangtong was offered mead and barley-beer by the master of Tsari.[6] The same regions produce wheat and rice: rice at Chamdo, at Gyamda in Kongpo, from Ngemda to Chödzong, and in Ngari. Ngari is also famous for its jujube fruit and apricots, and the Tsethang district in Yarlung for its apples and pears.[7]

Besides its grapes, nuts, peaches and small apples, its good pastureland and its horses, Dakpo is remarkable for the shrub, a

---

[1] 24, p. 10; 196, *shang*, p. 27. For Kongpo, oral information.
[2] 193, f. 18*b*; 203, *hsia*, f. 15*a*.
[3] 192, T'ai-tsu, hung-wu, 7th year, 7th moon.
[4] 64, p. 13.
[5] 177, f. 92*a*.
[6] 135, f. 68*a*.
[7] 203, *hsia*; 194, *hsia*.

species of *daphne*, whose fibres are used in making Tibetan paper (*dvags-shog*), for junipers, and for the pines that produce resin for a well-known glue. Kongpo produces bamboo (the shoots are eaten,

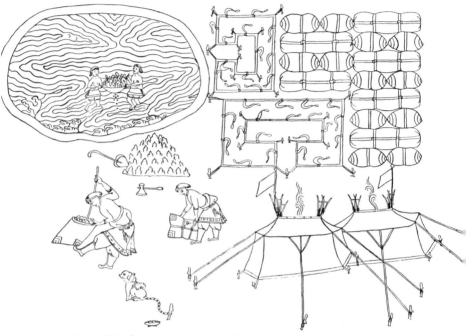

FIG. 1. Herdsmen gathering salt from the Changthang lakes. Yak-fold and bales of salt. Foreground: tents, with muskets fastened to the poles.

and the wood made into bows, arrows and spears) and cinnamon. Powo is famous for its bamboo and spices too. The gathering of medicinal herbs plays a large part there, as it does in the wooded mountains of the Sino-Tibetan border.

From these few examples may be seen what variety exists throughout. The alternation and overlapping of varied habitats, the juxtaposition of different ways of life and at times the coexistence of distinct ethnic groups impart a duality—sometimes a yet more complex structure—to Tibetan civilization.

PEOPLES

It is its civilization that unifies Tibet. In doing so it overlays a wide

26

assortment of elements, as we know already in connection with sub-climates, plant life and dwelling sites, dialects and customs. Much the same is true of ethnic make-up. Different racial types live side by side or coalesce. The predominant strain in most cases is Mongoloid, but many travellers have been struck by the prevalence of what they describe as a 'Red Indian' type (in Kongpo, among the Hor nomads, and in Tatsienlu). Others have noted a European, 'Hellenic' or Caucasian element which seems sometimes to be identical with the preceding type, and sometimes to denote a separate type altogether, especially in north-eastern Tibet. A dwarfish type occurs in Chala, a district of Kham. Though all these are but impressions, the fact that different groups exist is plain. According to travellers with no special claim to scientific knowledge, the brachycephalic type predominates in the farming communities of the Brahmaputra valley and in the south-east. In Ladakh, it would appear to have been superimposed on a dolichocephalic strain (no doubt Dards). Northerners, as in the Changthang lakes region—the Hor and Golok people—are themselves dolichocephalic, on the other hand. However, anthropologists merely distinguish two types: one distinctly Mongoloid and of slight build, spread throughout Tibet, and the other, of taller build, typical of Kham. Blue-eyed 'blond' types have also been observed in the north-east.

The explanation really is that different populations have occupied various parts of Tibet in the course of history, and to a certain extent remain there still. We have mentioned the 'savages' of the Amdo forests and can include also the Lo (written *Glo* or *Klo*) of Kongpo who still controlled the road to Tsari and the iron mines in that district during the fifteenth century before being 'tamed' by the sage Thangtong. The herdsmen living in the pasture-lands are often of a different ethnic group from the others, and the name given them (Drokpa, spelt *'brog-pa*) is often contrasted with Pöpa (*Bod-pa*), 'Tibetan', as though it referred to foreigners. This fact struck the Moslem traveller Mirza Haidar when he visited Ladakh in 1531.[1] In that region, the term might well describe the Dards.

The origin of the Tibetans is still a mystery. Theories put forward about it are based on all sorts of observations—ethnographic, linguistic, etc.—and postulate various migrations of different peoples. We shall confine ourselves here to the picture that can be

[1] 90, pp. 90–92.

sketched out at the dawn of their history when, around the seventh century or slightly earlier, Tibetans became recognizable as such.

According to their own legend, the Tibetans' first ancestors were a forest-monkey and a demoness of the rocks. Sothang (*Zo-thang*), the meeting-place of this couple, is generally thought to have been in the valley of Yarlung, south of the Tsangpo. But this identification is probably motivated by a wish to place the nation's origins in the district where the first kings appeared. Other traditions set the story in Poyül (Powo), further to the east but equally famed for its forests. The Chinese of the latter half of the eighth century even seem to have believed that the place was considerably further north. It is in the south-east, again, that tradition places the spot where Nyatri Tsenpo, the first legendary king, came down from heaven. The place hallowed by his descent is a sacred mountain. About this too tradition is uncertain. It is usually thought to have been north of Yarlung. But even in ancient times this 'mountain where the god descended' (*lha-bab ri*) had been localized further north between Nyang and Kongpo, where there is another mountain, Ode Kunggyel, connected with the same legend.[1]

Later, when the death of Trigum brings the first break in the celestial line of kings, the legendary setting shifts to the three south-eastern provinces. The king's corpse is cast into the Nyangchu and floats as far as Kongpo. His three sons flee from the usurper into Kongpo, Powo and Nyang. And the son who restores the royal line, when the usurper is killed, is fetched back from Powo.

Tradition, in short, suggests that the first Tibetans had their homes in the south-east, in mountainous country covered with forests (inhabited by monkeys) that was comparatively warm and suitable for agriculture—the first cultivated field was at Sothang, and we know from other sources that Yarlung is the most fertile district of Tibet. It was also the cradle of royal power.

According to other Tibetan traditions from Amdo, the land of monkeys and rock demonesses was Amdo itself. The forest zone does in fact stretch the whole length of eastern Tibet. Moreover the six 'original clans', the first descendants of the ancestral monkey and she-demon, may all be placed more or less in the east of the country. But, although the Tibetans consider them their ancestors, they always describe them as 'wild' people, or non-Tibetan aboriginals.[2]

[1] 115, pp. 82–84.
[2] 115, pp. 27, 32, 48.

Here the opinion of ancient Chinese historians comes in. According to them, the Tibetans proper, the T'u-fan, whose kings united the country at the beginning of its history, are a branch of the Ch'iang. The Ch'iang are mentioned in Chinese sources from about 1400 B. C. to modern times. To start with, they were the western neighbours of Shang and Chou dynasty China at her north-western extremity. From the beginning of the Christian era they lived on the Sino-Tibetan marches from Koko Nor to Szechwan. By the time the Tibetan (T'u-fan) royal line appeared in Yarlung, two important nations with Ch'iang populations occupied the region that is now Kham, eastern Tibet. These were the eastern 'Land of Women' (there was another in the west), and the land of Fu (originally something like Biu). The Ch'iang were in contact with another people of north-eastern Tibet, the Sumpa (Tibetan) or Su-pi (Chinese); while further north, in what is now Amdo, they mingled with a Turco-Mongol race from Manchuria, the Asha (Tibetan) or T'u-yü-hun (Chinese), who had established a kingdom there. This mixed population, whose country the Tibetans called Minyak, lived in the region of Koko Nor and north-west China, and set themselves up as the state of Hsi Hsia from 1032 to 1226. In the same region earlier on, before the arrival of these Turco-Mongol tribes, the Ch'iang had absorbed the remnants of an Indo-European people, the Yüeh-chih, who had been driven west at the beginning of our era. These Tokharians or Indo-Scythians founded important states whose traces survive on the western boundaries of Tibet. Ch'iang groups still live today in the mountains of the Sino-Tibetan borderland. And their language, beliefs and customs are akin to those of Tibet. As early as the seventh century they claimed to be descended from a monkey, as Tibetans did. A considerable portion of their ideas about Heaven and ancestry, in which a white sheep and a monkey play leading parts, is shared with the Tibetans. From the seventh century onwards Chinese historians associate these people with monumental stone structures, like towers or fortresses, which are still often found among them, but are also to be seen in Kongpo and Lhotrak (in south-eastern Tibet), and are apparently the prototypes of Tibetan architecture in general.

The picture we should have of the early Tibetans, then, is somewhat different from that frequently evoked by talk of nomads, yak-herds and horse-breeders, on the steppes of the high northern plateaux. We have rather to imagine hill pastures, above thick forests, and men at home in both environments. Not that the great grazing-lands of the north were slow in being absorbed by Tibetan civilization. Once the royal line at Yarlung had sprung into existence, its power spread rapidly to the north-east. Sumpa and Asha were conquered and rapidly absorbed (seventh and eighth centuries), ending up as no more than Tibetan clans and districts. Hence it comes about that texts of a slightly later date give long folk sagas of the hostility between the horse and the yak.

FIG. 2. Muleteer wearing Nyarong herdsmen's hat. The two leading mules of a caravan.

Our name 'Tibet', still unexplained, may be the result of confusion arising from the overlaying of the Turco-Mongol races of the north-east by Tibetans from further south. The name Tibetans give their country, *Bod* (now pronounced Pö in the Central dialect, as we have seen), was closely rendered and preserved by their Indian neighbours to the south, as Bhoṭa, Bhauṭa or Bauṭa. It has even been suggested that this name is to be found in Ptolemy and the *Periplus Maris Erythraei*, a first-century Greek narrative, where the river Bautisos and a people called the Bautai are mentioned in connexion with a region of Central Asia. But we have no knowledge of the existence of Tibetans at that time.

The Chinese, well informed on the Tibetans as they were from the

seventh century onwards, rendered Bod as Fan (at that time pronounced something like B'įwan). Was this because Tibetans sometimes said 'Bon' instead of 'Bod', or because 'fan' in Chinese was a
common term for 'barbarians'? We do not know. But before long,
on the testimony of a Tibetan ambassador, the Chinese started using
the form T'u-fan, by assimilation with the name of the T'u-fa, a
Turco-Mongol race, who must originally have been called something
like Tuppat.[1] At the same period, Turkish and Sogdian texts
mention a people called 'Tüpüt', situated roughly in the north-east of
modern Tibet. This is the form that Moslem writers have used since
the ninth century (Tübbet, Tibbat, etc.). Through them it reached
the mediaeval European explorers (Piano-Carpini, Rubruck, Marco
Polo, Francesco della Penna).

Settlement of new races among old, then, is clearly responsible for
the complex anthropological picture we have today, which can only
be understood by taking population movements into account. The
map of Tibet given here (Map II, pp. 86–87) only serves as a general
frame of reference. Dozens more would be needed to show how the
situation changed over the years. Regular marriage-links existed
between different peoples. The (Tibeto-Burman) Ch'iang and the
(Turko-Mongol) T'u-yü-hun or Asha exchanged brides one with the
other; and the clan-name T'o-pa, originally Tubbat, occurs in both.
The same relationship held between the Sumpa and the Ch'iang of
the eastern Land of Women. These Sumpa, in turn, carried their
raids as far as Khotan and Chinese Turkestan. They must have been
in touch with the western Land of Women, of which we shall have
more to say later.

Political and administrative developments also brought about
shifts of population. After their submission to the Tibetans of the
Yarlung royal dynasty, the Sumpa were assigned to guard the
eastern frontier in Minyak, now Amdo, facing China. In the ninth
century, the remnants of the Tibetan army sent against the Bhata
Hor (Uighurs) of Kanchow turned into nomadic tribes. The Chinese
present them as a group of communities dispersed from Kanchow
in the north to Sungpan in the south. Little groups speaking the same
dialect (*wa-shul, wa-skad*) seem to be their modern counterpart. They
are not a homogeneous grouping in one territory but scattered and
dotted among other groups over a considerable area.

[1] 197B, f. 1*a*; 191, *shang*, f. 18*a*.

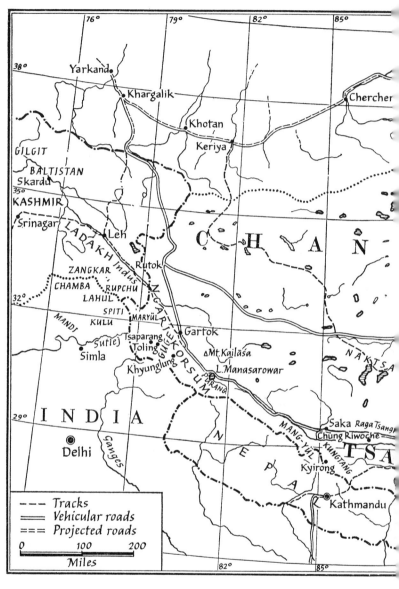

I. Modern Tibet and her neighbou

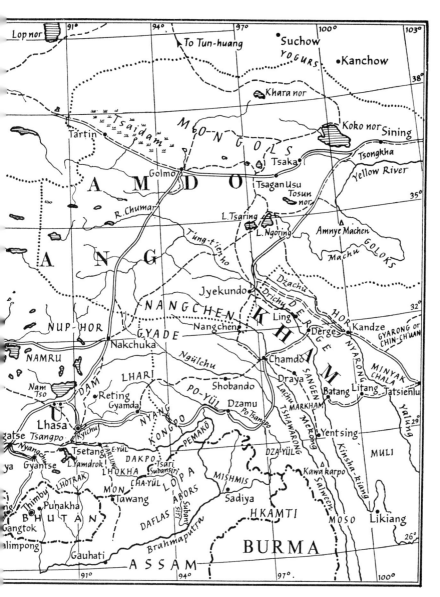

eas and communications

Other movements took a south-westerly direction. The ruling family of Minyak which had founded the Hsi Hsia dynasty emigrated to Ngamring, in northern Tsang, when that dynasty was destroyed and the country conquered by Genghiz Khan in 1127. It took with it the name given to its country (the 'North') and its religious folklore. Other noble families of central and western Tibet must have travelled a similar path; for they trace their more or less legendary origins back to foreign populations in the north-east.[1] Racial names add to the confusion. The name 'Hor' was given at first to the Uighurs, found in Kanchow about A.D. 800. The modern nomadic Horpas of the West (Nup Hor) may still bear their name. But 'Hor' was later used for the Mongols of Genghiz Khan, and it is from these that the five Hor principalities of Kham (around Kandze and Beri) claim their descent. Apart, though, from a few Mongol words such as the title *tarqan*, their speech is related to the aboriginal language of Kinchwan. On the other hand, the name of the Sok (spelt *Sog*), nomadic tribes of Mongol origin who live in the Koko Nor region and still spoke Mongolian quite recently, certainly means 'Mongolia' in the later Tibetan chronicles. However, it seems to be derived from that of the ancient Sogdians (*Sog-dag* in early Tibetan).[2]

The speech and the racial affinities of a population are not necessarily associated with the particular cultural features it presents. The Horpa of today inhabit districts in the east (Derge, Kandze) and the centre of Tibet (Nup Hor) that share two apparently un-'Tibetan' characteristics. They are: the sets of menhirs and tombs arranged in stone circles in the lake region on the southern fringes of the Changthang; and the 'animal style' in the decoration of metal objects (knives, stirrups, buckles, etc.) practised at Derge and in Amdo, which is similar to that of the Ordos bronzes and the 'Scythian' art of the steppes.

To revert to our survey of Tibet's population as it was at the time of the first kings (sixth to seventh centuries). We have looked at the state of *Biu and the Land of Women, in the east, and the Sumpa and Asha peoples in the north-east. The south, whose inhabitants had not thus far been organised into states, was lumped together under the name 'Mon'. The term covers all sorts of aboriginal tribes of the wooded Himalayan hills (e.g. Mishmi, Abors) and is possibly related to the word 'Man' used in literary Chinese for all southern

[1] 121, pp. 6, 737.
[2] 127, n. 34.

'barbarians'. But even in the earliest texts mention is also made of Mon peoples in the east, along the Sino-Tibetan border. In the west, the name is given to other low-caste communities in Ladakh; and lastly, it is applied to Sikkim and Bhutan.

Westward of the Yarlung Tibetans, at first, lay Tsang, the valley of the upper Tsangpo. This region, including the land of Myang or Nyang, was annexed to the kingdom of Yarlung in the early seventh century, after Dakpo and Phenyül (near Lhasa). Then, further west, the Tibetans encountered a distinctly foreign nation—Shangshung, with its capital Khyunglung. Mt. Kailāśa (Tise) and Lake Manasarowar formed part of this country, whose language has come down to us through early documents. Though still unidentified, it seems to be Indo-European. The part played by Shangshung has been an important one, for in Tibetan tradition it is the home of *Bon*, a religion adopted by Tibetans before Buddhism. Geographically the country was certainly open to India, both through Nepal and by way of Kashmir and Ladakh. Kailāśa is a holy place for the Indians, who make pilgrimages to it. No one knows how long they have done so, but the cult may well go back to the times when Shangshung was still independent of Tibet.

How far Shangshung stretched to the north, east and west is a mystery. It seems to have dovetailed into two countries mentioned by T'ang historians as Lesser and Greater Yang-t'ung. It is hard to picture them as organized states, as these historians claim, when their own descriptions force us to situate them on the high, practically desert, Changthang plateau. They doubtless formed a bridge between the eastern and western parts of Tibet.

To the west and north-west, these countries bordered on Khotan and on Gilgit and Hunza (Tibetan Drusha: the name—spelt *'Bru-zha* —is related to the Burushaski language spoken in Hunza). They also adjoined a mysterious region mentioned by Chinese and Indians: Suvarṇagotra (the Golden Race) or the western Land of Women (Strīrājya). These are the countries referred to in our old legends about the ants' gold and the Amazons whom Alexander was unable to conquer. The abundance of gold and the political power of women caused a certain amount of confusion between these places and the eastern Land of Women, which had the same characteristics. Nevertheless, it may well have been that real connections existed between the two separate regions.

Tibetan civilization owes a great deal to the western districts. They border on Gandhāra, Uḍḍiyāna (Swāt) and other countries through which ancient Greek, Persian and Indian cultural influences reached Tibet.

An inscription of the Kushān (first or second century Indo-Scythian) emperor Vīma Kadphises has been found at Khalatse in Ladakh. Further east at Drangtse, near Lake Pangkong, there are Nestorian inscriptions in Tibetan, Kuchean and Sogdian, probably dating from the ninth century. Like Shangshung and Tasik (*Ta-zig*: Iran, Arabs), the Drusha country and its language play a leading rôle in

FIG. 3. Horpa herdsmen. Tobacco-pouch and sword at their belts.

the traditions of the Bon religion and in those connected with Padmasambhava, the great saint of Lamaism who came from Uḍḍiyāna.

Nepal to the south and Khotan to the north were in touch with Tibet very early on, and the influence of their ancient Buddhist civilization remains, in art and religion.

Finally, less well known but significant connections linked the kings of Yarlung with Yünnan and the Burmese frontier. In the ninth century, Tibetans (T'u-fan) went regularly to the Sino-Burmese frontier to buy large gourds, grown by the tribes there. According to the Chinese historian who mentions this, the Tibetan king's 'military tent' (seat of administration) was 'not far' from there, although elsewhere he places the Tibetan frontier sixty days march to the north-west of Yung-ch'ang (between the rivers Mekong and Salween).[1] The kingdom of Nan-chao which then occupied Yünnan, itself Buddhist, had close connections with Tibet at the time.

So, in spite of its isolated appearance, Tibet has in fact been wide open on every side since its earliest days. Only on our own early maps does it feature as a white patch, and only in our history books as a country cut off from world developments.

TIBETAN DESCRIPTIONS

After this summary of our knowledge of the country, it may be helpful to consider how the Tibetans themselves view it. Most of their ideas are only known to us through relatively late documents, dating from a time when Buddhism was firmly entrenched. Many of them are also of Indian provenance.

Like the people of Nepal, Kashmir and Khotan, Tibetans believe that in the prehistoric era, central Tibet was one large sea or lake, of which the numerous existing lakes are remnants. This is what a sixteenth-century historian[2] has to say:

'We read in the *Mañjuśrīmūlatantra*, "A hundred years after my death, the lake in the Land of Snows will have dwindled and a forest of *sāl* trees will appear there" In accordance with this prediction, a hundred years after the death of the Master (the Buddha), the lake that once covered the Land of Snows finally dried up. The saying that a *sāl* forest would grow corresponds with the Tibetan tradition that formerly the country was entirely covered by a juniper forest. A short time after the country was formed in this way, Avalokiteśvara and our lady Tārā, in the semblance of a monkey and a rock-demoness, had first of all monkey offspring. Gradually, these became men. The first village they made is commemorated in (the saying): "Trena (monkey-beginning) in the land of Kongpo, (the first) district of the land of men".'

[1] 191A, ff. 7b and 28b.
[2] 143, f. 97.

37

HABITAT AND INHABITANTS

In 1748, the great polymath Sumpa Khenpo summarizes:

'Tampa Sanggyê (an Indian sage, died 1117) must have visited Tibet seven times, to believe many people. On the first occasion, all the lands of Tibet are said to have been covered by water, but on the second the waters had (already) receded. Men speak (in this connection) of "Tshona" (lake-beginnings), meaning by this name that the two "turquoise lakes" of the south (Lake Yamdrok) and the north (Lake Namtso/Tengri Nor?) once communicated with each other.'

Like a good scholar, the author next quotes the *tantra* passage that we have just read, but gives it a rationalistic explanation:

'The meaning of this *sūtra* is that in Tibet the "turquoise lakes" of the north and south were larger than at present, while "Tshona" illustrates that there were still many other small lakes which have by now shrunk a little. Particularly, there was in Kyishö (the plain around Lhasa through which the Kyichu flows) a small lake in the Plain of Milk (Othang), which has also shrunk. On these (dried-up lakes) "temples" etc. (gloss: "trees") appeared. It seems that (all this happened) at the period when the Religion spread. One must not conclude that, Tibet being wholly filled with water, there were no human beings at all.' (II, 147).

This semi-rationalist's line of argument is based on another legend, already told in the *ma-ṇi bka'-'bum* (I, 169), which may date from the twelfth century. Songtsen Gampo (died 649 or 650), regarded as the first king to have introduced Buddhism, and an incarnation of Avalokiteśvara, was thought to have built the Jokhang temple in Lhasa over a lake. To this day, a stone is shown in the temple which is supposed to lead to the subterranean lake through a hole beneath. An ear laid against it detects a sound similar to that heard in a sea-shell.

The political centre had moved. While before it had been in the south-east (Kongpo, Yarlung) from the mythical epoch of the earliest Tibetans to the legendary kings, it was now at Lhasa. The lake in the Plain of Milk where the first Buddhist king built his temple represented the heart of a she-demon lying on her back. The she-demon is Tibet itself, which had to be tamed before it could be inhabited and civilized. Her body already covered the whole extent

38

of Tibet in its period of military greatness (eighth and ninth centuries). Her outspread limbs reached to the present boundaries of Tibetan settlement. The conquering and civilizing function of the first king, once he was established at the centre, was performed in accordance with Chinese ideas: in square concentric zones, each boxed in by the next and extending farther and farther from the centre. Temples erected at the four corners of three successive squares stand for nails driven, as it were, into the limbs of the demoness, crucifying her. The land is held firm and made fit for habitation.

'To keep the limbs of the prostrate she-demon under control, twelve nails of immobility were driven into her,' says a chronicle of 1508,[1] before listing the thrice four temples that were built.

Another square-based system expresses Tibet's relationship to her neighbours. Tibetans attribute it to the time of the legendary kings, but the place-names it contains must date from the epoch of military power. The concept derives from an early Buddhist tradition that was taken over and given fresh currency by Moslem writers in the ninth and tenth centuries. In it, Tibet is surrounded—and threatened —to the east by China; to the south by India; to the west by Persia (*Ta-zig*) and Byzantium (*Phrom, Khrom*) or Rūm in the sense of Anatolia; and to the north by the Turks (*Dru-gu*) and the Uighurs (*Hor*), or by one *Ge-sar* of *Phrom* (Caesar of 'Rome' transferred to a new setting). To the east lay the land of divination and calculation, to the south the land of religion, to the west that of wealth, jewels and trade, and to the north that of horses, weapons and war.

This arrangement was first seen in the reign of a king who brought military glory to Tibet. He 'subjugated the two-thirds of the world' over and above the third he already ruled in Tibet (early ninth century). The concept was then parallelled by another schematic application of the four cardinal points. The conquered members of four tribes which later became great noble families (Shüpu, Tshepong, Belnön and Nanam) were absorbed into the army. They were the 'falcons' faces' to the east, the 'donkeys' feet' to the south, the 'cats' tails' to the west and the 'hares' (or donkeys') ears' to the north.[2] The same fourfold classification was used over and over again. After the administrative organization of the country under

[1] 179, ff. 57–58.
[2] 177, ff. 58–59; 114, p. 249.

HABITAT AND INHABITANTS

Trhisong Detsen (about A.D. 800), the tributary kings were those of Nam, 'king of ointments (?)'; of Pelpo (Nepal), 'king of brass'; of Sumpa, 'king of iron'; and of the Mon, 'king of bamboos (?)'.[1] Later, people considered the Myang (Nyang) district as having 'four gates' corresponding to four routes: to the east the 'route of the Law', to the south the wood route, to the north the iron and to the west the barley.[2] We shall see that even the pattern of the first holy place was conceived in this way.

The posting of troop detachments according to the four points of the compass is revealing. It corresponds to the military organization —already in evidence in early chronicles—into four 'horns', wings or banners (*ru*), identical with the first 'square' of the conquered she-demon. This square, called Runön ('conquering of the horns'), subdued the four 'provinces' (*ru*) of central Tibet. Centuries later, the great Tibetan hierarchs still lived in military encampments, the sacred sovereign motionless at the centre, unseen by the common people, while all around him tents were drawn up in squares something like the concentric fortifications of a walled town.

As was the fashion in China, the Tibetans imagined themselves at the centre of a square made by other lands, at 'the navel of the earth', as they say. At the same time, unlike China, they maintained a surprising humility that sprang from the dominance of Buddhist beliefs. They always regarded themselves as savages living in the north of the world. This attitude led to the transference of North Indian place-names to places in north Tibet. They speak of the 'little-known country of barbarous Tibet',[3] they describe themselves (like the 'wild' Horpas) as 'red-faced flesh-eating demons'[4] and many a time call themselves stupid, rough and dull, all this of course in relation to the civilizing influence of Buddhism. The *Ma-ṇi bka'-'bum* (I, 160) makes a list of the virtues and vices of the Tibetans. From their monkey ancestor the first inhabitants inherited hairy bodies and red faces, and from their demon ancestress the absence of tails and a taste for meat. Some inherited devotion, zeal, wisdom and kindliness from their father. Others acquired from their mother the lust to kill, physical strength and courage.

[1] 142, *JA*, f. 20*b*.
[2] 120, vol. IV, i, p. 59.
[3] 165, f. 4*b*.
[4] 174 = 117, I, pp. 78–83.

In this position at the north of the world, Tibetans sometimes confused their own barbarian condition with the sort of Gog and Magog (*Hor* and *Phrom*, 'Turks' and 'Tartars') that was supposed to reign north of their country, in the region of horses and lawlessness. Their own land thus became a curious jigsaw of overlapping zones or 'degrees' of barbarism. 'The three lands of Dakpo, Kongpo and Nyang (south-eastern Tibet) are the most harmful in the *Khrom Ge-sar* land of the north, in the land of the *preta* (ravenous demons), *Pretapuri*, Tibet.' Or in another place: 'This Land of Snows, Tibet, was unconquered, harmful and restless. As a *sūtra* describes it: the land of *Phrom Ge-sar* of the north, Tibet, the land of meat-eaters on the borders, the land where men eat human flesh.'[1]

Indians, on the other hand, regarded the Himalayan snows to their north as the home of the gods and of the *vidyādhara* (*rig-'dzin*), a kind of supermen gifted with special knowledge, particularly the understanding of magic. This belief appears to account for the occultist tradition and the popular European picture of Tibet as the dwelling-place of immortal sages guarding the ultimate secrets. The Tibetans themselves accordingly transferred this whole geographical and religious complex to the north of their own country, to Khotan or just somewhere in Turkestan. It is there that the mythical country of Śambhala lay, to be approached by routes at first real, then imaginary.

Like a world in miniature, the narrower sphere of the inhabited locality was thought of now as a square, now as an octagon or circle. In the second case, the sky was an eight-spoked wheel and the earth an eight-petalled lotus—both of them Buddhist symbols. At the same time, there was a three-tiered vertical scheme: sky, earth, and the world under the earth. Often the two systems fused and were mutually complementary. The principle of an arrangement in tiers is taken a stage further on the middle of these levels, the only one occupied by man, which is thought of as a ladder between the other two: each rung of it represents a botanical or zoological type.

The occasion of the legendary advent of the first king gives us an instance of this kind of habitat. In an account based on Indian

[1] 178, p. 15.

sources Rupati, an Indian prince, was exiled and fled to Tibet. A native version sees him as a Sky god. In both stories, he came down from the peak of a sacred mountain that was pictured as a ladder linking heaven and earth; a Tibetan ladder, that is to say a tree-trunk with notches cut into it for footholds. Sometimes the mountain is Gyangtho in Kongpo, and sometimes Yarlha Shampo in Yarlung. The descent took place on a plain called Tsenthang Goshi, 'King's Plain with Four Gateways', essentially square, therefore, like a fortified camp or a *maṇḍala*. Twelve chieftains who had come there to pay religious homage to the mountain met this being from on high and took him as their king. They are described as herdsmen, hunters, local inhabitants, twelve petty kings or twelve Bonpo priests, holy men or chieftains. Their number fits in with the square lay-out.

The earliest history we have (probably ninth century) says of this spot:

> 'It was the centre of the sky, the middle of the earth and the heart of the country. An enclosure of glaciers; the head of all rivers. High mountain, pure earth, an excellent country. A place where wise men are born heroes, where custom is perfected, where horses grow swift.'[1]

In the Mongolian version of the legend, the mountain is called a 'ladder with nine steps', and this peculiarity it shares with heaven itself. The rungs or storeys each correspond to a separate natural environment, represented by its own characteristic animal.

The seven, or nine, 'storeys' of heaven were associated with the first king's ancestors, prior to his descent to earth. Only some of them are known: the plane of the sky, the clouds, the rain. Conversely, the planes or storeys of the mountain are classed with the successive legendary descendants of the first king, each one being the place where the tombs of a given period were constructed, in a graded downward sequence.

The first seven kings were the 'seven Heavenly Thrones'. The names of their queens are evocative. They begin, successively, with the syllables *Nam* (sky), *Sa* (earth), *So* (place ?), *Dog* (ground ?), *Dags* (sunny slope of the mountain) and *Srib* (shaded slope of the mountain). The two latter terms correspond exactly with the primary meaning of the Yin and Yang of Chinese systems. Those who go

[1] 6, p. 81.

across the pass leading from western China (Szechwan) to Tatsienlu see the force of the Tibetan metaphor. The Chinese mountainside, cold and damp, is wrapped in mist; the Tibetan slope is dry and sunny; and the two aspects are divided with extraordinary sharpness, as though there were a wall between. In a text concerning funeral rites,[1] a series of metaphors sets out the associations of ideas belonging to these contrasted landscapes extremely well. Heaven and earth are seen as king and people; a mountain's bright side (*dags*) and dark side (*srib*), as husband and wife (in China too Yin and Yang originally denote the shaded and sunny sides of a mountain respectively and are contrasted in sex); right and left as maternal uncle and sister's son; head and body as father and son; and the upper (*phu*) and lower (*mda'*) parts of a valley, lastly, as master and disciple.

The seven Heavenly Thrones had their tombs in the sky. Those of the ensuing dynasties were sited progressively lower in this order: 1. slate and clay; 2. where slate and pastureland meet; 3. river; 4. (missing); 5. plain; 6. valley bottom.[2] With a few variations, this topographical classification has remained in use to distinguish the kinds of natural surroundings that exist alongside one another virtually everywhere, determining the structure and development of society. First, on the heights, there are glaciers, home of the white 'lioness' with her turquoise (blue-green) mane, the symbol of Tibet. Then come the rocks where the eagle dwells, the clayey slopes where the wild yak roams, pasture or grass lands with their deer, streams and lakes full of 'golden eye' fish, and lastly, the forests, domain of the tiger.[3] Sometimes, very rarely, there is also the plain, home of the wild ass (kyang). That is the only terrain that occupies a separate geographical region—the north—instead of being an integral part of the general gradation from the valley-head to its lowest reach.

The head and lowest end of a valley are always carefully distinguished by special names (*phu* and *mda'*). But the Tibetans also employed this image for the general orientation of their country. The expressions 'high' (*stod*) and 'low' (*smad*) were applied to large areas and this came to mean 'west' (high) and 'east' (low). In this way they not only recognized an upper (western) and a lower (eastern) part of any given province, but could also say:

[1] 187, II, f. 50*a–b*.
[2] 141, f. 11*b*.
[3] 152A, f. 30*a*.

Ngari up above (in the west), Kham down below (east); or India above, China below. An alternative mode of orientation was based on the idea, familiar in China, that the sovereign lived in the centre, facing south: so that the Left Wing meant the east (for instance, Yarlung) and the Right Wing the west (e.g. Tsang).

This is how Tibetan civilization stands as far as place is concerned. Now let us see how it looks in time.

2

Historical Survey

Tibetan civilization does have recognizable characteristics of its own, but its social expression has undergone changes, needless to say, over the centuries. Since we shall be concerned with its manifestations at several different periods, it is time we knew something of the broad outlines of its history.

It is not a history to which any dates can be assigned earlier than the sixth century of our era. The Tibetans have their tradition on the subject, however—myths and legends—and these are the more noteworthy for the rationalistic view of social evolution they assume. Society is conceived of as passing through successive stages of development, whose rudiments we may safely accept. To try to date them would be a mistake, though, for it is quite clear that they have been more or less arbitrarily assigned to various periods by the scholastic historians of a later age whose records have come down to us.

TIBETAN IDEAS

On the history of mankind, as on that of the inhabited world, Tibetans took over the Indian Buddhist views. Some of their ideas also coincide with Chinese theories about the beginnings of civilization under the first sage-kings of long ago.

From Buddhism came the idea of a series of Ages, and the progressive degeneration of mankind. Men were radiant heavenly beings to start with. Their radiance gradually dimmed, and their bodies grew dense, as the earth itself took shape: to be precise, it resulted from their tasting, first, the sweet cream of which the pre-earth consisted, and afterwards other kinds of food. According to legends, which the Tibetans knew from translations of Buddhist scriptures (the Kangyur), human society with all its inequalities—king and subject, rich and poor—came into existence step by step through quarrels about food. The origin of the Tibetans themselves was imagined in the same evolutionist spirit.

We have already learnt how their earliest ancestors were a monkey and an ogress of the rocks whose children were half-man, half-ape: standing erect, but covered with hair, with flat, red faces and, say some (though others deny it), still possessing tails. The parent monkey set aside the southern forests for them to live in, and there they mated with female monkeys and multiplied. 'In summer, they suffered from the rain and sun; in winter, from the snow and wind. They had neither food nor clothing.' Moved with pity, the original monkey, really the deity Avalokiteśvara, brought them the 'six kinds of grain' (buckwheat, coarse barley, mustard, etc.; though earlier the same text speaks of five kinds—barley, wheat, rice, sesamum, and peas).[1] In this way the first fields were cultivated at Sothang, in the Yarlung valley, and the men-apes slowly took on the shape of man.

The earliest tribes are referred to as *mi'u*, a name which in its present form means 'dwarf' or 'little man', but which perhaps came from a Chinese term, 'mi-hou', denoting the monkeys from whom the ancient Ch'iang were said to be descended. These tribes were six in number, and sprang from the first six children of the monkey and the demoness. They were subdivided into four 'elder brothers' and two 'younger brothers'. A seventh tribe, that of the 'maternal uncle' (*zhang*), is generally added to the list. It derives from the radiant gods of heaven, or from a primordial egg to which other legends trace the descent of mankind. Tibetan authors combined two population groups in their scheme of classification. One consists simply of foreign countries, Shangshung, Sumpa, Asha and Minyak. The other comprises populations still encountered in the historical period and whom the Tibetans themselves regard as non-Tibetan. Actually, from the analysis of certain traits, we can group them with the aborigines of the Sino-Tibetan borderland, and in particular with the Ch'iang. In T'ang dynasty Chinese descriptions (evidence from A.D. 600 to 800), the Ch'iang and the T'u-fan Tibetans have many cultural features in common. The difference is merely that

---

[1] 139, f. 225*a–b*: the six cereals (*'bras drug*) are staples in the Nyenkar district; cf. 6, p. 116.

some Ch'iang tribes—though not all—are described as more nomadic and pastoral than the T'u-fan.

The Tibetans distinguish a series of seven or ten periods preceding the advent of the first mythical king. Each of them is characterized by a particular species of demons or lesser deities, by a different name given to the country, and by the first appearance of certain inventions or institutions. In the most usual list,[1] the first period is marked by 'powerful (or violent?) kinsmen', the second by the 'red-faced eaters of meat', the third by 'the little white one dwelling in water', the fourth by weapons, arrows and spears, the fifth by the use of horses for riding and by ear-rings, the sixth by rules of etiquette. The rulers given for this sixth period are the 'twelve minor kings'; and they probably correspond to the twelve wise men, herdsmen or chieftains who are represented as greeting the first heavenly king. For his reign is the seventh, and last, period.

Besides the twelve chieftains, we often hear of another twenty-five or forty. The numbers are purely a matter of convention; and this example may give us some idea of the schematic treatment of historical data by later authors. The twelve kings they enumerate are taken from a much longer list that survives in original manuscripts of the eighth and ninth centuries, discovered at Tun-huang. There we find the names of twelve kings, plus a thirteenth, twenty-four ministers, plus a twenty-fifth, twelve castles plus a thirteenth, and twelve countries plus a thirteenth. These early chronicles themselves are no models of historical exactitude. Already, apart from a portion written with the chronological precision of Chinese annals, they have the epic manner.

The kings and their castles probably date from the sixth century; but tradition has set them in the legendary age of the first heavenly king. In those days 'there was no distinction between people and ruler', and so these twelve worshipped the holy mountain, and welcomed him who came down from it in order to have a king. A centralized monarchy was needed, we are told, because the four great countries mentioned earlier—China, India, Iran and Hor or Gesar (Trhom, spelt *Phrom*)—dominated the four points of the compass.

This was 'the age when the kings of the four directions spread out in their respective regions. At that time, the men of Tibet were without a ruler. Moreover there were stout castles on all the hills and

[1] 177, f. 18a (= 56a).

steep rocks. Clothing, food and treasure were laid up in safe fortresses. At that time (no one) was able to win disputes, and armies were few in number. A time when, lacking power oneself, no support could be found by joining together (?).'[1]

Hence the need for a leader. Messengers were sent to heaven saying, 'For men, the black-headed ones, who are without a ruler, a leader must be appointed.' Thus reads an account in the Tun-huang manuscripts, which ends with the words: 'The divine king of Great Tibet, of magical power, came from the gods as ruler of men; as ruler of men, the black-headed ones.'[2]

Attention has already been drawn to the manner in which the first line of kings, the Seven Thrones, was correlated with various types of habitat through the names their queens bore. It is a peculiarity of these kings that their names are derived from those of their mothers. They are thus, perhaps, to be included in the seventh tribe, described as 'maternal uncle', evidently in contradistinction to the twelve sages who welcomed the first king and were termed 'the six clans of father's (side) subjects'.[3] These first seven kings could be more accurately described as gods, exercising an earthly function: living on earth by day, but returning to their celestial abode each night. The final return was at their 'death', which always took place as soon as their son had learnt to ride a horse (at thirteen as a rule). The ascent was performed with the aid of a rope; and the name applied to this rope, *dmu*, was also used both for the sky, i.e. heaven, and for the king's maternal family (whose home it was). His body dissolved into the rope, which resembled a kind of rainbow extending from his head to the sky. The period is thus distinguished by the absence of earthly burial places or, as it is sometimes put, by '*dmu*-style tombs'—tombs in the sky. For all its mythical character, features of later times are erroneously projected back to this stage. They include the earliest royal castle at Yumbu Lagang, in upper Yarlung; several Tibetan clans; and even states, like Sumpa and Shangshung, that were regarded as foreign.

A new period, of two reigns, follows the tragic end of the first royal line. Trigum, son of the last of the Seven Thrones, was a god in human form still. But filled with bragging arrogance, he took it

[1] 177, f. 56*a*.
[2] 63, No. 16.
[3] 142, *JA*, f. 6*b*.

1. Kongpo: confluence of the Tsangpo and the Nyangchu. Fields, forests and glaciers. *Photo: H.R.H. The Maharaja of Sikkim.*

2. Defence towers in Kongpo. *Photo: H.R.H. The Maharaja of Sikkim.*

3. The Dalai Lama's camp in 1939, on the Lhasa plain. *Anonymous photo, courtesy of H. Richardson.*

into his head to challenge the nine paternal and three maternal clans, his own subjects, to a duel. None dared accept, save one: Lo-ngam, described as a 'herder of horses', and probably a foreigner. He features in one sober chronicle as 'subject' and 'princeling' by turns, in the context of an athletics tournament held after a Tibetan victory against Khache (Kashmir).[1] 'Lo-ngam' is a generic name, encountered under king Trhisong Detsen's administration, where we find seven herdsmen—including the 'horse herders of Lo-ngam'—listed among the secular working population, along with the seven saddlemakers of Karong and the five tea-merchants of China. The place Lo-ngam appears to have been in the Myang (or Nyang) district of Tsang. The contest took place near Mount Kailāśa, and its sequel at Shampo in the grazing-lands (*ro*) of Nyang (see historical map, pages 86–87).

It was during this magical struggle that king Trigum inadvertently severed the *dmu* string that connected him with heaven, thus becoming the first king to leave a corpse, for which the first tomb was built at Chhinga Taktse. The king's three sons, Shatri, Nyatri and Chatri, fled to the three districts of Dakpo, Kongpo and Powo. But the queen had another, miraculous son by the god Yarlha Shampo, the holy mountain, who appeared to her in the guise of a white yak. This son, Rula-kye, killed the usurping Lo-ngam and brought back prince Chatri from Powo to enthrone him as Pude Kunggyel, himself becoming the first of a series of seven wise ministers. However, only the two sons Shatri and Nyatri are known to one Tun-huang chronicle and to an ancient inscription at Kongpo (*ca.* 800).

This is the period in which later tradition (fourteenth century onwards) places the rise of the Bon religion, which is invariably linked with foreign lands such as Tasik (Iran) and the Asha, Shangshung and Drusha (Gilgit), or a country called Gurṇawatra situated on the borders of India and Iran (see pages 231–232, below).

Along with the introduction of Bon to a 'Tibet' confined to Yarlung, two other religious techniques are traditionally supposed to have developed during this period: that of the story-tellers (*sgrung*), and that of the genealogists and singers of riddles (*lde'u*). At the same time material culture is stated to have made great strides, thanks to the first two of the seven wise ministers, Rula-kye, otherwise known as Lhabu Mönshung of the Khu clan, and his son

[1] *Ibid.*, f. 7a.

Lhabu Gokar. Once again it is plain that we should not attempt to date these discoveries, arbitrarily apportioned as they are between the various reigns. Not only do the texts conflict, but the very number seven is merely a product of scholastic fondness for numeric classifications. In the Tun-huang manuscripts the same names are encountered amongst a much larger number of ministers. Still, here are the inventions credited to them that have relevance for the history of Tibetan civilization.

'Rula-kye subjected cattle to the law (doubtless he took a livestock census for purposes of taxation) and prepared grass for the winter by making sheaves (presumably of straw or hay). He turned (the earth of the) grassy plains into fields and occupied the crests (?) of the mountains (built houses there, as we shall see). Before him, there was no harvesting of grass or grain in Tibet'.[1] According to other accounts, Rula-kye 'made charcoal by burning trees; he used it to smelt ore and extract gold, silver, copper and iron. Making holes in wood, he fashioned ploughs and yokes. He dug out the ground and drained the water from the upper valleys into channels. He harnessed two plough-oxen as a pair (but the older work, attributing the invention to a later king, says, 'he harnessed hybrid cattle, *mdzo*, and oxen, *glang*, in pairs'). He ploughed the grassy plains into fields. On the unfordable rivers, he built bridges.'

This memorable reign was followed by a line of six 'Lek' kings. Under the first, Isho Lek, the second wise minister Lhabu Gokar 'counted the fields by pairs (*dor-kha*, two oxen harnessed to a single yoke, a western technique still found in Tibet) and grazing-land by hides (*thul*: probably for taxation).' He also 'drained the water from the valley-tops into channels and made irrigation channels in the valley-bottoms, thus causing progress to be made in tillage'.[2] According to the oldest account this second sage was the minister of king Trhinyen Sungtsen, who reigned much later: 'He diverted the lakes to drain their waters into channels. He gathered the water from the upper valley and counted this water, (gathered?) by night, in the daytime (no doubt the distribution of water, captured at night in collecting ponds, was regulated during the day, as is still the case in Ladakh).'

The next dynasty, of the eight De kings, is not distinguished for any inventions but is associated with an important constitutional

[1] 175, ff. 110*a*–111*a*.
[2] 142, *JA*, f. 9*a*.

development. Until its end, all queens are held to have been deities who left no corpse at death. Consequently the crown princes, their sons, were called 'divine sons' (*lha-sras* or *lde-sras*). The five Tsen kings, who come next, married among their subjects, to whom they thus became related, a state of affairs described by the chronicles as an 'admixture', presumably in the sense of an improper match.

Under Thogje Thoktsen, the fourth king in this line, 'the panpipes, music of the gods' are said to have been invented or introduced. Down to the end of this period, i.e. during the twenty-seven generations of legendary rulers, the kingdom is held to have been 'protected', ruled or sanctified on the religious level by the story-tellers, singers of riddles and Bonpos, through their ritual powers.

It is in the reign of the 'god' (*lha*) Thothori Nyentsen, the last of the Tsen, that tradition places Buddhism's first appearance in Tibet. A casket, containing the *Karaṇḍavyūha-sūtra* (devoted to Tibet's patron Avalokiteśvara), another book and a golden stūpa, fell from the sky, it is said, on to the palace of Yumbu Lagang. These gifts from heaven were preserved as treasure without being understood.

After another four kings, of whom little is known, we come to history documented by trustworthy Chinese and Tibetan sources. Some of the discoveries we have already mentioned are ascribed to these reigns. The second wise minister, we are told, invented irrigation, etc. under Trhinyen Sungtsen, the son of Thothori Nyentsen. Under his grandson, Tari Nyensik, the third sage invented charcoal, etc. Others, however, credit him with the origination of vessels for measuring grain. Several accounts associate the beginnings of military expansion and the introduction of Chinese science with this king's son, Namri Songtsen; but older sources place these events in the reign of *his* son, Songtsen Gampo. The last named was Tibet's first great historical king, and soon came to be regarded as an incarnation of Avalokiteśvara. At his death, legend relates, he dissolved into that patron-deity's statue and thus became a kind of sacred talisman of the kingdom, standing at its centre.

The historian Pawo Tsuk reckons the reigns of the first twenty-seven kings, from Nyatri up to but not including Thothori Nyentsen, at six hundred and sixty years, and one hundred and fifty years for the succeeding five kings, from Thothori Nyentsen to Namri Songtsen. He doubtless allowed twenty-five to thirty years for each reign, and I shall studiously refrain from basing any chronology of proto-history on these figures. One Bonpo chronicle allows only eight hundred years for the whole period from the Heavenly Thrones to Lang Darma (died 842). We have, on the other hand, a short undated history which considerably extends matters, with Nyatri entering Tibet in 599 B.C., King Thothori being born nine hundred and sixty-five years later in A.D. 367, and a hundred and ninety years elapsing between him and the birth of Songtsen Gampo in 557.[1] King Songtsen Gampo, then, is the first to whom we can put an exact date. He died in 649 or 650. From then on the chronology is fairly reliable; but there is still doubt over certain basic dates. Our Tibetan documents do not always agree among themselves, or with the Chinese sources.

Although we are dealing with real history now, we have not yet seen the last of the schematic view of things. The list of discoveries and inventions ascribed to each reign continues. The great kings Songtsen Gampo and Trhisong Detsen made such a strong impression that they rapidly turned into stock heroes, and events may have been transferred from one to the other. In the stylized scheme of events, Songtsen Gampo is said to have borrowed techniques from the four great countries of the four points of the compass. 'In the east, from China and from Minyak, he took books of technology and of divinatory calculation (others say: medicine and calculations of the five elements). In the south, from India, he translated the holy religion. Westward, in the land of the Sok and in Nepal, he opened the treasuries of foodstuffs, wealth and goods. In the north, from among the Hor and Yugur, he took books of laws.'[2] In any case, if India is always the land of religion, the country of secular laws (*khrims*) is China. This pattern stems from the theory of the Four Sons of Heaven, which we have already seen projected back to primitive times, and it reappears under Songtsen Gampo, with the building of the twelve temples on the she-demon's body. The architects or 'overseers' (*lag-dpon*) of the four temples erected at the farthest borders were all foreign. They came from the Minyak (east), the Thogar (south), the Hor (north) and Nepal (west), respectively. Under the same ruler the fourth of the seven wise ministers, Thönmi Sambhoṭa, invented the alphabet. A Tun-huang chronicle already

---

[1] 178, p. 40; *dPal-ldan Shar-kha'i yig-tshang*, MS, excerpts compiled by *Tshe-dbang nor-bu* (1698–1755).
[2] 142, *JA*, f. 18a, quoting the *Thang-yig chen-mo*.

declares, in epic diction: 'Tibet, of old, had no writing. But it was invented in this king's reign. And thenceforth there appeared, in the time of King Trhi Songtsen (Songtsen Gampo), all the excellent texts of Tibetan usage, Tibetan sciences (or religions) and the great laws, the hierarchy of ministers, the respective powers of the great and the small (or of the elder and younger brothers), rewards for good deeds, punishments for evil and wrongdoing, the counting of skins for pasturelands and yokes for fields, equalization in the use (?) of rivers, duties levied by (fixed) units of volume, weights, etc.'[1]

As we have seen, some of these boons have been attributed to culture-heroes of an earlier date. In other cases, later kings receive the credit. Under Me Aktsom (Trhide Tsukten), the fifth of the wise ministers is stated to have invented units of volume and weights, as well as rules governing trade and the making of agreements. Under his successor, Trhisong Detsen, the sixth 'brought down the mountain houses to the river valley. Thus, crops and houses were together, on the slopes at the edge of the fields. The plains having been tilled into fields, water was brought into the fields. Hitherto, castles and houses had occupied the crests (?) of the mountains.'[2]

In the following reign, we are told that the seventh sage appointed 'guardians' of the four directions (on the borders) in the king's service, and organized warriors (*rgod*) into 'groups of a thousand' (*stong-sde*) to guard the frontiers. Within the kingdom he compelled the 'weak' serfs by law to supply the king's needs, and organized them too into groups of a thousand.

At this point the catalogue of inventions comes to an end. The schematic view of history makes a final significant appearance in the Fifth Dalai Lama's chronicle, however, to sum up the end of the monarchy in the ninth century. Power is fragmented now. No longer does the line of Nyatri reign over all Tibet. Right until the last king, Ösung, the histories supply each king's name and the whereabouts of his tomb. With Ösung the custom of building tombs dies out.[3]

---

[1] 6, p. 161.

[2] 175, *loc. cit.* The early, but poorly preserved chronicle of *Ne'u Paṇḍita* (*sNgon-gyi gtam me-tog phreng-ba*, fourteenth century?) credits the seventh sage with these inventions: 'He brought the mountain houses (*ri-khyim*) down into the valley; he built castles on the lofty heights (*spo-thon*) and houses at the end of the fields. Previously people had lived on the mountain ridges (? *do-bo*).'

[3] 141, f. 45b.

At this point precise dates become available. For the early period they are supplied by a chronicle from Tun-huang, written in the Chinese style (from 650 to 747), and by the Chinese annals; for the middle period, up to the eighteenth century, by later Tibetan histories and Chinese annals; and for the modern period by other Chinese sources, Tibetan accounts and some European observations.

Some mention must still be made of Tibetan historical concepts, for these have influenced the manner in which events are described and sometimes even their dating. And we must remark at the outset that from now on these are Buddhist concepts.

The standard chronicles divide Tibetan history into four periods. The first is characterized by the absence of royal authority and of Buddhism. The Tibetans themselves are 'stupid' barbarians, their country 'dark' and gloomy. King Songtsen Gampo, an incarnation of Tibet's patron saint Avalokiteśvara, 'tames' the country—civilizes it by introducing Buddhism and establishing the monarchy at Lhasa, its centre. He ushers in the second age, that of the 'earlier spread' (snga-dar) of Buddhism, which ends in the mid ninth century with the persecutions of the wicked king Lang Darma. The latter represents the type of ruler one constantly comes across in Chinese history, as the emblem of the end of any dynasty.

No Tibetan chronicler ever succeeded in settling the exact length of the period of political and religious chaos that intervenes between this king and the beginning of the next age, that of the 'later spread' (phyi-dar) of Buddhism, and no independent source allows it to be fixed. The uncertainty turns on the number of sixty-year cycles, reckoned at one, two or sometimes three.

For something of prime importance for the dating of history took place during this period. In the ancient chronicles, all that was used was a cycle of twelve years, each bearing the name of an animal (rat, ox, tiger, hare, dragon, snake, horse, sheep, monkey, cock, dog and pig). The system, invented in China, had been taken over by the Turks. But, to lessen the possibility of confusion, the Chinese had combined this cycle with another of ten signs, so that a given composite year-name only recurred every sixty years. The Tibetans subsequently adopted this system but with the ten signs replaced by the five elements—each divided into male and female. At the same time, to avoid confusion, they numbered their cycles. But unfortunately they nearly always forget to mention the number.

Now the first sixty-year cycle only starts in the year 1027 (fire-hare). That is the traditional date of the introduction to Tibet, or translation into Tibetan, of the 'Kālacakra' (Wheel of Time) philosophical system. As yet this system has received little study. It is traditionally accorded a northern origin (in the mythical land of Śambhala) and linked with prophecies in which Islam plays an important part. Some have held it to contain Manichaean elements. The fact remains that later historians, groping hesitantly in the dark, reached divergent conclusions when they took events hitherto only dated by the twelve-year cycle and tried to date them accurately in terms of the sixty-year cycle. Their perplexity was soon to be increased when, from the thirteenth century on, they became acquainted with dated facts, in translations from the Chinese annals, which did not always agree with their own tradition.

Another theory led to fresh discrepancies of dating. The sūtras contained prophecies of the degeneration of mankind, and of Buddhism in particular. They divided the period of decline (*snyigs-ma'i dus*, 'tainted time'; Sanskrit *kāliyuga*, 'evil age') into five, six or ten phases of five hundred years starting from the Buddha's *nirvāṇa*. During the final phase, that of times yet to come, barbarians—foreign peoples (now Muslims, now Mongols or Chinese)—will destroy Buddhism. That is the age in which people will have to take refuge in the 'hidden countries' (*sbas yul*), a kind of earthly paradise, always in thickly wooded lands like that of Pemakö in the great bend of the Brahmaputra. In those days, Tibetans hope for the arrival of a king and a general from the fabled northern land of Śambhala who will vanquish the 'barbarians' and unbelievers.

To work out the dates of Tibetan history in terms of the five hundred year periods, the date of the Buddha's *nirvāṇa* had first to be established. But nobody knew when this was. Various dates have been claimed, none of them agreeing with the one preferred by modern scholars (about 480 B.C.), though the date of Singhalese traditions comes very close to it (543 B.C.) and was known in Tibet. Because of the number of five-hundred-year periods assumed and the supposed imminence of the evil times that come at the end, it was necessary to set the Buddha's date further back. Some authors must have known the tradition in Chinese Buddhism that the Buddha was born in 1029 B.C. (in the reign of King Chao) and entered *nirvāṇa* in 950 (in that of King Mu). But they differ from it somewhat.

HISTORICAL SURVEY

The Buddha's birth is variously dated 1027, 957 or 959, and 880, with the *nirvāṇa* eighty years later. Others, however, place the Buddha in 2217, 2132 or 2133, or again in 2073: in other words, they reckon ten periods of five hundred years. According to different authors, three thousand one hundred and seventy-five years had elapsed in the year 1043 of our era, or three thousand five hundred and sixty-two in 1429; or again three thousand eight hundred and twenty-five years in 1752 and four thousand one hundred and seven years in 1891. The end of time (10 × 500 = 5,000 years) had to be at hand on each occasion.

THE ANCIENT MONARCHY

Knowing how Tibetans thought of time and their place in it, and what uncertainties beset their traditional accounts, we can now attempt an outline of their history. Reliable landmarks are provided here and there by the Chinese sources.

It is no accident that dated history begins around A.D. 600, with King Songtsen Gampo. For it was then that Tibet shared and even strikingly influenced the destiny of the great Asian nations. Tibet's era of politico-military greatness and territorial expansion began as soon as she appeared on the international scene, and lasted nearly three centuries. Most of the neighbouring states were giants, but all had their weak points. Their names are preserved in a standard list which we have already discussed.

In the east, China was in the process of acquiring a new dynasty, the T'ang (618–906). It excelled in art, science and literature, was powerful enough to conquer distant countries, but was also periodically convulsed by revolts and palace plots. It was often dependent on help from abroad, and was unusually eager for imported novelty in the way of religion, art and folklore.

To the north, in present-day Sinkiang, Tibetans found at first a string of small oasis states, Indo-European in race and language, and Buddhist by religion, from which they received a strong leaven of civilization. Turfan, Kuchā, Khotan, soon subjected to Chinese suzerainty, presented no threat. But further north, east and west were mighty warriors who made themselves felt even in China: the eastern Turks (by the Orkhon river, in Mongolia), and the western Turks (around the Ili, in northern Sinkiang). Later came the Uighurs, another branch of the Turks, who settled in the oases north of the Tarim (Turfan, etc.) and then, around 872, in the Kanchow region. In Tibet, their names were associated with the idea of armies and horses, barbarity and violence, somewhat like the mediaeval Gog and Magog. The name of the Turks, Tʻu-chüeh (ancient Turkut) in Chinese, became Trugu or Truk (spelt *Dru-gu, Drug*) in Tibetan, while that of the Uighurs became Hor (short for Ho-yo-hor).

Another place-name, vaguely applied but pregnant with associations, was the legacy of changes to the west. Tasik (spelt *Ta-zig*) denotes, roughly, Iran. It is often linked or interchanged with Trhom (spelt *Khrom* or *Phrom*: the east Iranian Hrōm or Frōm, Chinese Fu-lin), which originally denoted Byzantium and later, in the tenth century, the Seljuks of Anatolia. In Iran the great Sassanian dynasty collapsed in the seventh century under the Arab onslaught; and Arabs soon occupied the regions of Bukhara and Samarkand, the homes of the Tokharians and Sogdians. Their Chinese name of Ta-shih (ancient Tasig) comes from the Tajiks, an Iranian people, whence in turn we have the Tibetan *Ta-zig*.

But between Tibet and Iran there were other countries whose cultural influence has been carried to Tibet: Gilgit or Bolor in the north (Chinese Po-lü; Tibetan Drusha), Kashmir, and the ancient lands of Gandhāra and Uḍḍiyāna (Tib. *Udyan, U-rgyan*). Here, Indo-European Buddhist populations had been conquered by Turkish and Indian rulers.

Lastly, to the south lay India, split into minor dynasties after its invasion by the Hephthalites. Of interest to Tibetans at the time were two of these kingdoms, both Buddhist: those of Harṣa, at Kanauj (on the upper Ganges, north-west India), and of the Pāla rulers in Bengal. They had no military power with which to confront the Tibetans but conquered them with their religion, Tantric Buddhism.

The Tibetan tradition of Songtsen Gampo's building temples as far as the Chinese borders may be no more than a pious reconstruction. However, the king undoubtedly had great power. As soon as he ascended the throne, in 634, he defeated the Tʻu-yü-hun in the region of Koko Nor and received a Chinese ambassador. Soon afterwards, having demanded and been refused a Chinese princess in marriage, his armies pursued the T'u-yü-hun northwards from Koko Nor, annexed various Ch'iang peoples and encamped on the Chinese frontier. The credit for these operations went to the king's minister, of the Gar clan, Tongtsen Yülsung (Lu Tung-ts'an in Chinese), who eventually created, for a while, a sub-dynasty of his own in eastern Tibet. The Emperor of China now yielded up the desired princess. This was Wên-ch'êng *kung-chu*, known to the Tibetans as Münshang Kongjo or Önshing Kongjo, or just Kongjo. She propagated Buddhism among them and built the Ramoche temple at Lhasa. To please her, as a Chinese, the king forbade the Tibetans' custom of smearing their faces with red, and he built her a palace and a wall. In her turn, she prompted the king to send young people of noble rank to the Chinese court to study the Chinese classics (especially the *Shih ching* and *Shu ching*). The king and his Chinese bride also asked for and were given silk-worms, and workmen trained in the manufacture of alcohol (rice-alcohol according to the Tibetan histories), mill-stones, paper and ink (Tibetan accounts add glass).[1] Writing was obviously indispensable for an organized state. According to the Chinese annals, Tibetans still did not know how to write, and the king invited Chinese *literati* to conduct the official correspondence with China.

But Songtsen Gampo had also married a Nepalese princess, again Buddhist, and the Tibetans had certainly made contact with India. In the lifetime of princess Wên-ch'êng, a Chinese pilgrim went from China to India by way of Tibet, in an ambassador's entourage. The first description of this route was published in China as early as 650. The famous pilgrim Hsüan Tsang had made a long stay in India and had aroused Indian interest in China. The king of Kāmarūpa (Assam) had asked for a statue of Lao Tzŭ and a translation of the *Tao tê ching* (one was made, but it is not known whether it reached Assam). Harṣa Śīlāditya, the king of Magadha, had sent a mission to China; and China had responded with the embassy of Li I-piao and Wang Hsüan-ts'ê, which probably travelled through Tibet, and is commemorated by inscriptions at Rājagṛha and Bodhgayā. On his second journey, meeting an unfavourable reception from Harṣa's successor, Wang Hsüan-ts'ê sought and received the assistance of Tibetan and

[1] 23, pp. 187–188; 197A, f. 2*b*; 201, years 640, second moon, and 641, first moon; 142, *MA*, f. 11*a*, based on Chinese sources.

Nepalese armies. The Tibetans had thus made their appearance in northern India around 647. They had also overrun Shangshung in 645, and they must similarly have learnt something of Indian civilization from that source. Songtsen Gampo died in 650. Soon afterwards, Tibet took from China the Buddhist Indo-European kingdoms of Turkestan which were largely dependencies of Indian civilization—Khotan, Kuchā, Karashahr and Kashgar (665–666).

According to Tibetan tradition, Songtsen Gampo sent a young man of the Thönmi or Thumi clan, Sambhoṭa son of Anu (or Drithorek Anu), to India (in 632?) with other youths, to learn the alphabet. The pattern chosen was the script of Kashmir. At all events, the ancient annals of Tun-huang record against the year 655 that 'the text of the laws was written'. It is staggering to realize that, in a couple of decades, not only was the Tibetan alphabet invented, but the script had been adapted to the Tibetan language by a highly complicated orthography, and used for the writing of documents. Thönmi is also said to have composed, no doubt later on, a very learned grammar on the Indian pattern.

The Tibetans were not so 'stupid' and 'barbarous' before the introduction of Buddhism as their tradition paints them. They were both worthy and intelligent. Tibetan pupils trained amongst the Chinese were as brilliant as those returning from India. In 663, the Tibetan minister known to us by his Chinese name of Chung-tsung had been entrusted with a mission to China. In 672, on a fresh mission, he astonished the Emperor with the cleverness of his answers. In his youth he had been a pupil at the T'ai-hsüeh national school at Changan, the Chinese capital, and he read and wrote Chinese extremely well. Back in 641, the minister Gar Tongtsen, more noted as a great strategist, distinguished himself with his gifts of repartee when negotiating the marriage of the Chinese princess in the capital of China. The Emperor was so pleased that he offered him a princess in marriage, too. Tibetans continued to attend the state school in China, along with other foreign noblemen. In 730 Chinese classics and a collection of literature (the *Shih ching, Tso chuan* and *Wên hsüan*) were sent to Tibet at their request. Amongst the Tun-huang manuscripts one finds not only adaptations or translations of Chinese literature (*Shu ching*, legend of Hsiang T'o, etc.) but Chinese texts transcribed in Tibetan characters, doubtless for the use of school-children (the school book *Ch'ien tzǔ wên*, and others).

While adopting a script and forging a grammar on the Indian pattern, the Tibetans could not remain unaware of India's religions. We shall see how Hinduism or Shivaism may have played a part in the Bonpo religion of Shangshung. But it is Buddhism that concerns us most. It was promoted by King Harṣa, and Buddhist Tantrism was flourishing in Bengal when the Pāla kings had to pay Tibet tribute around 755. It was Buddhism again that Tibetans found in the oases of Central Asia which they occupied from 666 to 692, as well as in the kingdom of Nan-chao, in Yünnan, which they controlled from 680, and which recognized their suzerainty after 703 and then again from 750 to 794. Most probably it was the same in the small states to the west, such as Serip (Chin. Hsi-li[1]), a hot country south-west of Tibet whose king was captured in 709, or Drusha (Gilgit, Greater and Lesser Po-lü) which yielded to Tibet in 737. Not to mention Nepal, of course, and above all China.

At first, perhaps, it was no more than a making of contact, not implying any real insight into Buddhism, even at the court. That at least is the impression Chinese sources give. The Chinese pilgrim Hui-chao asserts, in 792, that king and people were ignorant of Buddhism and that there was no temple in Tibet. He speaks, it is true, from hearsay only. However, the Tibetan tradition that takes the introduction of Buddhism back to Songtsen Gampo is supported by an inscription of King Sena Lek (804–816) which refers to the temple of Rasa (Lhasa) and others built in the time of Songtsen Gampo, to temples erected by Tüsong (676–703 or 704) at a place that seems to be Liangchow in north-west China, and to a temple built near Samyê by Trhide Tsukten (704–755). The silence of the Chinese annals proves nothing. They also ignore the foundation of Samyê in 775 and the religious debate ordered by the king; yet these facts are well vouched for by early documents.

During the same period, sketchy ideas of other foreign religions may have reached Tibet: Manichaeism through the Turks (Uighurs), Sogdians and Chinese; Nestorianism by way of Iran; and Islam through the Arabs. The same applies to certain items of folklore. The New Year rites and the mythology of the lion travelled from Iran to Turkestan (Samarkand, Kuchā, Turfan) and thence to China and Tibet.

At the same time, foreign influences were at work in the sciences.

[1] 6, pp. 41–42.

China and India supplied various techniques of divination and astrological calculations and, most important, medical science. But interestingly enough, the latter was also represented by the Greek tradition from Iran. In fact a very serious chronicle, which devotes a chapter to the history of medicine in Tibet, informs us that an Indian physician called Vajradhvaja, a Chinese physician called *Hen-weng Hang-de*, and a physician from Trhom ('Rome') in Tasik (Iran) called *Ga-le-nos*, were invited to Tibet in the time of Songtsen Gampo's Chinese wife (Wên-ch'êng, seventh century). Works representing their respective schools were translated, it goes on, but only the 'Galen of Iran', *Ga-le-nos*, was named king's physician or physician-in-chief (*bla-sman*) and gave instruction to pupils 'without taking the higher or lower rank of their family into account'. Later still, when princess Chin-ch'êng (eighth century) revived the translating of medical works from India and China, she too is stated to have invited from Trhom the physician *Bi-chi-tsan-ba-shi-la-ha*, whose name actually contained the Persian word for a doctor. And once again, it is this 'Greek from Iran' rather than a Chinese or Indian who is called the king's physician (*lha-rje*, an expression the chronicle explains as 'lord of the king', *rgyal-po'i rje*), with the privilege of sitting at the centre of the assembly on an 'excellent carpet' and being venerated as superior (*blar bkur-ba*) by all the others.[1]

That so much should have been possible within about a century, was due to the Tibetans' having a swift and powerful striking force at their command. The old chronicle from Tun-huang shows kings and ministers constantly journeying long distances from one meeting-place to another. Consequently, the horse is much celebrated in its pages. The king's steed subdues the four frontiers. Just as the king's body possesses supernatural powers (*'phrul*), his horse is so swift that its hoof-prints cannot be seen. According to the Fifth Dalai Lama's chronicle (f. 13b), King Namri Songtsen, the father of Songtsen Gampo, found his excellent horse, endowed with wisdom, on the shores of Lake Traksum Dingma during a wild-yak hunt which led him to discover salt. This was probably one of the many lakes in North Tibet. Perhaps it was no accident that apart from the conquest of

[1] 142, *TSA*, f. 46a.

the 'herders of horses' in Nyang, to the west, during the legendary period, the first expansion from Yarlung was north-eastwards, towards Koko Nor by way of the great plain of Yarmothang, and further east to Amdo—in the process subjecting and assimilating the Tomi, the Sumpa, the Asha or T'u-yü-hun and the Ch'iang. This whole region bred horses of high repute. At the outset, as we have seen, the Tibetans had the sturdy strains of Kongpo and Powo at their disposal.

Those same southern districts were producers of iron. But iron was also the distinctive tribute of the Sumpa. Iron or leather breast-plates and excellent iron swords were the speciality of the Ch'iang of Amdo (Namdong, Dong Sumpa, etc.)[1] The fifth Dalai Lama's chronicle (f. 11*b*) states that armour was introduced from Kham, though it places this advance in the time of the legendary king, Trigum. The Chinese annalists marvelled at the quality of Tibetan equipment. 'Their armour is excellent. They clothe their entire body in it, except for eye-holes. Even powerful bows and keen blades can do them little harm,' they wrote. Or again: 'They have bows and swords, shields, spears, suits of armour and helmets. . . . Both men and horses are covered in coats of mail of excellent manufacture'.[2] In Tibetan, from ancient chronicles to modern rituals of the warrior deities, the idea of power is expressed by the phrase 'having a firm (or powerful) helmet' (*dbu-rmog btsan-po*), hence 'exalted'; and a warrior's arms and armour, like his horses, all have names of their own.

But the royal family had to enforce its authority if these assets were to do it any good. It succeeded only slowly, and for a brief span, in doing so. And when the dynasty fell apart through internal conflict in the middle of the ninth century, that was the end of Tibetan military expansion. We shall be considering the feudal ties between the king and the great families later on. Loyalty was often unreliable. The kings' conquests were matched by diplomatic marriages. Songtsen Gampo had five wives: besides the princesses from China and Nepal, one wife was a daughter of the King of Shangshung, another, from the Ruyong clan, daughter of the King of Minyak, and a third came from Mong (though other lists exist). Five generations later, King Trhide Tsukten (704–755) took three wives: the Chinese princess Chin-ch'êng (Kyimshang Kongjo) who

[1] 115, p. 38.
[2] 197B, *hsia*, f. 1*b*; 200, f. 8*a*.

came to Rasa (Lhasa) in 710, a lady from Jang (Nan-chao) and a third born in Nanam. His successor, Trhisong Detsen (742–797 or 804) again had five wives, this time all from Tibetan noble families.[1] These great clans supplied the ministers. But rivalries between the king's family and his relations by marriage, as also between the different wives and their families (struggle for succession), led to great political instability.

It will be recalled that King Songtsen Gampo's success was largely due to his minister Tongtsen Yülsung of the Gar clan. The Chinese Emperor lavished favours upon him. Was the object to set him off against the king? Tongtsen knew how to stand aside; however, in a romance of which he is the hero he is suspected of having seduced the Chinese princess before delivering her to the king. The king placed the administration of Tibet proper in his hands whilst other ministers governed Shangshung and the Sumpas. Tongtsen Yülsung was on the frontier at the time of his sovereign's death, and came post-haste to the capital to chant his funeral oration. He himself did not die until seventeen years later, in 667.[2] His five sons divided the real power between them, helped by the insecurity of the royal succession. Songtsen Gampo's son, Kungsong Kungtsen, reigned for five years only (he died at eighteen); and his son, Mangsong Mangtsen, for only fifteen more. The dynasty of the Gar ministers flourished at their side for about thirty years. The more powerful of the five Gar sons had ensconced themselves on the Chinese borders and were thus in control of the T'u-yü-hun and the gateway to Amdo. King Tüsong (676–703 or 704) determined to end this parallel rule. When he was eight, he had accompanied his uncle to Yang-t'ung to raise troops, and the great minister Gar Trhindring (Chinese Ch'in-ling) was pressed to seize the opportunity of enthroning the king's younger brother, who was in his army. He wisely refused, and Tüsong was enthroned with his assent. But suspicion was bound to persist, and the minister's wisdom was perhaps dictated by the defeat he had just suffered at the hands of the Chinese at Koko Nor (678). Tibet at that stage reached as far as Liangchow, Sungchow and Maochow on the Chinese frontier, and Tali lake in south-west China. Princess Wên-ch'êng, when she died in 680, had lived through four reigns.

Tibet's power was not uncontested, however. The Chinese won

[1] 142, *JA*, ff. 25*b*–33*b*, 70*a*–*b*, 198*b*; 183, p. 46.
[2] 142, *JA*, ff. 65*b*–67*b*; 6, p. 14.

battles on several occasions and the Tibetans strove in vain to secure a peace treaty. To counterbalance Tibetan influence in Turkestan, the Chinese set about forming an alliance with Persia. In 692, they regained the 'Four Garrisons' of Turkestan (Kuchā, Kashgar, Yarkand and Khotan) from the Tibetans.

Soon afterwards Tüsong, now a man, decided to smash the Gar clan's power. The royal army defeated Gar Trhindring, who committed suicide (699). His son and brother surrendered to the Chinese, who received them with open arms—giving them titles and responsibility for guarding the frontier. The king did not gain a great deal by Gar's defeat. In 703, Nepal and the Himalayan parts of India rose in revolt, and the king died while on a campaign against them (according to the Tibetans his death took place in the land of Jang).[1] The succession was disputed between his sons, until Trhide Tsukten, alias Me Aktsom, was proclaimed king. He married a woman from Jang, by whom he had a son. The Tibetans had several times previously asked for a Chinese princess in marriage. Not until 710 was one granted. Intended originally for the king's son, who died in infancy, she was married to the father instead. According to some sources, she gave birth to a son who was the great king Trhisong Detsen (born 742, enthroned in 755–6) (though others say she died in 739). However, another wife of the king, born of the Nanam clan, is said to have brought him up and claimed the child was hers. Under his father things were in a precarious state. The Arabs had resumed their onward march: India and Tibet were obliged to seek Chinese help. The Tibetans tried to secure their western flank by upholding their authority over Drusha but that country, whilst accepting Tibetan suzerainty and a marriage alliance, turned towards China. Nan-chao also attacked Tibet. The peace treaty won from the Chinese in 730–734 was only too welcome to the Tibetans.

The situation improved under Trhisong Detsen. Nan-chao, hard pressed by Chinese armies, formed a new alliance with Tibet (750). The Pāla kings of Bengal had to pay tribute (755–6), and the Tibetans may also have invaded India in search of relics of the Buddha in Magadha, set up an iron column to mark their frontier on the Ganges, and left men behind to found a great city—but this account is admittedly legendary.[2] In any case, a Tibetan thrust in the direction

[1] 142, *JA*, f. 70*a*.
[2] 183, p. 44.

4. Fields at Khampa-partsi, seven miles from where the Tsangpo and Kyichu meet. *Photo: H.R.H. the Maharaja of Sikkim.*

5. Fields in front of Gyantse fort. *Photo: H.R.H. the Maharaja of Sikkim.*

6. Yaks used for threshing grain at Rong Champa, Lake Yamdrok region.
Photo: H.R.H. the Maharaja of Sikkim.

7. Threshing with flails at Rong Chutsen (hot springs), in the same region.
Photo: H.R.H. Maharaja of Sikkim.

of China was now also possible, thanks to that country's internal troubles. For the Chinese had annoyed the Uighur allies who had helped them put down the revolt of An Lu-shan. The Tibetans took the opportunity to invade the capital, Changan, and place another Emperor on the throne (763). It was a mere fifteen days' flash in the pan, but the fleeting coalition of Tibetans and Uighurs may have had an unexpected consequence—though this is pure hypothesis. The Uighurs had by then encountered Manichaean priests at Loyang and adopted Manichaeism, and the Tibetans could have made its acquaintance.

Fortune continued to favour Tibetan arms, with some ups and downs, for half a century. Constantly threatening the west of China, even driving the Chinese out of Bēshbalīq, in Turkestan (789–790), Tibet had to contend with Nan-chao when it was won over to China (794–808), and with the Arabs (under Haroun al Raschid) in Turkestan (791 onwards).

However, the decisive event for Tibetan civilization in this period was the king's official adoption of Indian Buddhism. Of course, as we have said, this decision is unlikely to have arisen *ex nihilo*. Tibetans had had many opportunities of acquainting themselves with Buddhism in all its forms, in China, Nan-chao, Khotan and India. But isolated contacts are one thing; official patronage by the king and part of the nobility is another. The Chinese annals are silent about the king's conversion, and the whole chronology of this period is uncertain. Even so, the accounts of the Tibetan chronicles have been confirmed by ancient documents from Tun-huang and by inscriptions. We shall keep mainly to the oldest account, which claims to go back to contemporary evidence though it has undergone subsequent adaptation (the *sBa-bzhed*, twelfth to thirteenth century?).

The king's father, Me Aktsom, had already displayed interest in Buddhism after the discovery of a prophecy heralding it. To start with he had sent two men to India and invited monks who were engaged in meditation at Mount Kailāśa (in Shangshung, then occupied by Tibet), but they contented themselves with sending him sūtras. The king had even built five temples. These measures, however, were met with hostility from some of the ministerial clans associated with the Bon religion. A certain Sangshi, of the Ba clan, was sent more or less surreptitiously to China and brought books back. He was obliged to hide them on his return to Tibet, for the old king had died, his heir Trhisong Detsen was still a minor, and a clan hostile to Buddhism was in power. Princess Chin-ch'êng had been stricken with ulcerous sores and ministers' children had died. These calamities were sure to be ascribed to the favour shown to Buddhism (according to the *Prophecy of Khotan*, the princess had let in the monks, from Khotan or Nepal).

When King Trhisong Detsen took charge on attaining his majority, and learnt what had taken place, he interested himself in Buddhism with the discretion called for in view of the hostility of some of the clans. Chinese and Indian Buddhist books were translated, it is said, and Selnang of the Ba clan made his way to India where he visited Mahābodhi and the great university of Nālandā. Afterwards, we are told, he brought the Buddhist monk Śāntarakṣita from Nepal and was ordained a monk by him with the religious name of Yeshe Wangpo. He had to go into hiding at Mang-yül near the Nepalese frontier. It was in Nepal, again, that he is said to have met the famous saint Padmasambhava who became the patron of the non-reformed orders of Tibet. Since Mashang Trompa-kye, the principal opponent of Buddhism, had been killed in an ambush, it was feasible to call in Padmasambhava and Śāntarakṣita. The former specialized in magical practices, but soon had to leave the country, pursued by the adherents of the Bon religion. Tibetan tradition makes him a native of the land of Uḍḍiyāna, which was famous for its magicians. It also links him with the land of Zahor where Tantrism flourished, a country sometimes described as being in north-west India, sometimes in Bengal. Such is the obscurity surrounding this personage that the prolific scholar Sumpa Khenpo, writing in 1748, assumes that there existed a 'true' Padmasambhava who had spent a long time in Tibet subduing all the local gods and demons, and a 'false' Padmasambhava who was just a Nepalese medium and only stayed a short while in Tibet.

However that may be, a great complex of Buddhist temples was built over a period of twelve years at Samyê at an undecided date (*ca.* 775?). An Indian temple at Otantapurī (or at Nālandā)[1] is regarded as the pattern used. The chief ministers and the five queens are stated to have contributed to the work with their offerings. Not long after, perhaps in 779, seven intelligent men were picked from

[1] 177, f. 58*a*.

66

the nobility (the 'seven chosen ones', *sad-mi*), to be ordained monks by Śāntarakṣita. The lists vary with different authors, and the number seven is doubtless due to a liking for numeric classifications, as was the case with the 'seven wise ministers'. But the prominent rôle played by Indian teachers at the time must not lead us to over-look the equally strong influence of Chinese Buddhism.

It was a period when Sino-Tibetan relations were good. At the Tibetan king's request China sent two Buddhist monks, skilled in preaching, in 781. They were to be replaced by others every two years, as a permanent arrangement. Shortly after, probably in 791, the king issued an edict setting up Buddhism as the official religion. The text was carved on a pillar near Samyê, where it remains to this day. According to tradition, two queens and three hundred people took religious vows, and the king decreed privileges for those in holy orders, with the promise of providing for their needs by dona-tions. We shall have more to say about this first step towards the wealth of the monasteries. So much success was not achieved without hindrance, ministers raising objections to an excessive number of ordinations. And the success of Buddhism had been primarily that of Chinese quietism, Ch'an ('Zen' in Japanese), which set little store by good works and the slow, difficult advance towards sainthood. Its popularity worried the Indian teachers, who had chiefly preached simple rules of moral conduct and the principle that good or bad actions are rewarded in a future life. This straightforward Buddhist moral code, the ten virtues and the ten sins, has even been ascribed to the period of Songtsen Gampo, and it is the moral aspect of Buddhism that Trhisong Detsen refers to in his edict.

Faced with the ensuing outburst of doctrinal antagonism between adherents of Indian and Chinese Buddhism, the king decided to cut short the proceedings with a religious disputation, the kind of rhetorical and theological duel that was then in vogue in India and China; a duel which meant not merely disgrace and humiliation, but sometimes even death, for the loser. China was represented by the Chinese monk Mahāyāna, and India by the monk Kamalaśīla, who had been invited for the occasion. The text of the historic contest has been preserved for us both in the works of Kamalaśīla (in Sanskrit and in Tibetan translation) and through a Chinese record found among the Tun-huang documents—the town fell into Tibetan hands about 787. The debate seems to have taken place at Samyê in

792–794 in the king's presence. The Chinese upheld the 'sudden path', the identity of what is beyond any phenomenon (Emptiness or *nirvāṇa*) with the phenomenal world (*saṁsāra*), and the pointlessness of good works at that doctrinal level. The Indians, though not unaware of the doctrine, which was in keeping with Mahāyāna and Tantrism—and accepting it, as we shall see, under certain conditions —championed the 'gradual path', the slow journeying towards perfection in which good works play an important part. The Chinese lost and were forced to leave the country, in no gentle fashion. The king proclaimed that only the doctrine that had been maintained by the Indians was to be recognized in Tibet.

Actually the triumph of Indian Buddhism was only temporary and incomplete. The Chinese doctrines have left their mark on certain works and schools down to the present day. The anti-Buddhist section of the aristocracy, moreover, had not given up the fight, and the king had to reckon with them. The minister Tara Lugong, a Bon devotee, had been 'exiled to the North'. In reality, he was the general who took possession of the meditation school of the Bhaṭa Hor, a tribe of Uighurs in the Kanchow region, and is reputed to have brought back Pehar, the guardian deity of the treasures of Samyê. He is listed among the eminent persons who built stūpas at Samyê, though it is true that his was a black one, no doubt because he was a Bonpo. An inscription (probably of 762–4) extols his services to the king and contains the royal edict granting extensive privileges to him and his descendants.

The great king died shortly after the debate, in 797 or 804, and the chronology of his successors is jumbled and obscure. He had two or three sons. The first-born was poisoned by his mother after a reign of almost two years. Tradition asserts that, grieved by the disparity between the offerings of the rich and the poor, he thrice tried in vain to bring about an equal distribution of wealth among his subjects. His younger brother succeeded him (for those who believe there were three sons, the second was exiled for murdering a minister's son, and then himself murdered). This was Trhide Tsukten, also known as Sena Lek. His son and successor Trhitsuk Detsen, or Relpachen, is the last Buddhist king (reigning 815–838). He signed a peace treaty with China in 821–822 of which the Tibetan and Chinese texts are still preserved on a pillar at Lhasa. We shall see that the progress of Buddhism had not eliminated earlier beliefs. And yet this king did a great deal for Indian Buddhism. Hitherto, Buddhist texts in several languages, including Chinese, had been made use of.[1] Now Sanskrit was chosen as the official religious tongue. Moreover, the vocabulary used in translations was revised, and the rules of translation were laid down in detail by royal decree. A 'new language' was created in this way that was more suited to translation and closer to real Tibetan than that of the first translations, which were often so literal as to be incomprensible.

The king carried his devotion to the extent of becoming a monk. The gifts and privileges heaped upon the clergy aroused strong opposition, which culminated in the king's assassination (according to one source at least).[2] It was a wonder that he came to the throne at all, since he was the youngest of three brothers. The eldest, Tsepa or Tsenma, had not succeeded in taking power and had been assassinated in the south of the country, on the Bhutanese border. After Relpachen's death his son Tsangma, a monk, was exiled to Bhutan and his elder brother Lang Darma took the throne. Tradition accuses this king of every sort of crime because he persecuted Buddhism. He reigned for only a year and a half according to one source, however, though others make it six or even thirteen years.[3] He was killed (in 846, according to Sato) by a monk, Pelgyi Dorje of Lhalung, who fled to the neighbourhood of Hsünhwa, south of the Yellow River in Amdo, where we shall have occasion to meet him again.

Tibetan glory and the royal power were at an end. Tradition sees persecution of Buddhism as the reason. However, internecine power-struggles and external military setbacks might also be considered. The Chinese frontier towns were lost, in particular Tun-huang (occupied from 781 or 787) and Shachow (851); and the high minister in command on the frontier was eventually beheaded (866), the scattered remnants of his army forming the nucleus of a population spread all along the borderlands. About the middle of the ninth century the Tibetan presence in Turkestan was brought to an end by Turks, Uighurs and Qarluqs.

For a century and a half or so, the Tibetan chronicles yield only dry lists of successive kings, partly without dates. To make matters

[1] 183, p. 73.
[2] 183, p. 77; *Bod-kyi rgyal-rabs* quoted in 123, pp. 311, 314.
[3] 166, f. 211*a–b*: thirteen years.

worse, this is the period affected by the 'gap' of sixty or a hundred and twenty years referred to earlier. The Chinese annals do speak of Tibetans (907–932) sending missions to China, but significantly they are always local chiefs from the Koko Nor region.

Lang Darma had two sons, Yumten by his first wife (said, however, to have been stolen from another woman), and Ösung by his second wife. They competed for power and reigned separately, the former over the Centre (Ü) and the latter over the 'left wing'. A great conflict or revolt ensued (929, or according to Sato 869) and ended in the desecration of the royal tombs or at least the abandonment of the custom of building them (in 937, or according to Sato 877).[1]

Pelkhortsen, Ösung's son, is portrayed as a pious Buddhist who built a hundred temples. He was slain by his subjects and lost the central kingdom of Ü and Tsang. Thus ended the dynasty of Nyatri, his legendary ancestor. His two sons took western Tsang, and the three lands of Ngari, respectively. The son and grandson of the first founded local princely houses at Kungthang, and in Nyang, Amdo (at Tsongkha), Yarlung, etc. The sons of the second reigned separately over the three lands of Ngari—Mar-yül, Purang and Shangshung or Guge. A branch descending from the prince of Purang carved out the principality of Yatse, capital of the Mallas, and probably in the north-western corner of present-day Nepal.

THE EVOLUTION OF MONASTIC POWER

When the curtain lifts once more and a few gleams of light fall on the scene, Tibetan civilization is definitely taking on the aspect it has retained till modern times. History is no longer concerned with kings but with monasteries and religious orders. The princes or heads of noble houses are now no more than benefactors and partisans of one ecclesiastical establishment or another. It is the eleventh century.

In China, after the fall of the T'ang (907) and the intervening period of the Five Dynasties (907–960), the Sung dynasty (960–1276) was established. But in the north-west of the country a new state had taken shape: Hsi Hsia or, in both Tibetan and its own Tibeto-

---

[1] 141, f. 46b; same dates and information found already in *Tshal-pa Kun-dga' rdo-rje*'s *Hu-lan deb-ther* (mid-fourteenth century).

Burman language, Minyak. It soon stormed the Chinese towns occupied by the Uighurs (Shachow, Kanchow, and so on, in 1038), but in the west it collided with a recently formed Tibetan kingdom in the Sining region (Chinese Ch'ing-t'ang; Tibetan Tsong-kha), that was headed by one Gyelsê (Chinese Chüeh-szŭ-lo, 997–1065), whom the Tibetan chieftains of the region had travelled westwards to find, probably in Mar-yül, among the descendants of the royal line. This state, which lasted till about 1100, was Buddhist. Monks, some of them from Khotan—occupied by the Muslims since 1006—played a major political part. They had dealings with China and the Uighurs, both those of Kanchow, who later settled further south in the Nan Shan range where they still live under the name of Yogurs, and those of Turfan who were Buddhists and Manichaeans.

So it was to these parts that Buddhist monks made their way, fugitives from the persecution and decadence in Central Tibet. Three monks set out via Ladakh and the Qarluq Turks to the west, passing through Hor (Uighurs) in the north, to end up in Amdo, on the Yellow River. Gerap Sel of the Musu or Musi clan, an ex-Bonpo from Tsongkha, was converted to Buddhism (832–915). His ordination as a monk required the presence of five existing monks. Three Tibetans were found further south, at Longthang in Kham, and two Chinese were added to make up the quorum. Others came to join the nucleus thus constituted, which soon approached King Trhi of Yarlung with the intention of renewing links with Central Tibet. The ruins of Samyê were restored and other monasteries were founded.[1]

A new upsurge of Buddhism meanwhile took place in the west through the efforts of the kings of Ngari. King Khorre had abdicated in favour of his younger brother Song-nge, and taken the robe under the name (Lha Lama) Yeshe Ö. He decided to send young men to study in India, for the monastic tradition had been lost, and irregular practices had caused the spread of doubt. In the tenth and eleventh centuries, married Tantrists had taken the instructions of certain Tantras literally. These 'robber-monks' (*ar-tsho bande, a-ra-mo ban-dhe*) kidnapped and killed men and women, ate them, drank alcohol and indulged in sexual intercourse. In the face of such developments, the need to be assured of a sound tradition was felt. The kings as patrons of the established religion were concerned for

[1] 151, ed. Das, pp. 177–178 and *Re'u-mig*; 183, pp. 87–88.

the upholding of public morals, just as in Trhisong Detsen's day. The Tibetan monks they sent to India and the Indian teachers they invited to Tibet, however, were all firm adherents of the Tantrism then flourishing in India, not only among isolated yogins, but in the great monastic colleges such as Nālandā and Vikramaśīla. They were simply careful to offer a symbolic interpretation, especially to the uninitiated and to lay people, of ritual acts which taken literally would offend common morality. Their reform consisted mainly of a rigorous distinction between the types of behaviour expected at different levels of mental training and holiness: ordinary men had to regulate their conduct according to ordinary morality. Not for nothing was the most violent diatribe against Tantric abuses delivered by Lha Lama Changchup Ö, prince of Purang.[1] Reform aimed at the re-establishment of monastic discipline.

Two figures dominate this period in western Tibet. Rinchen Sangpo (958–1055), who was sent to India and Kashmir, showed tremendous industry as a translator and founded several temples in Guge—Toling in particular—as well as, in all probability, Tabo and Nako in Spiti. Atiśa (982–1054), invited to Tibet, was the founder of the great Kadam-pa order, from which later came the Geluk-pa order, the official or Yellow Church of the Dalai Lamas and Panchen Lamas.

Atiśa, also known as Dīpaṁkara Śrījñāna, is described as the son of a king of Zahor, a country noted for Tantrism. He studied all the schools of Buddhism, including Hīnayāna, but above all the Tantras. These works were taught by the famous *siddhas* or yogins such as Ḍombhi, Nāro-pa and Avadhūti-pa, all of them teachers revered in Tibet. Offered a large quantity of gold to come to Tibet, by Changchup Ö, nephew or grand-nephew of Yeshe Ö, the king of Guge, he arrived in 1042 and died there in 1054. He found Buddhism in the process of renewal through the work of monks from Kham who now became his disciples. The composition of this group of disciples is significant. The three leading members, Khutön, Ngoktön and Dromtön, were natives of Ü who had brought back the tradition of the Vinaya or monastic discipline from Kham, while the four others were all yogins (*a-mes* or *rnal-'byor-pa*).

It was in Kham, at Longthang in the land of Den, that a wandering monk from Nepal, Smṛiti, had founded a school for the study of the

[1] 151, ed. Das, p. 393.

Abhidharmakośa, before moving on to Liangchow. He taught Dromtön. The latter, at the age of seventeen, returned to Ü and founded the famous Reting monastery (north of Lhasa) in 1057. He became Atiśa's principal disciple. Smṛiti had taught Sanskrit to Setsün who, in turn, was the teacher of Atiśa's three chief disciples, and who founded an important faculty of theology at Öka on the model of the school at Longthang.

But, in the same part of Kham, the spiritual lineage of Padmasambhava had also been kept alive through the agency of the translator Vairocana, exiled to Kinchwan, where the daughter of a king of that region became his disciple. This lineage is that of the Dzokchen-pa order, which belongs to the 'ancient' (Nyingma-pa) unreformed school, and teaches a form of Tantrism in which some material from Chinese *Dhyāna* (Ch'an, Zen) is preserved. A former Bonpo, Yasi Pöntön, and his teacher, Aro, were also there at that time. This Aro, likewise established at Longthang in Den, had received the teachings of seven lineages of India, together with seven lineages of China. A point of interest is that, alone among Tibetan writings of this period, it was his chief work, *Entering into the yoga of the Mahāyāna*, that Atiśa is recorded as having liked and praised. So we are hardly surprised to find that Dromtön was followed on the abbot's throne at Reting, from 1065 to 1078, by a great yogin (*a-mes*), Changchup Jungnê, who was born at Tsongkha in 1015.[1]

Tantric teachings, with some variations, took root everywhere. On the basis of particular techniques and teachers, different orders and great monasteries were founded in this period. Drogmi, 'the man of the grazing lands' (992–1074), acquired from great yogins in India the teaching known as Lamdrê (*lam-'bras*, 'the path and fruit of action') that made use of sexual practices for mystical realization. His disciple Könchok Gyelpo in 1073 founded the great monastery of Sakya whose future hierarchs were to become so important.

Marpa (1012–1096) also went to India where he learnt, among other things, the art of transferring the conscious principle into another body or a paradise (*'pho-ba*, *grong-'jug*). But above all he brought back and handed on to his disciple Mila Rêpa the mystical songs (*dohā*) of the Tantric poets of Bengal, and the doctrines called

[1] 99, II, p. 1000; 50, p. 703; 146, f. 129*b*.

Mahāmudrā, the 'Great Seal'. Out of the disciples of the poet hermit Mila Rêpa (1040–1123) was formed the Kagyü-pa order, whose two main branches were to have extensive influence. Khyungpo the Yogin, born in a Bonpo clan and brought up initially on Bonpo and Dzokchen-pa doctrines, founded the branch at Shang in Tsang, dying in 1139. To the east, in Dakpo, Gampo-pa (1079–1153)—also called Dakpo Lharje ('physician, or medium, of Dakpo')—founded the Dakpo branch, maintaining doctrinal links with the Kadam-pa. A little later the school produced major subdivisions whose hierarchs and monasteries played an important political rôle: the Karma-pa, Drigung-pa, Tshel-pa, Phagmotru-pa and Drukpa. All these names are derived from the names of monasteries, the suffix -pa denoting membership of a group, or place of birth.

The incredible religious and philosophic ferment of the eleventh century does not stop at that. We have already mentioned the Dzokchen-pa tradition which had been kept up since the ninth century in Kham. Now people tried to link up with that period and with Padmasambhava by discovering 'hidden treasures' (gter-ma). These were writings which a modern historian would class as apocryphal like prophecies, but which were said to have been concealed in the time of Padmasambhava. Some, it should be added, may have been adaptations of genuine documents if we are to believe their description as rolls of yellow paper, which agrees with the appearance of the Tun-huang manuscripts. From its beginning at this period the fashion grew over subsequent centuries, with Nyang Rel Nyima Öser, ruler of Nyang (1136–1203), Guru Chhöwang (1212–1273) and many others, including Mingyur Dorje of Kham in the seventeenth century. We should also recall that at the same period the Kālacakra and the sexagenary cycle were introduced (1027). Two other doctrines and practices which were to play a great part in Tibet (zhi-byed and gcod) were spread at that time by an Indian yogin, Tampa Sanggyê (who died in 1117), and more especially by a remarkable Tibetan woman, 'the Mother' (ma-cig) Lab Drönma (1055–1145 or 1153).

In the following century, this intellectual activity was translated into social or political reality. We know nothing at all about the noble families and local principalities, and only a little about the conditions that allowed the flourishing of rich and powerful monasteries. We shall hear of one feature later on: the succession of abbots from paternal uncle to nephew within a noble family, one brother getting married, the other becoming a monk. In any case, by the twelfth century monasteries are everywhere, some of them being particularly powerful. A century later and they are battling for temporal power; and these internal feuds, in combination with the rivalries of noble houses and the absence of central authority, prepare Tibet for the fate that will henceforth be hers. On re-entering Asian history in the thirteenth century, her participation is no longer active as in the past but passive. Submission to foreign powers is all that will now be possible.

Let us take a look at the forces confronting one another when the Mongols first appeared on the scene. The great Khön family, which had supplied prominent members of the religious community since Trhisong Detsen's time, had made its home at Sakya. Like other great noble clans, it claimed divine descent. It was allied with the Che family whose divine ancestry accordingly had much in common with theirs. The family connection was carried on in the relations between monasteries. The Khön founded Sakya in 1073; the Che had founded the monastery of Shalu, not far away, in 1040. Some centuries later their rulers established marriage ties with the lords of Gyantse.

Another important noble family with the indispensable distinction of divine origin, the Phagmotru, was connected with the great Lang clan and, through it, with the Gar family that was already powerful in Kham and later to reign at Derge. The Phagmotru family originally came from Kham where its forbears occupied a district in the valley of the Drichu (Di Chu, the Upper Yangtze), but it took the name of the region where the branch's founder settled. This 'precious protector of beings', the 'great man of Kham', born in 1110, was a pupil of Gampo-pa (Dakpo Lharje) and of one of the Sakya-pas. In 1158 he founded the monastery of Thil or Thel at the place called Phagmotru, in the Ön district (the south-eastern corner of Central Tibet), and in 1170 he died. He won the territory of the 'king of Tsharong' at a game of chess. His religious order derived from both the Kadam-pas and the Kagyü-pas. The monastery was a bone of contention between the abbots of Drigung and those of Talung.

The office of abbot was handed down from uncle to nephew. But the family did not attain political power till later, in the fourteenth century.

Drigung monastery, on a tributary on the Kyichu far to the north-east of Lhasa, was first set up by Minyak Gomring, a disciple of Phagmotru-pa (abbot in 1167); however, its real foundation was the work of Drigung Rinpoche (1143–1217), a monk from Den, in Kham, in 1179. The order was attached to the Kagyü-pas. The administration, modelled on that of Sakya, comprised an abbot assisted by a civil and military governor who, despite his functions, bore the title of 'great meditator (or hermit)' (*sgom-chen*).

Another monk of the Kagyü-pa order, Shang (spelt *Zhang*) Rinpoche (1123–1193), founded the monastery of Tshel (1175) and the temple of Tshel Kungthang (1187) on the Kyichu a little east of Lhasa. This monastery became the seat of the Tshel family who were soon to take part in the struggles for power.

One last important counter on the political board remains to be introduced. This is the Karma-pa order. Its founder Tüsum Khyenpa (1110–1193) was another native of Kham, from the district of Tao (Taofu), and a follower of Mila Rêpa's disciples—Gampo-pa, Rêchung, etc. He first founded, in 1147, the 'Karma seat' or 'southern camp of Karma', east of the river Ngomchu in Kham, between Riwoche and Derge. Subsequently in 1155 he established the Karma monastery of Tshur Lhalung (already begun in 1154 by Dakpo Gomtsül in Tölung), then in 1185 that of Karma Lhadeng, and lastly, in 1189, that of Tshurphu, the modern seat of the Karma-pas and also in the Tölung valley north-west of Lhasa. The order, which stems from the Kagyü-pa, owes its name to a black hat of *ḍākinīs'* hair in which are brought together all the works (*phrin-las = karma*) of all the Buddhas. With the abbots of Drigung, the Karma-pa 'Black Hat' succession claims to have started the system of successive reincarnations of the same person, which was later adopted for the Dalai and Panchen Lamas. Its representatives reign to this day and formerly recognized a related line of incarnate hierarchs, the 'Red Hats', starting with Trakpa Sengge (1283–1349).

While these monastic authorities were being set up at the religious, economic, political and military level, the 'kings' or heads of principalities left scarcely a trace. In the west, our sources only provide incomplete lists of the kings of Guge and Ladakh. They had turned towards Nepal and the outlying parts of India (Kulu, Purang and Kashmir). In the east, Gyelsê's sons were competing for mastery in Tsongkha, facing the powerful Hsi Hsia kingdom, and part of their domain seems to have formed the nucleus of a principality which was to play its part later on—Ling. With its neighbour, Beri, this little kingdom had been in existence since the end of the twelfth century if isolated references are to be believed. For the rest, there is silence and obscurity.

But now the Mongols appear on the scene. Genghiz Khan, king of the Mongols (Tibetan 'Sok') in 1189, got as far as Central Tibet by 1206 according to Tibetan sources. Greeted by the regent Jorga, a descendant of the Yarlung royal family, and by Künga Dorje, head of the Tshelpas, he received Tibet's submission from them. But we are also told that, before leaving, he sent presents to Sakya and invited its abbot, Künga Nyingpo, to come and preach the religion in Mongolia, thus offering himself as a 'donor' or patron. By surrendering to alien suzerainty, Tibet was able to preserve her autonomy. In order to wield power in the interior, it was necessary to have a foreign patron. Sakya had been preferred to the Tshelpas, though other candidates were waiting in the wings. And the political game grew more complex by virtue of the division of the Mongol empire between several brothers, on the death of Genghiz Khan in 1227.

According to a Mongol work the first Karma-pa, Tüsum Khyenpa, tried to convert Kublai Khan. Perhaps this is merely a pious anticipation, but it does show how, from the outset, the Karma-pas were going to be the Sakya-pas' rivals at the court of the Emperors of China —first Mongolian (Yüan) and later Chinese (Ming). In 1221–1222 a Karma lama, Tsangpa Tungkhur-wa, was invited to Minyak, i.e. to a Buddhist, Tibetanized Hsi Hsia. He was still there when Genghiz Khan conquered that kingdom and died there (in 1227), and received an edict of approval from the queen. Karma Pakshi (1206–1283) was sent for by Kublai, while still a prince, and met him in Amdo in 1255. Urged to stay with him, he refused, in expectation of conflicts between the Mongol princes. This attitude was to earn him persecution by Kublai Khan and exile to South China, but prior to that he continued his journey as far as Mongolia (1256). There he took part in theological contests between Buddhists and Taoists at the court of the Emperor Möngke whom he had converted from Nestorian

Christianity to Buddhism. However, Möngke died in 1260 and Kublai took power against his young brother Ariboga. Karma-pa had lost his patron.[1]

The Sakya-pas were more fortunate. The 'great scholar' Sakya Panchen (1182–1251) had the reputation of having worsted the 'heretics' in theological debates in India. So that he might do the same in Mongolia, he was sent for in 1244 by Güyüg and Godan, the son and grandson of Genghiz Khan, who had made their headquarters in Koko Nor. In 1244, accompanied by his young nephews Phakpa (1235–80) and Chhana, he met Godan. The invitation was 'supported', it seems, by a raid under the general, Dorta, whose army advanced as far as northern Ü, burning Reting monastery and killing monks, but apparently sparing Drigung monastery. Sakya Panchen gave Godan religious initiation, and is credited with devising a Mongol alphabet. Godan in 1249 gave him an order conferring the rulership of Ü and Tsang on the Sakya-pas. After the deaths of Godan and Sakya Panchen there was a fresh Mongol invasion of Tibet (1252–1253). But Kublai became patron of the Sakya-pas and granted them rulership over all Tibet's 'thirteen provinces': this was in 1253, or in 1260 when he was proclaimed Emperor. The recipient of this authority was Phakpa, under the title of 'Teacher of the Emperor' (*Ti-shih*). He originated a Mongol script, derived from Tibetan writing, which continued in use for nearly a century.

If the Sakya-pas had thus officially received the regency of all Tibet, other monasteries did not stand idly by. Profiting by the splitting up of Mongol power, each tried to have its own patron. The Tshelpa, Gara, had performed rites for Ariboga, son of Möngke, about 1260, but was later arrested by Kublai Khan at Shangtu, the Mongol capital, where he died. Even so, Kublai became patron of the Tshelpas. Meanwhile Kublai's elder brother, Hülä'ü, had founded the Ilkhan dynasty (1258–1335) in Iran. Despite some partiality towards the Christians, he was a Buddhist. He was chosen by the Drigung-pas as their patron, which he became as early as 1267. Their aim was to turn the tables on the Sakya-pas. They received offerings from Hülä'ü, gained control of Ü and founded the fief of Neudong which was to be very important later on; and in 1285 they descended in force on Chayül, in southern Tibet, and

---

[1] 151, xyl., f. 275*b*; 89; 142, *MA*, ff. 17–18.

78

brought an army of Iran Mongols against Sakya. However, the Sakya-pas won, helped by an army belonging to Kublai's son Temürbukha and an army from Tsang, and burned the temple of Drigung in 1290; though Drigung was soon restored at the Sakya-pas' own request, and received gifts from the Emperor. This was the first expression of the opposition between Ü and Tsang which was often to be manifested over the centuries.[1]

The Mongol Emperors of China exerted a fairly loose suzerainty over Tibet. They had instituted population censuses (1268, 1287) and tried to set up an administrative organization. But the real power was still contested among great monasteries backed up by important noble families. Sakya-pa influence lasted only three-quarters of a century. The Phagmotru-pa family had at first been linked with the Drigung-pas and their patron Hülä'ü. But in the fourteenth century, under the 'Great *Si-tu*' Changchup Gyentsen and his grandson, the family came to power in southern Tibet, where it was now allied with, now opposed to the Sakya-pas and Drigung-pas. In the meantime, the Karma-pas continued to be welcomed at the Chinese court and took firm root in Kham and south-east Tibet. Here they were to occupy a leading position for centuries, alongside the Sakya-pas.

One of the countries in Kham which had close relations with the Karma-pas was the 'kingdom' of Ling, which in those days included modern Derge. When the Ming dynasty in China took over the Mongols' policy of bestowing honorary ranks and titles on various heads of religious orders, around 1400, Ling and Gonjo received the title of 'kings' and golden seals, on a par with the Phagmotru-pas, the Drigung-pas and the Taktsang-pas of Tsang. The Karma-pas went to China in great numbers. They occupied themselves in bringing their moral authority, but often too the force of their military camps, to bear in pacifying the countless feuds and quarrels between indigenous tribes and minor states, followers of Buddhism and Bon.

Meanwhile a great yogin-type saint, Thangtong Gyelpo (1385–1464), celebrated for the building of iron suspension bridges, had opened the route to the Kongpo aborigines (the Lo), and from them he obtained supplies of iron and rights of passage for Tibetan

---

[1] 142, *MA*, f. 21*a*; 143, ff. 160–172; 132, ff. 39*b*–88*a*; 95; 142, *MA*, ff. 17*b*–37*a*. [cf. p. 117–JESD].

pilgrims wishing to visit the holy places of Tsari. He had also founded Derge monastery.

In Central Tibet, Phagmotru-pa power was on the wane and a new antagonism between Ü and Tsang was taking shape. The political leaders of the Phagmotru-pas reigned in their capital of Neudong, in Yarlung, south of the Tsangpo; their abbots at Tsethang, a little further north. Their ministers, the princes of Rinpung, then took power at Samdruptse (modern Shigatse in Tsang). They made war upon Ü (1481), while another war took place between the Karma-pas (on the Tsang side) and Geluk-pas (Ü).

For, in the meantime, an event of major importance had taken place—the foundation by Tsongkha-pa (1357–1419) of the Geluk-pa order. Not that the 'reformation' for which he is commonly praised really included any basic innovation in doctrine or ritual. No more than Atiśa, whose teachings he followed, did he neglect the Tantras with all the rituals and meditations that go with them which he had studied with the Karma-pas and Sakya-pas. But, like Atiśa and his Kadam-pa order, he insisted once more on the need for monastic discipline and the gradual path (morality, etc.), for the generality of men and even as a preliminary to total liberation. After a retreat at Reting, the Kadam-pa monastery where in 1403 he composed his great work in two volumes (*Lam-rim* and *sNgags-rim*), he took the decision to mark the renewal of the discipline by founding a new order. At first, this was called 'new Kadam-pa', but later Geluk-pa ('those who follow virtuous works') or Ganden-pa, from the Ganden monastery, founded in 1409. His reputation as a great theologian and debater earned Tsongkha-pa an invitation to China from the Emperor (1408). Being too busy, he sent his disciple, Jamchen Chöje Shakya Yeshe, who received the title 'king of religion' and soon afterwards (1419) founded the great monastery of Sera. Another disciple, Jamyang Chöje Trashi Pelden, had founded—in 1416—the third great monastery in the neighbourhood of Lhasa, Drêpung, on the pattern of a Tantric monastery in India. These monasteries were regular university cities and they all contained a variety of faculties, some of which specialized in the Tantras.

Despite the importance of this maintenance of Tantric tradition at the religious and philosophical level, it was its reforming side, its insistence on discipline, that set the movement's tone and political direction. Its affinity with the early Kadam-pas drew it towards the

8. Forests of Powo (Pome).
   Photo: V. Sís/J. Vaniš.

9. *rGya-ma*, reputed birthplace of Songtsen Gampo. *Photo: H. Richardson.*

10. Potala Palace. Top, roofs as on Chinese tombs or temples, and tree branches. *Photo: H. Harrer, Liechtenstein Verlag.*

11. Samyê temple. Foreground: high ground marked by pile of stones, trees, rags and 'wind horses'. *Photo: H. Harrer, Liechtenstein Verlag.*

Phagmotru-pas. The fact that their chief monasteries were situated in Ü reinforced this closeness through the territorial opposition between the forces of Ü and Tsang. Geluk-pa monasteries were founded at Chamdo (1436–1444) in Kham, and at Trashilünpo (1447) in Tsang, but the order was unable to gain the upper hand in either of these regions of Karma-pa predominance. The princes of Tsang built a fortified monastery at Shigatse, close by Trashilhünpo, and even succeeded in keeping control of Lhasa for twenty years (1498–1518) through the instrumentality of the Karma-pas. The 'Red Hat' Karma-pas allied themselves with the governors of Tsang, who had succeeded the Rinpung princes (sixteenth century).

There were many wars. The monks of Drêpung attacked the 'people of the camps' (*sgar-pa*), i.e. the Karma-pa military camps, in 1546. The reason was that in 1537 the fifth Red Hat had formed an alliance with Drigung and the governor of Tsang, designed to suppress the Geluk-pas and their best patrons, the princes of Ganden. The uncertain fate of these temporary alliances and local struggles was to be decided by a fresh Mongol irruption onto the political and military scene.

The influence of the Karma-pa and Sakya-pa hierarchs at the court of Genghiz Khan and his successors did not amount to an actual conversion of the Mongols to Lamaism. The eighth 'Black Hat' Karma·pa had fleeting contacts with Dayan Khan (1470–1543) who was then reigning over the Mongols. However, their real conversion was the work of Geluk-pas at the time of Altan Khan, Dayan's grandson and king of the Tümed Mongols. The head of the Geluk-pas in those days was the abbot of Drêpung, later known as the Third Dalai Lama, Sönam Gyatso (1543–1588). The royal patrons of his order, the house of Phagmotru, were then split into two hostile branches. In spite of the support he received from several feudatories of this royal house, even in Tsang, the ruling family of Tsang were still a serious threat, along with the Karma-pas, to Ü and the Geluk-pas, particularly after they occupied the important position of Samdruptse. So it was understandable that Sönam Gyatso should approach foreign patrons, as other hierarchs had done in the thirteenth century. Some Tibetan monks had been taken prisoner during expeditions led by Sechen Hung Taiji of the Ordos Mongols in 1566, and by Altan Khan in 1573. To revive the policies of his illustrious ancestor Kublai Khan. Altan Khan now issued an invitation to Sönam Gyatso, and met him in 1578. With gifts heaped upon him, Sönam Gyatso secured an edict abolishing the Mongols' blood-sacrifices, as well as receiving his famous title of Dalai Lama (*dalai*, meaning 'ocean' in Mongol, is a translation of the 'gyatso' which occurs in the names of all the Dalai Lamas). The reason he is reckoned the third of the line is that his two previous incarnations were given the same title retrospectively. These were Gedün-trup (1391–1474), a personal disciple of Tsongkha-pa and the founder of Trashilhünpo in 1447; and Gedün Gyatso (1475–1542), the first of his incarnations to be recognized as such, who had been abbot of Trashilhünpo in 1520, Drêpung in 1517 and Sera in 1526.

The Third Dalai Lama travelled a great deal throughout Kham, Amdo, the Koko Nor region and Inner Mongolia, winning the patronage of the Tümed, Chahar and Khalkha Mongols for the Geluk-pas. This the Mongols doubtless saw as a political advantage, for the Third Dalai Lama had scarcely died before his reincarnation was discovered in the person of a great grandson of Altan Khan. He was recognized by a delegation from his Drêpung monastery and the princes of Ü, which had gone to Kweisui (Köke Qoto, Inner Mongolia) to meet him in 1601.

The Fourth Dalai Lama, Yönten Gyatso, was duly installed on the throne of Drêpung; but he was still threatened by the rulers of Tsang—who were aiming at hegemony and whose dependency the fief of Lhasa then was—and by the Karma-pas. The latter had not omitted to find a patron of their own among the Mongol princes— Ligden Khan of the Chahars. But at the same time they weakened their authority through an armed quarrel between the Amdo 'Black Hat' and the 'Red Hat' who was in alliance with the governor of Tsang. At this juncture the Karma-pas had first to sustain an attack by Arslan Khan of the Khalkhas (battle near Dam in 1635), who subsequently turned against the Geluk-pas, and then once more against the Karma-pas. Arslan was executed by his father, and the Karma-pas' remaining ally, Ligden Khan, died of smallpox on the Koko Nor plain.

Mongol troops had opposed the armies of Tsang several times since 1621 in defence of the young Fifth Dalai Lama, Ngawang Lopsang Gyatso (1617–1682). But the final blow to Tsang power and the triumph of the Geluk-pas were due to the intervention of Gushi Khan. Having established himself at Koko Nor in 1637, he first crushed the principality of Beri, in Kham, whose religion was Bonpo, and then came to the aid of Derge, which was by now enlarging itself at the expense of Ling. He went on to subdue the whole of Kham as far as Yünnan (Likiang), where the Karma-pas, till then (1641), had been powerful. A year later, the Tsang sovereign was defeated and killed. The Dalai Lama received authority from Gushi Khan to reign over all Tibet, but at the same time he had a 'governor' (*sde-srid*), nominated by the Mongol, imposed on him.

THE MODERN ERA

Throughout this period the Tibetans had had dealings to the westward with Islam. Successive invasions and wars in the direction of Kashmir and Turkestan had failed to jeopardize the existence of the kingdom of Ladakh—the Sultan Saïd Khan of Kashgar and his general Mirza Haidar had, for instance, penetrated to Central Tibet in 1531–1533. Baltistan, however, had become Muslim in the sixteenth century. Despite successes against Guge (overthrown about 1630), Ladakh then had to face the Moghuls of Kashmir and, on the east, the governors of Tsang. This was the period when Roman Catholic missionaries appeared in western Tibet. Father Antonio d'Andrade was welcomed (1624) at Tsaparang, the capital of Guge, where he was able to remain until 1631. Two other Portuguese missionaries, Cabral and Cacella, were equally well received by the governor of Tsang at Shigatse (1626–1632). The former had come from Bengal via Bhutan, and returned there by way of Nepal. A branch of the Kagyü-pas, the Drukpa order, had gained a footing in Ladakh, in particular at the great monastery of Hemis (built 1602–1642). This order was strong in Bhutan, to which it gave its Tibetan name. The Kagyü-pas had also gained religious control in Sikkim. The Karma-pas went on making use of their 'military camp' (*sgar-pa*) allies to war on the Geluk-pas. Though accepting the Dalai Lama's authority, they retained numerous monasteries in the border regions.

The issue was one of political antagonisms. There was no schism over doctrine: the Fifth Dalai Lama's works show the extent to which he was steeped in the Buddhism of the Tantras. On the other hand, despite his political ascendancy, further strengthened by a distinct preference for him on the part of the first Emperor of the new Ch'ing (Manchu) dynasty in China, and despite his undoubted personal ability, Tibet's unification under a single religious authority was far from being achieved. The Fifth Dalai Lama took another census of the monasteries and regulated their revenues and taxes. He also instituted the high office of Panchen Lama of Trashilhünpo although the monastery's first abbots had not been looked upon as incarnations. It had been founded by the disciple of Tsongkha-pa who was later regarded as the First Dalai Lama, while the (in retrospect) Second Dalai Lama was its abbot in 1512. Now, the abbot of Trashilhünpo, Lopsang Chhökyi Gyentsen (1570–1662, enthroned as abbot in 1600), who had helped the Fifth Dalai Lama, was declared an incarnation thanks to the 'discovery' of 'hidden texts'. His previous incarnations were promptly traced back to an immediate disciple of Tsongkha-pa, Khê-trup (1358–1438). It is he that Tibetans regard as the First Panchen Lama, Lopsang Chhökyi Gyentsen being the Fourth. From that time onwards the elder of the two hierarchs, the Dalai and the Panchen Lama, always initiated the other. The Panchen Lama was considered—prior to his human life as Khê-trup—the incarnation of Amitābha; the Dalai Lama, beyond Gedün-trup, that of Avalokiteśvara. The latter choice is readily accounted for: he had long been the patron saint of Tibet, earlier incarnated in the Tibetans' monkey ancestor and in their first great Buddhist king, Songtsen Gampo. His statue was part of a sort of Holy of Holies at Lhasa, the centre of the realm. That statue and Songtsen Gampo's both bear an image of Amitābha, the 'father' from whom Avalokiteśvara sprang, on their heads. It was in Amitābha's presence that Avalokiteśvara took his bodhisattva vow— to help all beings, and Tibet in particular. The event is the start of a series of incarnations ending in the Dalai Lama, according to the account published by the Fifth Dalai Lama as a 'revealed text'.[1]

To continue Songtsen Gampo's tradition, the Fifth Dalai Lama built the Potala palace (between 1645 and 1694), named after Mount Potala, the abode of Avalokiteśvara. His reign and that of his 'regent' or governor Sanggyê Gyatso (in office between 1679 and 1705) were noteworthy for their upsurge of literary activity and of cultural and economic life. Numerous foreign travellers, both scholars and traders, thronged Lhasa—Indians, Kashmiri Muslims,

[1] 162, *ZA*, f. 19*b*; 121, p. 134.

Chinese and Mongols. Numerous inventions and institutions are attributed to the 'Great Fifth', as Tibetans call him.

But the old animosities had not vanished and the Mongols were once more to intervene. Gushi Khan's descendants had settled in the Tsaidam and Koko Nor regions after his son (another Dayan Khan), proclaimed 'king of Tibet', helped the Fifth Dalai Lama to suppress a revolt in Tsang (1659). But now, the line of Qośot Mongols from Koko Nor had a rival in the person of Galdan, king of the Dzungars (1676–1697), who had founded a kingdom in Turkestan (Ili). The Regent Sanggyê Gyatso, as it happened, had made an ally of King Galdan; whilst Lhapsang Khan, the then Qośot king, was allied with the Emperor of China (K'ang hsi), who had just been at war with the Dzungars. And the young man whom this same Regent had recognized as Sixth Dalai Lama, Tshangyang Gyatso (1683–1705 or 1706), went around with women and wrote love-poems. Using this behaviour as an excuse, Lhapsang Khan attacked Lhasa, with K'ang hsi's agreement; killed the Regent; and kidnapped the Sixth Dalai Lama, who died soon afterwards on the way to China. He then tried to force a Seventh Dalai Lama on the Tibetans, one who had not been recognized as the authentic incarnation by the religious authorities. The Tibetans appealed to the Dzungars. The latter invaded Tibet and defeated Lhapsang Khan, who was killed at the end of 1717. China reacted at once. An army dispatched by K'ang hsi entered Lhasa in 1720. The real Seventh Dalai Lama, born at Litang and recognized as incarnate, was enthroned at the Potala (Kêsang Gyatso, 1708–1747 or 1757). The walls of Lhasa were pulled down, a Chinese garrison was installed at Lhasa, and Kham (with Batang, Litang, Tatsienlu, etc.) annexed to the Chinese province of Szechwan. The Chinese protectorate, which was to last till the end of the Ch'ing dynasty (1912), was established.

Italian missionaries, whose reception was favourable, had meanwhile built a church at Lhasa, and written Tibetan treatises in justification of their faith after studying the language and religion in the Tibetan theological schools (the Jesuit Ippolito Desideri, 1716–1721; the Capuchins, 1707–1711, 1716–1733 and 1741–1745). In the meantime, Sikkim had been converted to Lamaism by Lhatsün (1597–1655), a member of the Dzokchen-pa order; several monasteries and temples had been built there; and the first Mahārājā, Phüntsok Namgyel, had been proclaimed in 1657.

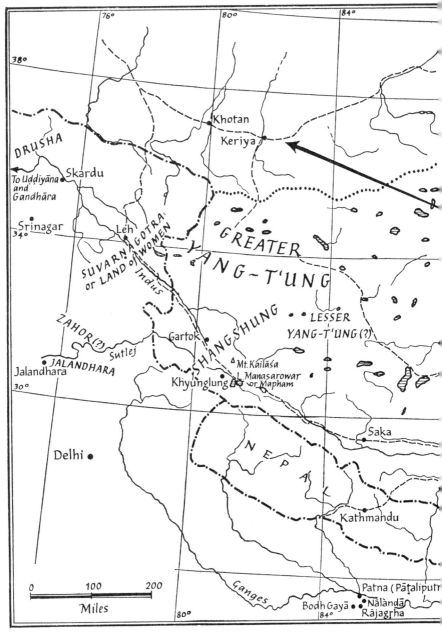

II. Ancient Tibet an

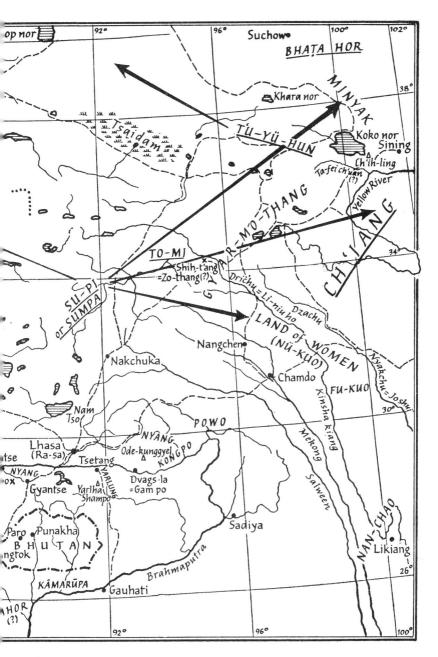

op nor

92°

96°

Suchow

BHAṬA HOR

100°

102°

MINYAK

Khara nor

38°

Tsaidam

TU-YÜ-HUN

Koko nor

Sining

Ch'ih-ling

Ta-fei ch'uan (?)

Yellow River

CH'IANG

GYAR-MO-THANG

34°

TO-MI

Shih-t'ang =Zo-thang(?)

Drichu=Li-niu ho

Dzachu

LAND of WOMEN (NÜ-KUO)

SU-PI or SUMPA

Nangchen

Nakchuka

Chamdo

FU-KUO

Nyakchu=Joshui

30°

Nam Tso

POWO

Kinsha kiang

Lhasa (Ra-sa)

NYANG

Ode-kunggyel

KONGPO

Tsetang

NYANG

ox

Gyantse

Yarlha Shampo

YARLUNG

Dvags-la =Gam po

Mekong

Salween

NAN-CHAO

Sadiya

Paro Punakha

BHUTAN

ngtok

KĀMARŪPA

Brahmaputra

Gauhati

Likiang

26°

HOR (?)

92°

96°

100°

ghbouring areas

The Chinese protectorate was sufficiently mild and flexible to be accepted by the Tibetan government. Admittedly the eastern and north-eastern provinces (Kham and Amdo) were largely lost. After the revolt of a Qośot prince in Koko Nor, the whole region was made into a Chinese province (Tsinghai) in 1724. Throughout eastern Tibet the Chinese tolerated principalities headed by indigenous rulers (*t'u szŭ*), who were invested with a seal and a diploma. At Lhasa China was represented by two ministers (*amban*) and a small garrison. The 'king' or governor of Tibet was no longer appointed by the Chinese after 1750, and the Dalai Lama was tacitly recognized as sovereign of Tibet, with the exception of Kham and Amdo on the one hand and, on the other, Ladakh—which was at first under Moghul suzerainty before being annexed by Kashmir after the Dogra war (1834–42). China henceforward defended Tibet against foreign invasions (notably that of the Gurkhas, 1788–1792), but reserved the right in future to superintend the choice of a new Dalai or Panchen Lama, dictating a set of candidates from whom the final selection was to be made by lot in the presence of the *ambans* (1792). In addition, the Emperors loaded Lamaism with favours in China and Mongolia where they set up temples and monasteries and issued invitations, often permanently, to great incarnate Lamas of the Geluk-pa order, which had become the established Church.

This is the dawn of modern times, when Tibet gets mixed up in Great Power politics despite herself. While her patron and protector, Imperial China, was crumbling under the blows of the European powers and Japan, British India and Russia to the north gradually manœuvred themselves into positions of strength—the former with more success than the latter. In Tibet, seemingly stable and content, the little game of plots and squabbles went on unchanged.

The Dalai Lamas from the Eighth to the Twelfth were unimportant, or died young (1758–1875). In contrast, some of the Panchen Lamas earned distinction. Lopsang Pelden Yeshe (1738–1780), the Third Panchen (according to European works; the Sixth, for Tibetans), had dealings with the Emperor of China's Counsellor, the high Lama Changkya Hutukhtu, featuring the identification of Kuan-ti—Chinese god of war and patron of the dynasty—with the Tibetan warrior gods, and the epic hero Gesar. It was said that Gesar was to come back at the head of an army from the mythical land of Śambhala, in the north, when Buddhism and Tibet were

88

faring badly. But, for others, the general would be an incarnation of the Panchen Lama. The Third (Sixth) Panchen Lama took an interest in this: he wrote a work about the half-mystical, half-real road leading to that country, incorporating information about the geography of Asia. He had in fact negotiated with Warren Hastings, as Governor of India, through his envoy Bogle (at Trashilhünpo 1774–1775). The Rājā of Bhutan had then invaded Cooch Behar (1772) and negotiations were carried on under the arbitration of the Panchen Lama, at that time tutor to the young Dalai Lama. The Panchen was next invited to the court at Peking (1779), but died there soon afterwards. His successor, Tenpê Nyima, enjoyed great prestige at the Chinese court.

With the second half of the nineteenth century we find a certain fellowship growing up, more or less in opposition to the Dalai Lama, between the Panchen Lama, or the Regent, and China. The Thirteenth Dalai Lama, Thupten Gyatso (1875–1933), had a fortunate reign to start with. China was at bay. Britain had set up her protectorate over Sikkim and secured the opening of a trade mart in Tibet, at Yatung in the Chumbi Valley (1893). Russia, several of whose Mongol nationalities (Kalmuks, Buriats) were Buddhist, had an influential advocate with the Dalai Lama, the lama Dorjieff. Britain tried to restore the balance in her favour. After fruitless attempts to negotiate, she decided on war and occupied Lhasa in 1904, Russia's attention being then absorbed by her war with Japan. The resulting treaty (1906) recognized China's suzerainty over Tibet, but opened up Tibet to trade with Great Britain. The Dalai Lama had fled to Urga. He was subsequently to visit Peking (1908), where he tried without success to gain a greater degree of independence for his country. On the Empress Tzŭ hsi's death, he returned to Tibet. China then set about reorganizing and modernizing Tibet in order to re-assert her own position. There was armed intervention in Kham to convert it into a Chinese province. Britain, whose aid was besought by Tibet, could do nothing. The Chinese army advanced on Lhasa and the Dalai Lama fled to India (1910). The protests of the Great Powers were without practical results for Tibet. But revolution broke out in China, and with it a period of anarchy. The Chinese army had to withdraw from Tibet, and the Dalai Lama went back to Lhasa. Regarding China, he proclaimed himself freed from the ties of vassalage which were only attached to the person of the Emperor, and looked upon himself as sovereign. But China declared that Tibet formed part of China. A Sino-British treaty (1914) provided for the division of Tibet into two parts: Central Tibet, from Ladakh to Chamdo, under the Dalai Lama's administration, but with a Chinese representative, accompanied by a small escort, at Lhasa; and the eastern part, Kham, under Chinese administration, but with the Dalai Lama retaining control over monasteries. This treaty was never ratified by China.

Whilst the Thirteenth Dalai Lama was ruling with authority and skill, accusations of pro-Chinese partisanship obliged the Panchen Lama to flee to Mongolia and China. Republican China lacked the strength to force herself upon Tibet, but she was allied to the great European powers in both world wars. Neither they, nor apparently Tibet, would or could declare Tibet's independence. Imperturbably devoted to its mediaeval structures in a modern world, the Tibetan government made no effort to adapt. From fear of modernization almost no aliens were admitted, and even the young Tibetans who came back from a course in England with technical knowledge were prevented from doing anything. But suddenly China had regained her strength. As soon as the Communists had achieved power in China (1949), they set about controlling Tibet effectively. They swiftly occupied the country and, with India's agreement, signed a treaty incorporating Tibet in the People's Republic as an ethnic minority enjoying internal autonomy, maintaining the privileges of the Dalai and Panchen Lamas, and respecting religious tradition.

This time Chinese authority worked. Motor roads were completed in a short time (see map I), the Tsaidam was exploited for oil, an electricity generating station was established at Lhasa and others were built elsewhere. Schools and hospitals were set up, and key staff trained in China. Corvée and obligations to supply free transport were abolished and co-operatives set up. Officially, religion was respected, though the Church feared it would not be so for long in view of the new education to which youth was subjected, and the fact that the traditional civilization was in danger of vanishing. In circumstances that are not wholly clear, an armed revolt broke out in 1959, owing much to the Khampas, proud warriors who had many times before resisted China. It was quickly broken, and the Dalai Lama fled to India with his Cabinet, soon to be followed by thousands of Tibetans.

For some time, the Tibetan government of the Dalai Lama tried to gain support from the United Nations for their claim that Tibet was an independent country, or at least in obtaining some kind of censure of China as an invader. But no great power was willing to back it, not least because the Chinese nationalist government in Formosa, that was recognized by the United Nations, maintained a claim to sovereignty over Tibet similar to that of the communists on the mainland. Though kindly received and given assistance by India, the Dalai Lama did not succeed in winning recognition as head of the Tibetan government in exile, either.

In the meantime, China's grip on Tibet was increasing. Her promises of religious toleration were not kept. The Panchen Lama, who had remained in Tibet and tried to get on with the Chinese, was not able to continue co-operating with them and has now disappeared. The Cultural Revolution has carried its turmoil into Tibet, and reports of fighting between different factions have reached the outer world. It is no wonder that the flow of Tibetan refugees to India is still continuing today; for they know that in India Tibetans have organized themselves and got together in an effort to maintain their traditions in religion, language, literature, art, crafts, medicine and other branches of knowledge. It is there and in certain small communities overseas that Tibetan civilization can still be seen alive.

The tragedy is that of a civilization under threat of death for not having been able to adapt itself gradually to the changes taking place around it. If I have tried in this book to portray it in its hour of fearful crisis, I do so because it has been far too little known till now and deserves—with its beauties and despite its shadows—sympathy and survival.

3

Society

The structure of Tibetan society may be analysed on two planes. First in terms of the basic groups common to the whole population, the families or clans; and secondly by social classes—the common people and the nobility, for the older Tibet, and the people, the nobility and the clergy from the ninth century onwards. That is the most obvious classification, though it admits of gradations or subdivisions which have altered in the course of history. For one thing, there are conceptual and institutional differences relative to the ways of life of cultivators and stock-breeders. And for another, the term 'people' covers at least two distinct groups: well-to-do families, owning herds or land; and labourers lacking such property, subordinate either to the better-off families, or directly to an overlord (nobility, monastery or State), or to both at once. A further division may be added, between the great mass of non-specialist workers, performing all tasks and providing all services without distinction, on the one hand, and a few skilled craftsmen, on the other. The clergy, too, are of two kinds, though both are privileged by comparison with the common people. High-born, wealthy or learned ecclesiastics contrast with the impoverished lower clergy, who are generally illiterate and burdened with all manner of tasks. A small class of yogins or meditators is marginally associated with these monks. There is no 'middle' class—except for a few rich merchants from better-off plebeian families, especially in modern Tibet, and stewards, who are remarkably well informed. Apart from foreign merchants, large-scale commerce is in the hands of the State, nobility and clergy; while petty trading is an occasional pursuit shared by all sections of society. On the fringe of this society are certain other occupations that are generally looked down upon. In some cases this is due to the influence of Buddhism, e.g. fishermen, butchers and smiths. There are also the entertainers (musicians, actors, story-tellers, and wandering bards), and the beggars.

Obviously this is only a brief survey that is chiefly applicable to the last three centuries. We shall have occasion to mention a few variations. Some Tibetan works give lists of the elements that constitute society. Classes, social rôles and degrees of kinship are set side by side as though they were things of the same kind. The upper classes are listed as follows, in the epic: 'The Lama who has blessings, the great man who has power in public affairs, the rich man who has

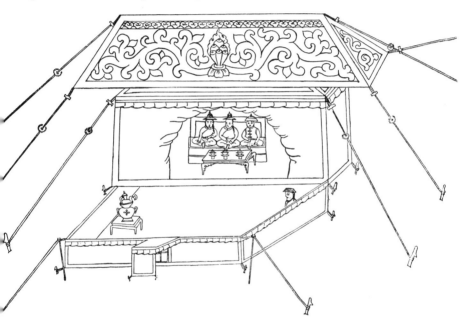

FIG. 4. Noblemen drinking tea. Ceremonial tent, itself sheltered by a canopy (*lding-gur*).

means, the chieftain.'[1] A similar work enumerates—one after another—heads of tribes, chieftains, young warriors, leaders of men, relatives on the father's side, servants, children, brothers and sisters, rich men, stewards, mothers-aunts, and daughters-in-law.[2] The occasion for these lists is always a gathering attended by all strata of

[1] 152B, I, 25*b*.
[2] 180, f. 41*a*.

93

SOCIETY

society, usually arranged hierarchically. Hymns sung at these meetings invoke successively the yogins, Bonpos, sorcerers, physicians, craftsmen, wise men and elders, lamas, soothsayers, chiefs, old men, young men, women, children and servants.[1]

One feature of social morphology sufficiently common to be significant may be expressed in a formula, equally applicable to the family group and to the structure of political power. It is the co-existence of two principles which are both interdependent and antagonistic: egalitarian joint ownership and hierarchy. Plotted diagrammatically on two co-ordinates, the horizontal axis would represent joint possession, i.e. non-individualization, group solidarity and cohesiveness; while the vertical axis would be hierarchy, i.e. the subordination of some to others.

THE FAMILY

To the principles just stated must be added the dichotomy resulting from the rule of exogamous marriage. The patrilineal stock (*brgyud*), constituting the clan (*rus*) descended from a common ancestor, is exogamous: a clan member cannot marry within his own clan. This kind of relationship is called 'bone' (*rus*), whereas that through women, by marriage, is given the name 'flesh' (*sha*). Certain features of kinship nomenclature have led to the over-simplified supposition that Tibet, at a proto-historic period, knew 'cross-cousin' marriage (where cousins born of siblings of opposite sexes may marry, and are even encouraged to). As in China, the word for maternal grandfather or uncle (*zhang*) also means father-in-law. The corresponding term *tsha*, or *dbon*, denotes both the grandson and nephew (on either side) and the son-in-law. In a proper name, on the other hand, it implies a uterine filiation (for instance '*Jang-tsha*, the son of a lady born '*Jang*). In the historical period, there are only faint traces of a possible matrilineal descent. But whichever form of filiation is preferred, it coincides with the domicile: the patrilineal family is also patrilocal.

Within the clan each generation is treated as a compact, homo-geneous, undivided group. The set comprising the father and his brothers (the paternal uncles) is called 'fathers-uncles' (*pha-khu*), or else the senior of them is called 'elder father' and the others 'younger

[1] 52, pp. 166–169.

94

fathers'. The set of the son and his brothers (the nephews), called 'elder brothers-younger brothers' (*phu-nu*), includes brothers, half-brothers and cousins (*spun*, a word derived from *phu*, 'elder brother') indiscriminately. So marriage between first cousins is considered incestuous and forbidden by law, the avenging of a murder is the brother's or cousin's responsibility, and male and female cousins call one another brother and sister. The exogamous clan is called *pha-spun* (or *spad-spun*), which expression may be translated 'fathers and cousins' or 'cousin-brothers with the same fathers'. Its unity is sometimes reflected in the shared cult of an ancestral god (*pha-lha* or *phug-lha*). The collective character of each of these groupings is so strong that the terms for them also denote all persons of the same generation or age.

In epic poetry, the expression *pha-khu*, 'fathers/uncles', denotes all the old men in the country, and *phu-nu*, 'elder brothers/younger brothers', all the young warriors (Gesar's thirty or thirty-three 'brothers' are his trusty knights), whilst all the old women are referred to as *ma-sru*, 'mothers/maternal aunts'. Similarly, in polite language of the present day, *a-khu*, 'paternal uncle', means any old gentleman (sometimes with a shade of familiarity) and *a-ne* or *ne-ne*, 'paternal aunt', any lady. The terms *a-jo*, 'elder brother', and *a-ce*, 'elder sister', are used in the same way. Thus too, the *pha-spun* group widens to an association of friends or companions who become 'sworn brothers' through an oath backed up by a sacrificial rite.

If the terminology underlines the collective character of a generation so very well, it also reflects the complementary principle of hierarchy and descent. When speaking with reference to the family's continuity in time, the idea of ancestors is expressed by the term 'fathers/grandfathers' (*yab-mes*) and that of descendants by the word 'sons/grandsons' (*bu-tsha* or *sras-dbon*). The eldest brother is also set apart from the other brothers. The word that denotes him (*a-jo* or *jo-jo*) also means 'father'. It is a respectful term whose primary meaning is 'lord' (*jo-bo*; feminine *jo-mo*) or head of the family: a child sometimes calls his father *pha-jo*, 'father-lord'.[1]

The two principles are complementary, though they often cover a certain antagonism. This seems to have been quite strong at the dawn of history but soon overcome through compromise. Tibetan texts,

[1] 145, *s.v.*; 134, ed. De Jong, p. 55, l.3.

particularly the epic, are full of passages decrying 'internal defilement' (*nang-dme*), viz. the sometimes violent conflicts between members of the same family. The combining of the two principles is illustrated by the rules governing marriage and succession or inheritance.

In modern Tibet, over the past three centuries or so, and in early Tibet—at least in the royal family—three forms of marriage are encountered. First, monogamy, which seems to be prevalent in Amdo and is fairly widespread elsewhere, although perhaps a relatively recent phenomenon. When King Songtsen Gampo's minister was in China to bring back the Chinese princess promised to the king, the Emperor of China wanted to offer the minister, too, a princess in marriage, as a mark of distinction.[1] He refused, saying that he could not repudiate his wife, who had been bestowed on him by his parents. His refusal, it is true, is probably to be explained not by an objection on principle, but by reluctance to appear to be in competition with the king.

A second form of marriage, polygamy, is confined to the rich and the nobility. For the early kings and local chiefs, it was a political means of binding noble clans to themselves by matrimonial alliance. The principle of joint possession by the group often asserts itself: the women a man marries are sisters (sororal polygyny) or, if not so in fact, they are considered to be. Sometimes, such a group of sisters is not married outright, but remains available should one of their number die. The mother of the twelfth-century Talung-thangpa having died soon after marriage, his father married his 'maternal aunt' (*sru-mo*, a word denoting both mother's sister and brother's wife); then, as she did not like the child, he married yet another 'maternal aunt'.[2] It can also happen that sexual relations other than marriage extend to several sisters or several women of the same generation. These practices counterbalance the effects of polyandry by taking up the considerable surplus of women.

Besides his two foreign wives, from China and Nepal, king Songtsen Gampo had three others from three different clans, two of them again from recently conquered foreign lands (Minyak and Shangshung). King Trhide Tsukten (Me Aktsom) had three wives— two foreign princesses (from China and Jang, i.e. Nan-chao) and one

[1] 201, year 641.
[2] 99, p. 610.

12. Heap of white stones and tree, on a height facing the Potala. *Photo: H. Harrer Liechtenstein Verlag.*

13. Tree-branches, rags and 'wind horses' on the roof of a house (note the ladder, a notched tree-trunk). *Photo: V. Sís/J. Vaniš.*

14. *Above:* Geluk-pa *homa* (*sbyin-sreg*) ritual at Ghoom, Darjeeling.
15. *Below:* Same ritual, wig representing yogin's long hair. *Photos: R. A. Stein.*

other, regarded as senior, from the Nanam noble clan. His son Trhisong-Detsen took five wives: though born in different clans, they were described as 'five sisters' (*jo-mo mched-lnga*).[1] A high minister of king Relpachen, having carved himself an independent fief in Amdo, also married five women,[1] a patently political marriage intended to win over the population. But a polygamous marriage may also have a quite different explanation, this time a religious one. Marpa, the great Tantric teacher, had eight wives in addition to his principal lady. They were needed for the 'circle' (*cakra*) of participants in the rites devoted to Heruka.

But the characteristic form of marriage seems to have been polyandry. It is practised everywhere, by cultivators as well as herdsmen. It would appear to be lacking, however, in Amdo, though certain travellers claim to have found it there. Normally, and always in theory, it is fraternal polyandry. But in practice a woman may marry several unrelated men. Or else she may, after marrying a single husband, persuade him to agree to others. The norm, however, is for a group of brothers to marry one woman. If, in other cases, friends share a wife, they are regarded as sworn brother-cousins (*spun-zla*). The hierarchic principle of primogeniture intervenes however, for it is the eldest brother alone who chooses the wife, and the marriage is sanctioned by a single ceremony, the other brothers becoming *ipso facto* her husbands. They form an indivisible group with their brother, while he represents the group. The offspring of the marriage all count as the eldest's children, whichever the actual father may be.

This group is bound up with its dwelling-place. Its cohesion is broken if a younger brother sets himself up with his own wife, land and house. In such a case, he loses the right to his elder brother's wife, and to the family property. But normally the land is occupied by one family: it is indivisible and inalienable. The group of brothers share wife, house and land, though their collective ownership is concentrated, as it were, in the person of the eldest one. Even their landless agricultural labourers, as well as aged parents or other relatives who only have a little plot of land allotted by the head of the family, all belong to the indivisible property of the family. In practice, the group of brothers living together is often reduced. Generally younger brothers have become monks. But the house they may have at the monastery is family property and, even as monks, they retain a potential share in the wife and land. About 1800, Tshepel Namgyel, a lama of Hemis monastery in Ladakh, returned to secular life on the death of his elder brother, the king, married his widow and inherited the throne. The above rules are meant to prevent the splitting up of property (land or cattle). The cohesiveness of the fraternal group is so strong that it sometimes prevails against the hierarchic principle of seniority. If the eldest brother has left no son, but a daughter, the latter inherits. She then marries a husband who takes her name—the name of her land or house—and lives at her home. Such a husband/son-in-law (*go-mag*) has an unenviable position, on a level with that of a serf. He is merely an instrument to ensure the succession. That was the case with, for instance, the famous saint Thangtong (*ca.* 1400). Still earlier, king Trhisong Detsen's law-code[1] decrees: 'If there are many sons, let them take the estate successively in order of seniority, and the youngest enter religion! Let those who have no sons invite a son-in-law for their daughter!' And so it often came about that daughters inherited a throne and reigned (Golok, Derge, Gonjo, Ngom, Lhatse, Poyül, etc.). Another means of safeguarding the line of succession is by adoption. But younger brothers of the deceased father may regain their rights. If an eldest brother has had a daughter, but no sons, his younger brother may object to his adopting a child or to his daughter's acquiring a husband/son-in-law. He may ask to succeed the elder brother himself, even if he is a monk. He may even set aside his elder brother during the latter's lifetime, if he has remained childless, and take a wife of his own (either his elder brother's, if she is not too old, or another).

The strength of the fraternal group's cohesion explains several customs, and the levirate in particular (where a younger brother marries his elder brother's widow). This is also known among the ancient and modern Ch'iang. For ancient times in Tibet, Chinese annalists[2] allege a custom of still broader scope: on his father's, uncle's or brother's death, a man would marry his stepmother, aunt or (elder) sister-in-law. Perhaps that is just an 'ethnographic' formula intended to describe all 'barbarians'. Though it may be that it corresponded to an actual state of affairs. 'Oblique' marriages are

[1] 170, f. 113*b*.
[2] 199; 200.

rare, but perfectly respectable, in modern as in ancient Tibet. In these, a son shares his father's wife (not his real mother, but a stepmother) or a father his son's (his daughter-in-law)—a union known as 'half-beam, half-rafter' (*lcam-ma-gdung*). Sometimes too an uncle shares his nephew's wife, or else a mother and daughter may have one husband/son-in-law in common.[1] The difference from the Chinese formulation is that the union takes place without waiting for the other partner's death, and that the obliquity operates in both directions, not only from the young to the old, but also vice versa. The mechanism seems designed to overcome the latent antagonism between the two generations (father and son, paternal uncle and nephew), between the principle of the undivided group and that of hierarchy.

In fact early Chinese texts use yet another expression (it, too, is unfortunately now a mere cliché applied to barbarians) about the Ch'iang and Tibetan societies of antiquity: 'they esteem the young (vigorous) and despise the weak (old)'. However, this trend, coupled with the murder or abandonment of the old, is better attested among the Turco-Mongols. Perhaps it is not by chance that, in modern Tibet, the custom has been noted in areas (Amdo, the Horpas) strongly influenced by the presence of Mongol tribes. But a few traces may be detected in early Tibet. Tradition avers that the first seven legendary kings' reigns ended as soon as each one's heir was grown up, 'able to ride a horse' (theoretically at thirteen), and that they then went 'to the sky'. The verb used in this context (*yar-bkum*) connotes a violent death, and the same verb is employed in a Tun-huang chronicle for an old man who 'warms himself in the sun' while awaiting or preparing for his end.[2] Thirteen was the very age at which King Songsten Gampo came to the throne: some say it was on his father's death,[3] others, that the father renounced the throne in favour of his son. On the other hand, the very peculiar succession of the first seven mythical kings is accompanied by another curious fact: each son's name was derived from his mother's. In Ladakh, according to some, the king used to abdicate on the birth of a son, and ministers then governed in the son's name

[1] 12, pp. 20, 47 n. 77, 102; 60, vol. II, 4, p. 43 (*Lu-ho kai-k'uan*); *Kan-tzŭ hsien t'u-ti jên-min tiao-ch'a lu*, in the magazine *Pien-chêng*, No. 3, 1930; verbal communication from H.R.H. Prince Peter of Greece.

[2] 142, *JA*, f. 6*b*; 6, p. 108.

[3] 142, *JA*, f. 14*a*.

(in ancient Tibet, the ministers were often the king's maternal uncles, or at least belonged to his mother's clan). Others say that the prince joined his father in ruling at the age of thirteen. In the time of King Thothori, two legendary physicians are said to have come to Tibet from India. Seeing an invalid being carried out of a house, they asked whether it was customary in Tibet to drive out the sick. They were told: 'If children are ill, father and mother do not turn them out of doors; if father and mother are ill, the children turn them out.'[1]

The practice of getting rid of the old, if it existed, must soon have been mitigated or forsaken under Buddhist influence and that of China. Songtsen Gampo's sixteen-point moral code (*mi chos*)[2] and the code of Trhisong Detsen both stress the obligation 'not to return evil for the kindnesses of father and mother' in the words of the former, and the need to 'protect the aged with respect, without causing them annoyance' (another reading: 'to venerate them and satisfy them with food and clothing') for the latter. Under these two kings elementary works on Buddhism and some Chinese classics had been introduced to Tibet. In spite of that, a certain setting aside of the old survives to this day. As soon as the eldest son has married and so taken the undivided family property into his hands, the old parents are pushed into the background. They keep only a small allotment and their living quarters, and are thus treated as sub-tenants on the same basis as the 'servants' (*khol-po*). The father or paternal uncle accordingly stands aside as soon as the son marries and becomes head of the family. It even happens that a father bears a name that only makes sense in terms of his son. In the epic poem, the hero's elder brother is called Rongtsa, 'uterine nephew of Rong', after his mother, née Rong. His father is called Trhagen of Rongtsa. An eleventh-century adept, Khyungpo Neljor ('the yogin of the Khyung clan') was born in a tiger year. But it was his father that was known as Ta-kye, 'tiger (year) birth', perhaps on account of this son.

Though antagonism between father and son is rare, that of paternal uncle and nephew is common. The paternal uncle, the father's younger brother, may try to get hold of the succession for his descendants. If polyandry and the levirate mean that the younger

[1] 135A, f. 30*a–b*.
[2] 167, I, ff. 163*b*, 227–230; 162, '*A*, f. 7*a*; 170, f. 113*b*.

succeeds the elder brother, the principle of patrilinear succession
and primogeniture require that younger brother to step down as
soon as the elder has a son. Now it often happens that a younger
brother wants to set himself up on his own. Moreover, there may be
polygamy to complicate the situation. 'Junior' wives and their clans
may try to transfer the succession to their sons, particularly in the
nobility.

King Trhisong Detsen had five wives. But the first three confined
themselves to religious activities and had no 'portion', whilst of the
remaining two only the fourth, of the Tshepong clan, had a son
(some say she had three sons, others that the king had three sons in
all but it is not known by which wife). Before dying, the king ordered
his son and heir to marry his fifth wife, of the Phoyong clan: she was
most probably still young. The fourth wife, Tshepong, then tried to
murder the fifth, but the latter was protected by the crown prince,
who perhaps had already married his stepmother. The Tshepong
lady nevertheless succeeded in murdering first the young prince
(Mune, aged seventeen), after a reign of seventeen months, and then
the Phoyong lady. Succession to the throne then passed to the
second son, Muruk.[1] What motives were at work the sources do
not tell us. It is possible that rivalry between sons (brothers)
was added to the antagonism between wives (mothers: from different
clans, but called 'sisters'). According to a Bonpo chronicle,[2] Trhisong
Detsen had three sons (Mune, Muruk and Mutik) by his two
'elder' wives, a Chinese and the lady born Tshepong. However,
deserting Tshepong and the two later sons, he went off with
his first-born to live with a 'junior' wife, born Drang, who had no
sons. Tshepong, doubtless the titular queen, sent the second son
Muruk to his father and elder brother to avenge her. Muruk killed
his elder brother, while Tshepong caused the king-father to be
killed by magic. It was Muruk, apparently, who succeeded to
the throne.

So, in this instance, the father wished his eldest son to marry the
youngest of his wives (perhaps actually during his lifetime). In
another case, the father appropriated a wife intended for his son.
King Trhide Tsukten (Me Aktsom) had married a lady of Jang
(Nan-chao) in addition to his senior wife, the queen, who was from

[1] 183, pp. 68–69.
[2] 186, f. 116.

the Nanam clan. The latter had no sons, whereas the Jang lady had one. This was Jangtsa Lhawön, whose name links him with his mother—'uterine nephew of Jang, divine nephew'. A Chinese princess, Chin-ch'êng, was given to this son whilst he was still very young. But he fell from horseback and was killed when the Chinese was on her way. The father then married the princess intended for his son. The future King Trhisong Detsen, who was born of this union, received the name Gyatsa, 'maternal nephew of China', on account of his mother. He had the further name of Yum Ngösung, 'recovered by his own mother', because the child was first carried off by the father's senior wife, the Nanam lady—who claimed to have given birth to him—and was only later restored to his real mother.

If we turn now to the latent antagonism between the paternal uncle and his nephew, an antagonism which the rules of good behaviour aim at overcoming, we can ascertain how it relates to the rules of succession.

That opposition is one of the Epic's chief themes. The young hero's real father is a god, and his only bond of consanguinity is with his mother. She lives with her son in the palace of the old king of the country, who has received her as spoils of war. The king's younger brother, the hero's paternal uncle, who had hoped for this booty, tries to do away with the boy. He wants to prevent his nephew from coming to the throne, in order to take power himself. He also wants the young woman the hero is intended to marry, either for himself or for his own son. Despite his supernatural powers, the hero never tries to get rid of his paternal uncle once and for all, but limits himself to repeatedly punishing and making fun of him. Nor does the paternal uncle, although a powerful sorcerer, ever succeed in killing off his nephew. He does, however, cause the death of the hero's brother (by a different mother), who is in a way his double—also of divine birth but vulnerable at a weak spot on his body. The hero, who has several wives but no children, adopts a child of this half-brother as his son.

Two biographies of eleventh and twelfth-century saints provide other examples. Before dying, Mila Rêpa's father entrusts his wife and children (Mila and his sister) to his younger brother. That was the rule: the younger brother must take the elder's wife and goods. Though, be it understood, only until the son's majority. It is sometimes mentioned that Mila Rêpa's mother (the elder brother's wife) had to marry his uncle (younger brother), she not being above the age of twenty-four. Mila's uncle, then, wanted to take his elder brother's wife, either for himself or for his son (our sources differ).[1] She refused. But Mila Rêpa's uncle took their property and made the mother and two children work for him. The mother, however, had kept a field which was tilled by her brother (Mila's maternal uncle). She was able to sell it and use the proceeds to send Mila Rêpa to study under a sorcerer, in order to get vengeance. The uncle was then ruined by hailstorms, brought on by his nephew's magic. He was forced to restore the mother and son their patrimony. Later, when Mila Rêpa renounced the world and his mother was dead, it was his paternal aunt, the uncle's wife, who cultivated his land and supplied him with food, ending up by buying the property.

Curiously enough Rêchung, Mila Rêpa's disciple, had a rather similar fate. He was only seven when his father died. His mother was then married to his paternal uncle, doubtless willingly since both of them ill-treated him. He fed them with the payments in food which he received for reading books aloud. He also had to work as a domestic servant for his paternal uncle, more particularly at ploughing the fields.[2] The sixteenth-century saint Drukpa Künlek, too, says in his autobiography (*KA*, 3–4) that he, an elder son, was very happy to start with, as the Drukpa estate was extensive. But, 'My paternal uncle (*a-khu*) posed as the continuer of the family (literally as its representative, *gdung-tshab*) and took advantage of war to have my old father murdered by the people of Nel. For myself, I was taken away by Sangpo, the cup-bearer of Kongkarnê, the husband (or lover, *bza'-rogs*) of my maternal aunt (*a-ne*). In this way I ended up as the servant of Küntu-sangpo, the lord (*mi-dbang*) of the Rinpung-pa domain (who belonged to his own clan).' He stays on as a servant for six years, then travels to Ü. 'My mother had become my uncle's wife (*chung-ma*)'. He then gives his sister his jewels, the cup-bearer his horse, and sets off to rove the kingdoms.

When the Eighth Karma-pa (1507–1554) was born, his paternal uncle tried to proclaim him a demon, and gave him poison: he got away with an outbreak of pustules.[2]

[1] 99, p. 427; 143, f. 144*a*; 151, ed. Das, II, p. 364.
[2] 142, *PA*, f. 190*a–b*.

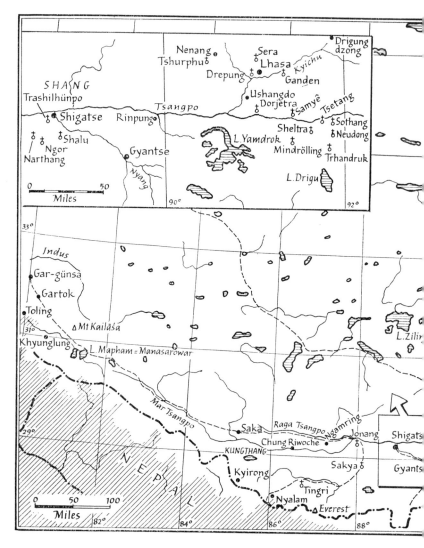

III. Modern Tibet: places a

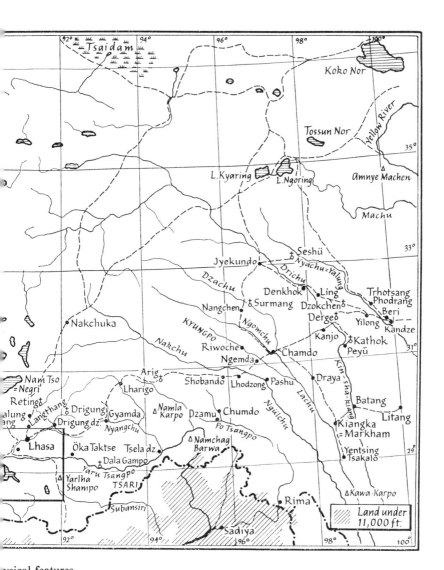

ysical features

If all goes well, however, the relationship of paternal uncle and nephew is the same as that between father and son. In both cases they may share a wife; an orphan is brought up by his uncle as in the case of Tampa Dorje (1230–1303),[1] and when a youth wishes to enter a monastery and needs a reference and guidance from an older monk, it is generally the paternal uncle who fills this rôle. Succession from paternal uncle to nephew, in the case of high ecclesiastics, often replaces that from father to son which is appropriate to laymen.

With the growth in influence of the religious orders, succession to power in a noble family took effect on two levels or in two lines. A married brother transmitted secular power and the family estate from father to son; another brother, a monk, passed on religious power and the property of the order from paternal uncle to nephew. In the non-reformed orders where the abbot can marry, one hierarch could combine the two functions. With the Sakya-pas and Phagmotru-pas, and sometimes too with the Drigung-pas, the elder brother became abbot and the younger married. Succession to power went from paternal uncle to nephew. When the great missionary Sakya Paṇḍita visited the Mongol king Godan, in 1244, he took with him his two nephews Phakpa and Chhana, aged ten and six. On his death in 1251, Phakpa continued his mission. In the branch of the Gar clan that reigned at Derge,[2] the eldest son became head of the monastery and combined political and monastic power. He did not marry, but seems to have had the opportunity for relations with his younger brother's wife. It was this second brother who married, became head of the family and ensured the continuance of the line. If there were other brothers they became monks. If there was only one son, he both married and took the robe, being then head of the monastery and the family together. The same rule prevailed in the little principality of Muli (south-eastern Kham), and elsewhere. In the twelfth century there were two clans, Begu and Negu, on the Gyer estate in Yarlung. In the Begu clan, and especially in the Khangsar ('New House') family, the 'nephew-line' (dbon-brgyud) of Trhandruk was transmitted. The general Könchok Kyab had two sons, Chhöseng and Chhödor. The elder, who as a monk took the name 'Yogin of Gyer', became head of the

[1] 188, p. 705.
[2] 150, f. 191a; 153.

'nephews' of Trhandruk. The younger married and inherited the post of general from his father. He had five sons. The eldest became a monk, was initiated by his paternal uncle the 'Yogin of Gyer', and received the name 'Sanggyê the Nephew'. The second son, Tang-re, married and had three sons. The third and fifth are unknown, but the fourth, Gompo, also had two sons, the elder of whom became a monk with the name 'Nephew of Gyer'. The youngest son of Tang-re became, as a young monk, the disciple of 'Sanggyê the Nephew', his eldest paternal uncle. He in his turn was the teacher of his cousin 'Nephew of Gyer' who thus continued the line of 'nephews'.[1] Paternal uncle to nephew (*khu-dbon*) succession, which is characteristic of the transmission of monastic power, corresponds to the spiritual succession from teacher to disciple expressed by the terms 'father' and 'son'. Probably too this is the reason certain adepts of the Tantric type (*sngags-pa*) bore the title 'nephew' (*dbon-po*) or 'uncle-nephew' (*a-gu dbon*).

It will have been noticed that a person's names sometimes indicate his status or birthplace. A man is identified by a personal name (generally connected with some circumstance attending his birth, or with a parent or ancestor—teacher in the case of a man of religion); by the name of his house or estate, which takes the place of a family name; and by the name of his clan. Such, at any rate, was the rule in ancient Tibet. In the modern period, the clan name has disappeared or rather been replaced by the name of a territory or house, while among nomads the name of the tribe is added to the personal name.

We have still to glance at affinity on the female side, the 'flesh' (*sha*, as opposed to *rus*, 'bone') or 'noble household' (*cho-'brang*). Marriage has to overcome a certain opposition, sometimes marked by hostility. The ceremony includes a mock struggle or kidnapping, and a go-between is indispensable. Among the Horpas and in the Kandze and Litang districts, a form of marriage involving previous abduction of the woman, followed by payment of an indemnity, is reported. The abduction can lead to a vendetta. In the wedding, the bride's maternal uncle (*zhang-po*) plays a dominant role. His agreement is essential. Proverbially, he is 'the owner of half his niece, as half the material in a gown belongs to the sleeves'. Hence marriage between maternal uncle and niece is forbidden. In the

[1] 99, pp. 890–894.

commonest rite for the confession of sins,[1] 'love of the minister—maternal uncle (*zhang-blon*) for the stepdaughter' (or daughter-in-law: the word *mna'-ma* refers to the young bride in relation to her parents-in-law) is duly included. The terminology is explained by the fact that a woman may marry her cousin on the mother's side, her maternal uncle's son: a marriage not merely permitted, but frequent. On the authority of the excellent historian Pawo Tsuk (*JA*, 11*a*), the maternal uncle was referred to, in the legendary past, as 'lord' (*jo-bo*); and it was King Trhinyen Sungtsen, son of Thothori, who first used the term *zhang* to denote his mother's clan. We know that the latter term also refers to the father-in-law. An early inscription (*ca.* 800) speaks of the 'wise' maternal uncle taking an active interest in the king's birth or childhood, and uniting in joy 'father/son, elder brother/younger brother, mother/son, superior/inferior'. Elsewhere it is asserted that during the Crown Prince Sena Lek's minority, a wise minister (*blon*) or three 'ministers/maternal uncles' (*zhang-blon*) were appointed to govern on his behalf.[2] Now once he had reached adult years, the king married a lady whose maiden name was Dro, and appointed a member of that clan as his minister. The same clan had already provided a queen for his father, and for his great-great-grandfather (Mangsong Mangtsen). The exact meaning of the composite term 'minister/maternal uncle' is not too clear. The two elements are also used separately, and then, according to T'ang Chinese sources, denote the ministers who belong to a queen's family (*zhang*) and those belonging to the king's family (*blon*).

We can thus appreciate the importance of 'flesh' kinship, despite the lack of precise descriptions. It is on a par with the Tibetan woman's exceptionally independent character and status—they are very free, both economically and from the sexual viewpoint. They have their own property, which makes divorce easy for them. They often manage their husband's finances. Their economic position is as strong among the herdsmen as the cultivators. Some say even more so.

We have seen how Mila Rêpa's mother was able to pay for her son's studies, and hence seek vengeance, thanks to her personal field, tilled by her young son's maternal uncle. When the wife of Marpa decided to help Mila Rêpa against her husband's wishes, she gave

[1] 185, f. 12*a*.
[2] 94, II. p. 2 and n. 2; 183, p. 69.

108

him her turquoise of great price, which had been 'well hidden' (*phag-nor*, usually *phug-nor*, personal wealth). To her husband's complaints, she replied: 'This turquoise never belonged to you. When I was sent into your presence by my father and mother (at marriage) they gave it to me as a personal possession. They told me, "Since the lama is a man of violent character, you may need it if you should divorce; so don't show it to anyone—keep it!" '. Women have movable property (personalty) as distinct from the real estate held by the head of a family. When the possessions of Mila Rêpa's father were seized by his paternal uncle, the latter took the 'male wealth' (*pho-nor*) and the aunt the 'female wealth' (*mo-nor*). Further on we shall see how the first must have been the fields and house, the second the utensils and articles of value.

WAYS OF LIFE

As we have said, the idea often entertained of the Tibetans as nomads engaged solely in pastoral stock-raising is inadequate. But now it has rightly been pointed out, in a recent work, that 'the economy of Tibet derives from patterns of cereal agriculture and animal husbandry developed by the early civilizations of the Near East, with a few variations that can be best explained in terms of the high-altitude environment.'[1] Indeed the habitat, by its very nature, gives Tibetan life a dualistic form. Sometimes this governs one and the same group in a seasonal rhythm (summer and winter), and sometimes two groups live in symbiosis.

Now it may well be that, as regards the amount of land occupied, the areas devoted to pastoral stock-breeding exceed the agricultural areas; but the greater part of the former was occupied by non-Tibetans at the dawn of history, as it was once more in the modern period. On the other hand, it has been estimated that in modern Tibet five-sixths of the population are engaged in agriculture. We may suppose it possible to explain the rise of the first monarchy by its control of the most fertile agricultural regions. Nowadays, as in ancient times, the political and cultural centres are in districts of intensive cultivation. Let us recall, too, that since at least the eleventh century 'Tibetans' (*Bod-pa*) have been contrasted with 'pasture-land people' ('*brog-pa*), as though the latter were foreigners.

[1] 12, p. 5.

The king of Ladakh, at Thoding, asked Dromtön (1004–1063) how many houses there were in Tibet (*Bod*) and how many tents in the pastoral regions (*'brog*). The answer, at least in the form that has come down to us, is certainly erroneous and probably a scribal error (105,000 houses (?) as against 2,400,000 tents and 55 monasteries, with a population of 30 million men, 40 million women, and 40,000 monks), but the contrast between the two population groups remains. It is in fact taken up by another fairly ancient work.[1] Even in the land of Nyang, in Tsang, the local chronicle distinguishes between the ordinary, sedentary inhabitants and the herdsmen (*'brog-pa*). In 1531, a Muslim author states that Tibet's inhabitants are divided into Bolpa (= *Bod-pa*), who live in villages and towns, and Canbah (Khampas, elsewhere referred to as 'dolpah', i.e. *'brog-pa*) who are nomads. From quite recent Chinese estimates, it appears that Tibet has 4,500,000 inhabitants, 1,000,000 of them in Central Tibet—600,000 'agricultural serfs' as against 200,000 'pastoral serfs', together with 150,000 monks and 50,000 nobles, merchants, craftsmen and beggars. Censuses have often been taken in Tibet, though their results, at least as represented by our sources, usually seem impossible or incomplete. But we are told of the Sakya-pas' investiture as heads of the 'thirteen provinces' of Tibet, that they received power over 'the inhabitants of Tibet who have wooden doors (*shing-sgo can*, to their houses)' and that, in addition, a military census was taken among the Tibetan tribes (*Bod-kyi-sde*) of Dokham (Amdo). And when population censuses were held under the aegis of the Mongol kings (1268, 1287), 'Tibetans' (*Bod*) were carefully distinguished from 'nomads' (*'brog*).[2] The same distinction was observed in the 1384 census held by the lord of Gyantse.[3]

Caution should be observed. Certain tribes of pastoral herdsmen originated in a previously sedentary population. The phenomenon is vouched for in modern Amdo. We also hear of similar developments in the early period, in the same area. The troops despatched to guard the Tibetan frontiers in the north-east were demobilized on the spot after the campaign against the Bhaṭa Hor (about A.D. 800). Dispersing locally, they apparently developed into shepherd tribes (*'brog-sde*) with their own clan name (*dBas*). A set of nomadic

[1] 162, '*A*, f. 4*b*; 139, chap. XV.
[2] 162, '*A*, ff. 13*b* and 5*a* (= 121, p. 251).
[3] 121, p. 665.

110

tribes in the same region, the Goloks of modern times, also seems to have been formed from various elements that had come from elsewhere. One of their regular occupations was attacking caravans, and they boasted of their courage and warlike gifts. Other nomads ('*brog-pa*), in southern Tibet (Öka district), also practised highway robbery in the fourteenth century.[1]

There is no question of minimizing the role of the inhabitants of the grazing-lands, who are to be found everywhere and contribute an essential part of Tibet's diet (meat and dairy products) and clothing (wool). But for all that, a certain predominance of the agricultural areas is evident, at least in the cultural centres. We have already seen that by tradition the first, forest-dwelling, Tibetans received from their monkey ancestor the five, or six, cereals, including barley which is the staple foodstuff. The first inventions this tradition ascribes to wise ministers are mainly concerned with agriculture and irrigation, and if the yoke for two animals is there too it is because such cattle form part of farm economy.

In the administrative outline attributed to Songtsen Gampo,[2] six 'appointments' (*khos*) are distinguished, split into two subsets based on the contrast between the country's borders and cultural centre. Three ministers were put in charge at the centre: a 'head of appointments', the famous Gar Tongtsen Yülsung, governed Tibet (*Bod*), and two others Shangshung and Sumpa. Meanwhile, three 'groups of warriors' mounted guard at the frontiers. This way of dividing up the country was superimposed on another. On the one hand there were the warriors (*rgod*), organized as sixty-one 'groups of a thousand' (*stong-sde*): they were 'the best subjects, engaged in military tasks'. On the other hand were those liable to statute-labour (*g.yung* or *kheng*): they were the 'working people', organized as groups of men who had, below them, their own servants (*yang-kheng*, *yang-bran* or *nying-g.yog*). A Tun-huang chronicle informs us, in fact, that in 654 the great minister Tongtsen instituted a census with a view to a major organization into 'appointments'. To that end he divided the people into soldiers (*rgod*) and labour force (*gyung*). The reason there is no mention here of herdsmen is probably that those 'liable to statute-labour' were as much tillers as stock-breeders, having pasture-land and cattle, but not necessarily being

[1] 135, f. 60*b*.
[2] 142, *JA*, ff. 18*b* et seqq.; 126, pp. 77–90.

nomads. The ancient chronicle tells us further that Songtsen Gampo and the wise minister Tongtsen Yülsung levelled up the units of hides and units of yokes for fields and pasture-land. It was most probably a matter of regularizing taxes. The same source also mentions numerous censuses between 653 and 758, whose nature is still in part unknown. In order of importance, and omitting unknown terms, confiscated goods, extinct families, etc., we find: fields (ten times), grazing-land ('*brog*, five times)—sometimes both in the same territory (Tsang); then, armies (five times), fallow land or that intended for winter fodder (*sog, sog-ma*, four times), diseases of cattle (*gnag*, the yak, twice) and hunts (of yak and of deer, twice).

The same chronicle preserves a song of the minister Gar Trhindring (in 694–696) in which he uses fourteen metaphors to say that a large number of mediocrities cannot prevail against one person's excellence. It contains a good sample of the images of life that would impress themselves on a man of that period. Here they are: many small birds are killed by one hawk, many small fish by a single otter; despite his branched antlers the stag cannot withstand the yak with his short horns; a hundred-year pine is overthrown by a single axe, a river crossed by a little boat; barley and rice (*sic!*) sprouting over an entire plain are ground by one water-mill; the stars are eclipsed by the sun; one fire lit at the bottom of the valley burns all the trees and grass of mountain and valley; the waters of one spring can transport all the trees (felled) in mountain and plain; a single stone (a roller?) crushes all the lumps of hard earth on a plain; a whole load of grass rots more quickly than one neglected piece of iron; a cauldron full of water takes the flavour of salt put in it; much grass is cut by one sickle; one slender arrow is capable of killing a large yak. Agriculture, forestry and hunting— these are the preoccupations. Not a word about pastoral husbandry and nomadism.

In another song, King Tüsong alludes to irrigation channels drawn from the Yarlung river. Shortly afterwards, inscriptions give lists of hereditary possessions of noblemen and monks. There enumerated we find liegemen (or serfs, *bran*), fields, pastures ('*brog*), fallow land (or fields for winter fodder, *sog*) and parks or groves.[1] Later still, under Trhisong Detsen (eighth century), Padmasambhava, accused

[1] 6, p. 121 (translation, p. 168) and p. 119, 1.8; 93, p. 30; 94, II, p. 3; 92, p. 62.

of misdeeds, recalls the good he has done Tibet in these words: 'In the sands of Ngamshö, meadows and groves have appeared. As far as Tra, Doltog-la and Phülso, at all places where there was no water, there now is. In all the stony places I have made fields, to feed all Tibet.' And he promises the ministers, who want to kill him, to make fields. Then they offer him many presents, saying 'Fields will be all right at Yarlung'.[1] Curiously enough, Padmasambhava

FIG. 5. Threshing and winnowing. Four-walled threshing floor. Pillars along the rear wall support a shelter, for eating under.

came from Swat, and in his religious influence some have thought to recognize Iranian elements absorbed in his native country. And here again, in Tibetan agriculture, experts see the prototype of some of these techniques in the Middle East or in Iranian lands.

[1] 183, p. 25.

SOCIETY

When King Sena Lek (*ca.* 800) ordered the building of a large temple in the region of the great northern pasture-lands, pleading the extent of this territory, his ministers raised objections: they, like the king, had their property in Central Tibet, and such a temple in the north would therefore remain empty. They advised its building at Nyang, in Tsang. Then again, when that king's elder brother, Mune, tried three times to obtain equal contributions from all his subjects, rich and poor, for his temple at Samyê, he appointed officials charged with carrying out this levelling in the 'Four Horns', that is, in Ü and Tsang. Then, a fairly early chronicle tells us, 'the tillers of fields deserted their ploughs', and 'the tillers destroyed the system of irrigation channels to come and make their offerings.' Not a word about nomads. Besides these peasants, the chronicle only mentions merchants and travellers, together with huntsmen (or murderers?) and thieves. The king forbade the former to carry supplies of flour for use while travelling (he sold it to them, for payment in kind); the latter, he even prohibited from obtaining food.[1]

About the year 1300 at Treshö, in the region of the five Hor principalities in Kham, a Bonpo chieftain undertook, in the event of a son being born to him, to give the mother 'all that is necessary as property in fields/land and serfs/servants.' And when a son was born he gave, as promised, three villages.[2] If livestock is not mentioned here, that does not of course mean that stock-raising was neglected, but that the beasts were part of the farm.

The history of Mila Rêpa's family, in the eleventh century, is very significant in this respect. The ancestor was a Nyingma-pa 'sorcerer' of the Khyungpo tribe, a tribe of herdsmen (*'brog-pa*) from the North. Arriving in Tsang on pilgrimage, he succeeded in curing a sick man possessed by a *mi-la* demon and hence acquired his family (*gdung*) name of Mila. The fortune he gained from fees for effecting cures was squandered by his son. The latter started a sort of duel at dice in which the stakes were progressively raised until he pledged his fields, house and chattels . . . and lost the lot. Deprived of their estate (*yul-gzhis*), the Mila father and son had to leave the country. They took up residence in Mang-yül, near the Nepalese border. There they got money, the father by his far-famed

[1] 183, pp. 69, 67.
[2] 154, f. 18*a*.

114

exorcisms, and the son by trading in wool, which he obtained from Nepal in winter and from the northern herdsmen in summer. The son then married a well-born girl of that country. He bought a large field, and a ruined house nearby which he turned into a castle. He subsequently married his son, Mila Rêpa's father, to a daughter of the famous noble clan of Nyang and marked the occasion by building a new three-storied house near his palace. It had a granary on top, and a kitchen, as well as an inner reception court with four pillars and eight beams. The family had become so influential that

Fig. 6. Crops of four different cereals. Stacks covered with paste made from moistened ash, on which seals are stamped. If any is stolen the paste slips and the seals break.

'We were allied to the nobles of the country and had made the "weak" (the common people) our subjects (*'bangs-su 'khol*).' And so, when Mila Rêpa's father died, his written testament dealt with the following possessions: herds—yaks, horses and sheep—at the head of the valley; fields at the bottom of the valley; cattle—cows, goats and asses—on the ground floor of the house; and upstairs, furniture and utensils, gold, silver, copper, iron, turquoises, silk and the cornloft.

The ancient Chinese texts bear out this picture of pastoral or domestic stockbreeding and agriculture in juxtaposition. In this context they discuss the central Tibetans (T'u-fan) and their related neighbours to the east and north-east, the Ch'iang. Broadly speaking, the Ch'iang are classified as stockbreeding nomads: 'They have no fixed dwelling and move about depending on the water and grass: their country lacks cereals, and their occupation is pastoral stockbreeding.' The Tang-hsiang, who are Ch'iang people, have no agriculture (they import wheat to make beer); they breed yaks, sheep and oxen, but also pigs. Like the T'u-fan, they love to die on the battlefield; like them, they think highly of the strong and valiant, and a murder only necessitates the payment of blood-money. Other Ch'iang, the Tang-ch'ang, also rear pigs along with yaks and sheep. Some, the Pai-ma, have fields of hemp. Others, the A-kou, have stone houses, and palaces. Some of the Tang-hsiang, too, are sedentary, others have houses covered with skins (but not tents), others again have stone defence towers. All, like the Tibetans, are horsemen and warriors. Like the Tibetans, too, they are descended from a monkey ancestor.

As for the T'u-fan, say the Chinese annals, although they live in a cold mountainous country as the Ch'iang do, they cultivate wheat, barley, buckwheat and beans, but not rice. They eat tsampa (roasted barley flour) and fix the beginning of the year at the moment of the wheat (or barley) harvest. They often have high flat-roofed houses and large stone tombs. They have but few 'cities', or only small 'cities', and do not reside there, but usually live on the move, the nobles in tents containing more than a hundred people. The animals they keep are yaks, pigs, dogs, horses and sheep; and they make sacrifices of sheep, dogs and monkeys, or horses, oxen and asses. They are warlike, have coats of mail and swords, and make bridges of iron chains.

Livestock is thus as important as crop-farming, but it is not solely a question of nomadic stockbreeding and grazing. In the texts we have just summarized, the Chinese use a different expression for the true nomad Ch'iang ('Their occupation is pastoral stock-breeding') and those Ch'iang and T'u-fan who know agriculture ('They breed—literally, feed—oxen and sheep'). The presence of pigs is equally characteristic: to this day large herds (up to 200 or 300 head) of pigs are bred in Dakpo. They are taken to the forest by swineherds and brought back to the farm at night; but they can also be left day and night on wooded islands in the Tsangpo, where there are no wild animals. That livestock is indeed important, appears from the old expression for a loyal vassal's gifts to his king, which means literally 'curds and meat' (*zho-sha*).[1] But we shall see that the stock concerned returns annually to winter quarters in the village. Another interesting point is that the date of the New Year was determined by agriculture. In modern Tibet the old 'farmers' New Year' (*so-nam lo-gsar*) in the tenth or eleventh lunar month was still distinguished from the new 'king's New Year' (*rgyal-po lo-gsar*) which is the same as in China (first lunar month): it was probably introduced by the Mongols, whose name is preserved in the calendar (*Hor-zla*). One and the same Tibetan word (*lo*) means both 'year' and 'crop', as was the case in archaic China. Such a concept would not have been expressed in its language by a society of nomads.

Two other early neighbours to the eastward, also related, shared the characteristics of the ancient Tibetans, according to the same Chinese sources. The Country of Women is cold, and people there hunt, breed yaks and horses, and sacrifice men and monkeys. The queen and nobles live in houses with up to nine storeys, and they have more than eighty 'cities'. The land of Fu (anciently Biu) is cold, too, but millet is grown there. Sacrifices of oxen and horses are performed. There are no 'cities' there, but very high stone defence towers. The natives are warlike.

Certain particulars are only apparently contradictory. The term commonly translated 'city' (*ch'êng*) is the counterpart of the Tibetan word for fortified castles (*mkhar*), as we know from a dated Sino-Tibetan gloss (741).[2] If we are told that the nobles hardly ever

[1] 94, I, 1.20 and frequently; cf. the expression *zho-shas 'tsho* for servants: 139, f. 244*b*.
[2] *mkhar lCags-rtse* = T'ieh-jên ch'êng or Shih-p'u ch'êng; 202, *ch.* 962, f. 15*b*. 6, p. 51; 117, part III, pp. 42–43.

stayed there, but lived in tents, it is because they were primarily warriors. We see them at work in the Tun-huang chronicle: the king, queens, ministers and nobles have estates equipped with fortified castles or palaces, but they are constantly on the move. They spend their time riding long distances, holding different local meetings in summer and winter, and taking perpetual censuses over the whole vast territory. Here is the explanation a Tibetan ambassador, formerly a pupil at the Chinese court, gave the Emperor of China in 672: 'The (Tibetan) king moves about each spring and summer at the dictates of grass and water: only in autumn and winter does he live in the fortified city but, even there, he pitches his tent and does not live beneath a roof.' The last part of the sentence is no doubt exaggerated: the ambassador was highly sinicized (he bore a Chinese name) and on this occasion was anxious to belittle his country by representing it as poor and barbaric.[1]

The position must have been comparable to that in eleventh-century Europe where the king had to travel about constantly in order to keep the country under control, watch over the levies, and consume the proceeds of taxes in kind at the point of origin.

It is the life of warrior horsemen they led, consequently, that explains how the Tibetans could be both sedentary and constantly on the move. We have seen how warriors were regarded as the best members of the population. It is not surprising that the Chinese only saw them in tented camps. Most of the Chinese emissaries' audiences with the king, recorded by the Tun-huang chronicle, took place in summer, outside the palace. The Chinese say that the noblemen's great tents were called 'fu-lu': probably this is a transcription of the Tibetan word *phru*(-*ma*), which meant 'palace' or 'military camp'. And in fact, the camps described by the Chinese were organized in the style of a fortified enclosure. In 822, the summer residence of the kings (so they had another for winter!) was north of the Tsangpo, according to Chinese texts, in the 'Valley of the deer'. It was probably the same place as the Tun-huang chronicle's 'deer park' where the Chinese princess Chin-ch'êng took up residence, in 710, on her arrival at Lhasa. According to the Tibetans, there were two temples and a stone palace in Lhasa at that time, though the Chinese never allude to them.

The 822 camp was pitched in an inhabited plain. It was bounded

[1] 197B, *Ch.* CCXVI A, ff. 3–4.

118

by a stockade in which a hundred spears were inserted every ten paces. It clearly comprised three concentric enclosures, for we are told of three successive gateways at a hundred paces' distance from one another, guarded by soldiers and sorcerers or priests who escorted the visitor. In the centre was a great standard and a high platform surrounded by a balustrade adorned with precious stones. This supported the 'golden tent', i.e. the tent of the king and his command, set off with gold.

It was, therefore, a sort of mobile palace or city, thought of as a capital. The use of these camps has been kept up right through Tibetan history. A well-known case is that of the great Karma-pa hierarchs from the twelfth to the seventeenth century. They commanded a whole court of officials and soldiers forming camps (*sgar-pa*). These camps were very large. The hierarchs lived at the centre, like a Chinese Emperor, invisible to the common people save at the time of the New Year theatrical performances, with a throne and the statue of a protective deity—neither of them easy to cart about. Yet these camps were always on the move, most of the time engaged in warfare. Scarcely a year passed without the hierarch and his camp removing once, if not oftener.[1] A photograph of the Fourteenth Dalai Lama's travelling camp (opposite page 49) gives some idea of the arrangement in concentric enclosures.

In early Tibet extreme mobility, especially among the warring aristocracy, went hand in hand with the principle of basing one's power firmly on an estate defended by a fortified castle. The period preceding the country's unification, projected back into legendary times, was characterized by 'little kings' or princelings who were not strong enough to confront the large countries in the four principal directions. 'They fought amongst themselves and loved to kill', and 'there were strongholds on all the hills and all the steep rocks'[2] (see chapter II). And so the first king to bring this anarchy to an end begins by building his family's first castle, Yumbu-lagang in Yarlung.

And indeed, every one knows the magnificent, daring stone buildings typical of Tibet—palaces, castles, temples and even private houses. Such technology is not the work of nomads. The prototypes of this architecture are reported in the Land of Fu and the Country of Women, in eastern Tibet, in the sixth century: nine-

[1] 142, chap. *PA*, and 132.
[2] 177, ff. 55*b*–56*a* (= 17*b*–18*a*).

storied houses and defence towers, some 75 to 90 feet in height. These towers, which are often octagonal, are still characteristic of the Ch'iang and other districts in Kham, in the modern period; they are also known in Kongpo and Lhotrak, where they have nine or ten stories and are sometimes octagonal, sometimes square, with very thick walls. A similar nine-storied tower is reported in Kongpo, back in the early twelfth century.[1] Among the Tibetans and Ch'iang of today, as is known, even the dwelling-houses are fortress-like. Closed to the outside, they open on an inner courtyard. They have three or four storeys, with animals on the ground floor, living rooms in the middle and a chapel above. As in ancient times, the roofs are flat and sometimes function as a threshing-floor for grain. Sometimes the house contains an upstairs granary, but there are also winter granaries underground, equipped with a ventilation system at surface level. When they are not isolated but grouped into villages, houses are built up the slope of the mountain-side and form such a compact group that the roof of one house communicates with the courtyard of the next, somewhat as in a North African Kasbah. In some parts of Ladakh and the western Changthang, villages even consist entirely of cave-dwellings, giving the impression of a bee-hive.

At the time of the thirteenth-century Mongol censuses, a family was defined as a house, four pillars in size, containing six persons: the married couple (their children, no doubt), manservant and maid-servant. The household included domestic animals and fields.[2] It is significant that the inhabitants are described by a figure of speech derived from the architecture of a house, not a tent. We have seen how the phrase 'beam and rafters' typifies a particular kinship

---

[1] 135A, f. 106b (spe'u dgu-thog); cf. p. 150 below for the nine-storied tower Mila Rêpa had to build for Marpa at Lhotrak.

[2] 180, Appendix.

FIG. 7. Home of a well-to-do family at Dam. Agriculture and stock-breeding. Fields (wheat, barley) surrounded by yak-dung walls, and a fold: yak cows milked by a nomad woman ('brog-mo). Ewes, and shepherd wearing the Horpa hat. In the courtyard, a large black tent (sbra-gur) and two small white ones (phying-gur). Behind the house, the kitchen-garden and, left, the garden and a stack of wool. Race-horses in the courtyard. Outside, the stallion, and mares being milked to make liquor (a-rag, rta-chang). The sacred mountain Nyenchen Thanglha, shaped like a Chinese temple roof, and rivers.

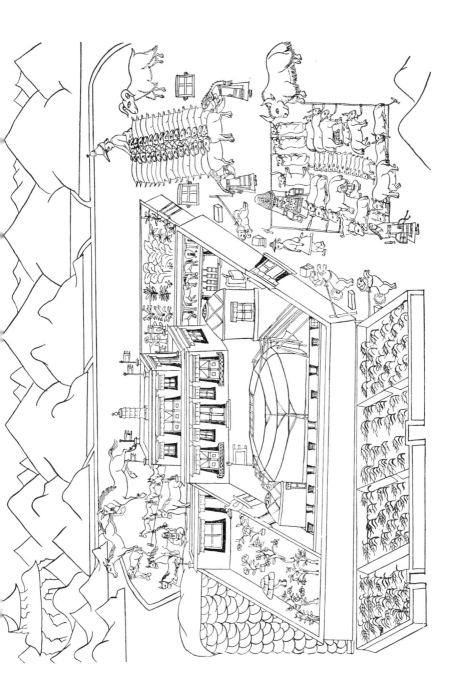

structure. The word 'beam' (*gdung*) also denotes a pedigree. These metaphors were applied to spiritual descent in a religious school, (also expressed, as we know, by the father-son relationship). The principal disciples of Marpa are the 'Four Pillars', the disciples of Mila Rêpa the 'Eight Brothers'. Those of the Nyingma-pa Lama Gyawo-pa are labelled 'Four Pillars, Eight Beams, Sixteen Rafters and Thirty-two Planks'. A similar classification was applied to the noble house of Shalu and its estates: four pillars, eight beams, or rather nine counting the northern one with a 'maned lion' (probably the pillar-capital), and seventy rafters.[1]

The house-dwelling, sedentary population is very mobile, however. All Tibetans like to travel about, and when doing so live, if they can afford it, in tents. Pilgrimages are made to holy places and journeys undertaken for trade, over very great distances and in spite of highly unreliable roads infested with brigands. Even the monks of any given monastery have always spent a large part of their life travelling in quest of initiations and knowledge from various teachers and in scattered libraries. Not to mention all the itinerant professions—smiths, physicians, astrologers, musicians, storytellers, actors and bards. We shall return later to the opposing tendency of authority, which consists of settling them and giving them land, to ensure the regularity of their services.

But chiefly, it is the seasonal duality that accounts for the way sedentary life goes hand-in-hand with a life of removals. In winter the Dalai Lama resides at the Potala, though in summer he lives in a park outside the city. The population, though normally occupying houses of stone or beaten earth, likes to take to its tents, enjoying protracted picnics or camping out, in the spinneys, as soon as fair weather allows. However, primarily, it is economic life and the type of ecology that compel them to a dual way of life, different in summer and winter. In the west, for instance, only women and children stay at the village in summer. The men go to the grazing-lands (*'brog*) with the livestock and only come back to their houses in winter. Authority accompanies them in the person of the district head man, the 'head of the military camp' (*sgar*). The village of

---

[1] 99, p. 118; 121, p. 658; cf. also 136, f. 9*b*, for the disciples of *'Gos locā-ba Khug-pa lHas-btsas*: four Pillars of the mother-lineage (*ma-rgyud*), eight Beams (*gdung-ma theg-pa*) of the teachings, Joists (*lcam*) and Laths (*dral-ma*) of those who know the texts.

Gartok as found on the map is the Gar Günsa ('winter military camp'). It is matched by the Gar Yarsa ('summer military camp'), the former being warmer and at a lower altitude. Other place names marked on our maps, too, only mean 'summer' or 'winter' residence (e.g. two large villages in the Khangpa valley, between Sikkim and Nepal). In the eleventh century, the heads of various groups of the Lang clan dissuaded the yogin Changchup Dreköl, of the same clan, from settling near Lake Manasarowar, in the following words: 'These eighteen great valleys of the South (in Kham) are our birth-places, ours, your sons' and grandsons'. When, in summer, we go to the pasture-land ('*brog*), we find there good grass ('*grogs*, a term in current use for pasture-land in Amdo); when, in autumn, we go to our "country" (*yul*, the village), we find there good land (? —*zhim-sa*).'[1] At the same period, the young Mila Rêpa and his sister are working at their paternal uncle's: 'In summer, servants of the uncle during work in the fields; in winter, servants of the aunt during work with the wool.' When the Sakya hierarchs were made leaders of the country by the Mongols, the edict concerning their administration stated that in summer they occupied mountain pasture-land in the north, but in winter they resided in Ü and Tsang.[2] In 1769, a monk from Horkhok, in Kham, begs for alms 'in summer in the pasture-land ('*brog*), in autumn and winter in the cultivated valleys (*rong*).'[3] He was evidently following the population.

This duality is evidenced everywhere in the modern period, even among the tribes of pastoral herdsmen in Amdo. Of course, many local variants are encountered. There are agricultural villages with pasture-land nearby: the livestock is led out in the daytime and brought back at night to its stabling, where it remains in winter, and is fed on the fodder gathered in the autumn. On other farms animals spend the whole summer grazing, guarded by shepherds living in tents, and are only brought back for the winter. Often a tribe is split in two: a group of farmers in the cultivated valleys (*rong*) and another of purely pastoral herdsmen on the upland pastures ('*brog*). Both groups have the same tribal name and the same chief. Conversely, in Amdo, pastoral groups have a very restricted grazing territory and permanent winter quarters, with houses, where the

[1] 180, f. 37*b*.
[2] 142, *BA*, f. 7*a*: *ri she-pa byed*; *she-khag* = '*brog-hkag*.
[3] 154, f. 36*b*.

123

whole group—scattered in summer—gathers in winter. These houses have cattle-sheds and nearby, for each family, a field of oats, which is harvested green and used as fodder. In any case, agricultural and pastoral districts almost everywhere are very near to one another, and contact between shepherds and farmers is close and constant, for they naturally exchange produce: they often form part of one and the same village community or family group. Even when a single tribe is divided into herdsmen living nomadically over a limited territory and agriculturists, the latter still have upland pastures where their beasts are taken in summer, besides their fields and houses. In such a tribe, the duality is thus doubly expressed. In that instance, moreover, the village, the group of agriculturists, controls not only its fields and hill grazing, but also the fallow land, woods, roads, and water supply used by the herdsmen who make up the other part of the community. In assessing the relative importance of 'nomadic' herdsmen and sedentary farmers, therefore, one must add to the latter the considerable portion of land taken up by forest, which we have noticed in the case of ancient Tibet. Cities also must be added, for the modern period, and monasteries since at least the eleventh century, the places on which intellectual life centres.

It is true that the nomad tribes of Amdo proudly regard themselves as the real Tibetans, and the purest ones. But we know that many of them were formerly aliens. In plays, the naïve, uneducated man who makes people laugh is not—as in the West since Rome—the peasant, but the shepherd, 'the wild man from the north', from the Changthang where the most homogeneous groups of true nomads live.

A work that seems to date from the eighteenth century gives us, in the form of a learned poem, an actual treatise on Tibetan agriculture. It speaks volumes for the latter's importance, the degree of technical refinement it has reached and the interest an educated representative of Tibetan society attached to it. Here is a short extract:[1]

> 'Next we examine the types of land. One sows in accordance with the three forms, "moist", "soft" and "coarse", conforming in each case to the custom of the district, but manuring is suitable for them all. On the other hand if the ground is hard, at the end of

[1] 161, pp. 1–6.

the winter, the water and moisture being frozen, (the soil) will become pliant and soft (with the thaw). Soils which do not become soft even in this way, those of mountain or woodland, will become very spongy when manure has been put on them. . . .

'Goat- and sheep-droppings, human excrement, dung and urine of oxen, dogs, pigs, cross-bred oxen, yak-cows and donkeys, in great quantity, with (in addition) chaff, straw, tree-leaves and *ra-thal* (?) completely burnt, all this is accumulated year by year and mingled without distinction. These remains of materials, all specially pressed down by other manures, will cause the first green shoots, well born, to spring from these materials. . . .

'Upon (the fields), one sows seed in good condition and without blemish, according to custom, in seed-holes. In each small hole five grains are thrown. The depth of the seed-hole and the number of worms are noted. When the disc of the sun is bright, water is mixed in. If the seeds are spoilt by drought or frost, they must be planted afresh.'

POWER AND PROPERTY

Two principles exemplified in the family are found again when we turn to consider the structure of authority: cohesion and the strength of the group, on the one hand; the hereditary authority of one person and a keen sense of hierarchy, on the other. Time and again one has the feeling that the second of these principles has won the day, but that the first continues to counterbalance it.

Two other salient features should be added. The bonds of dependence have a personal character; and they are repeated all the way down the social scale, giving a recurrent, nested effect. In Tibetan thought, the various fields in which the principles of hierarchic structure can operate merge into one. We have seen an example (page 43), where the relations between prince and subjects (*rje, 'bangs*), husband and wife (*khyo-po, chung-ma*), maternal uncle and nephew (*zhang-po, tsha-bo*), father and son, and teacher and disciple (*slob-dpon, slob-ma*), are found side by side.

This hierarchic structure is strongly expressed in the language. The latter is altogether different when talking to a superior, an equal or an inferior; and that is true in all spheres of human intercourse— government, the family or spiritual relations. The whole vocabulary

125

is affected: not only by joining on honorific words, as in the polite speech of China and elsewhere, but by a different set of nouns and verbs, as in Japan.

Here to start with are the social rules which have applied in modern Tibet, for the last two centuries approximately. The village is administered by a village headman, who collects taxes and passes them on to his overlord. He is usually elected, e.g. for three years. His

FIG. 8. Sowing in the third month: two yoked pairs of *mdzo* oxen. Labourers' provisions: beer jar, quarters of dried meat, stacked bowls with different foodstuffs, tsampa bag, bread basket, pepper and salt box.

prestige, wealth and influence often enable him to be re-elected several times in succession. Frequently the job even becomes hereditary. But the council of elders, by whom the headman was elected, takes part in administration (justice, etc.). Besides the fields belonging to families individually, some land is common property of

126

the village or a group of families. Such, in particular, are woodland and hill-pasture, fields reserved for the upkeep of the temple, and fields whose income is used for a communal feast to reward villagers who look after the irrigation channels. The same holds for the shepherd tribes, not only the agricultural section of the tribe, when there is one, but also the purely pastoral part. The tribe is led by a chief, but the pastures—regarded as the tribe's common property, livestock being the individual property of each family—are distributed to different families each year by the chief and council of elders. This council of senior members of the tribe, or elected leaders, also administers justice. The leader of the whole tribe may be elected (in his turn) by the elders.[1] He may also hand on his office to his son, but only if the latter is a man of ability. There are even said to be small tribes without any chief, governed solely by a group of elders.

The other villages or tribes come under an overlord in charge of a wider area within which they happen to be. This lord may be an independent prince (the kings of Ladakh, Derge, Poyül, etc.), a religious leader (e.g. at Chamdo), or the central government (the Dalai Lama). The nesting of jurisdictions may be single or multiple: single if the territory is directly subject to an overlord (Dalai Lama, king), multiple if the immediate overlord is himself subject to, or has accepted, the authority of a higher overlord (e.g. Derge, set under Lhasa's authority only in 1865). The hereditary principle is here only in evidence with kings, princes or other secular overlords. In the case of lords of the church, it can still be seen in those who can marry, and in uncle to nephew succession. In other cases, and particularly that of the Dalai Lama, the principle of incarnation replaces inheritance. The power of these rulers is checked, however, by a group of ministers. The Dalai Lama is assisted by a cabinet of four ministers (three laymen and a monk) and by an assembly of dignitaries convened on special occasions.

The stratification of power is paralleled by that of land ownership. The land is regarded, in the aggregate, as essentially the overlord's property. It is assigned or lent to a temporary owner in exchange for services (statute-labour, etc.) and taxes. Usually, although the higher overlord (e.g. the Dalai Lama) farms out most of the area to a lesser lord (noble family. local prince, etc.), and so on down, part of the

[1] 100, p. 151

land remains under the original overlord's direct authority. For instance, the Dalai Lama's government has direct tax-payers—landed peasants—as well as granting land to noble families who, in turn, have their own landed tax-payers. The direct tax-payers (*khral-pa*) have labourers or older relations under their orders, both types of dependant receiving a plot of land on a sort of sublease.

The land 'given' or rather lent by the overlord, directly or indirectly, is essentially indivisible and non-transferable. It is tied to the name of the occupying family, itself represented by its senior member. It is inherited, but possession is governed by a reciprocal obligation between giver and recipient. Although land belongs to the overlord in principle, he cannot resume it at will. An edict of the prince of Gyantse, in 1440, states that the lord could not take back the land (and the house that went with it) if there were an heir.[1] It must be added that the giver cannot take back possession as long as the holder pays his taxes and renders service. For the gift, or loan, of land by the overlord calls for services and taxes in return. In the event of flight or lapse of payment, the recapture of the fugitive, so that he can have his land (and the obligations that go with it) again, is preferred to confiscation and reassignment. Even the little allotments assigned to agricultural labourers by the senior representative of the family holding an estate cannot be taken back by him as long as the labourer pays for it with his service, and especially if he has built his own house.

The overlord seems therefore to have all the rights of land ownership, but he needs services, and these are tied to the hereditary possession or usufruct of the land. When the lord, whether great or small, wishes to ensure the regularity of an income or service, he grants a piece of land which takes the place of a salary, since part of its income accrues to the holder. In this way a landowner gives land to highly itinerant tradesmen in order to pin them down and attach them to himself—sorcerers, physicians, musicians and smiths. As a rule a subordinate can refuse his services, on pain of losing the land and being condemned to a wandering life (or the lord may deprive a beneficiary of his land in the event of misconduct, e.g. rebellion by a noble family against the king or government). Service is in effect a tax, just as a piece of land is equivalent to a salary. Some villages are exempted from taxes because they specialize in a service (a theatrical

[1] 121, pp. 667, 668.

17. Dalai Lama's dancer. Note the bells. *Photo: V. Sis/J. Vaniš.*

16. The 'ransom king' (*glud-'gong rgyal-po*) at the Lhasa New Year, his face half white, half black. *Photo: H. Harrer, Liechtenstein Verlag.*

18. Clowns (atsara) representing Indian saints. End-of-year masked dances
('*cham*) at Gangtok, Sikkim. *Photo: R. A. Stein.*

19. Nyingma-pa yogin (*rtogs-ldan*) or wandering Tantrist (*sngags-pa*), with skull
cup, pilgrim's staff, feathered spear and bag of ingredients. *Photo: H. Harrer,
Liechtenstein Verlag.*

or acrobatic troupe, the weaving of certain fabrics, etc.). For noble families enjoying an estate but exempt from taxes, the return payment consists in the obligation to provide the government with officials and soldiers. This obligation is plainly very light in comparison with the privileges, but the principle holds. The only exceptions are monastic estates, which are exempt from tax and service. Their rulers can be regarded as independent overlords, though the monasteries provide the government with officials. The Church will consequently require separate treatment.

In this system, where work is not paid for directly and private property is tied to service, the representative of authority, at any level, obviously had a hundred and one ways of abusing his power to force excessive services and taxes from his subordinates. The decree of 1440 mentioned above gives a long list of such exactions. And abuses did not fail to occur. But apart from any value judgment, the structure imposes limitations and seems a harking back to earlier times, when personal ties involved mutual obligations and the power of a group limited that of its chief.

The picture we have painted is inevitably simplified and provisional, though. It is based on travellers' accounts. The Tibetan and Chinese sources only occasionally give practical details, and there is no book of regulations, or even a systematic description. The modern position was never studied in the field. The principles laid down above are probably not absolute and unchanging. In the early period we have seen Mila Rêpa's ancestors buying and selling fields. In our own time, according to information from Tibetans, a tax-paying landowner could sell his land, but the new owner would then have to till the land—in person or by delegating someone to take his place —and was subject to the same taxes and services to the overlord as his predecessor. In the unlikely but possible event that the land was not cultivated, through the occupier's flight or negligence, the lord would take back the land. He could then either reassign it to another landowner on his territory, who would then fulfil service and tax payments, or—if there were no taker—incorporate it in the territory belonging to him personally, which was cultivated by the whole body of tax-paying landowners of his estate. For modern times, Chinese influences are possible. In the present state of Tibetan studies, one can only assume a certain diversity of institutions according to region and period.

SOCIETY

The Tibetan epic poem is a good mirror of society, though it certainly idealizes it, and though the institutions it describes are not all historical. In it we see an old king put very much in the shade, and his ambitious brother who covets the throne. Decisions, however, are always submitted to a gathering of the 'people', called by a very old man who is the embodiment of wisdom and the repository of laws and traditions. At certain important junctures the wishes of the king's brother are thwarted by this elder statesman's decision, as approved by the assembly. Now the latter contains all elements of society, from young and old warriors of the noble clans to beggars. But the hierarchy of their social positions is clearly shown by the position they occupy in the assembly (to left or right, in front of or behind the king's throne) and by the height of their seat (three carpets, nine, etc.), exactly as found in real life. Although succession to the throne is hereditary, it is stressed that, in the hero's country, throne, treasures of state and wife are bestowed on the winner of a horse-race in which all classes of society including the very beggars take part. Another work describes the rules of behaviour of a good society: the elders' advice must be asked and 'even one who is powerful himself, accords with the interests of the community.'[1] Despite this 'tribal' or communal organization, which recalls that of Tibetan nomads, the epic emphasizes the need for a leader to settle the quarrels to which clans or tribes are liable. It is because everything is going wrong in the country without a leader and because it has thus been put in the power of mighty neighbours, that the elders decide to ask the gods for a leader—the hero.

It is in exactly the same fashion that tradition sees the coming of the first monarchy. There too, the first king is the son of a god, coming down from heaven or the sacred mountain, welcomed and elected king by shepherds, chieftains, priests and representatives of the clans, or a group of 'kinglets'. This election ended the 'absence of distinction between people and ruler' and the incessant civil wars between isolated lords, based upon fortified strongholds (chapter II).

It does seem that the king was elected by his peers: the expression for any enthronement means 'to be elected to the throne' (*rgyal-sar bskos*). On the other hand, what were called 'subjects' or 'people' were not necessarily always the common folk. These words (*'bangs, dmangs*), together with those which in classical literature and the

[1] 180, f. 38*b*.

language of today mean 'slave' or 'serf' (*bran*) and 'servant' (*khol*), in ancient literature are also applied—at least occasionally—to nobles.

We turn now to the position in antiquity. We have seen that, under Songtsen Gampo, the 'tax-payers' among the people (*'bangs*) had 'second-order serfs' (*yang-bran*) or 'servants of oneself' (*nying-g.yog*) under them. They themselves could accordingly be described as 'serfs' or 'servants'. Similarly, in Trhisong Detsen's law-code, the 'black-headed ones' have servants. They correspond, therefore, to the modern 'tax-payers' (*khral-pa*)—'rich peasants' as they have been called—possessing land and houses vouchsafed them by an overlord or the state; deriving a family name from this property; and paying services and taxes in return. But at the same period the word *khral*, 'tax', also denotes the services each noble family owes the state (supply of officials and soldiers). There is no structural distinction between the two.

When Trhisong Detsen's succession was disrupted by the murder of his eldest son, 'the whole people (all his subjects) held a council and transferred power to the younger brother Trhide Songtsen'. They also elected a minister to be responsible for 'the law' (justice and administration), and that minister attended to 'the affairs of all the subjects (of the whole people: *'bangs*)'. Such is one chronicle's account, but according to another, a Bonpo one, it was the council of ministers that placed the younger brother on the throne.[1] The word 'people' or 'subjects' thus refers equally to noblemen, such as ministers. Conversely, the ancient epithet of ministers, the 'wise' (*mdzangs*), has taken on the meaning of 'nobility' (*ya-rabs*—according to the dictionaries). 'The king is mighty, the ministers are wise', says the old Tun-huang chronicle (Bibliography, no. 6, p. 81). Later, other chronicles often speak of 'wise ministers', and we already know a list of seven. 'The divine king (the word "king", *btsan*, can also mean "mighty") is he whose courage is capable of difficult deeds. Those who perform miracles through wisdom are known as the three maternal uncles and the four ministers,' says one of them.[2] Those ministers have, in truth, an almost magical (*'phrul*) wisdom and

---

[1] 183, pp. 68–69; 186, f. 117*b*.
[2] 139, f. 254*b*.

knowledge, enabling them to invent new techniques and win duels of magic and illusion. The king, too, in his capacity as a 'god' is referred to with the same attribute (*'phrul-gyi lha btsan-po*).

The king thus emerges as a *primus inter pares*. In the seventh or eighth century his domain simply adjoins the eighteen other domains (*dbang-ris*) of different noble clans. The ministers are very close to him. They all bear the names of great noble clans and a good many belong to a queen's clan (hence perhaps their title 'maternal uncle'). They also threaten the king's authority with a parallel power. In the administrative organization attributed to Songtsen Gampo, the 'wise men' have credentials and emblems of rank (*yig-tshang*). Chinese chronicles inform us, and the Tun-huang manuscripts confirm, that these proto-bureaucrats had insignia (*yi-ge*) of different precious substances according to their station. Now, on Chinese authority,[1] their responsibilities were hereditary: 'For any post, the son succeeds on his father's death, and if there is no descendant the nearest relative replaces him; they only succeed (or replace) one another inside their own clan.' Trhisong Detsen's code, later, distinguishes three upper and three lower classes within the King's Law (parallel to the Religious Law—*rgyal-khrims, chos-khrims*). In the first category come (1) the good, wise 'venerables' (monks), (2) the young warriors who subdue enemies and (3) the artisans, wise men and credential-holders (*byas-gzo mdzangs dang yig-tshangs*).[2] As in modern Tibet, official posts must have entailed a title to land and a family name, both of these hereditary. The hierarchy of posts implied greater or lesser privileges, e.g. with regard to the punishments laid down by law.

The bonds between the king and his subjects, the nobles, were personal and based on exchange—the granting of land, titles and benefits by the king against the performance of services by the 'subject'. And these bonds are repeated, at a further remove, between the vassal or noble 'subject' and his subordinate, vavasour or liegemen. The king has subjects who are 'near to his heart' (*snying-nye; glo-ba nye*), i.e. faithful or loyal, and others who are 'distant from his heart' (*snying-rings; glo-ba rings* or *'dring*), disloyal and rebellious. They regularly exchange oaths of fealty, a minor one every year and a major one every three years: animals are sacrificed and deities

[1] 200, f. 8*a*; 199, f. 69*b*.
[2] 139, f. 230*a*.

called to witness (page 200). Not only does subject swear fealty to king, but the king on his side swears to uphold the subject's possessions and privileges, for him and his descendants. Such oaths have been carved on pillars, and the inscriptions are known to us. Moreover, the Chinese testify, 'the ruler and his subjects enter a pact of friendship embracing five or six persons who are called "common destiny" (life-and-death). When the ruler dies, they commit suicide to follow him in his tomb.' Another text states that many other relatives and faithful followers were buried at the same time. In late Tibetan chronicles this bond is weakened, but retains its basic ingredients. For Songtsen Gampo's funeral, the king and his two queens, on their death, were coated with gold and the treasures were put on display. The whole was guarded by ministers who behaved 'like dead men' and were thus enshrined as 'servants of the corpse'. And since living and dead must stay apart, they were banished like outcasts from the society of ordinary men. They were no longer visited by anyone but members of the royal family, save on the occasion of sacrifices. Neither men, horses, nor cattle might approach the confines of the sepulchre. If they strayed, they were seized by the (pseudo-) 'dead', the guardians of the tomb and, once touched by them, must not go back to the living any more. Stamped with the sign of death (or of the simulated 'dead men', probably as a mark of ownership) they became 'slaves' or 'serfs' of the tomb-guardians.[1]

The Chinese word I have translated 'subjects' (ch'ên) also means 'minister', and it is clear that the men who shared the king's fate were nobles. In their personal relations with the king even nobles were regarded as 'subjects', 'people', 'serfs' and 'servants'. Let us see then how this bond grows up, how the king binds a retinue of loyal clients to himself by a kind of magnetism inherent in his virtue and his godlike quality. An early chronicle from Tun-huang (no. 6, chapter III) gives an exact picture of the process.

The king is residing at Chhinga Taktse on the River Yar, in Yarlung, 'A man, ah yes, son of a man; but son of a god, yes, he dwells! A true prince, yes, one loves to serve; true saddle, yes, one loves to bear!' The verb 'to serve' (bkol) used in the text is only another form of the word 'servant' (khol), which also denotes the servants of plebeians liable to statute labour. But here it refers to a nobleman. This theme will be found to recur.

[1] 197B, f. 1b; 197A, f. 1b; 177, f. 73b.

Two noble lords, Ta-kyawo and Trhipangsum, live on their respective estates. The former is a bad lord. From pride, he refuses to listen to wise (ministers) and loyal subjects, but gives ear to flatterers. He hates the wise and valiant, and makes arbitrary and unseemly decisions.

'When prince, above, is violent, the servant is afraid, below,
When prince, above, is lunatic, the servant is wily, below.'

Confidence no longer subsists between them, and the subjects harbour malice against their leader. The minister then cautions the lord and predicts the decline of his power. However—as in so many Chinese stories, too—the lord will not listen, accuses him and dismisses him from office. Displeased, the minister goes over to the other lord, Trhipangsum, and kills his own:

'When the mule is overburdened, the saddle breaks.'

The murdered lord's land is then added to Trhipangsum's estate, but a quarter is given in bondage (*bran*) to the minister. But now it is his turn to behave badly. Among the 'serfs' (*bran*; but the text has 'serfs' land') given to him were a man of the Nyang clan, and another of the Mön clan. Despite their subservience (*bran*) to the minister they were plainly noblemen since they bore well-known clan-names and had land. Anyway, while doing his services, Nyang is humiliated by the minister's wife:

'She weighed him down with her arrogance; she approached him in a sinful way (?); she showed him her private parts.'

The 'serf' Nyang complains, not directly to his new lord, but to the latter's lord Trhipangsum. He, however, does not accept the complaint. For one thing, he values the minister above all else; for another he declares the mistress without blame, she having authority to do much more even than she has. The 'serf' Nyang is then disheartened and very displeased. There we have one factor tending to bring about a new situation.

It happens that Trhipangsum also wields power over two other noblemen, of the Wa and Shen clans respectively. They quarrel, and Shen kills Wa. Wa's elder brother asks his lord what blood-price (*stong*) he will give for the murder. The lord's reply, plainly siding with his ministers, is very odd. Shen, he argues, is a minister (the same as the unnamed minister involved earlier on?). Now 'when a

134

"virtuous" person (*dge-ba*) kills an "unvirtuous" one, (the matter) ends with the murder'. Wa is displeased and disheartened. And there we have a second potentially disrupting factor.

The custom of 'man's price' (*mi-stong*) was still practised in modern Tibet. Its object was to avoid the endless vendettas the relatives were driven to. At nineteenth-century Litang, 'in the event of armed robbery (the guilty party) was sought and killed. If he was taken alive, it might be that his supporters came and asked for him to be set free. There was then a discussion on the amount of damages, which were always nine for one. It was the same in case of murder. It was what was known as "life price". Thus, even if the murder went back decades or even several generations, the indemnity had to be paid if the other party, no longer weak but strong, came to claim the life price. Otherwise the desire for vengeance raised up arms, and wars never ceased.'[1] It has been supposed that this institution was due to some humanizing influence on the part of Buddhism. Nothing of the kind. The ancient Chinese annals speak of it as linked with the warlike temper of the Ch'iang: 'They regard (the use of) force as (a sign of) heroic (valour); in the event of manslaughter, an indemnity is paid for the person killed, but there is no other punishment.' Trhisong Detsen's legal code, or one version of it, sanctions the custom in these words: 'In case of murder, its price (*stong*) is paid'; while another has: 'For homicide under the law, murder price (*stong*) and consolation price (?—*gsos-thang*).'[2]

But, to return to our story, it seems that the lord was held responsible for the murder committed by his minister. This type of responsibility presupposes an imaginary bond of kinship. The two malcontents reach an understanding and leave together for their estates. They look for a new lord and very naturally think of the king. Nyang expresses his intention in veiled words:

> 'Beyond, ah yes, the river, river,
> Beyond, ah yes, the River Yar,
> A man, ah yes, son of a man,
> But son of a god, yes, he dwells.
> A true prince, yes, one loves to serve,
> True saddle, yes, one loves to bear.'

[1] 190, *shang*, f. 25*b*.
[2] 139, f. 230*a*.

So does the second, Wa, who vows: 'Nothing is truer than what you say. Since I, too, have never undergone anything more unpleasant, my thoughts are no other than yours.' So they swear fealty to the king (are 'near to his heart'). The king probably had to give them a reward. An early inscription instructs us that according to the 'usage of olden days' the lord had to bestow some favour upon a vassal who, being 'close to his heart', had come to make him an offering of 'curd and meat'.[1]

Now observe, though, how their vengeance is prepared, to the king's advantage. Each first associates other men with himself. Wa administers the oath to his maternal uncle Nön, and then to the latter's son when he dies. These relatives formed part of the entourage of their lord Trhipangsum. As for Nyang, he puts a man of the Tshepong tribe on oath. The latter communicates the plan to the king by 'whispering in his ear'. The king declares his assent although his sister is living with the lord in question. Whilst oaths are being exchanged at the king's castle and the attack is being prepared, the king dies. His two sons then administer the oath anew to the six conspirators, and further members of the Nyang, Tshepong and Wa clans are brought in. Then the new king sets out with a large army. The lord's castle is captured and he himself 'ruined'. His territory is put under the king's authority. Nyang and Wa are pleased: 'Of a true prince, yes, the servants; with a true saddle we're saddled.' As for the subjects of the newly conquered country, they and others extol the king and give him his reign name: 'His reign is higher than the sky (*gnam*), his helmet stronger than a mountain (*ri*).' Hence he is called Namri Löntsen. Then the plotters hand over the vanquished lord's domain to the king, who rewards them by allotting them fiefs. The four chief conspirators, who had been the first to swear, receive lands and fifteen hundred serfs (with their houses or families, *bran-khyim*) and are appointed ministers. The others, who were only accessories to the oath, receive neither land nor serfs but are appointed to the king's immediate entourage. At once, the king's increased prestige makes him a focus of attraction and other lords submit to him. A man of the Khyung clan cuts off the Lord of Tsang-Pö's head and surrenders that country's twenty thousand families to the king. The king returns them to him in reward for having been 'near to his heart'. In the east, however, Dakpo (which

[1] 94, I, 1.20.

used to be subject to the king) revolts. A general conquers it and receives in return the men of Serkhung and its pasture-land. And all ends in a 'feast of joy' presented to his subjects by the king, at which the exploits are celebrated in song.

Services rendered, then, were rewarded. Although it was only a moral obligation, the lord's reward and favour were expected in return. And the subject, though accepting the constraint of vassalage, saw to it that the benefits of his loyalty should become hereditary. In an inscription of 764, the great minister Tara Lugong boasts of having foiled the treachery of two ministers who had caused the king-father's death, and of having become the faithful servant of his son Trhisong Detsen. So the king vowed that Tara Lugong's descendants should never hold lower rank than that of the silver-emblem, that one of them should always be in the king's personal service, and that none of them should ever lose their lives or property for any offence, save that of hostility to the king. In the absence of an heir their serfs, estates and livestock should not be confiscated by the king, but given to the closest relative.[1]

At that early period we may certainly speak of feudalism, founded on a knightly ethic. The vassal is a 'serf' and accepts his servitude as the horse his saddle. But his lord must be a 'true' prince, a 'true' saddle. Otherwise the overladen mule breaks its saddle. Arrogance, in particular, is not tolerated, any more than abuse of power and despotism. That, at least, was the theory. In practice ministers often took advantage of the king's youth to monopolize power. We have seen an example with the Gar ministers. The ancient Tun-huang chronicle often emphasizes treachery and the use of poison. Much later the dual-power phenomenon reappeared with the Dalai Lamas' regents. Just as the Gar minister hid King Songtsen Gampo's death for a long time by parading his statue in a veiled carriage,[2] so too the regent Sanggyê Gyatso concealed the Fifth Dalai Lama's death and ruled in his name.

On the other hand, if the subject accepts the lord's authority it is because the king, according to one standard history, has duties: 'to erect a temple for his tutelary deity, establish his subjects in peace

---

[1] 93, pp. 26–31; cf. also the Kongpo inscription (Richardson, 'A ninth-century inscription from Rkoṅ-po', *Journal of the Royal Asiatic Society*, Oct. 1954).

[2] 142, *JA*, f. 68a.

and, himself, risk his life leading the army.'[1] How anxious the subjects were to have a leader is shown by the case of King Relpachen's minister (page 23) who carved himself out a fief in Amdo where he had been sent to collect taxes. That country's subjects, liable to the exactions of both Tibet and China, made him their chief (*dpon-po*) and offered him tribute of gold, silver, silk, horses and cattle. He thus became rich and powerful, and allied himself with the local clans by marrying five women belonging to them. His descendants were still reigning in 1773. Later, in the thirteenth century, we find Rinchen of Chayül (lower Yarlung) gathering local chieftains together and so driving out the Mongol army. For this exploit the local chiefs elected him their head.[2] The process recalls the manner in which a village head, at first elected for a period, then for life, may end up by handing on his authority hereditarily.

Tibetan society has changed, of course, but certain patterns have held their own. The most important stages are marked by the end of the central monarchy in the tenth century and the growth of organized religion which eventually resulted in an ecclesiastical state. But the break was never total. For hundreds of years, practically until the eighteenth-century Chinese protectorate, monastic hierarchs merely continued the life of the lords; not to speak of the independent states ruled by local princes. Religion played such a leading part, however, that we must examine it separately.

ORGANIZED RELIGION

Tibet has often been described as a theocratic state. That is true to the extent that, in recent centuries, a central government has been headed by the Dalai Lama: the incarnation—indirectly, it is true—of Avalokiteśvara, Tibet's patron bodhisattva, whose statue stands in the capital. There was a precedent for this: the same deity had already been incarnated in Tibet's first centralizing king, Songtsen Gampo, who at his death dissolved and melted into the same statue. It would be more accurate, however, to speak of an *ecclesiastical* state: first, because other hierarchs have ruled the whole or part of Tibet, some also incarnations and others not; but mainly because the Dalai Lama is not, any more than the Panchen Lama or any other incarnate lama,

[1] 183, p. 70.
[2] 141, f. 120*b*.

Avalokiteśvara's direct incarnation, repeated every time. Like all the others, he is the rebirth of the historical figure he was in his preceding life, a link in a chain that starts in history and leads back through legend to a deity in mythical times. The First Dalai Lama, Gedün-trup (1391–1474), was already the 51st incarnation; the teacher Dromtön, Atiśa's disciple (eleventh century), the 45th; whilst with the 26th, one Gesar king of India, and the 27th, a hare, we are in pure legend. True, it is always Avalokiteśvara, still present in each succeeding Dalai Lama. The dogma is hard to explain, but Tibetan texts always say that a given Dalai Lama was the incarnation of his historical predecessor and not directly of Avalokiteśvara: we are told for instance that the Sixth was indeed the reincarnation of the Fifth, but reminded that in the beginning Avalokiteśvara made a vow to be reborn many times for the good of Tibet.[1]

Tibet, then, is an ecclesiastical state, as regards both the central government at Lhasa and the more or less independent local states. Every lay official has a monastic counterpart. The practice of putting younger brothers into religion ensures tight control and community of interests between secular authority, at all levels, and the monasteries. Not to speak of the deep and sincere faith which Tibetans all imbibe, like mediaeval man, from top to bottom of the social scale.

Population statistics give a good idea of the place monasteries occupy in society. Whereas the present-day population of Lhasa has been estimated at some 40,000 inhabitants (about 1910 a Chinese source suggested 50,000),[2] the three great monasteries in the neighbourhood, Ganden, Sera and Drêpung, contained about 20,000 (a very rough figure: for Sera, 7,000–10,000 monks were claimed at the end of the nineteenth century; there were only 2,850 in 1697). At Chamdo (12,000 inhabitants), monks are said to have made up a quarter of the population. A census of 1663, under the Fifth Dalai Lama, speaks of 750 monasteries of 'moral conduct' (chiefly Geluk-pa) with about 50,900 monks; 400 monasteries of medium conduct and 650 of married monks and yogins of both sexes, with 20,000 monks and nuns. In all: 1,800 monasteries with 100,000 monks and nuns. But around 1885, one observer noted 1,026 Geluk-pa monasteries with 491,242 monks, estimating that the total of other orders must come to slightly more (altogether about 2,500 monasteries with some

---

[1] 162, *ZA*, f. 19*b*; 181.
[2] 196, *shang*, p. 24.

760,000 inmates, or a fifth of the population). The estimates are clearly not very reliable. According to an eighteenth-century Chinese source, the registers of the Li-fan yüan (ministry of foreign affairs) at the time of K'ang-hsi and the Sixth Dalai Lama (viz., *ca.* 1700) recorded some 3,150 monasteries and temples with 302,000 monks under the Dalai Lama's control, and 327 monasteries with more than 13,700 monks under the Panchen Lama. In the eighteenth century, the figure was about 341,200 'red' and 'yellow' monks, i.e. belonging to the non-reformed and reformed sects.[1]

Since monasteries are exempt from tax and services they can be regarded as independent overlords, for they own land and serfs yielding them taxes and services, and discharge all the functions of authority (justice, etc.). Sometimes a monastery is a positive fortress. Revenue is further increased, as with other overlords, by trade and money-lending. To these is added a source of revenue peculiar to them: payments for rites performed at a private individual's request. The recipient may be a monastery collectively, with its management in the hands of experts, or it may be a hierarch, especially an incarnation, acting individually. Like the nobles, the monasteries supply the government with officials, and their dignitaries receive titles in accordance with a hierarchic scale. On the other hand social classes are maintained inside the monasteries. Private property is allowed there and can be increased by private trade or private fees for the performance of rites. Rich monks own property and have poor monks for servants. The different sections or houses of a monastic town or city belong to a family or a village: some houses belong to the family of the monks living there, others are reserved for monks from a particular district. In non-reformed orders that allow marriage, the married monks live in the village and till their family's fields; even in other orders, the poorer monk often comes back to the village and helps in agricultural work. It will be recalled that a monk may also return to the lay condition and get married, if that is necessary for the perpetuation of the line. The impoverished lower clergy cannot usually follow the lengthy studies needed to reach high monastic positions, and often even remain illiterate. In addition to the duties of every kind with which they may be burdened at the monastery (cooking for the monks, music, preparing offerings, etc.), they supply —in some large Geluk-pa monasteries, like Sera—quite an army of

[1] 195, f. 271*b*.

athlete or warrior monks.[1] These monks (*dob-dob* or *ldab-ldob*) are subjected to a regular training (jumping, quarter-staff, races, etc.); fight duels (often over a minion); take part in sports contests between monasteries; and serve high-ranking ecclesiastics as bodyguards on their travels, or the monastic proctors (*zhal-ngo*) as servants (*dge-g.yog*) at the Great Prayer (*smon-lam*) festival in Lhasa . . . on which occasion they exert political pressure backed up with force. They form a fairly close-knit body which keeps up its esprit de corps by peculiar customs. Although, like all monks, they must have their head shaved whilst living at the monastery, they adopt another hairstyle when they serve outside: the hair shaved at the middle of the skull but long, curly and coiled like ram's horns above the ears. The better sort are regarded as wandering Tantrists with extraordinary powers (*grub-thob*, Sanskrit *siddha*). Others, looked on with disfavour and liable to penalities if they should re-enter the monastery, go in for roving about at will, with their hair long and carefully curled, leading a reckless improvident life, free from constraint (*snang-ba skyid-po*). Little is known of them, and still less of their history. But despite certain distortions and some abuses, we can recognize in them the tradition of the warrior monks, so important in China and Japan, and the taste for unconventional behaviour. The latter, though of little importance in the official (Geluk-pa) church, we shall meet again among certain adherents of the unreformed orders.

Such broadly is the situation in the modern period. Its genesis dates back to the beginnings of Buddhism's official adoption as state religion by King Trhisong Detsen.

According to one chronicle the king wished the queens, other than the titular ruling one, and those sons of ministers (*zhang-blon*) who were Buddhists, to take monastic vows. The ministers objected that, once monks, they would have nothing to live on and would fall foul of the law through failure to supply military service and taxes. The king replied that he would make them his 'objects of worship', i.e. provide for their needs. So the abbot of the newly created monastery of Samyê, Yeshe Wangpo, asked for privileges and authority even higher than those of great ministers with golden insignia. His request was granted and he was placed 'at the head of the superiors', whilst other monks, belonging to the noble clans of Nyang and Trenka, were appointed ministers with a higher rank than the

[1] 39A.

141

'great ministers' and the 'maternal-uncle'.[1] At a reception in the royal camp, a monk bearing a glorious title ('*dpal chen-po*) sat on the king's right (honourable side) on the actual dais, whilst the ministers sat below that dais:[2] their inferiority to the monk was thus unmistakable. Yeshe Wangpo had no need to invent. He merely imitated the pattern found in India where tax-exempted donations were the rule and where there also existed monasteries that were literally university cities of several thousand monks (Nālandā, etc.).

Donations were graded at Samyê and sanctioned the administrative positions and university grades. On the authority of the chronicle we have been quoting, abbots received 70 loads of grain a month, professors 35 and pupils 12. Or else the abbot and the 'eternal support

FIG. 9. Athlete monk (*dob-dob*). On his arm, a piece of cloth held in place by a rosary. Curled hair above the ears.

[1] 183, pp. 51, 53–54.
[2] 202, *ch*. 981.

of religion' (the monastery as a whole; another chronicle has 'for the temples, images, etc.') received 100 families of subjects, and each monk three (in his own right). These 'subjects' (and no doubt their land) made up 'domains of the gods' (*lha-ris*: in modern Tibet, *lha-sde*) and were not 'subject to the power of superiors' (the king or the government), but to that of the clergy.

Another chronicle[1] gives a more detailed list. The domain (probably of the temple) contained 150 (or 250?) peasants (?). Each of the abbots was entitled, each year, to 75 loads of barley, a garment of nine lengths of material, 1,100 ounces of butter (and?) incense (doubtless for lamps used in worship), 4 bundles of paper, 3 sticks of ink and salt as required. Below them, the 25 hermits of Chhimphu (near Samyê) each got 55 loads of barley, 800 ounces of butter, a saddle-horse and a garment of six lengths of material. Lower still, the thirteen lecturers got 55 loads of barley, a six-length garment and 800 ounces of butter apiece. Lastly, the ordinary independent monks were given 8 loads of barley, two bundles of paper and a piece of ink, and each of the 25 pupils was given 25 loads of barley and a garment of three lengths of material.

Several inscriptions of this period state that, even if the line of succession were broken, 'authority over servants, villages, etc., will not be taken over by the rulers or entrusted to others'; that a register of the donations made will be kept in two copies in two different temples; that the donations will not be reduced; and that 'the subjects and property making up the monastic estate will not be subject to tax'.[2] King Relpachen (815–838) granted each monk seven families of subjects for his maintenance.[3] From that time on we see monks playing a political part as ministers or ambassadors and above all as mediators. Under Relpachen, the peace of 821–822 was negotiated by Tibetan and Chinese monks.

The privileges, moreover, do not stop at property, but extend to the province of the penal code. Although Trhisong Detsen's code is only known to us, in poor preservation, through much later historians, it is worth quoting. That code distinguishes between 'religious laws' (directed to the monks) and 'royal laws' which related to 'the general affairs of all the subjects', to which are added, without explanation,

---

[1] 183, p. 63; 142, *JA*, f. 122*b*.
[2] 92, p. 60 (*mTshur-phu* inscription), p. 56 (*sKar-chung* do., 1.49).
[3] *La-dvags rgyal-rabs*, ed. Francke, pp. 33–34; 183, p. 74.

'laws by decree' (? *thang-khrims*). In the 'religious laws' a strict distinction is made between 'ordained monks' subject to domestic discipline (the *Vinaya*), and 'Tantric monks';

> 'Let the abbot administer vows to the monk, with the discipline; let him act as it is said in the *Tripiṭaka*! For thirst, let the monks drink tea and "the white" (milk); for food, let them eat grain, treacle, honey and butter; for clothing, let them make themselves an under-robe and a red robe; for dwelling-place, let them live in the temples (monasteries); let them not indulge in black beer, meat and excess of food!

> 'Let the Tantrists (*sngags-pa*) act in accordance with their vows and as it is said in the Tantras! For thirst, let them drink beer, (but) let them not steal the monks' property; for food, let them eat what they wish but let them not taste the poison of enjoyment; for clothing let them have the white, red and black clothes of the Tantrists; for dwelling-place, let them take the houses of meditation (the type that aims at the creation of a deity, *sgrub-khang*) and (by this means) make benefits increase; for the protection of religion, let them apply themselves to those meditations (*sgrub*, Sanskrit *sādhana*)!

> 'By way of good works, let the monks celebrate "yellow" sūtra feasts, the Tantrists "Tantric" maṇḍala feasts, and let the "black men" (laymen) make gifts to the monasteries of both doctrines! . . . Let the two doctrines not be mingled, and let each keep to his own!'[1]

The 'religious law' stipulated that 'Men shall not have their eye plucked out; women shall not have their nose cut off; those accused shall not be killed. The whole people shall obey the sovereign's orders, but sovereign and people shall venerate and bow to the monks.'[2] It also laid down that 'He who shows finger (?) to a monk shall have his finger cut off; he who speaks ill of the monks' and the king's Buddhist policy shall have his lips cut off; he who looks askance at them shall have his eye put out; he who robs them, shall pay according to the rule of the restitution of eighty times (the value of the article stolen)'.[3] This rule is repeated in the Code: theft of the sovereign's goods, hundredfold payment; theft of the clergy's goods, eighty times;

[1] 170, f. 114*b*.
[2] 183, p. 51.
[3] 183, p. 76.

144

20. Yak dance. Shepherd's part played by the narrator, wearing mask of 'hunter (*rngon-pa*). *Photo: H. Richardson.*

21. The 'hunter' and one of the 'goddesses' (*a-che lha-mo*) of the drama. Free-lance strolling players, at Gangtok.

22. Scene from a play at Lhasa: presentation of gifts and scarves at the end of the performance. *Photo: H. Richardson.*

23. Inaugural rite of the drama. 'Hunters' and 'goddesses' around the altar, tree planted at the centre.

of an ordinary man's, nine times. Actually, the provisions of the Code are ill-preserved and sometimes contradictory. The following paragraph occurs in it:

'If any one does not act as though bound by my Religious Law, he will be punished without fail by the Royal Law. (In the following cases:) a monk towards his abbot, a disciple towards his (Tantric) teacher, a servant towards his master, a son towards his father and mother, a younger brother towards his elder, a wife towards her husband: whoever misbehaves, kills or acts as an enemy shall be burnt in fire and thrown in the water.'

Despite the obscurities, it does seem that bodily punishments were not to be applied to monks. And the clergy is almost at the sovereign's level, if we consider the rates of reimbursement in case of theft.

Regardless of persecution and in spite of the decline of the monarchy, the church retained privileges and quickly recovered considerable wealth. In the west and east of the country, as we have seen, the monks had soon found protectors. About 1250, the hierarch of Drigung thrice received large gifts from Hülä'ü, the Mongol king of Iran, as well as from the kings of Ceylon, Tirahuti and Yatse. In giving the Sakya-pas kingship over Tibet, the Mongols at the same time granted them tax immunity for their monasteries, not to mention the concession of three thousand *tarqan*, officials exempt from taxes (the Tshelpas got two thousand). To this day the Sakya lay officers, who succeed from father to son, have kept this title of *tarqan*. In the mid-fifteenth century, the Seventh Karma-pa, too, received offerings from nine different kings of Tibet (Tsang, etc.) and abroad (Mon, Kashmir, Nepal, Purang, Guge and Mang-yül). All the religious leaders hastened to send 'tributes' and missions of obedience to the Chinese court, taking with them a retinue of hundreds, sometimes thousands. They received valuable presents and engaged in a trade that was all the more lucrative in that the Chinese court paid the expenses of all their people during the journey. The cost had become so heavy that China was obliged to restrict the frequency of the missions and the size of the convoy. As chaplains to the Emperor, high-ranking lamas had even taken up permanent residence in China, from Yüan to Ch'ing times (thirteenth to twentieth centuries), and often enjoyed a privileged position there. Chinese men of letters protested against the luxury and excesses of some of these dignitaries.

So it is not surprising to find that the endless feuds between great monasteries and religious orders nearly always had economic and political reasons. With a few exceptions, they do not involve any doctrinal divergence: they were not religious wars, but struggles for ascendancy between ecclesiastical overlords, or even quarrels between land-owners. During the building of the great temple of Talung in 1224–1228, the carpenters of that order met with refusal from the Drigung monks, when they wanted to seek wood in the Nakshö (forest region). They were later allowed to, but a war whose cause we do not know broke out between Talung and Drigung soon afterwards.

Political and economic motivations should not however let us forget the part played by certain high ecclesiastics, who were disinterested saints. Their religious and moral prestige was such that they were ideal candidates for an important job in Tibetan society, that of go-between (*gzu-ba*). When there had been a murder, theft of animals, a fugitive 'serf' running away or any other dispute, the go-between was called in and accepted by both sides to avoid endless vendettas, and he received gifts for his services.

About 1074, during a great war in Kongpo, the soil-god of the place entrusts the task of go-between to Chhökyi Sherap of Ma. The saint then proceeds to the battle-field and waves a religious garment between the two armies, threatening them with nine kinds of fearsome demons and calling the soil-god to witness his mediation. Violent storms break out at an appointed moment, and the soldiers leave off battle.[1]

At the close of the twelfth century Shang Rinpoche, observing that Tibet was 'without law and falling into pieces', stamps the mountains, valleys and roads with his 'seals' (*rgya*), adding a fearsome rite. This was a way of forbidding hunting and highway robbery. Denouncing armed strife, he instigates negotiations. A lay chieftain taking part in one of these meetings for the settlement of conflicts (*'khrug-gral*) sees the face of the wrathful deity Demchok (Heruka), created by the master.[2] The procedure of prohibiting violence by stamping mountains, rivers or roads with a religious seal, as a sign of prohibition, was very

[1] 99, p. 874.
[2] 142, *NA*, f. 37a.

frequent. The roads were extremely unsafe, as they have remained till modern times. At the beginning of the thirteenth century we find another saint 'sealing' mountains, rivers and streams and building a sort of hospice (*'gron-khang*) which he endows with 'food for the guests' (or travellers, *'gron-zan*). Such hospices already existed two generations earlier: the sick were tended in them.[1]

Midway through the fifteenth century, the Seventh Karma-pa acts as go-between and in this way halts fratricidal conflicts (*nang-dme*) at Ling. The word used denotes as a rule conflicts within a clan, which morality strongly disapproved of. But here the result of his mediation was that the saint put the 'divine population' (*lha-sde*, serfs subject to a monastery) and the 'human population' (*mi-sde*, serfs dependent on a lay lord) each in its place. He similarly puts a stop to feuds between Buddhist and Bonpo monks (*ban-bon*) at Ling and Kathok, releasing prisoners and enforcing peace. He also intervenes in actual tribal wars in the neighbourhood of Tatsienlu: he satisfies all the 'human' and 'divine' populations there, both with sermons and material goods. Intervening in feuds among the Goloks, he receives from them the 'tax on roads' (*lam-khral*) and presents.

But despite the impartiality of those saints, they could not help becoming the object of disputes themselves, precisely because the possession or control of such a saint was a source of revenue and political prestige. When reincarnation determined the succession, the struggle might centre on the choice of the next rebirth: this was the case with the Seventh Dalai Lama, when the Chinese court had to make up its mind to persuade the Tibetan government to hold a lottery between several candidates lest certain families should monopolise the succession.

In the sixteenth century, a dispute set the partisans of the Eighth Karma-pa in opposition to those of another incarnation from Amdo. It was open warfare waged by the military camps (*sgar*) and their commanders, who in those days constituted the court of any high-ranking Karma-pa. The Eighth Karma-pa succeeded in stopping the conflict by performing miracles. The Tenth Karma-pa was born amongst the Goloks. The child was transferred to the camp of the 'Red Hat' Karma-pa leader, who initiated him and conferred the status of 'Black Hat' upon him. He was then placed upon the 'lion throne' and given the black hat, seal, parasol, etc. The camp then

[1] 99, pp. 986, 997.

147

wanted to keep the young incarnation. But the Goloks, especially the child's family, 'fearing a loss of money', refused. For his part Kholoji, king of the Amdo Mongols, also sent the young dignitary and his father an invitation. But there again the Goloks were afraid that the Mongols, with the connivance of the people of the Red Hat's camp, would kidnap the Tenth Karma-pa. Some years later, after several journeys by the Karma-pa and invitations to him to visit the Amdo Mongols and Yünnan (Jang), the Goloks again suspected that he would be snatched from them and 'took great precautions as though against enemies'.[1]

We must accordingly reckon with a certain difference between the ecclesiastic community and the individual prelate. The former tended to hoard and accumulate wealth and political power. The latter was often a factor in their circulation, in both a centripetal and centrifugal sense. Not all prelates were saints, to be sure, and many merged their own power with that of their monastery. The distinction should be retained, however. It also coincides, at least in part, with that between 'Tantrists' (of the wandering yogin type) and other followers of the religious life, as it appeared as early as the law Code of Trhisong Detsen summarized above. Even in the modern period, when a marked institutional sclerosis had set in evidenced by the preservation of established positions in wealth and privileges, we are informed that the 'living buddhas' (incarnate lamas in Chinese parlance), as opposed to the monasteries, regularly made distributions of alms, once a year, amounting sometimes to half their capital, and contributed to the costs of the religious ceremonies of their monastery and the state.

But it is in earlier periods that we find a greater circulation of wealth, especially with wandering holy men of yogin or contemplative type. To understand the situation, one must first grasp two principles that the Tibetan Buddhists inherited from their Indian teachers. The first is subordination, the disciple's absolute obedience to his spiritual master or teacher (Sanskrit *guru*) which we shall need to speak of further. The second requires that every initiation be paid for dearly. It is not our concern to explain why the Indian teachers demanded such payments. Doubtless one reason was that certain Tantric rites, especially the maṇḍalas, required large amounts of precious materials for offerings. To that we must add the great difficulties experienced by Tibetan devotees in search of books and initiations. The journey to

[1] 142, *PA*, ff. 195 seqq., ff. 223 seqq.; 132, ff. 169–178.

India was long, the manuscripts were scarce, the teachers scattered. An identical situation soon arose in Tibet: to learn a new doctrine or study a new commentary, you had to go from teacher to teacher.

The Tibetan chronicles abound in stories showing devotees busy amassing large quantities of gold in Tibet before setting out for India in quest of books and oral teachings. The large quantity of gold collected by Changchup Ö to ransom his great-uncle Yeshe Ö, when a prisoner of the Qarluq Turks, was used—on the captive's advice—to invite Indian teachers to Tibet. A little later, Drogmi was given much gold to bring teachings from India. He' was only partly successful. The remaining teachings were supplied to him in Tibet by an Indian master on payment of a considerable sum, thus ensuring his monopoly of that teaching. So it is not surprising that Drogmi in his turn required large presents from his disciple Marpa.

Marpa was born in the fertile district of Lhotrak, in southern Tibet, of parents who were very rich 'because they possessed both "country" (*yul*, village and fields) and pasture-land.' Since he had a violent character, his parents sent him away to the Lama Drogmi's school, giving him as 'religious provisions' (*chos-rgyags*) enough paper for a sixteen volume *Prajñāpāramitā*, two pack-animals, an ounce of gold, a measure of silver, a good horse with an acacia-wood saddle, and a roll of silk. Marpa gave the paper and the two pack-animals to the teacher Drogmi and asked him for initiation. But he only received lessons in Sanskrit and Indian vernacular, which he learnt in three years. Unsatisfied, he thought that he would need fifteen yak-cows for each of the four initiations of Nairātmya, and a cow and a yak for each of the permissions to worship Ekajaṭī, so that he would do better to go to India. He offered part of his remaining possessions to Drogmi so that he would not be vexed with him, and exchanged the rest for gold. He went home to his parents and demanded his whole share (*skal*) of riches, fields and house (*nor zhing khang*). His parents and brothers agreed, but asked him to stay with them, devoting himself either to religion or agriculture. Marpa refused, took his portion, and exchanging it all for gold, except for the fields and house, he obtained eighteen ounces. He knew that he must have gold in India: 'If, for the sake of religious teachings, one goes to India without having much gold, it is like drinking water from an empty bowl.' After twelve years' residence in India, having obtained numerous teachings and spent

149

all his gold, Marpa returned to Tibet to amass some more. Nyö, his rival and travelling companion, offered to strike a curious bargain in return for an ounce of gold and a maṇḍala: 'You be the master of the mother lineage (*ma-rgyud*, the Mahāmāya doctrine, etc.)! I shall be the master of the father lineage (*pha-rgyud*, Guhyasamāja).' This wish to corner the teaching market had already moved Nyö to throw the rare books Marpa was bringing from India into a river.

Back in Tibet, Marpa received an invitation from a member of his clan, Marpa Golek, a rich chieftain of stockbreeding nomads in the North (Dam). He was given many offerings (horses, cattle, armour) and much gold (eighteen ounces). He added to that the gold he received for effecting cures and giving initiations, and from working a mine in the north. On his return to Lhotrak, he was offered all the land he wished. Now famous, surrounded with servants, he married several wives and had several sons. Eventually he was able to fulfil his vow and set out for India again with fifty ounces of gold. His hagiography[1] naturally stresses his religious concerns, but as one chronicle puts it, 'in the eyes of ordinary people, he reared a family, quarrelled with his countrymen and only occupied himself with agriculture and building.'[2] His disciple Mila Rêpa's biography, in fact, shows him surrounded by agricultural workers and many shepherds, complaining that the people of Talung attack his disciples in Ü and Tsang and so prevent him receiving their offerings, and asking Mila Rêpa to send them hail with his magic. He also asks him to build a castle or defence-tower which should have nine storeys, with a cupola as the tenth, a covered walk with twelve pillars, and a chapel. The biography emphasizes that that was one of the trials Mila Rêpa was put through to purge him of his sins. But it admits that it was also a dodge to build this tower at a strategic spot (a gorge) where the members of his paternal clan (*pha-tshan kun*) had sworn not to build any castle, without however including Marpa in the oath. So the 'cousins' raise a force of armour-clad men to demolish the fort. But Marpa succeeds in frightening them with his magic: they present him with offerings, and become his sponsors and subjects ('*bangs*).

Mila Rêpa, who was poor, had to work to have food and lodging at his teacher's home. Marpa repeatedly prevents him from taking

[1] 133, ff. 3–5, 26 seqq.
[2] 99, p. 404.

part in initiations because he cannot offer the 'initiation price' (*dbang-yon*). And Mila Rêpa, telling himself that whichever way he turns 'it is impossible to dispense with offerings; without wealth you don't get religion', falls into despair and tries to commit suicide. Then his total gift of 'body, speech and mind' ends his trials, and he is initiated. Another disciple of Marpa, Ngoktön, already half initiated, comes to ask the teacher for 'particularly deep instructions' and especially those dealing with the 'manuscripts of the oral transmission' (*snyan-gyi shog-ril*) which bear the seal of prohibition. For that, he has to bring the whole of his possessions (*nor-dgu*), 'external' (livestock) and 'internal' (precious stones, silks, etc.): no doubt a symbolic gift—he has to go and look for an old lame nanny-goat he had left at home—but the principle of total allegiance to an indissoluble personal bond remains.

A contemporary of those figures, Chhökyi Sherap of Ma—whom we have already met as a go-between in armed conflicts—goes home after receiving the teachings of his master Tampa, and renounces his servants and possessions to become a meditator (Sanskrit *sādhaka*). Another pupil of Tampa's, able to subdue demons in order to cure the sick, takes very high fees and thus becomes extremely rich. He uses his wealth to buy land, an estate (*gzhis*). There he installs his parents and brothers, who have been obliged to beg for their living after a famine, and he marries off his brother. Furthermore, he offers his teacher three ounces of gold and a good stallion, which he has received as fees for his cures. His biography adds a significant detail: the gold offered to the teacher was carried off by a goddess to cover the cost of a ritual circle (*gaṇacakra*). These 'circles' consisted of great feasts uniting a throng of male and female contemplatives.

The yogin must not keep riches. He receives them, then uses them. Such is the principle at least. A fourteenth-century yogin, Samten Pelpa (1291–1366) has many disciples and accumulates foodstuffs and wealth. 'Though there was hardly a kind of property which did not reach his hands, he personally did not own even a single needle and thread. . . . All the teachers and disciples subsisted on begging rounds only, and did not own even a field of the size of a blanket for the upkeep of the monastery.'[1] Yet gifts sometimes reached a con siderable size. Gyer the meditator (1144–1204) offered his yogin

[1] 99, p. 884.

teacher and his wife (*yab-yum*) a hundred and three different possessions, including in particular fifty large families (of 'serfs'), a manuscript of the *Prajñāpāramitā* and three horses.

The chronicle presumably stresses these cases as examples of saintliness which, perhaps, contrasted with other cases less notable for their altruism. But the distinction between the monastery's wealth, which is not criticized, and personal property still holds.

Though they may only have been a minority at any time, some monks took their religion's commandments seriously and translated them into deeds. They were even spokesmen for criticism of society's excesses. Frequently the criticisms were expressed in stern tones: they were especially directed by the reformed order against the older schools. We have already alluded to the violent diatribes of Lha Lama Yeshe Ö (eleventh century):

'Since the growth (of rites) of "liberation" (killing), goats and sheep no longer have rest. Since the growth of (rites of sexual) "union", people mingle without regard for bonds of kinship.'

Or again:

'Your practices, you "village abbot" Tantrists, may seem marvellous to others if they hear of them in other realms. But those practices which make you say "We are buddha" are even less merciful than the God of Karma. You are greedier for meat than hawks and wolves, more lustful than asses and bulls, greedier for decay (?) than ruined houses or a corpse's breast. You are less clean than dogs and pigs. Having offered excrement, urine, semen and blood to the pure deities, you will be reborn in (the hell of the) swamp of rotten corpses. The pity of it!'[1]

Much later, in the eighteenth century, one volume of sermons appears to aim its criticisms at all orders, including the reformed.

'Nowadays, some monks do have religion constantly in their mouth, but it is seen from their behaviour that in fact they don't think of it at all. They desire something fat (?); they are greedy for

---

[1] 151, ed. Das, II, p. 393 = xylograph, f. 248*b*.

meat, beer, etc. . . . The moment there are songs, (opportunities for) profitable trade or (exhibitions of) athletic or warlike (feats) anywhere, they are delighted and rush up.'

Or again:

'As soon as there is an opportunity to hold a ceremony for themselves or others with sacrifices and meetings of lay-people, the lamas of today kill animals and taste their meat and blood, yet without feeling the slightest shame.'[1]

The voices of these harsh critics of current religious practice had little chance of being heard outside clerical circles by the people, however. Sermons are unknown and the faithful take no part in worship. Popular criticism existed, but most often found expression in songs and jokes. King Trhisong Detsen's Code contains a curious item: 'Hatred must not be shown to Tibetan or Indian translators and scholars, even in poems.'[2] We shall see later that in early Tibet there were religious specialists, akin to bards, who expressed themselves in enigmatic poems or songs: veiled criticism was thus possible.

It happens that the religious circles which inherited this taste for songs and allegories, and developed them, also played an important part in drawing attention to the defects inherent in Tibetan society. These are impecunious wandering yogins characterized by unorthodox behaviour. In Tibetan they are known as 'madmen' (*smyon-pa*), a word implying both eccentricity and 'divine' inspiration. They have a liking, and an undeniable talent, for poetry, song and dance. They are fond of laughing and joking. They mix with the people and take their part. So they violently criticize the abuses of society, including the 'Church' and all the religious orders.

The great saint and poet Mila Rêpa (1040–1123 or 1052–1135) was already imitating popular songs, gaining notoriety with his pranks and calling himself 'mad'. He delighted in mocking the monks. This is what he has to say about the theologians or 'logicians': 'Your belly filled with pride, you belch vanity and vomit jealousy. You fart contempt for others and excrete sarcasm!'[3]

We know other saints of this type, who may be compared with St. Francis of Assisi and his order during its early history. Of one of

[1] 158, ff. 6a–b, 14b.
[2] 139, f. 229a.
[3] 134A, ff. 192a–196a.

them, Drukpa Künlek (sixteenth century), we fortunately possess a detailed biography. That saint mingles with the people at the festivals of the sacred mountain, gets drunk and sings with them, reproducing the style and phraseology of popular songs. He dances to his own guitar accompaniment, and spends his time roving from district to district in this manner. And in his songs we find criticism of all the religious orders of his time. He protests at the mechanical performance of rites as though they were external actions bereft of meditative content (as with the masked dances or the fearsome practices of 'chö'), but also denounces other errors.

'In the great meditators' schools, every one has a *vidyā* (Tibetan *rig-ma*, a woman representing, essentially, wisdom) to whom he is attached. As for me, the yogin, I refrain: I should be afraid of becoming a family man one day.' And: 'In the schools of logic every one has a young monk to console himself with. As for me, the yogin, I refrain: I should be afraid of committing the sin of ejaculating.' Or in the sphere of economic interests:

'I have visited the monasteries of Druk. In those in Upper Druk, there were internal quarrels about landed property (*gzhis-byes*). As for me, the yogin, I refrain: I should be afraid of stirring up strife between cousin-brothers (*pha-spun*, members of the same clan).'[1] We saw earlier on how he was treated by his family.

As in an analogous situation in Europe, the monks' incontinence was as common as the jokes about it. A very widespread ritual for confession of sins gives a whole list of sexual relations regarded as 'incestuous' or forbidden (*nal*): among them are those between teacher and disciple (*slob-dpon gyis lha-nal*).[2] In the modern period, travellers have often noted relationships of monks with women outside the monastery and, especially, some homosexuality inside. As one might expect, the latter is particularly frequent in the rather close-knit body of warrior monks we have already discussed: the abduction of a boy can be grounds for a fencing or boxing duel.

Drukpa Künlek and other 'mad' saints like the famous Aku Tömpa have become beloved popular heroes. They are the protagonists in countless jokes, usually very crude, about monks and nuns. By this expedient it has been possible to express awareness of social abuses in a popular style. The one truly popular work of

[1] 131, f. 67*a–b*.
[2] 182, f. 5*b*.

literature known to every one, the Gesar epic, is likewise full of jokes and gibes about the excesses of the great and the clergy. The author, though still unknown, was surely one of those singing poet adepts, of the 'mad' or inspired type.

'The lama, the godlike, is learned in sermons: possessions are impermanent, bubbles on the water's surface, says he; life is impermanent, a play of lightning, says he. But his acts are different from his words. Is he pleased? That depends on the amount of the offerings. Does he find fault with some one? That depends on whether they are handsome or ugly. Wealth, he considers, is for his control. His hand clasps it in the knot of avarice.

'The prince, the superior, is learned in law: the people must be made happy, says he; others' property should not be coveted, says he; dishonesty falls foul of the law, says he. But his acts do not agree with his words at all. Destitution and famine, he inflicts on his subjects. Have you money? He fixes punishments in writing, but it suffices to send him fine riches in secret, for the most guilty to escape the law.'[1]

Not long ago at Lhasa again, there was a famous jester with a talent for singing, a sort of ballad-monger, who could venture political satires without risking punishment. He was known by the nickname 'Aku Tömpa', thus being likened to one of those waggish saints we have discussed. We shall be seeing later that the clowns who appear in the masked dances also represent grotesque saints (a-tsa-ra). But whilst, as in China, up to the tenth century, and elsewhere, certain noted individuals of comical yet sacred character specialized in criticizing corrupt practices by means of jokes, it became quite a widespread game in modern Tibet, under the name of 'destroying religion' (or 'destroying the realm', bstan-bshig). In the intervals of the masked dances, for instance, monks stage skits on organized religion (the soothsayer who invents lying oracles, etc.). At receptions and picnics in the parks, the nobles do not mind doing the same in the secular sphere, to make their guests or companions laugh. It would be wrong, then, to take these criticisms and jokes as a first sign of unbelief and rebellion. They simply amuse, and do not rule out a profound faith. They call in question not the structure of society, which is always accepted, but only particular

[1] 152B, II, p. 30.

cases regarded as incidental deviations. When a radical upheaval is contemplated it is represented, not as the utopia of a better world, but as a sign of the end of time. Thus, a Bonpo chronicle describes the end of our evil age by saying that there will then be no difference between prince and people or between lord and servants, that slaves will have power and rule over masters, that monks will be generals and hermitesses have children.[1]

The political and economic aspect of organized religion should not allow us to forget its no less extensive role in the country's intellectual life. Practically all cultural activity has taken place within its purview, at least since the fall of the monarchy.

In the modern period, monasteries were still really universities or monastic colleges on the Indian pattern (Nālandā, Vikramaśīla), as they were in ancient Tibet. Besides religion and philosophy, all the traditional sciences were pursued there: medicine and pharmaceutics, astronomy and astrology, grammar and prosody. Art too—painting and sculpture. From monasteries lastly, as in mediaeval Europe, came the book, as manuscript or xylographic block-print, edition and impression. We have seen monks establishing hospices. Others were technologists: the famous saint Thangtong (c. 1400) worked iron-mines in Kongpo and the homeland of the Lopa aborigines, and built iron bridges.

A certain dichotomy can be detected in monastic activity: study on the one hand, practice on the other. It corresponds to two basic aspects of Buddhism which we shall be returning to. We have already encountered, in Trhisong Detsen's legal code, the carefully-drawn distinction between followers of the *sūtras* and the *tantras*. In modern Tibet, it has more or less crystallized into the two great groups of religious orders: study, with the 'reformed' school (Geluk-pa); practice, with the 'unreformed' (Nyingma-pa, Kagyü-pa, etc.). Not that Geluk-pas neglect the *tantras*. They teach esoteric as well as exoteric Buddhism: the Geluk-pa monastery of Ganden has two large Tantra faculties (*rGyud-stod* and *rGyud-smad*). Conversely, great scholars, learned in all the sciences and philosophies of Buddhism, have come from the unreformed orders. But as a whole

[1] 186, ff. 133*b*, 135*b*.

156

the distinction is valid. In the Geluk-pa order the two Tantra faculties are only open to monks who have already obtained the highest doctor's degree.

In both sorts of religious order, the monk's career is that of a student moving from grade to grade by way of examinations. With the 'reformed' school the examinations test book-learning and the handling of formal logic; with the others they concern supernatural powers acquired through yoga and meditation practices. Examinations properly so called, with questions and answers, examining board and proclamation of the doctorate, tend however to be a Geluk-pa speciality. Among the others, individual initiation seems to play a more important part (just as it does in the 'Tantric' part of Geluk-pa teaching).

This division is echoed by another between teaching based on books, which is bound up with discursive thought, dialectics and formal logic, and the secret, initiatic oral teaching, which corresponds to the practices of meditation. It is true that this distinction does not match the division into 'reformed' and 'unreformed' schools. The Nyingma-pas never tire of proclaiming their scorn for books and the uselessness of learning: they have an extensive literature none the less. We can best understand this dual aspect of monastic instruction by going back to the ancient period. Remember the donations made to the Samyê community under Trhisong Detsen. The monks received paper and ink annually, but not so the 'hermits' or meditators.

In modern times paper—made from the fibre of the shrub *daphne cannabina*—was produced in Dakpo and Bhutan, both close to Samyê. It must have been rather rare or costly in the ancient period: in the Tun-huang manuscripts the text is often written on the back of a Chinese sūtra or even between the lines of such a text. In the late eleventh century, Sochung-wa was obliged to write the lineage of the fifty-four Siddhas in the margins—probably cut off (*shog-ras*)—of a *Prajñāpāramitā* belonging to somebody else. Later, when he left them in his mother's charge, she made leaves of family registers (?) out of them, so that eight lineages are now missing.[1] Printing with carved wooden blocks, probably introduced from China about this period, was not yet, or little, used. Stress was laid on the possession of a mantra ('*om arapacana*') that prevents one

[1] 99, p. 878.

forgetting things: Thönmi Saṁbhoṭa was able, with its aid, to write out all that king Songtsen Gampo had said, on a roll of paper; and Denma Tsemang, all that had been said at Samyê under Trhisong Detsen.[1] In our own times, pupils used to recite it at school. Cases of extraordinary memory are recorded among the Chinese and Indian translators, and it is known that important texts were transmitted orally.

It is true that the vast labour of translation carried out under Trhisong Detsen and Relpachen all had to be written down, and systematic catalogues came into being at that period. None the less teachers refused as a rule to transmit esoteric teachings other than by word of mouth and in a manner that linked teacher and disciple personally (see chapter IV). After subjecting the disciple to tests, the master, satisfied with the candidate, promises him a doctrine: 'He took him to the house. Joining their pillows for many days, he spoke much to him of the religion and satisfied him with the teachings in full.' Another teacher does the same: 'Joining their pillows, they stayed (together) about a month.' This was in the twelfth century.

Other eleventh and twelfth century instances show the distinction between study and practice, as well as the appearance of written notes even in the book-scorning orders. The great Indian master of 'Chö' (*gcod*), Tampa Sanggyê (died 1117), had two Tibetan disciples, Kyo Shakya Yeshe and Mara Serpo. The latter committed six teachings to writing, leaving out the secret oral instructions (*zhal-gdams*). Fearing the lineage might come to an end, Kyo bestowed the instructions on Sönam Lama who, in turn, transmitted four of the six precepts to Ma-chik Lab-drönma. Mara likewise did not at first entrust them to any one, but then, in his old age, he handed them on to his disciple, the 'madman' (*smyon-pa*) Bere, charging him to practise them himself, not to bestow them on any one else. So much for the practice.

But now we have another master, Shatön. He has a college (*gra-sa*) with two teachers, Chetön and Phuktön. When Chetön falls ill and it is known that Bere 'the madman' practises Chö (which cures the sick) Shatön advises him to go to him and ask for the precepts. But Phuktön thinks that Chetön cannot receive these Chö precepts because he 'is engaged in studies'. He, Phuktön, on the

[1] 167, I, f. 244*b*; 177, f. 116*a* (= 92*a*); 162, *ZA*, f. 33*a*.

other hand, being a hermit or practising meditator, might be given them. So it is he who goes to request them for his friend Chetön. Bere is suspicious at first. He is surprised that Phuktön knows he has the secret and asks him if he really intends practising it. On his replying that he does, Bere gives him the six books of precepts with the oral precepts and explanations. Phuktön then starts practising them. Next he goes to Shatön and gives him three of the six teachings whilst he gives all six to a teacher from Kham. The latter's 'copyists' then 'write them down'. Later, another monk, Sherap Ö of Rok, also wishes to acquire these teachings. He invites the yogin's copyist to be his guest. But the latter no longer has the books (or does not want to give them). So Rok turns to Phuktön, but only receives one of the six teachings from him. 'Aren't there any others?' he asks. 'Yes', says Phuktön, 'but I only gave three to Shatön, and he would be displeased if I now gave the complete precepts to somebody else.' But why didn't he give them all?— Because this is a very profound (secret) teaching. Now Shatön, having a school, had many pupils at his residence who used to write teachings down. Also there were many who were not devoted to the teacher (*guru*, Tibetan *bla-ma*) but had only come there to 'get books'. That is why he had taken care not to give the whole teaching. Since Rok asks for them and he recognizes him as worthy to receive them, he finally gives him all six teachings, together with the oral precepts, but on one condition: he must not commit the oral precepts to writing.[1]

Sochung-wa, another pupil of Tampa, had asked and been granted permission to write down the teaching of the fifty-four Siddhas. To this day it is necessary first to obtain the 'power' (*dbang*) and the authority to read (*lung*) such and such a work before being able to study it (still more so the oral precepts that go with it). Certain works too, although printed, still contain, at the end, mention of 'seals' and the need for silence.

Despite the importance of the oral precepts for everything to do with the practices of meditation and yoga, books and book-teaching have played a considerable part in these. We have already seen how much gold or other commodities the quest for books and teachings required. As in the European Middle Ages, one had to go from college to college, from teacher to teacher. Each was a specialist

[1] 99, p. 997.

and some guarded their teaching quite jealously as a kind of monopoly. As in Europe too, the scarcity of books was another reason for travel. Sometimes you had to sit at a teacher's feet and take notes: lecture notes of this kind have been published. Sometimes you needed to go a long way to consult some work in a library. Until quite recently the Sanskrit manuscripts of works that had vanished from India were preserved at Sakya. Others, which originated with Atiśa, were at Reting monastery, chained and sealed. To this day the copyist's job is essential, though it was yet more so at first. Even when printing had become familiar, it was often easier and cheaper to borrow a work and have it copied. So we have to distinguish between original manuscripts and manuscript copies: the majority of handwritten texts are only copies of printed works. To get anything printed, you had to approach the, often very distant, monastery where the woodblocks were kept. You had to procure the paper and ink, engage and pay monks to do the printing, and finally find a caravan-leader who would provide transport. Manuscript copying was commonly resorted to, therefore.

It gave rise to a large number of mistakes, especially as the scribes, like those in Europe under the same conditions, had taken to abbreviating many words, sometimes contracting several into a single ligature. Colophons accordingly mention the corrector, as well as the scribe, of any book. Both copying and printing were encouraged by the fact that a donor could acquire religious merit by having them carried out. Hence it is that we find beautiful manuscripts, sometimes in different scripts and with black and red ink, sometimes on black or blue paper with silver or gold ink, and often embellished with illuminations. For this reason, too, printed editions mention the person or persons who paid for their preparation, and often state how much it cost them. Sometimes the encomium even extends to a complete history of the donor's family.

We shall have occasion to speak of Tibetan Buddhism's doctrines and its enormous literature further on. Here we must devote a few more words to an institution that has a long history, viz. the religious disputation. In the modern period where monastic life has taken on a fixed character, these debates are peculiar to the Geluk-pa order and, within that order, to the schools of philosophy (*mtshan-nyid*). It is no longer anything but an exercise in essentially

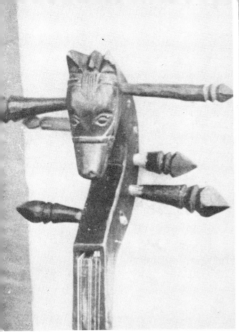

24. Horse-headed fiddle, Kalimpong. *Photo: R. A. Stein.*

25. Sea-monster (*makara*) headed fiddle, Darjeeling. *Photo: R. A. Stein.*

26. Horpa workmanship, animal style. Flint-and-steel pouch. *Photo: Philastre.*

27. Detail from a biographical painting: youth of the epic hero (Joru). *Photo: Musée Guimet.*

formalistic logic or rhetoric. Some features, however, show that the institution formerly had the character of a joust or duel in the same way as other ritual contests.

The disputation (*rtags-gsal*) proceeds by question and answer, either as a daily exercise between fellow-pupils, or as an examination between teacher and pupil. The mode of argument, which can also be utilized for solitary reflection, provides for three positions closely corresponding to our thesis, antithesis and synthesis: 'propounding one's own thesis' (*rang-lugs-bzhag-pa*), 'overthrowing the other party's thesis' (*gzhan-lugs 'gag-pa*) and 'abandoning (probably = rising above) the dispute' (*rtsod-pa spong-ba*). In the now stereo-typed state of the practice, discussion seems to be conducted entirely with quotations from canonical works, aptly and artfully deployed. But the thing that strikes every traveller is the outward appearance of these disputations. The petitioner, who asks the questions, is on his feet in the attacking posture; his opponents, who answer them, remain seated. The questioner accompanies his on-slaught with actions, governed by a code, which attempt to put his adversary out of countenance: he squares his shoulders, claps his hands, raises his rosary and gown; he accentuates the last word in a question, stamping on the ground and shouting; he lifts his right hand and claps it on his left palm, stretched out in his opponent's face. The questioned candidate may himself leap to his feet and, instead of answering, ask a question. The winner of the debate is borne in triumph on his colleagues' shoulders, sometimes, it seems, humiliating the loser (in Sikkim, the loser has been known to get on all fours, with the winner riding on his back and spurring him on with his heels). The Italian missionaries witnessed this performance at Lhasa in the early eighteenth century and were astonished. The violence of the gestures has persisted till the present day, in spite of the distaste expressed by Tsongkha-pa, founder of the order: 'When he stayed in the colleges of logic, he urged that no one should engage in the running and jumping dances, or the clamour of contemptuous contradiction (*gzhan khyad-du gsod-pa'i ca-co*).'[1]

There can be no doubt that the disputations had a ritual character that allies them with other more popular religious contests. They have to take place in the open air, near a tree (in one detailed description, near several trees surrounding the temple of a

[1] 99, p. 1075.

FIG. 10. Examination-debate in courtyard (*chos-ra*). Two 'abbots' as examiners. The monk on his feet questions the candidate seated in the foreground.

deity).[1] The epic describes a religious debate between the lamas of China and Ling, matched by a whole series of contests or jousts— conjuring, hand-to-hand fighting, horse-racing, dice, archery, beauty contests.

Although the disputations are now a mere exercise within a uniform group, they gave currency to real antagonisms at one time. An eighteenth-century work vividly describes a 'deliberation' (*sgro-gling*) at the foot of a tree, between a great contemplative (hermit) of the Yogācāra school and the representative of a heresy.[2] Sometimes a savant might be challenged by posting up questions, just as in mediaeval Europe. In the early fifteenth century, the Fifth Karma-pa posted up questions in Kham. No monk of Ü could answer them and the Karma-pa won the day.[3]

The custom of debate was well known in India and China. It sometimes entailed death or at least banishment for the loser, or else the obligation to espouse the winner's doctrine. Kings, there-fore, resorted to these 'trials by ordeal'. The invitation sent to Sakya Panchen by the Mongol king was probably inspired by his reputa-tion as winner of theological disputations with Indian heretics. The Mongol Emperors had contrasted Nestorians, Muslims and Bud-dhists or Taoists, or again Buddhists and Nestorians, in this way. Karma Pakshi, too, took part in religious tourneys with Taoists and Nestorians at the Mongol court. But in these another factor can already be seen. The contest is no longer purely dialectical; it also embraces competitions in magic and 'miracles'. We have seen that it was by a duel of this kind, between Chinese and Indian monks, that King Trhisong Detsen decided which doctrine to promote officially in Tibet: the adherents of the Chinese Dhyāna school were expelled, and violence ensued (according to the Tibetan chronicles). The same king also presided over a tussle between Buddhists and Bonpos: the contest was both magical and theological.[4]

[1] 82, pp. 141–142.
[2] 158, f. 48a.
[3] 99, p. 883.
[4] 183, p. 27.

4

Religion and Customs

❧

Tibet's religion, as we all know, is Great Vehicle (Mahāyāna) Buddhism. And that religion profoundly affects the country's every institution and inhabitant. It has taken a peculiar form, which is not shared by the Mahāyāna found elsewhere in the Far East—except for that of Mongolia, Sikkim and Bhutan. This form is often called 'Lamaism' from the important part played by the Lama (*bla-ma*), a term not denoting just any monk, but a person's spiritual master or teacher (*guru*) alone. We shall find that his rôle is indeed uncommonly important, even from a doctrinal viewpoint. So I do not feel it necessary to depart from this nomenclature.

There can be no question of giving even the most incomplete overall account. It is a whole world, immensely complex, embracing many aspects: a rich and subtle philosophy, with its own dialectics and metaphysics; a very advanced depth-psychology linked to techniques of meditation and the control of psycho-physiological functions (yoga); an enormous pantheon; countless rituals; popular practices; cosmological speculations; systems of divination. The Tibetans have devoted thousands of volumes to all these sides of their religion, which is further complicated by the fact that their conceptual bases derive from India (and to a slight extent from China). In consequence I shall only be able to go over a few topics, attitudes and modes of behaviour that to me seem peculiarly significant.

To embark on a complete account is all the more impossible in that it is essential not to neglect two other religions which have contributed to Tibetan civilization. The first is Bon (with its adherents, the Bonpos), Buddhism's predecessor. The second is the whole body of ideas and customs belonging to the indigenous tradition: a religious, but an unorganized, churchless, doctrineless, priestless and almost nameless, whole. Not that we could lay hands on such a religion in its pure state. Buddhism's influence is everywhere, overlaying or infiltrating native or other non-Buddhist beliefs, exactly as Christianity did in Europe. All the same, beneath the Lamaist veneer, and in early documents, we can discern vestiges of it.

European authors have frequently confused this nameless religion with Bon, describing both as 'primitive'. The Tibetan historians contributed to the confusion insofar as, for them, everything that is not Buddhism is necessarily barbarous and demonic. They did, however, preserve a vital distinction between the 'religion of the gods' (*lha-chos*) and the 'religion of men' (*mi-chos*). The first means, or has successively meant, Bon and Buddhism, whilst the second denotes folklore.

LAMAISM

Essentials of the doctrine

Hard as the task may be we must first give some account of the doctrinal groundwork.

Two Indian schools dominate Lamaic thought and have been officially accepted in Tibet regardless of divergences of school or order. They are the Mādhyamika (Tibetan *dBu-ma*, 'middle way') of Nāgārjuna (second to third century?) and the Yogācāra ('practice of yoga') or Vijñaptimātra (*Sems-tsam*, 'consciousness-only') of Asanga (fourth century?).

To simplify a complex situation, it is tempting to see in the relative importance these two systems have in Tibet a further instance of the study-and-practice polarity we noted earlier. The first-named school may be thought to carry more weight with the 'reformed' Geluk-pas, the second with the Nyingma-pa 'ancients' and associated orders. At first sight, the Geluk-pas, are more typified by philosophy (*mtshan-nyid*: literally 'characteristics', Skt. *laksana*) and theoretical discussion, the others more by meditation and psychic experiences. But the Mādhyamika school recognizes swift, direct experience (sudden enlightenment or purification) too; whilst the Yogācāra, conversely, accepts the gradual path to perfection and excels at philosophy. Atiśa and Tsongkha-pa, the two masters of the reformation, stressed reconciliation of the two systems. Meditation and tantric ritual are not absent among

Geluk-pas, and the Nyingma-pas are no strangers to theoretic study.

What both schools are concerned with is the nature of the *Noumenon*, that which is beyond *phenomena*—which I shall in future refer to, for convenience, as 'the Absolute': it is this that must be attained to ensure salvation. Reason alone cannot bring us there, but it can prepare the way by destroying appearances and conventional concepts: it has a negative side. Psychical technique, on the contrary, can lead to the goal through an ineffable realization, not to be grasped by discursive thought, but positively experienced.

For both schools 'things', the elements, however subtle, of our phenomenal world, have no reality of their own, in themselves (*niḥsvabhāva*). The only true Reality is 'the Absolute'. It cannot be defined but, for want of a better name, it is called Emptiness (*śunyatā*), Own Nature (of phenomena, *svabhāva*),[1] That which is Thus ('Suchness' or Quiddity, *tathatā*: Tibetan *de-bzhin-nyid*), etc. For both schools this 'Absolute' can only be attained through yoga experience. The Mādhyamika has something of a negative cast: nothing can be affirmed of the 'Absolute', which is neither this nor that, and 'things' are 'empty', have no reality of their own. The Yogācāra has a more positive aspect: the inmost reality of the 'Absolute' is characterized as Thought (consciousness, *citta*) which penetrates everywhere, like space, and is likened to a pure, bright mirror reflecting nothing but its own light; it is Consciousness-only, where there is no duality between subject and object. The relative phenomenal world of 'things', on the other hand, is merely the projection of thoughts which are subject to causal laws and preserved in potential form, like seeds, in a kind of underlying psychic receptacle (*ālayavijñāna*, Tibetan *kun-gzhi'i rnam-par shes-pa*).[2] The passage from the 'Absolute', Thought-in-itself, to the Relative of thoughts or associations, or the linkage between one and the other, is too complex to be stated here, but in a way they are

---

[1] E.g., *svabhāva* equated with *tathatā* in Suzuki, *Studies in the Laṅkāvatārasūtra*, p. 456; and H. V. Guenther (trans.), sGam-po-pa, *Jewel Ornament of Liberation*, p. 1: 'ultimate nature (*svabhāva*) of *saṃsāra* is *śunyatā* and ultimate nature of *nirvāṇa* is (also) *śūnyatā*.'

[2] Though most authors confuse the two standpoints (e.g. S. B. Dasgupta, *An Introduction to Tāntric Buddhism*, pp. 13, 27, 78, 133), we should actually distinguish between *vijñaptimātra*, which is about epistemology, and *cittamātra*, which is about ontology.

only different aspects of the same thing. Return to the 'Absolute', the condition of salvation, is brought about by the kind of meditation that eliminates thinking (subject)—thought (object) duality from deep in the psyche. That is the 'consummation' (*nispatti*, Tibetan *rdzogs-pa*) which leads to 'whole' or 'perfected' (*parinispanna*) own-nature. We shall meet these terms again in meditation procedure and in the name of the principal Nyingma-pa order.

The Mādhyamika had to be defended from heresies. In asserting Emptiness, it had to steer a middle course between overstrong negation which would lead to nihilism (nothing exists, everything is over when the body dies) and a too restricted, purely theoretic negation, which would tend to allow something to remain (immortality of the soul): the just mean being to assert nothing about 'things', except that they have no reality of their own. The artful solution was to posit two kinds of truth. One is 'really true' (*paramārtha*, Tibetan *don dam-pa*), and from that point of view 'things'—the phenomenal world—have no existence. It corresponds to the 'Absolute', which is indefinable and beyond understanding: 'the silence of the saints'. The other truth is 'relatively true', conventional truth (*saṁvṛti*, Tibetan *kun-rdzob*), the relative reality of appearance. From that point of view 'things' exist. In other words the constituents of our world are empty of inherent reality, are illusory; but the illusion itself exists and is perfectly real, at any rate as long as one has not attained 'the Absolute' (*snang-stong*, the existence of phenomena or appearance—*snang*—which have no own-nature, are empty—*stong*—of substance). Our world exists, as an hallucination does. Someone suffering from an eye-disease sees hairs in his food: there are no hairs, but his illusion is real, and he can only realize this when he has been cured. And the hallucination is dangerous, for it leads the victim to inappropriate behaviour: seeing hairs, he refuses to eat as long as they are there and vainly tries to remove them.

This theory is crucial, since it allows the retention of morality and religious works for the common believer. Since quasi-scientific laws remain valid within relative truth, ordinary Buddhist concepts as to the consequences of action (karma) must continue to govern religious life. This is the side that appealed to the 'reformers', faced with the outlandish behaviour to which practical experience of the non-reality of phenomena could lead (such as eating faeces, killing, etc.)

RELIGION AND CUSTOMS

It is also worth getting two other aspects of Lamaist thought into our heads straight away. 'True' (*paramārtha*) truth corresponds to the 'real', or certain, meaning[1] (*nges-don*: equivalent to the Sanskrit *nītārtha*, 'proven meaning') which is derived from it. 'Conventional' (*saṁvṛti*) truth corresponds to the 'alleged meaning' (*drang-don*: Skt. *neyārtha*, 'that which has to be proved or interpreted') which is derived from it. Even within this 'straightforward meaning', the Tibetans further distinguish between ordinary (*thun-mong*) conduct and that which is not so (*thun-mong ma-yin-pa*). The former belongs to the lay believer who venerates Lamas and thinks how hard it is to obtain a human body (in the chain of rebirths), that life is impermanent, and that bad or good actions have their fruits. The second course is that of the ordinary monk who takes refuge in the Buddha, the Dharma and the Saṅgha, makes the vow of producing *bodhi* in himself, purifies himself of accumulated sins by confession, and makes an offering of his 'two accumulations' (stocks of knowledge and merit). As for the 'real meaning', it is reserved for those who practise meditation by means of the 'guru's yoga' (*bla-ma'i rnal-'byor*) of which we shall be speaking later.

Accordingly the seeker should rely on meaning (*don*: Sanskrit *artha*) and not words; on the doctrine (*chos*: *dharma*) and not on men; on absolute knowledge or gnosis (*ye-shes*: *jñāna*) not on perceptions (*rnam-shes*: *vijñāna*); on the 'real meaning' sūtras and not the 'straightforward meaning' sūtras. But not everybody can grasp both or even one of these truths; different levels of spiritual capacity are recognized.

Men are grouped into three categories, each capable of apprehending three of the paths to liberation, or 'vehicles' (*theg-pa*: *yāna*), in the most usual Nine Vehicle classification. Not that anyone is excluded, in principle, from supreme enlightenment: we all have the buddha-nature within us, in a potential, latent state, and can, in theory, realize it. 'The inherent nature (*rang-bzhin*) of thought (*sems*) is (everywhere and in everyone) the same, but its characteristics (*mtshan-nyid*) are different.'[2] According to their stage of development, after innumerable past lives, men have differing intellectual capabilities which are grouped into three levels—upper, middle and lower. For the lower minds are intended the three vehicles of the 'listeners'

[1] My translation reproduces the meaning of the *Tibetan* term in each case.
[2] 166, chap. XIII, ff. 181–192.

(*nyan-thos*, Sanskrit *śrāvaka*, Buddhist laymen), the buddhas for/ by themselves (*rang-rgyal*, Sanskrit *pratyekabuddha*, i.e. the Hīna-yāna) and the *bodhisattvas* (*byang-chub sems-dpa'*: ordinary Mahā-yāna). They were all taught by the historical buddha Śākyamuni.

The two other categories correspond to the *tantras*. The middle group is still 'outer' or exoteric: it consists of the *Kriyā-tantras* (*bya-ba'i rgyud*: chiefly magic), the *Upāya-tantras* or *Caryā-tantras* (*spyod-pa'i rgyud*: mainly ritual), and the *Yoga-tantras* (*rnal-'byor rgyud*).[1] The first were revealed on the Himalayas to human and divine 'knowledge-bearers' (*rig-'dzin*: Sanskrit *vidyādhara*); the second to gods in the heaven or paradise of Tuṣita (*dGa'-ldan* in Tibetan) and the last to gods and bodhisattvas in the heaven of the Thirty-three and the Akaniṣṭha (*'og-min*) paradise. In spite of this relatively exalted status, it is only the third category that is 'inner' or esoteric. It consists, according to the source we are following here, of *Mahāyoga*, *Anuyoga* and *Atiyoga*. A tenth vehicle (*sPyi-ti yo-ga*) is sometimes added, or even a fresh series of three vehicles (*sPyi-ti*, *Yang-ti* and *mTha'-chen*). It is impossible to go into the details here, but it is worth noting that the upper and medium vehicles are associated with the ten 'lands' (*bhūmi*) or stages of progress of the bodhisattva. The three middle vehicles (Kriyā, Upāya and Yoga) are taught to the saints of the third, fourth and fifth 'lands', and so on.[2]

'Relative Truth' which accepts the world and its laws is not just useful in that it encourages moral conduct in the 'lower' class of personality. It is also necessary as the bodhisattva's field of activity when he operates in this phenomenal world, out of compassion. The enlightened saint who has attained 'the Absolute', Emptiness, does not remain in that condition, but returns to the conventional world to help others.

But if, for some, acceptance of the phenomenal world carries the obligation of pure moral behaviour with the object of a slow, gradual ascent to sainthood (*lam-rim*), for others the discovery that things are void, and no other than Emptiness and Absolute Reality, leads to identification of the Absolute and the Relative and to emancipa-tion from common rules. This is the swift and instantaneous path,

[1] Indologists, basing themselves on the Sanskrit texts, tend to use the form *caryā-tantra*, but the Tibetans show a marked preference for *upa-* or *upāya-tantra*; see examples in 142, *THA*, f. 37*b*; 151, p. 389; and also in an ancient Tun-Huang MS. J. Hackin, *Formulaire sanscrit-tibétain du Xe siècle*, Paris, 1924, pp. 31–32.

[2] 166, *loc. cit.*; cf. 151, ed. Das, II, p. 384 = xylograph, f. 243*a*.

the 'deep doctrine' (*zab-chos*). For the saint dwelling in the state of Absolute Reality, *nirvāṇa* and *saṁsāra* (Tibetan *'khor-'das*) are one. For him, there can be no difference between good and evil. To make it quite plain that, all things being empty, there is no difference between them, he indulges in all kinds of unconventional behaviour. To attain 'the Absolute' it is, in fact, necessary to get rid of the chief obstacle, namely our discursive thought based on the fallacious impression of an acting and thinking I (*bdag-'dzin, ngar-'dzin*). Dialectics can be of some use to this end, through the destruction of conventional ideas it brings about and the bewilderment it arouses. But this technique is of limited application; religious behaviour, for instance faith, on which we shall have more to say, is more effective.

Tantrism went a step farther. It flourished in India at the time the Tibetans went there in search of their religion: a Buddhist Tantrism, its techniques shared with Shivaite Tantrism and yoga in general. In this system, 'the Absolute' involves two positive characteristics, not subject to proof by reason, but revealed by the psychic experience of meditation, accompanied by control of physiological functions. They are Bliss, or Great Bliss (*bde-chen*, Sanskrit *mahāsukha*), and Compassion (*snying-rje*: *karuṇā*). The former is inherent in 'the Absolute'. But the Absolute is regarded on two planes, as it were, partly as a unity and partly as embracing two complementary principles. Regarded as one, 'the Absolute'—perfect purity, the *dharma-kāya, tathatā*, the All—is the Mother (*yum*). But from another point of view a passive female principle, Wisdom (*shes-rab*, Sanskrit *prajñā*), needs, to become manifest, an active male principle, 'Means' or 'Method' (*thabs*: *upāya*). Method's sphere of activity is the phenomenal world when it withdraws, so to speak, from Wisdom, but its contrary tendency leads to mystical union (it should be noted that this is the opposite of Shivaite Tantrism where the passive principle is masculine, Śiva, and the active principle feminine, Śakti: but there too Śiva is realized through Śakti). Thus, in symbolic representations, the same word 'mother' (*yum*) also denotes the wife or spiritual consort. The union of the two yields Great Bliss or the Bodhicitta (*byang-sems*, 'thought of *bodhi*', but also likened to a 'drop', a sort of psychic counterpart of the semen).

This system accounts for the process of meditation or, contrariwise, is explained by it. The phenomenal world has a kind of usefulness. Emptiness (*śūnyatā*) cannot exist without active Compassion (*karuṇā*); Absolute Reality has no meaning without there being a world of phenomenal existence. But that existence itself cannot exist without Emptiness or Absolute Reality. The world of appearances is then compared to the bridegroom. Without him the bride Śūnyatā would be as if dead. But conversely, if the bride were separated even for an instant from her groom, he would be left in perpetual bondage.

So meditation is a technique of actualization (*sgrub*, Sanskrit *sādhana*) in that it repeats, if you like, the ceaseless, beginningless relationship between Emptiness or 'the Absolute' and phenomenal existence. It consists essentially of two parts: the phase of (mental) 'creation', starting out from Emptiness, which corresponds to phenomenal existence (*bskyed-rim*: *utpanna-krama*); and that of 'completion' or return to the unity of 'the Absolute' (*rdzogs-rim*: *niṣpanna-krama*). Only the first phase is (relatively) easy to understand and perform, at least in the purely Tibetan system. The second comprises psycho-physiological yoga practices (especially in connection with 'breath' and sexual energy).

The value of meditation, therefore, is that it allows a kind of experimental demonstration, a living experience not only of supreme Reality, Emptiness, 'the Absolute', but also of the nature of phenomenal existence which is only the latter's mental creation. The aim of the exercise, especially its second phase of achieving Emptiness or Great Bliss, is salvation, liberation. But it happens to have a side-effect as well—especially through its first phase of mentally creating phenomenal existence—a sort of by-product, viz. supernatural powers (*dngos-grub*: *siddhi*). They are not essential, but the saint may make use of them to convert people with miracles, to protect the religion against human or non-human enemies, and in general to 'benefit beings'. For realization of Emptiness through meditation is brought about for one's own benefit, but also for others': by active compassion (*karuṇā*), the resultant forces are placed at the service of all beings.

It is easy to imagine how, starting from this doctrinal basis and proceeding to logical conclusions, certain teachers or schools could have been led to very unconventional magical and ritual practices. But the fact is that even 'reformers' such as Atiśa and Tsongkha-pa studied and accepted these doctrines. To be sure, there are great Geluk-pa scholars, like Sumpa Khenpo in 1748, who look upon them with disfavour. Even he, however, closes his critical account of Nyingma-pa Tantric doctrines with the remark that the Second and Third Dalai Lamas (1475–1542 and 1542–1588) had studied them a little, and what is more, the Great Fifth (1617–1682) had taken a special interest in them 'owing to the fact that he had become the general Lama of all Tibet' (from the viewpoint of political power).[1] And sure enough, the second half of his Collected Works is entirely devoted to Nyingma-pa systems. It is true that this part was afterwards kept secret and became hard to get hold of.

Religious practices

We see at once a characteristic of Lamaism that proceeds from all this. Its central religious activity is the concern of monks and hermits. It is inaccessible to ordinary believers. Their deep faith depends upon the members of the monastic community. Lay Buddhists do not take part in rituals and religious services, save sometimes as mere spectators. They do not hear sermons and have no private prayers. Since they belong to the class of those whose grade of intellectual faculties does not permit them to escape 'conventional truth', they can only hope to improve their karma, the fruit their actions will bear in a future life. That is why their religious activity consists essentially of piling up merit (*bsod-nams*): by making gifts to monasteries or lamas and to the poor, by lighting lamps before the images of deities, by making pilgrimages or walking round sacred objects, and by asking lamas for blessings or charms. They know the principle of action and its rewards which leads to rebirth in one of six possible states: gods, titans, men, animals, hungry ghosts or hells. These spheres of rebirth are portrayed in the 'Wheel (of transmigration) of the World' (*srid-pa'i 'khor-lo*), the so-called 'Wheel of Life', paintings of which are seen everywhere. The punishments in the hells and the judging of the dead are popularized by strolling story-tellers who are supposed to have been to hell and come back alive (*'das-log*: known since the fifteenth century at least). Lastly, some of the masked dances present, for the edification of the faithful, the deities met with in the intermediate state between death and the next life (*bar-do*).

[1] 151, p. 388 = xylograph, f. 245*a*.

172

Laymen and illiterate monks can also have recourse to the recitation or visual representation of certain formulae, the *mantras*, which epitomize, as it were, a corresponding deity. Recitation may be actual or performed by mechanical means: wheels turned by hand, water or wind; moulds for shaping images. The most famous formula is *oṁ maṇi padme hūṁ*, invoking Tibet's patron Avalokiteśvara, but there are others. In Tantrism, such formulae are looked upon as having a power of evoking and materializing divinity which works

FIG. 11. The eight auspicious signs combined in the shape of a vase (*rtags-brgyad bum-gzugs*), a common ornament on ritual objects.

173

in a quasi-automatic fashion—provided they are pronounced correctly and accompanied by a suitable meditation. For the mass of Tibetan Buddhists, it is the act of faith which chiefly counts in recitation; and this faith makes possible a species of meditation and an obliteration of the ego. Though saying or writing the mani has become standard practice for the Buddhist masses in modern Tibet, formerly (twelfth century) this practice was, like everything else in the religion, the business of experts—in this case the *ma-ṇi-pa*, who were adepts equipped with Avalokiteśvara's initiation (that is, in Tibetan, the 'power' (*dbang*) to recite the formula). Nowadays the *ma-ṇi-pa* are strolling story-tellers who recite improving tales whilst showing the episodes on a painting, but they also perform rites (smashing a heavy stone on their chest, lying on the points of two swords) which show their unusual powers.

Otherwise, whenever religious intervention is necessary, the ordinary believers turn to specialists—for healing or exorcism in the event of illness or possession, help to the dead during the *bar-do* intermediate period, summoning good luck (*g.yang-'gug*) or long life (*tshe-'gug*) at weddings and other occasions, protection of livestock or crops, evoking or putting a stop to rain or hail—and yet other operations. Certain beliefs will concern us later: though all fully integrated in Lamaism, they have retained features that are not specifically Buddhist, and can be treated separately.

Faith and the teacher

There is one religious manifestation that ordinary believers share with even the most eminent men of religion. It is faith, whose absolute necessity countless texts declare. This might at first surprise us, given the absence of a God and the illusory character of all the divinities, who are only mental creations like any other phenomenon. But the reason for this need is clearly stated. It is that through the unconditional impulse of faith we can escape our ego and stop, at least momentarily, the activity of discursive thought which provides the illusion of this ego and is the chief obstacle to enlightenment. Of course, one can set up a distinction according to the object of this impulse. For all who move in the world of relative reality, faith can be directed at a 'deity'—buddhas, bodhisattvas, gods or goddesses. It hardly matters what support is used as the springboard. The divinities of the pantheon are only mental projections emanating from Emptiness, 'the Absolute', and representing it in an individualized form, so to speak. The power of meditation can create them, but that is a difficult process and the result of long training. Faith can take its place by producing an analogous concentration: it can produce a deity through intense emotion, and this deity will then be as objectively real and effective as if it had come forth from Emptiness through meditation.

It is related that the Fifth Dalai Lama had once, from the top of his Potala, seen the goddess Tārā regularly making a ritual circuit of that palace, a common devotional practice among Tibetans. After noting the exact times at which she went by and ordering an inquiry, he discovered that her movements corresponded to those of a certain poor old man. He sent for him and asked whether he knew that Tārā was accompanying him regularly on his circumambulations. Frightened, the old man replied that he did not. Questioned further, he disclosed that he had learnt Tārā's text by heart and had been reciting it regularly for forty years while making his daily circuit. He was asked to recite the text, and was found to have got it wrong. He was then made to learn the correct text. But as soon as the old man had learnt it and recited it in place of the other, Tārā ceased to appear. He was then authorized to recite the text as he had been used to, and Tārā showed herself as before. When he recites the faulty text, the Dalai Lama concluded, his mind is concentrated on Tārā, and she comes to bless him. But when he recites the right text his mind is attached to it. That is the difference.

No matter what focus is used, the concentration that results from faith, not only creates and brings before us faith's object, the deity, but generates the beneficent power of blessing which automatically ensues. By willpower and training, the meditator functions in the same way and gets the same results.

For the devotee in search of sainthood and enlightenment, faith can equally well bring about a sudden insight (here we must recall the remnants of Chinese Ch'an (Zen) doctrines which have been noted in Tibet). And a feature of Tantrism which we have not so far had the chance to emphasize as it deserves, may be added— utilization of the emotions. Despite the extraordinary discipline and iron will that meditation training implies in its adepts, they are often seen to dissolve in tears from the emotion roused by an impulse of faith and a sudden illumination. And this crisis often occurs after other violent emotions, especially wrath.

The impulse of faith may naturally centre on figures in the pantheon, especially in the case of laymen. But for all who enter upon the path to enlightenment, the object of faith is first and foremost the Lama or spiritual teacher (*guru*). For it is typical of Lamaism (as too of various Indian and other religions) that one's Lama (*guru*) is superior to all 'deities', even the most prominent.

'To venerate a single hair of one's teacher (*slob-dpon*) is a greater merit (*bsod-nams*) than to venerate all the buddhas of the three times (past, present and future)', a *ḍākinī* (a kind of fairy) tells the saint Gampo-pa (1079–1153). And by merit we must also understand usefulness, the resulting benefit. The *ḍākinī* goes on to inform him that he must not entertain doubt (*the-tshom*), or have discursive thoughts (*rnam-rtog*).[1] For the latter engender doubt by keeping alive the idea of a thinking 'I', whereas unquestioning faith enables one to abandon such thoughts and ego-attachment. The Lama's dominant position, higher even than the buddhas, is common to all orders including the Geluk-pas. No 'actualization' could be brought about without the '*guru-yoga*' (*bla ma'i rnal-'byor*): the disciple conjures up the tutelary deity (*yi-dam*) chosen for him by his Lama, with whom the deity is closely fused; then he himself merges with the Lama, who has absorbed, as it were, the deity. From him he draws the desired state of purification.

To see whether he can hand on his last secret to Marpa, Nāro-pa turns himself into Marpa's nine tutelary deities in such a way that Marpa shall see them clearly in front of him. He asks him, 'Do you bow to the *yi-dams*, or do you bow to your Lama?' Marpa, seeing only the deities, bows to them. Nāro-pa then says: 'As long as there is no Lama, there is not even the word *buddha*; even the buddhas of a thousand kalpas appear on the basis of Lamas . . . These gods are only forms of myself,' whereupon the *yi-dams* dissolve in Nāro-pa's heart. On account of this error Marpa will have no descendants.[2] 'The Lama is a buddha in person' (actually present), think Marpa's disciples when he admits Mila Rêpa to their number, and they are filled with faith.

So a disciple's absolute submission to his Lama is required, and

[1] 142, *NA*, f. 28*b*; cf. 30, pp. 87–90.
[2] 133, f. 50*a*.

176

28. Songtsen Gampo's
    Chinese wife.
    Jokhang, Lhasa.
    Photo: V. Sís/J. Vaniš.

29. His Nepalese wife.
    Potala.
    (*Hsi-tsang fo-chiao
    i-shu, pl.* 55).

30. *Above:* Lama.
Sera monastery.
(*Hsi-tsang fo-chiao
i-shu*, pl. 81)

31. *Below:* Lama
(*Bo-dong phyogs-
las rnam-rgyal*,
1306–1386 ?).
Shigatse fort
(ibid., p. 77).

the latter subjects him to a series of trials to test the strength of his faith. The bonds between them are predestined and indissoluble. They are characterized both by a father's affection for his son and a vassal's subjection to his suzerain: the terms used to denote them can be 'father' and 'son', but also 'master' (*slob-dpon*) and 'subjects, servants' (*slob-'bangs*).[1] 'He has no disciple more affectionate (*sha-tsha-ba*) and faithful (*snying-nye-ba*, "close to the heart") than you,' Mila Rêpa is told by his spiritual 'mother', the wife of his teacher. It will be recalled that the second expression is the same one used, in the oldest texts, for a vassal's loyalty to his overlord.

The disciple's submission is total. He makes his master the total gift of his person ('body, speech and mind') and possessions. Henceforth he belongs to him, and that teacher alone can lead him to salvation. If he wishes to listen to another, his own teacher must release him from his covenant (oath, *dam-tshig*). Since Marpa has refused to initiate Mila Rêpa, his wife forges a letter from him, ordering Ngoktön to do so. Mila then sets about meditating under Ngok's direction, but, 'Not having been released by Marpa's order, no mystical experience occurred,' Ngok, believing Marpa's order to be genuine, is amazed: 'Yet you came with faith in me, and in my (spiritual) lineage there is none who has not quickly gained the benefit of understanding, at least as long as no vow (*dam-tshig*) prevented it.'

The trials to which Marpa subjected his disciple Mila Rêpa are famous. Not only does he set him all kinds of useless tasks, but he rebuffs him in a thousand ways, strikes and insults him, humiliates him and drives him to despair. But Mila's faith rises above it all. It is spontaneous, unreasoning and emotive. When he turns up at the field in which Marpa is, without knowing that it is he, 'Scarcely had I seen him than I dwelt for a moment in a state of indescribable and immeasurable bliss where the fluctuations of this world's appearances were halted' (i.e. in a rapture leading to 'the Absolute', both emptiness-of-phenomena and bliss). Later, almost driven to despair by the harshness of the teacher, who has refused him initiation, he assures him in answer to his enquiry that he has withstood any 'revolt against faith' (*dad log-lta*). And when, finally, after all his tribulations, the master admits him and promises the teachings his heart is so set on—'At that moment I thought: "Is it a dream or is

[1] 133, ff. 26*b*, 40*a*, 73*a*, 75*b*, 76*b*.

it true? If it's a dream I should like never to awake!" A joy beyond measure filled me and, dissolving in tears through my excess of joy, I made obeisance to him.'

Mel Kawachen (twelfth century) had a similar experience, when looking for the teacher Tampa Gommön. One day he sees him at the edge of a field, preaching to a monk. 'Faith was born in him, his eyes filled with tears and, wide eyed with surprise, his mind became devoid of (discursive) thought (*sems mi-rtog-par song*).' In these favourable conditions, induced by sudden shock, the master says 'Loose your mind!', and at once contemplation or concentration (*thugs-dam*) is born in him.[1]

The highly emotional nature of saints is very evident. Marpa is a strong, violent man, much given to fits of temper, but he also often weeps in secret at his disciple's devotion and despair. Access to 'the Absolute' does not abolish the manifold forms of the phenomenal, including feelings. In the end, Marpa explains his unkind behaviour by saying that his anger was different from 'the world's' and that, despite appearances, he had actually 'walked in the path of *bodhi*'. This does not just mean, apparently, that the bad temper was always feigned in order to test the disciple. That comes into it as well, but Marpa undoubtedly had an irascible nature.

We often find emotions of any sort whatever made use of. Sochung-wa played all manner of tricks on Tampa Gommön, such as making him carry a bag of stones up a pass and then throwing them away. One day he went so far as to accuse him of stealing, in front of a stranger. Seized by a violent fit of anger, the disciple drew his sword and dashed towards his master. Barricading himself behind a door, the latter told him, 'Your mind (thought) is "achieved" (*rdzogs*) in anger: look at it!' Then, 'having looked, a pure full understanding was produced in him—an understanding that consisted of seeing really and in its naked state the Real Nature of Thought. Then, brimming over with joy, he grasped the flaps of his coat and began to dance and sing.'[2]

Doubtless taking his disciple's character into account—as one always must when making use of psychic forces—the teacher induces such anger that the disciple is as it were projected outside himself by giving way to it; his ordinary (discursive) thought obliterated;

[1] 99, p. 888.
[2] 99, p. 881.

and room thus made for the pure thought of contemplation which grasps 'the Absolute' directly. Translation is powerless to render the whole flavour of the text: the word *rdzogs*, which it uses to describe the engulfing of thought by anger, is a technical term denoting the afterphase of meditation and fusion with 'the Absolute'. Although his short biography tells us nothing about this disciple's character, we know that other saints of the same group (*gcod* and *zhi-byed*) were noted for their ill nature. Trubbe, the son of Lab-drönma—the patroness of *gcod* (chö) in Tibet—started out by being very violent, and a goat-stealer. His son, in turn, spent his youth in fighting. Mel Kawachen was 'very disagreeable' when he was young. Marpa, too, had a wild and violent nature and, in youth, was fond of a fight.

So the disciple's choice of a teacher is very important. For his part, the teacher bears the disciple's character in mind when initiating him. With the usual decided taste for numeric classifications, five chief emotions were singled out (anger, stupidity, desire, pride and envy) and associated with the five primordial buddhas who represent 'the Absolute' and the five initiation families corresponding to them (*vajra, tathāgata, padma, ratna, karma*). As a matter of fact they are not just associated with them, but are identified with figures in the pantheon, just as the phenomenal dissolves into 'the Absolute'.

The ability to proceed from any phenomenal aspect whatever to a corresponding aspect of 'the Absolute' results not only in the need to belong to one of the five families (*rigs*, Sanskrit *kula*) according to one's nature, but also in the manifold variety of the pantheon. Maṇḍalas and their deities vary with the 'family' to which they belong. The tutelary deity his Lama chooses varies with the disciple's intellectual and emotional predispositions. And it is by merging with the deity and Lama combined that the disciple attains 'the Absolute'.

The initiation conferred by one's master is the 'power' (*dbang*) to practise a particular group of meditations together with the official transmission and the 'authority' (*lung*) to read the texts in which these are described; to which are added the master's more precise instructions (*khrid*). He inherits this 'power' from his line of direct transmission (*bla-brgyud*), which invariably goes back to a supreme divinity. So, the meditator does not forget to invoke that lineage in his ritual practice, to ensure the validity of what he is doing.

179

Meditation and ritual

Countless rites for every sort of occasion, and with various aims, are performed by those experts, the monks and yogins. And there is no doubt that below a certain level these are merely a routine, the purely formal execution of ritual motions and recitations of texts. But when we read the handbooks of these rites we discover that in the main they only gain their effectiveness from the meditation that must accompany them and whose outward expression they are.

Meditation is in fact the essential practice of this monks' religion. The monasteries nearly always have affiliated meditation cells, in out-of-the-way mountain spots, where the monks are expected to withdraw and live in seclusion (*mtshams*) for a period. The retreat may last from a few days to some months, or several years (e.g. three, or twelve); it may even be for life. It may be limited to isolation in one room, but may also go as far as complete walling-in within a very restricted space, without light (*mun-mtshams*), only a small hatch making it possible to pass a little food through or communicate by signs with the disciple waiting nearby.

What a meditation consists of and how it proceeds are not common knowledge: those who have practised it are not talkative. But some items can be set forth as given in texts.

The basic texts of Lamaism, all Indian, like the *Hevajra-tantra* or the *Guhyasamāja-tantra*, always divide the process into two parts: *utpatti-* (or *utpanna-*) *krama* (Tibetan *skyed-* or *bskyed-rim*) and *niṣpatti-krama* (or *niṣpanna-*; also *sampatti-*, *sampanna-*: Tibetan *rdzogs-rim*). The first part is easier to understand. It is the gradual process of mental creation that consciously and voluntarily re-creates, as it were, phenomenal existence (*bhāva*). It consists of making 'the Absolute', the Noumenal, or absolute knowledge (*ye-shes*, Sanskrit *jñāna*) turn into the relative, the phenomenal, relative knowledge, or perception (*rnam-shes*: *vijñāna*). From the 'void', by mental generation, a deity with all its attributes is made to arise. To facilitate the European reader's understanding, the process might be compared to the creation of the world by a thinking God. Only there is no God, and no unique creation or beginning. The purpose of this type of meditation is not merely to gain an actual experience of the illusory nature of our world, but also to be freed

180

from it and thus win salvation by travelling in the opposite direction. By cancelling its 'creation', its mental production, we return from the phenomenal to the noumenal; we thus unfasten the bonds inherent in this phenomenal world (such as karma, etc.), and we rejoin and dissolve in 'the Absolute' which is Emptiness, Reality and Bliss.

This second part, the *nispanna-krama*, is less clearly explained. And with reason. The meditative process here includes, in Tibet at least, yogic psycho-physiological techniques which the texts only refer to indirectly. We can only, for the time being, get hold of external aspects that may give an idea of it. The word used for this process implies the idea of success, completion, fulfilment, perfection. It provides the name of the Dzokchen-pa order, within the Nyingma-pa school—the 'Great Fulfilment' they aim for is the state of buddha-hood or fusion with 'the Absolute'. Of the Nine Vehicles listed earlier, the process of 'production' (*bskyed-pa*) belongs to the lowest of the last three vehicles, Mahāyoga ('great yoga'), whilst that of 'great completion' (*rdzogs-pa chen-po*) is reserved for the third and last, Atiyoga ('yoga beyond').[1] We should not, however, suppose that these meditations are limited to the 'old' orders (Nyingma-pa). The chief work of Tsongkha-pa, the founder of the 'reformed' Geluk-pa order, is divided into two parts. The first and more widely known, the *Lam-rim*, takes care to distinguish men according to their faculties and to recommend the slow path of virtue to those of whom too much should not be asked, and in any case to everyone as a necessary preliminary foundation. But the end of the first, and all the second volume (the *sNgags-rim*) are devoted to the twin procedures of production and reabsorption.

We return, then, to the 'production' process. It underlies every ritual practice; for to have any effect a rite requires the presence of the appropriate deity, who thereby bestows a 'blessing' (*byin-rlabs*, Sanskrit *adhiṣṭhāna*)—the power of action—on the officiant. The term denoting these rituals (*sgrub-thabs*: *sādhana*) has sometimes been translated as 'coercion', giving a false impression of witchcraft and sorcery. 'Evocation' might be a better rendering. It is however true that this deity, once brought into being, may 'call' or forcibly summon up a demon, or the 'soul' of an enemy.

The rite of mental production or generation (also called *sgom-rim*,

[1] 157, f. 26*b*.

'meditation process' or *dmigs-rim*, 'imagination process') is analysed in greater detail in Tibetan Buddhism than in the Indian *tantras* on which it was grounded. It comprises two, or three, stages. First comes 'production in oneself' (*bdag-skyed*): the meditator imagines himself as a particular deity. 'Production in front of one' (*mdun-skyed*) follows, in which he projects the deity before him, having first visualized the universe as his palace, making it possible to worship him. Lastly may be added 'production in the vase' (*bum-skyed*): this time the deity is caused to enter a physical 'support', which thus acquires a power that can be made use of later.

Before 'production in oneself' properly so-called, all rituals begin with certain indispensable preparatory steps. Their order, number and type vary with different schools and with the purpose of the rite, but the following are usually found (often 'seven members', *yan-lag bdun*, are spoken of). The line of teachers that gives the rite its validity (*bla-ma'i brgyud*) is stated; refuge is taken in all the buddhas, bodhisattvas, etc. (*skyabs-su 'gro-ba*); the vow to reach enlightenment and use one's merits for the liberation of all beings (the bodhisattva vow) is renewed; one is purified of one's sins (*sdig-sgrib*) by confession and mantras.

Thus prepared, the meditator first re-creates the 'void'. From this void comes the rite's presiding deity, usually developing out of his own 'seed' syllable (such as *oṁ*, *āḥ*, *hūṁ*, *hrīḥ*, etc.). Then by an instantaneous leap (*skad-cig dkrong-skyed*) the meditator becomes identified with the deity in question. It is this state alone that enables him, for instance, to summon demons (*lhar bskyed-nas bgegs dgug-pa*),[1] etc. He then has a luminous, empty, divine body (*gsal-stong lha-sku*); he is indissolubly (*dbyer-med*) merged with the deity, through whom he partakes of Emptiness (*nyid zang-thal du bskyed-pa'o*).[2] 'My pure body, in *utpanna-krama*, appears luminous like a deity's body', says Drukpa Künlek.[3]

With the production of a deity in oneself, or oneself as the deity, that deity passes from the noumenal state, where it is one with 'the Absolute' or absolute Knowledge (*ye-shes*: *jñāna*), to the phenomenal state, known as its 'vow' (*dam-tshig*: *samaya*) form—because only in this form can it become manifest, so as to fulfil its vow to help all

[1] 144, VI, f. 7*a–b*.
[2] 138, ff. 100*b*–101*a*.
[3] 131, *JA*, f. 165*b*.

beings. This shift is brought about by assembling the deity bit by bit, as it were, with all its many attributes and attendants (requiring a vision that is very exact in the smallest details). Externally, this piecing together is matched by recitation of the corresponding iconography (*mngon-rtogs*: *abhisamaya*), which is used as a basis both for meditation and for depiction in painting or sculpture.

Paradoxically one might say that now the deity becomes really present—'really' in the western sense of the word. As proof of this it is related, for instance, that after a particular meditative evocation the deities represented on the painting came out, walked round in a circle and went back in: it was then noticeable that their clothes and appurtenances were out of order on the picture. The master Bodhisattva's contemplation (*ting-nge-'dzin*: *samādhi*) at Samyê was so intense that it rendered deities 'objectively' present before everyone's eyes: their statues came out of the temple, walked round it, and returned to their places.[1] That, too, is why in the Chö rite, which involves carving up one's own body, in meditation, to offer it to living beings, care must be taken not to do the imaginary carving whilst in the 'production in oneself' state: that would amount to cutting up the deity one had become, and be a sin. When Mila Rêpa, in desperation, wants to commit suicide, this is how the Lama Ngok dissuades him: 'The Lama grasped me and, shedding tears, he said, "Do not so, great magician! According to the doctrine of the secret mantras (Tantrism) which is the culmination of the teachings of the buddhas, our body with all its senses is inseparable from the gods. If we perform 'transference' (*'pho-ba*, passing from one life to another or into a paradise) before the right time, we commit the crime of killing the gods. Hence there is no greater sin than suicide." ' Similarly, Marpa's dying son, on the point of 'transferring' his own mind (*'pho-ba*), attained union, and 'my body, organs and senses became luminous, and of the nature of gods and goddesses'. It was, he says, because he was in the 'production process' (*bskyed-rim*) state. To effect the transference, he would need to have passed into the 'completion process' (*rdzogs-rim*) state. For, 'If I made the transference (implying the death of the body) in the "creation process" state, I should commit the crime of killing the tutelary deities (*yi-dam gyi lha*),' he explains. The presence of these gods in his body

[1] 183, p. 47.

was then so luminous, says the hagiography, that even ordinary onlookers could see them.[1]

One application of this principle of a deity's real presence is 'production in oneself' in a support other than the meditator's body. For example, in a fearsome rite intended to drive away demons, sacrificial cakes (*gtor-ma*) are made and thrown at them as offensive weapons. But they are only effective if they have received 'blessing', i.e. the power of the deity concerned. A small painting of him or her (the *tsakli*) is fastened to a stalk or arrow stuck in the cake. The deity is produced, by meditation, in the picture. His presence endows that receptacle with a power which will stay there even when the actual deity has left, One must be careful not to throw the cake-weapons whilst the deity is still there. They are only thrown when the stalk with its attached portrait has been taken out: an external operation corresponding, on the plane of meditation, to the deity's 'vanishing' (*yal*—like a rainbow fading away in space).

Having become a god oneself, it may be asked why that is not enough and why we move on immediately to projecting the deity in front of us—an operation always accorded a much more detailed treatment than the previous one by the handbooks of ritual, in which it features as the essential part. One text supplies a reason: 'production in oneself' is done *for* oneself, 'production before one' for the good of others, and 'creation in the vase' for the benefit of the gods.[2]

The meditator, therefore, produces the deity in front of him, still piecing him together in accordance with the iconography, along with all his attributes, paradises, attendants and suite: an exercise of unparalleled complexity and precision, requiring extraordinary concentration to accomplish. The vision must be so strong, in fact, that the deity and his retinue appear as though 'objectively' present, independently of the meditator, like somebody encountered in what for us is reality. He then makes him offerings and receives his blessings. He also requests the service which is the object of the rite—to give rain, drive away demons, prolong life, and so on. Once the rite is over and the meditation ended, the vision disappears. But a general purification and sanctity remain, as well as religious benefits. The whole may give the devotee the impression that the deities exist somewhere, come, and go away again.

[1] 133, ff. 88*b*–89*a*.
[2] 138, f. 19*a*.

This meditation is doubtless not taken very far in most cases, where the only object is the performance of a ritual for specific ends. But if it is followed all the way in the course of a retreat devoted to that sole purpose it can provide a practical experience of the nature of the universe. If the exercise is successful, in fact, the mentally created deity appears as though independent of its creator, objectively existing—not merely visible but accessible to all the senses. More, it can act and speak to the meditator as though it were somebody other than himself. If he finally believes that, he is surely lost. But if he remains aware that it is he who has created it, and reabsorbs it in his mind, will he not have experienced the very nature of our phenomenal world? It is as though a schizophrenic were aware of his condition and able to induce or end it at will.

It seems that the 'completion process' originally consisted of reabsorbing the deity, created in oneself, into 'the Absolute' and thus merging with the latter. In the *Hevajra-tantra*, when the officiant had attracted all the buddhas into his 'heart' in the form of so many Herukas (the type of supreme deity, representing 'the Absolute') and when he is thus consecrated (*dbang-bskur*), he is Heruka 'completed' or fulfilled in person, and that 'completed' (*rdzogs*) state is 'the Dharma space' (*chos-dbyings*), i.e. 'the Absolute'. In Tibetan usage, the 'completion process' always goes hand-in-hand with yogic practices and ends in a kind of transmutation. In some cases even the first phase, the 'production process', is associated with these practices.

There is no possibility of going into the principles of Tantric Buddhist yoga here, but we must review a few of its key terms. In the psycho-physiological entity that is man, it distinguishes a central channel or artery (to some extent confused with the spinal column) called *avadhūtī* or *suṣumnā* (Tibetan *dbu-ma*) flanked to left and right by two others, *iḍā* or *lalanā* (*rkyang-ma*) and *piṅgalā* or *rasanā* (*ro-ma*). They are attached to six 'wheels' (*cakra*, Tibetan *'khor-lo*) or psycho-physiological centres situated in the body, from the crown of the head to the base of the sexual organ. The two lateral arteries are associated with a series of complementary pairs: *iḍā* corresponds to white, the moon, vowels (*āli*), Wisdom (*prajñā*), semen; *piṅgalā*, to red, the sun, consonants (*kāli*), Means (*upāya*), blood. The two must be united in the central channel, and this union culminates in Great Bliss (*mahāsukha*), 'the Absolute', the *bodhicitta*. The conjunction itself is known as *yuganaddha* (*zung-'jug*). The system is shown symbolically in Tibetan paintings of deities, used as a support for meditation. At the top, over the main figure, is a pair of supreme deities in deep embrace (*yab-yum*); to left and right, a white moon and a red sun.

The process of fusion is sometimes purely meditative, but it is commonly accompanied by a technique that causes a 'wind' (*rlung*: *prāṇa*) or 'droplet' (*thig-le*) to rise into the central artery, and which can be practised either alone, or with a partner. Apart from realization of 'the Absolute', the procedure (with many variations from school to school) confers various powers, such as that of generating great internal heat (*gtum-mo*); levitation and fleetness of foot; and, above all, a 'rainbow-body' (*'ja'-lus*) which is indestructible as adamant (*vajra*), never dies, and thus enables one to 'die' (go to a paradise) without forsaking the body. Variations, as I remarked, are numerous and allow differing techniques. An eighteenth-century author outlines six 'completion process' methods attributable to six different teachers. One of them consists of the 'six teachings of Nāro-pa':[1] heat (*gtum-mo*), light (*'od-gsal*), illusory body (*sgyu-lus*), intermediate state, e.g. between death and the next life (*bar-do*), mind-transference (*'pho-ba*) and the art of taking over someone else's newly dead body (*grong-'jug*).[2] The sixth doctrine is usually that of dream (*rmi-lam*) and the last on the list we have just read is appended as an essential concomitant. The 'light' technique aims at sustaining a state that is conscious yet free from discursive thought, viz. meditation (*sgom*), even during sleep or after death. In the case of sleep, it enables one to observe, then direct, and finally abolish dreams and to remain in the luminous meditation state just mentioned. The object of this training is to preserve such a state even at the time of death, in order to succeed in catching the instant of intense light that supervenes, and thus to emerge from the cycle of rebirths instead of being dragged into *bar-do*.

Trances and dances

Such techniques are obviously only practised by an élite, but they nourish even the layman's religious life insofar as they are illustrated by countless hagiographic anecdotes. These are tales of famous

[1] 48A.
[2] 144, VI, f. 12*a*–*b*.

saints who have worked miracles for the benefit of common mortals to convert them and to convince them of the reality of the experience or effectiveness of the method. If it is effective it assures the believer an indirect share of divinity. Remember, from the fact of its identity with the creation or existence of this world in general, mental creation in the course of meditation cannot fail to have a quasi-physical effect on the world. The result is a 'blessing', i.e. a supernatural force that can be left in an object or person. To the extent that a Lama has received this, he can hand it on to the faithful, e.g. by laying his hand on their heads. He can also consecrate the images of deities—paintings which then bear the three monosyllabic mantras *oṁ āḥ hūṁ* (and sometimes the lama's foot- and hand-prints) on the back; or statues inside which are then placed rolls of mantras or an axis known as their 'life-tree' (*srog-shing*). These are the deities' 'bodily supports' (*sku-rten*). The believer worships them. For him, that is the only outward means of seeing and venerating the supreme deities, buddhas, bodhisattvas, etc. A distinction is drawn, indeed, between deities that have 'passed from the world' (*'jig-rten las 'das-pa'i lha*), which no longer incarnate themselves in a human support or vehicle, and those that have not yet done so (*'jig-rten las ma 'das-pa*) and can thus be directly manifested in a human being, visible to everyone. The latter group of deities are the 'protectors of religion' (*chos-skyong*, Sanskrit *dharmapāla*; or *srung-ma*). Hence they are generally of the fearsome warlike type, even when embodied in a woman. For they become incarnate in male and female mediums, who lose consciousness and go into a trance: the human ego is blotted out, and the medium's body is used as a support for the deity who fills him and speaks through his mouth. For this reason such mediums are called *sku-rten-pa* ('those who serve as support for the Body'), or else 'protectors of religion' like the deities themselves. They are monks or nuns who have been chosen by a deity and then given appropriate training. Each specializes in a particular deity. The usefulness of the manifestation lies in the opportunity to gather oracles from this deity's mouth. So the State, the Dalai Lama's Government for instance, itself employs some of them—such as the celebrated Nêchung medium who incarnates the god Pehar. That the trance is genuine is proved by the medium's behaviour. Not only is his face transformed—it swells and turns red, with bloodshot eyes, thick, lolling tongue, etc.—but he displays superhuman strength, supporting extremely heavy headgear, twisting swords, etc. In that state he mumbles words which are collected and interpreted by other monks. In addition, he blesses grain which is thrown to the faithful: by gathering it up, they can carry off a portion of the sacred being that has manifested itself.

There are yet other mediumistic specialists who incarnate minor deities and belong, in spite of their Lamaist dress, to the nameless religion of the people. These are shepherds, who have on some occasion been 'chosen' by a deity and from then on have been able to embody him. They go into a trance and sing, but they only incarnate local gods, of whom we still have to speak—gods of the sky (*lha*) and of the underworld (*klu*), gods of the soil, etc. From these they get their name: *lha-pa, klu-pa*. Oddly enough, they also incarnate the hero of the epic; at any rate, they did in the eighteenth century. Similar mediums called 'heroes' (*dpa'-bo*) compete with them and fall somewhere between them and the epic bards. Their name is of Buddhist origin. The word first denoted, as it still does, the dancers and musicians of Padmasambhava's paradise, who are also jugglers and athletes or warriors (*dpa'-bo, ging*).

The real bards also go into trances, either so as to see the epic heroes and scenes from their lives in some timeless sphere, and describe them in their songs, or so that such and such a hero may embody himself in them and speak through their mouths. In spite of differences what happens is, for Tibetans, essentially the same as in the Lama's meditation. In the latter, the deity moves from his 'knowledge body' (*ye-shes lus*), his Noumenal existence, to his visible phenomenal aspect ('vow' form), a process described in the words 'knowledge descends' or 'falls' (*ye-shes 'bab*)—on the support represented by the meditator, understood. Of the trances of Lamaic (*chos-skyong*) or popular (*lha-pa*) mediums it is similarly said that 'the god descends/falls' (*lha 'bab*), and of the bard in trance, 'the epic descends/falls' (*sgrung 'bab*). Conversely, when the trance is over and the god has left, it is said that 'the god of the epic has dissolved' (like a rainbow: *sgrung-lha yal-tshar*), using the same verb that denotes the deity's disappearance into the void during meditation. Moreover just as, in meditation, the 'creation process' necessitates the piecemeal building up of the deity, accompanied by the recitation of a corresponding iconography (*mngon-rtogs*), so too the bard, in order to put himself into a trance and evoke a hero in himself, begins by purifying himself with a prayer and chanting the hero's description. But the chief hero, Gesar, is never manifested in this way. Having 'become buddha' at the end of his life, he has since then been outside or beyond the world and can no longer alight on a medium. He can only be venerated in image form.

But to return to more exclusively Lamaistic manifestations: although rituals have to render the deities present and manifest through meditation, they are of course still invisible to profane eyes, save in tales of the lives of saints. But, partly to educate the lay-folk, partly too presumably because a mask has the property of making it easier for a deity to manifest itself, masked dances (*'cham*) have been invented and are publicly performed. Here we have what might be termed a mimed rite, in which the deities called up by meditation are at the same time presented by actors wearing masks. Scripts are attributed to visionary adepts of whom the best known is Guru Chhöwang (Chhökyi Wangchuk, 1212–1273).

Masks (*'bag*) were venerated at Samyê in King Trhisong Detsen's day, as well as statues. They represented only the 'protectors of religion' (*chos-skyong*),[1] not just any deities. This was not fortuitous: masks probably share with mediums the peculiarity of making it easier for these deities to become manifest. The 'protector of religion' Pehar is closely associated with a mask that was kept in his temple. When Sakya Paṇḍita and Phakpa met a young monk whose face resembled the mask in the Gorum temple at Sakya, they at once thought that Kurgyi Gömpo, the Sakya 'protector of religion', had incarnated in a man.[2] This mask, which bears the name 'Black able-to-fly' (*Nag-po 'phur-shes*), was still preserved at the same temple in the nineteenth century, and was venerated there as one of the four 'supports (*rten*) of miraculous manifestation'.[3] The deity it represents, a special form of Mahākāla worshipped at Sakya, is also—as we should expect—the principal figure in masked dances. The same deity appears in the form of Yeshe Gömpo. When, at the end of the fifteenth century, the Seventh Karma-pa ruler saw this Yeshe Gömpo's mask, known as the 'Black Sumbha', at Mönpa-thang, he also saw the Gömpo in person (*dngos-su gzigs*).[4]

[1] 183, pp. 36 seqq.; 179, f. 85.
[2] 154, f. 17*a*.
[3] 33, p. 63.
[4] 142, *PA*, f. 128*a*.

Thus, masks ensure the presence of certain protective deities. In the masked dances Mahākāla, in one form or another, usually fills the office of presiding deity (*gtso-bo*). Referring to the celebrants in these dances, Drukpa Künlek says: 'They say that they are the body of Mahākāla.'[1] Although the dances differ from one another in their style and pantheon, they are mainly performed for the rite of driving out evil. A human figurine (of dough, paper or hide)—naked, ugly, tied up and lying on its back—represents evil, the enemy, the devil, and is stabbed by the principal deity, then dismembered by an attendant (a stag). Previous rites, inside the temple, have inserted a demon or the enemy's 'soul' into it. But the word used for the execution means 'to set free, release' (*sgrol, bsgral*). It is an everyday term of Tibetan Tantrism denoting any ritual murder, from that practised by certain Tantric orders (the eleventh-century 'robber-monks' for example: page 71 above) to the execution of demons by the hero of the epic, a deity, or a 'sorcerer'. For they only kill the body and a demonic part of this 'soul'; but simultaneously they 'free' a sound part, the conscious principle (*rnam-shes*), by dispatching it to a 'paradise'. This crucial act is carried out in duplicate, by a masked actor representing the principal deity on the one hand, and by the celebrant of the actual rite on the other. The celebrant and his assistants are alone in not wearing masks. Indeed, it is they who call forth the deities who are present in mask form. They wear large black hats and a coat adorned with fresh human heads and dried skulls. Travellers tend to call them 'sorcerers' or even Bonpos. They are in fact the officiants: mantra masters (*sngags-pa*, 'Tantrists') who like to frequent cemeteries to perform their austerities.

The show usually lasts two days: an orchestra accompanies it and marks the dancers' steps, some slow and solemn, others quick and lively. Before and after the crucial moment of the enemy's 'liberation', the deities pass in procession before the crowd. But strange to relate, the terror that people might easily feel in the presence of so much that is sacred is frequently relieved by the antics of buffoons, who provide a safety-valve in the laughter they arouse. Masks are worn by these jesters, too, but in this case their function is to disguise the actors, realistically, as Indian philosophers (atsara). Venerated as they are, these saints make the Tibetans laugh merely by their grotesque foreign appearance, with dark faces and frizzy

[1] 131, *KA*, f. 56a.

hair. Yet while perpetrating a thousand freely improvised pranks they mimic every ritual action, even the most solemn, of the Tantric officiants.

TRADITION—THE NAMELESS RELIGION

Just as Christian missionaries adopted and adapted pagan Europe's festivals and sacred places, and figures from its pantheon, so Lamaism accepted, crowned with its authority and set its seal upon many features previously unknown to Buddhism, or even to Indian Tantrism. In this it did no more than continue what Buddhism itself had already done in India, where it had long been absorbing deities and practices from the area's other religions, together with foreign, as well as Indian, folklore.

It would be a mistake to suppose, however, that all non-Buddhist elements absorbed by Lamaism in Tibet were indigenous. Tibetan historians themselves have clouded the issue by constantly mixing up two separate points: the fact that Bon was there before Buddhism, and the judgment that everything preceding the latter religion was naturally 'barbarous', uncivilized and appropriate to an age of darkness. Hence the somewhat over-simplified conclusions drawn by early European students, who tended to present Bon as the primitive religion of Tibet. Further, by equating 'primitive' with 'savage', everything in Lamaism that seemed frightening, twisted, demonic or mediumistic soon came to be regarded as Bonpo and primitive. From that to describing it all as 'Shamanism' was but a step. The truth is more complex. It is often impossible to tell which of Lamaism's not specifically Buddhist elements is indigenous and which foreign, which one was really Bonpo and which was not. We shall have more to say about Bon, but we may remark at once that the Indian Tantrism that was introduced to Tibet, in spite of the kings' mistrust, already contained a great number of fearsome deities and rites, including animal sacrifices.

The 'religion of men': songs and legends

Tibetan historians of later times, including those who particularly stress Bon, tell us that before the introduction of Buddhism, during the legendary period of the kings Nyatri and Pude Kunggyel and before Songtsen Gampo, 'the kingdom was protected (i.e. ruled) by

191

the Bonpos, the storytellers and the singers'. Of these only the Bonpos are usually remembered, because they are better known than the other specialists. The latter must have had a religious character, their functions being parallel with those of the Bonpos. Still, the first sort (*sgrung*) were storytellers and the second (*lde'u*) singers of riddles, perhaps also of genealogies. Between them they must have presented what is known as the 'religion of men' (*mi-chos*) as distinct from the 'religion of the gods' (*lha-chos*), a term denoting at first Bon, and later Buddhism. The few examples of 'religion of men' that have come down to us under this name are merely wise saws, told by the old men of the clan and always uttered in a poetic style characterized by the use of metaphors, clichés and proverbial sayings. They also take account of religious beliefs, however; though without separating them from the code of social behaviour. Part of the reason is probably that the two great organized religions, Bon and Buddhism, incorporated the properly religious elements in their respective systems, leaving the 'religion of men' nothing but the morality that ought to act as a preparation for that religion. 'Basing oneself on the field of the religion of men, the religion of the gods (Buddhism) will grow there as a fruit', says a chronicle.[1] In this, the Tibetan missionaries were merely following the policy of Nāgārjuna, who is supposed to have encouraged and even written popular stories and a collection of wise saws much read and quoted in Tibet. 'Custom of men well adhered to, country of gods soon arrived at. Ladder of gods and men climbed up, shore of salvation within reach.'[2]

But the 'religion of men' *was* a religion (*chos*, though this word also has the meaning 'custom'). In the invocations to local gods of the soil, which have preserved indigenous deities to some extent, and more notably the ancient style of the songs, we are told that a given deity bore such-and-such a name in the 'religion of men' and some other new one in the 'religion of the gods' (Buddhism). The sacred mountain Nyenchen Thanglha, for instance, was called Yashur in the 'religion of men' and Pañcaśikha in the 'religion of gods', one of these rituals tells us. And in fact this name (*Ya-bzhur*) occurs among the ancient manuscripts of Tun-huang, both in a mythological or legendary tale and in a manual of divination.[3] It is

[1] 139, f. 245*a*.
[2] 164, f. 4*b*.
[3] 118, pp. 93, 140; 84, p. 570.

significant that Tibetans still did not ascribe it to Bon, but to the nameless religion which may be termed indigenous.

A fourteenth-century chronicle based on earlier documents informs us that the 'religion of men' was the sign of a king's good government. 'The nine basic forms of the religion of men belong to the pattern (or precedent) of the body of a lion. The right foot: reciting the manner in which the world came into being; left foot: relating the fashion in which living beings appeared; hindquarters: relating the divisions of the earth; right "hand": telling the genealogy of the rulers; left "hand": telling the genealogies of the subjects; "middle finger": telling the way in which the (Buddhist) doctrine was born; neck: relating the tribes (or villages) of each ruler (?); head: recounting the families of father and mother; tail: songs of joy with symbolic allusions.'[1]

The 'tales' (*sgrung*) certainly formed part of the narrative material described here as making up the 'religion of men'. A very sound historian cites the tale of Masang as an example.[2] The tale in question recounts the origin of the nine Masang clans (kinds of deity) with whom the Sakya noble family and others claim kinship. Formerly independent, it was incorporated in a collection of Lamaistic tales based on the Indian collection of Vetāla stories. But some of its themes are now found in the epic. The Masang 'King-of-Milk', an ox-headed man born from the union of a man and a cow, intervenes in a fight between a god and a demon, on the former's side, and as a reward is granted the sending of a celestial son to reign on earth. So no wonder that a seventeenth-century work[3] describes the legendary account of the Tibetans' ancestry as 'religion of men'. And we learn from a quite early chronicle[4] that, when the translation of Buddhist works had been completed under King Trhisong Detsen, 'the minister Gö said: "You have spread the religion of the gods (Buddhism). Now, what will you give men, as narrations of the religion of men?" Then they were given the genealogies of rulers, the local divisions of the people, the salutations and marks of courtesy towards the hierarchy and the Triple Gem (Triratna), tales and stories (*gtam* and *lo-rgyus*), virtues and diplomas (*dge* and *yig-tshang*)

---

[1] 139, ff. 279*b* and 244*a* (chap. XV).
[2] 142, *JA*, ff. 8*b*–9*a*.
[3] 156, *MĀ*, f. 114*a*.
[4] 183, p. 53.

The epic, and the genealogy of the great clan of Lang (*Rlangs po-ti bse-ru*), also cite significantly titled works on the creation of the world and its beings, as sources of their accounts. The head of state and the hero, in the epic, know everything through having certain 'mother' (*ma-yig*) or 'ancestral' (*pha-'bum*) books, on which oaths are taken—because they are sacred—and which set forth the origin of the world and the clans, together with their whole future history in the form of prophecies. One of these works was called the 'Great Opening of the Body of the World'. Perhaps this body was that of the lion with which the various traditions were associated, or that of a dismembered animal whose parts made up the country. Another work was entitled 'Oral Tradition, or Origin of Tribes': it dealt with the origin of the clans from an egg. Nowadays, this work is part of the Bonpo literature. But the epic quotes it, on the subject of the clans that came out of the egg, without breathing a word about Bon, and the same story forms the opening of the Lang genealogy. It is the 'genealogy of subjects', which is related after a brief mention of the 'genealogy of rulers': those, it will be remembered, were two of the nine topics of the 'religion of men'.

An egg appears, as the quintessence of the five elements. From its outer shell is born the White rock of the gods on high (masculine in Tibetan), from its inner fluid is formed the White lake of conch (feminine), and from the glutinous part in the middle come all beings. The soft part of the egg becomes eighteen eggs of which one (or six), in the middle, is as though made of conch. It is a shapeless man, without limbs or senses, but endowed with thought. In accordance with his wish, sense organs break through and he becomes a handsome young man, king Yemön or Sangpo Bumtri. He has a son by a queen. After some generations we reach gods, one of whom, Ode Kunggyel, is elsewhere regarded as the royal dynasty's ancestor, who came down from heaven to earth. Two generations later, with Thingge, we come to the ancestors of the great nations (Tibet, Hor, China), and then to the ancient clans, one of which gave rise to that of Lang.[1]

The beginning of the account is highly sophisticated and resembles Bonpo creation myths. Foreign influence, especially Indian and perhaps Iranian or even Chinese, is very strong: for an informed scholar from Drigung, in the twelfth century, this Bonpo chronology

[1] 157, f. 167a.

194

starting from an egg is a belief of the heretics (*mu-stegs*, brahmins) of India; and in fact it is found in the *Mahābhārata*. The remainder of the genealogy is as tangled and ill-preserved as most of the other genealogical legends, all constructed to the same pattern. The fact is that ancestral legends were like the armorial bearings of noble families. They would squabble over them, each family claiming divine origin and trying to annex famous ancestors. Fluctuations and variants were all the commoner because these legends were recited on the occasion of various contests at the festivals celebrated in honour of the god of the soil. The colloquies held to this day at horse-races, evidence for which goes back at least as far as the fourteenth century,[1] extolled clans or families in hymns and fine speeches. In one variant of the egg legend preserved in the epic, two birds are mentioned. There are eighteen eggs in their nest: six white, six yellow and six blue (the colours of the three levels of the world and their deities). From the six middle eggs come men. Then three smiths appear, each belonging to one of the three realms—of the gods on high (*lha*, white), on earth (*gnyan*, yellow) and under the earth (*klu*, blue). To these three is added a human smith who comes from the middle realm. Presumably they go on to fashion the eggs in some way, but there the narrative breaks off and only returns to the subject with scraps of other versions.

When historians regard the ancient storytellers as having 'protected the kingdom' on the same basis as the Bonpos, it is because the correct recitation of legends of origin was a religious act, necessary for upholding the order of world and society. The 'singers of riddles' (*lde'u*), named as the third type of specialists, must have had similar duties. We have specimens of their style, from a well-informed historical author: they are riddles. But the word's etymology implies question-and-answer songs dealing with the creation of the world and with human and divine genealogies. In the epic, experts in these songs (here called *le'u*) practise their art during the races that formed part of the festival of the holy place, and are meant to elect the winner as king of the country.

The ancestral legend of the egg provides, in the epic, the subject for alternating songs between boys from the land of Ling and girls from China. A Ling boy, 'Easy mouth' or 'Easy speech', has caught a girl and threatens not to let her go unless she can answer his

[1] 139, f. 230*a*.

questions. The riddle contest is then matched by a whole series of competitions: trials of strength, magic, conjuring, racing, dice and archery. The existence of different versions, and their fragmentary nature, are explained by the fact that the same story is told differently each time by each of the contestants, to bring out this or that ancestral connexion of the singer's; and also by poetic inspiration, inducing the singer to embroider around his subject. Whilst the subjects of the story and a set of clichés are constant, the free improvisation varies with the singer's gifts.

In the modern period, such alternating songs between boys and girls, turning on mythological issues or the origin of the dwelling-site, were performed chiefly at the New Year festivities. But they also formed an integral part of the marriage ritual. Boys representing the bridegroom, known as 'buyers' (*nyo-pa*) in Ladakh (but *nyi'u* among the Horpas), had to visit the bride's house. A group of girls barred the door, and only opened it when their sung questions had been bartered for the boys' sung answers: the songs were filled with metaphors and enigmatic expressions, and everything known about the world was their subject. In the course of a long exchange of songs, the bride's party challenges the opposing party in words like these:

'Since you say that you have come in accordance with the words of truth (*bden-tshigs*, a sworn oath possessing magical force), [tell us then]:

Who catches the wild yak by the horns?
Who seizes the tiger with his hand?
Who picks up water in his lassoo?
Who builds a castle out of sand?
Who strikes water with a sword and wounds it?
Which bird can give birth?
Which beast of prey can lay eggs?
Who follows the footprints of the pheasant running over the rock?
Who sews a cloak for the slaty ground?
Who accepts our challenge and recognizes us?'

And the answer:

'He who catches the wild yak by the horns,
    Is Makchen Rampa.
He who seizes the tiger with his hand,
    Is Saya Pechö.

196

He who picks up water with his lasso,
    Is the *yakṣa* Shongthok.
He who builds castles out of sand,
    Is the bird Karakukti.
He who strikes water with a sword and wounds it,
    Is none other than the water itself.
The bird that can give birth,
    Is the bat.
The beast of prey that can lay eggs,
    Is the weasel.
He who follows the footprints of the pheasant running over the
rock,
    Is no other than the grass.
He who sews a cloak for the slaty ground,
    Is Byishokara (Viśvakarman, artificer of the gods).
Those who accept your challenge and recognize you,
    Are ourselves, and isn't the answer good?'

The bride's party continue:

'Since you came yesterday, came to the castle,
Tell us three kinds of castle,
Tell us three kinds of space,
Tell us three kinds of lake,
Tell us three kinds of land! All right?'

And the boys reply:

'Since we came yesterday, came to the castle,
Khyunglung Ngülkhar, Tromo Semakhar and Mashang Tril-
bukhar, these are the three kinds of castle.
The boundless space of the sky, the unobstructed space of the
Dharma, the endless space of wealth, these are the three
kinds of space.
Maphang the bathing lake, La-ngak the poison lake, Gomo the
conch (?) lake, these are the three kinds of lake.
Tuṣita land of gods, Jambudvīpa land of men, Anavatāpta land
of *nāgas*, these are the three kinds of land.'[1]

These songs would be worth quoting in their entirety, but we lack
the room. Collected at the turn of the century, they blend naturally

[1] 36, pp. 48–50; Tibetan text, pp. 14–15.

together the standard concepts of Lamaism, some specifically Bonpo elements, the traditions of the epic and popular ideas. They treat of the three levels of the world, each inhabited by its own deities, the different realms of nature each with its representative animal (the white lion of the glaciers, etc.), the four *lokapālas* and the four legendary kings ruling over the four points of the compass. Despite their modernized appearance, these songs may give some idea of what the ancient *lde'u* were like.

The stories and songs, then, were supposed to 'protect the kingdom', like the rites of Bon, through their religious powers. They express the wisdom of the elders and their trustworthy nature lends its sanction to the social and world order, the structure of the environment and that of the group inhabiting it. The marriage songs begin with an allusion to the 'word of truth', a Buddhist term which in everyday speech has taken on the meaning of a formula for swearing and calling to witness, charged with magical energy (imprecation formula: 'As sure as . . . !', or 'May I be punished if what I say is not true!'). For the epic, exact recital is as important as it is for the rites and magical formulae in Buddhism. The epic, the songs and the race-course recitations, as also the plays performed at harvest time, gladden the god of the country (sacred mountain) and set up a communion between him and the group taking part in the festival.

To ratify the group's relationship with gods and ancestors, it is essential to go back in each recitation to the origin of such and such an institution, and the recitation must be absolutely authentic. This is the case even with Lamaist rituals which always refer to the origin, the mythical precedent, that justifies each rite. Curious to relate, these accounts in the ritual texts always have a dramatic nature and are remarkable for their very polished literary expression as works of poetry. In the epic, long poetical narrations are devoted to the origin and symbolic explanation of the bard's hat, or the hero's horse and sword. Wedding songs extol the origin of marriage, clothing, the hat and the 'sheep of good fortune'; racing hymns, the origin of the races and of the clans taking part in them. These accounts are frequently called *gtam-dpe*, a term whose second syllable combines the meanings of example, metaphor, maxim, tale and book. During the colloquies, 'sayings' (*dep*) of the elders are cited as authority. When describing the 'religion of men', the different parts of the lion's body are used as a pattern or metaphor (*dpe*) for different types of tradition. By conforming to the patterns and precedents laid down in the times when things originated, we take our place in the order of the world and thereby help to uphold it.

Take, for example, the ceremony of calling for good fortune (*g.yang-'gug*), for which a beribboned arrow, a mirror and a 'good-fortune bag' (*g.yang-khug*) are used: 'The material of the good-fortune bag is wool. The father was the sky sheep Reddish-white, the mother the earth sheep Reddish. These two united and had sons. Of five kinds were the lambs.' Or a ceremony (*bsangs*) in which clouds of sweet-smelling smoke are produced on high places: 'Song of the *bsangs*. Ho! The origin of *bsangs*, whence comes this origin? The origin of *bsangs*?—it comes from the sky. For its father, it had the great thunder ringing in the sky. For mother, it had the great light-ning running over the earth. Their son, a wild horse, is the glacier's essence; is the ocean's water-bubble; is the turquoise lake Mapham's foam; is the best medicine's power.'[1]

Those are only scraps of ancient songs which even Buddhist writers felt they must preserve. But, in the Tun-huang manuscripts, we have early texts of this type in which the accounts of origins are very long. They deal, for example, with the falling out and parting of the yak and the horse, and the horse's descent from heaven to the land of men. Unfortunately the archaic language of these documents makes them very hard to translate.

Oaths and tombs

Since Tibetan chronicles teach us scarcely anything about the old religion, let us see what we can learn from the T'ang Chinese anna-lists. They are unfortunately not very interested in religion or only know a few of the forms it takes. What little they tell us relates to the ninth century, when Buddhism had already come into contact with the native religion. Tibetans—they say—attach much impor-tance to demons and believe in wizards and witches. They worship a god who is a male ibex with large horns (*yüan-ti*, perhaps Tibetan *gnyan* which denotes both the ibex—*ovis Hodgsoni*—and a class of gods of the soil). They like the Buddha's religion, and utter imprecation formulae.[2]

[1] 172, *lhan-thabs*, f. 2*b*; 176, f. 11*a*.
[2] 197A; 197B.

When swearing the Sino-Tibetan peace treaty of 822, the Triple Gem (Buddha, Dharma, Saṁgha) and the Buddhist saints were called to witness, as well as sun, moon and stars. Sacrificial victims were offered. The text was read by a monk of ministerial rank (the *dPal-chen-po*) who performed a rite before the Buddha after the swearing, but the others had previously anointed their lips with the blood of sacrificial animals. On the occasion of another oath, taken at the Chinese capital in 756, the Tibetans said that they were not in the habit of going to the Buddhist temple for that purpose and that they anointed themselves with animals' blood. But according to a less official Chinese work the Tibetans, on two oath-taking occasions, brought a god's statue to swear by, and this statue was deposited in a Buddhist temple.[1]

Imprecations used to be read over water, which was then drunk; and this custom (*mna'-chu*) persisted in Lamaist ceremonies, where the celebrant 'binds by oath' minor deities who thus become his vassals or subjects (*'bangs-su mchi*).[2] We already know that the Tibetans used to renew the bonds of loyalty between vassal and sovereign by a small annual oath and a great oath every three years. Sorcerers then sacrificed victims (men, horses, asses, oxen, monkeys, sheep and dogs) and the imprecation consisted of vowing the same fate to whoever should violate the oath. Chinese annals state that the gods invoked in witness were the gods of sky and earth, or more specifically the sky, earth, mountains, rivers, sun, moon and stars. The Tibetan text of the oath of 730 also calls to witness the gods of the sky (the *lha*), of the watery subsoil (*klu*) and of the earth (*gnyan*); and the text of the oath of 822 names sun, moon and stars. The custom of sacrificing victims to confirm an oath (*mna'-grib*) is said to have persisted till the present day in Kham. The formula for taking to witness has likewise survived: 'The sky knows it.' The modern custom, reported in Kham and Sikkim, of setting up a stone at the time of oath[3] is already mentioned on the stele of 730 (*mtho-rtsig*) and in the old Tun-huang chronicle.[4] In the latter case, dated to the sixth century, the stone was erected on the tomb of the minister in whose favour the king pronounced the oath, accompanied by the

---

[1] 202, *ch.* 981, f. 9*a*; 204, *hsü-chi*, 6, f. 5*a*.
[2] 170, f. 104*a* = translation, 119, p. 244.
[3] S. C. Das, *Tibetan-English Dictionary*.
[4] 6, p. 109; 147, f. 25*b*.

sacrifice of a hundred horses. This stone must presumably have borne the text of the oath of mutual loyalty. On the pillar bearing the inscription of Trhisong Detsen, at Chonggyê (where the tombs of the early kings are), two discs can be seen above the text, perhaps representing sun and moon. The pillar with Trhide Songtsen's inscription, at the same place, bears swastika patterns and an anthropoid face. In Ladakh and Lahul, stones—sometimes anthropomorphous— are raised in memory of the dead.

It is possible therefore that early standing stones sometimes included a human face and represented the victim-witness or the tomb guardian (see above, page 133). Similar stones (*balbal*), representing enemies struck down by death, are known on the Turkic tombs of Mongolia (*kereksür*). In Tibet, it will be recalled, five or six 'common fate' friends were sacrificed in their lord's tomb. Where the Tibetan text says that the 'guardian of the tomb' behaved like the dead man and hence substituted for him, an early Chinese text asserts that after a warrior's death in battle a man used to be posted beside the corpse: he would answer questions addressed to the dead man and accept food and clothes in his stead.[1] The tomb of King Drongnyen Deru contained three 'subjects' who were buried there alive with the king's statue.[2] In modern Tibet, an image of the dead person dressed in his clothes received offerings during the intermediate period of forty-nine days between death and rebirth.

In early Tibet, the tomb was square, made of piled-up stones, with a flat roof. On top of it was thrown up a tumulus planted with trees of various kinds for use as a temple and place of sacrifice. In addition to the stone set up for witness (*mtho* or *tho*, nowadays a kind of altar of heaped-up stones), white stones would be handed over to the beneficiary of the oath, to be built into the foundations of his future tomb. According to one T'ang historian, the tombs of men who died on the battlefield—an honoured death—were rendered in white clay all round, and separated from other tombs. Another tells us that a red roof built beside the tomb carried the painting of a white tiger, the symbol of warlike valour.[3]

The tombs of the great Tibetan kings from Songtsen Gampo to Trhisong Detsen are described in later chronicles. They have been

---

[1] *T'ai-p'ing kuang-chi*, ch. 480, f. 24a–b.
[2] 122, p. 2; 177, f. 77a–b.
[3] 197B, *ch.* 216A, f. 1b and *ch.* 216B; 202, *ch.* 961, f. 15b.

identified and visited in Chonggyê district, in Yarlung. They are great square, or round, barrows. Much wealth was deposited in them, but the tombs were opened, and probably plundered, in the ninth century. It is possible that the early kings were inspired by great Chinese tombs. Elaborate rites accompanied the funerals. They were performed by Bonpos, and we shall discuss them later. We have seen (page 48) that the first mythical kings dissolved into the sky at death and had no tombs on earth. The custom of making tombs is said to have been introduced later by foreign Bonpos—just when King Trigum lost the ability to return to the sky—and kept up till the time of the last king of the line, Ösung (ninth century), after which it disappeared. That is precisely the period when the tombs were rifled.

Burial raises a difficult problem. Tradition seems to mention only royal tombs. It is known that in modern Tibet the dead are not buried, but exposed, cut up and eaten by vultures and dogs. Saints and high ecclesiastics are cremated or sometimes embalmed, whilst criminals are thrown into a river. However, burial was still practised in the twelfth century.[1] And the custom of feeding the dead to birds seems distinctly Iranian. The Parsee 'towers of silence', where vultures come to eat the corpses, are well known. In the time of Alexander the Great this custom was current at Taxila, in Bactria and at the mouth of the Indus, and was chiefly Parthian. When and how it was adopted by Tibet is not known. A T'ang Chinese text[2] ascribes to India the three modes of disposing of the dead at present known in Tibet (cremation, exposure to birds and animals, immersion). The problem remains.

The environment

The tombs of the kings were at the spot to which the origin of their line was traced. They tended to be called 'mountains'. We are told too that, 'touching the sky, similar to the sky', they 'increase (i.e. promote the growth of) the lineage of the kings'.[3] Elsewhere, the mountain is likened to a ladder or a *dmu* rope or cord (pronounced 'mu'), such as the first ancestor used for his descent from sky to

[1] 99, p. 458.
[2] 202, *ch.* 961, f. 2*a*; cf. Altheim, *Alexandre et l'Asie*, Paris, 1954, pp. 94, 98, 283.
[3] 187, II, f. 62*a–b*.

earth. The first kings had no tombs, or had their 'tombs in the sky' since they dissolved into the sky by way of the *dmu* rope, a sort of rainbow. The tombs of later kings were set, successively, on the natural steps leading from the sky downwards along the mountain slope. In the view of an eighteenth-century author, the tombs and palaces of the early kings were 'built in the *dmu* style', even after the cutting of the *dmu* rope in Trigum's reign, because all those kings were still Bonpo.[1] Even King Songtsen Gampo's tomb was known as 'brown Mu mountain' (*rMu-ri smug-po*: the *dmu* or *rmu* were brown in colour). The reason is probably that the king dissolved into light and merged with the statue of his country's divine patron, Avalokiteśvara. Mountain and tomb were analogous in character. Where human or stone 'witnesses' guarded the tombs of the historic kings, the tomb guardian of Yumbu Lakhar, the first royal castle, was the sacred mountain Shampo Kangtsen,[2]—most probably the same as the sacred mountain Yarlha Shampo from which the first king came down.

The sacred mountains are 'gods of the country' (*yul-lha*) or 'masters of the place' (*gzhi-bdag, sa-bdag*). They are regarded both as 'pillars of the sky' (*gnam-gyi ka-ba*), and 'pegs of the earth' (*sa-yi phur-bu*). The same function may be taken on by pillars erected near tombs or temples. Trhisong's tomb contained a pillar called the 'fixing peg': it was invisible because buried in the ground. A famous peg of the same type is found at Samyê: driven into the ground at the consecration of that temple, this 'earth peg' will herald the end of the world when it has completely disappeared in the earth. In the temple of Lhasa, on the other hand, there are two stones. One, the longer, is the 'pillar of the sky': the other, short, is the 'navel of the earth'.[3]

The sacred mountains are also warrior gods. They are denoted by terms meaning 'chief' or 'king' (*btsan*, like the ancient kings, or *rgyal*). They are regarded as mighty heroes who have died. One of the semi-historical kings has a significant name: *lHa Tho-tho ri-gnyan btsan*, 'god, boundary-post (or standing stone), sacred mountain, mighty'. Like the kings, the epic hero is called 'pillar of the sky', and his country, 'navel of the earth'. He combines the three levels of the world: the sky with its white gods (*lha*), the surface of the earth

[1] 159, ff. 132*a*, 142*b*.
[2] 177, f. 77*a*.
[3] 184, f. 27; 122, p. 5; 160, f. 13*b*.

with its gods of the trees and rocks (red *btsan* or yellow *gnyan*) and the subsoil with its black or blue aquatic gods (*klu*). The stones set up, in modern Tibet, in honour of the gods (*lha-tho*) are also associated with the colours of this three-storeyed world. In the legendary country where the epic is set, an altar is made of three rocks, black, red and white, laid one upon another. Sometimes, instead of being superimposed in this way, several *tho* may be set out in a line, each dedicated to a category of gods and coloured accordingly. In practice the red *tho* (consecrated to the *btsan*) seems to be the most usual: as the seat of the soil god, it is likely to be set up at the centre of the village.

The expression, 'Pillar of the Sky, Fixing peg of the Earth' also denotes the household god of the soil. No wonder, for the representation of the universe, like that of the human body, was modelled on the dwelling-house. Conversely, the human body, the house and the local environment are so many microcosms nested one inside the other, but of equal validity. They are closed, complete worlds which are all that matters for the individual or group (family, village, community). The world at large, the macrocosm, is only the projection or extension of this closed world of the immediate environment. Although this world has an ideal centre, it has living reality only as each person's centre in his own world. That is why, even when standing for the ideal axis of the world or the earth's 'navel', the upright stone—in all its forms—loses none of its significance as a witness and sign of taking possession. And the group's, or its leader's self-assertion at the centre of its world has a warlike victorious air, frequently expressed by the idea of height or loftiness, elevation and might, symbolized by the sky. *Tho* means 'register' and 'boundary mark', but through a trick of homophony Tibetans hear (and often write) it as 'high' (*mtho*, pronounced 'tho'). The image of sovereignty is the 'mighty helmet' (*dbu-rmog btsan*) or 'lofty head' (*dbu-'phangs mtho*). So the cult of height is expressed by stones, tree-branches or flags placed on roofs, passes or one's headgear.

At every pass crossed by a trail, the traveller finds a big heap of stones, white ones for preference.[1] Sticks are set in them bearing cords stretched to a tree or rock: on these are hung rags or pieces of paper bearing formulae or the 'wind horse' (*rlung-rta*). Strictly speaking, imitation weapons made of wood, especially arrows and

[1] 156, *MĀ*, f. 46*a*.

FIG. 12. Sacred mountains with shrines (*sku-mkhar*) to gods of the soil, a fragrant smoke offering (*bsangs*) before each. Centre, that of a fearsome deity (*rgyal-po, btsan*), whose face it bears. Glacier indicated by lions, lake by jewels and the 'golden eye' fish. In the caves, meditators.

spears, should be added to these heaps. Yak, or ram or ibex, horns or whole heads of these creatures are also often placed there, as they are on the stone-stacks or altars (*lha-tho*). Every traveller that crosses the pass lays a stone on the heap or, failing that, a bone, rag, or tuft of wool or hair. At the same time he calls out, 'The gods (of the sky, *lha*) are victorious, the demons are vanquished, *ki-ki so-so*!' The exclamations at the end are war-cries. They are accounted for by the warlike nature of the gods (*dgra-lha*) and the idea of passing through a difficult or strategic place. It is for this reason that other crossing places—fords and bridges—are marked in the same way (rags hanging from cords).

These heaps of stones are known as 'warriors' castles' (*dpa'-mkhar*: sometimes more specifically castles of the warrior gods, *dgra-lha*), and hymns of praise and taking to witness (*dpang-bstod*) are intoned to them. They are also called 'castles of the *btsan*' (*btsan-mkhar*; or *gsas-* or *bse-mkhar*). But their most usual name is 'laptsê' (*la-btsas, la-rdzas*), explained as 'a toll on roads and passes' (*lam-la'i sgo-khral*), or *lam-tho*, 'register/landmark of the road'.[1] Dimly, too, the heap of stones must have conjured up the idea of a tomb. The reader will recall the white stones that play a part in oath-taking, but are also used for the tomb of a king or a warrior killed in battle. In the epic, we find white stones used to bury a corpse.[2]

The heaps of stones represent warrior deities of the mountains. That is why they are also erected, whenever possible, at the summit. In a cellar of the Potala palace visitors are shown the laptsê of the 'Red Mountain' (*dMar-po ri*), the hill on which that palace is built. Such heaps can obviously be found only on accessible hills. The main thing is simply the concept of height, loftiness or elevation: the actual altitude does not count. The gods associated with sacred mountains and heaps of stones, the 'gods of the summits' (*rtse-lha*), 'gods of the country' (*yul-lha*), 'gods of the males' (*pho-lha*) or 'warrior gods' (*dgra-lha*), reign, too, over man's head and shoulders, the mighty helmet, and the roof. On the roofs of houses are to be found stone altars, flags, tree-branches, horns of animals and the little stove (*bsangs-thab*) in which juniper branches are burnt to worship those gods with their scented smoke. The 'god of the country' or 'master of the soil' is not necessarily a mountain, either. Where

[1] 149, *s.v.*; 131, *KA*, f. 80*a*.
[2] 152B, III, f. 53*b*.

there are none, he may be a plain, a tree or any topographical feature. In the village of Dzorge Nyima (Amdo) there are three little mounds of earth and weeds, the height of a man. You prostrate yourself in front of them and worship them with *bsangs*: one belongs to the head of the community, another to the Lama and the third to the whole population.[1]

The *bsangs* form of worship, burning juniper branches and invoking gods, is characteristic of the local deities. The style and pantheon of the old religion are found best preserved in its rituals. It was by offering this kind of worship to the sacred mountain, the god of the country (*yul-lha*), that the chiefs or elders who had no king asked the god of the sky for one: a son of the god then came down from the sky and from that mountain, and became the first king. It is the same with the hero of the epic. There too the country has no king, and it is the column of smoke from the *bsangs* offered by the elders that forces the sky god to send one of his sons to earth, the hero and future king of the country. Not counting the earthly pseudo-father who is only his mother's husband, the hero has two supernatural fathers: the heavenly father (Indra or White Brahmā), and a local holy mountain (Gendzo, *pha-yab*, *pha-lha*, *sku-lha*). Hence the sacred mountains are so intimately bound up with the originator of the line of the clan that they are venerated under the name of 'forefather' (*a-myes*). They date from the creation of the world, like the first heap of stones and like the old statesman in the epic, the 'universal chief' (*spyi-dpon*) who knows everything, 'old man of three generations of men, old god of three generations of gods, old man of the three created worlds, old ice-mountain of the world's creation, beginning of the world'.

Numerous traditions, differing in detail, but identical in structure, relate to the creation of the environment and the coming of the first chief or ancestor. Small wonder. People were not interested so much in the creation of the world as a whole—for that they borrow Buddhist cosmology—but in all the micro-worlds of environments and human communities living in them. Each clan or noble family has its ancestral lineage, the escutcheon that ratifies its nobility: each little country has its sacred mountain. The books devoted to *bsangs* worship contain whole catalogues of ethnic and geographic names, long lists of countries or inhabited centres with their mountains, rivers or other physical features of note, of clans and of tribes.

[1] 62, p. 56.

RELIGION AND CUSTOMS

These legends of origin have never been unified or systematized, and with reason: there was no organized Church, no priest invested with authority to do so. But the great religions have got hold of them, adopted and adapted them. Everything we know about them comes in Buddhist or Bonpo garb. The epics and genealogies of certain great clans have preserved a great many variations.

A Bonpo *bsangs* ritual is quoted in the sixteenth century by the 'mad' saint, and poet, Drukpa Künlek. 'Formerly, at the time when the world was made, the heap of stones (*la-rdzas*) was built on the white glacier. It is the road-marker (*lam-mtho*) of man's protecting gods ('*go-ba'i lha*, whom we shall speak of later). . . . Afterwards people built it in their own country or village—road-marker of the mighty god of the country (*yul-lha gnyan-po*); then by lake and rock —road-marker of the gods of the soil (*sa-bdag klu gnyan*).' Every item of this account is dressed up in a Buddhist interpretation, but we should notice its references to the four directions, zenith and nadir, together with the invocations of the gods on high (*lha*), below (*klu*) and in the middle (*btsan*).[1]

A similar ritual, in Buddhistic adaptation, brings out the warlike character of the gods of the soil whilst assimilating the myth of origin to an old Indian cliché. The very typical work which we follow here is entitled '*bSangs* of the gods, which honours kings (or victory)' (*rgyal-brngan lha-bsangs*), and the myth in question occurs in the chapter devoted to the warrior gods (*dgra-lha*). After a recapitulation of Buddhist cosmology ending with Sumeru, the central mountain of the world, the god Indra is described at its summit, and the lord of the asuras at its base. The latter covet the fruits of the tree growing on the summit of the mountain. A war between devas and asuras ensues. In the morning, the asuras have the upper hand, in the afternoon the gods. That these finally won, was because Vajrapāṇi pointed out to them that they needed a 'god of war' (*dgra-lha*), which they duly procured, together with weapons. 'There was created the white colour of the sky; was created the blue colour of the earth. Next was created the white mountain of ice. Then was created the outer ocean. In the midst of this ocean were created nine leather bags. These bags opened, and out came the nine weapons, appearing spontaneously, not fashioned by a smith.' They are given their names. 'Then, at the middle creation, were created the nine offensive

[1] 131, *KA*, f. 80*a–b*.

208

weapons of the created world.' Their names follow. 'Then, at the final creation: the grandfather was Luminous-White-Cloud, with noise of thunder and flashing of lightning, the father was the god on high (*lha*) Savage-Who-Lets-Fall-The-Thunderbolt and the mother was the underworld goddess (*klu-mo*) Protectress-Sea-Conch. There were created as their children the world's nine warrior-god (*dgra-lha*) brothers and sisters.' The names of these follow. By worshipping them Indra gains victory. The weapons were offered in sacrifice to serve as their 'support' (*rten*). It is of those weapons that wooden imitations are stuck in the heaps of stones.

The mythical precedent of the heap of stones is duly mentioned in the ritual text: it is the heap of stones of the world's creation. Assimilated to Sumeru, it is said to be the 'god of the country' (*yul-lha*). It is surrounded on the four sides by four symbolic animals: the white lioness in the east, the blue dragon in the south, the tiger in the west, and the wild yak in the north. With one difference (*garuḍa* eagle instead of yak), these animals also appear at the four corners of the picture of the 'horse of the wind', customarily fastened to heaps of stones and high places. But planted at the centre of the world, atop the mythical mountain, is an upright tree containing the nest of the bird Tungkyong-karmo (White *garuḍa* eagle). In the epic, this bird is the tutelary god who protects the top of the hero's helmet.

The Indian theme of the war between devas and asuras was substituted, in the Buddhist ritual, for an analogous native theme of which we know various forms. In the epic, the struggle in which one side is winning in the morning, the other at night, takes place between a god and a demon, both of them mountains, who assume the form of two yaks or two birds, one white and the other black. But what settles the victory of the white god, yak or bird over the demon is the intervention of a hero, the country's elder statesman: he kills the black demon, yak or bird. In reward, the god—who, as a mountain, is also god of the sky—promises the hero, at his request, to send one of his sons down to earth as a ruler of men, they having previously had none.

Other legends present the vanquished demon as a killed and dismembered animal: the different parts of his body become the corre sponding elements of the world, the country lived in or the ruler's palace. The most widespread image, through having been made use of in divination, is of Indian or Chinese origin: a turtle. But for other traditions, particularly those of the epic, the country originates from the dismemberment of a demon, apparently a ruminant; or from a toad, a 'milk-drinking, man-eating' tigress, or a lion. Each variant is peculiar to a clan, whose origin is linked with the creation of its homeland out of such-and-such an animal.

From another angle, the environment or holy place usually comprises two matched parts, a god (mountain, rock or tree) and a goddess (lake, spring or river). The two marry. They are sometimes confused with the supernatural father and mother of the hero or king, the mountain representing both the sky and its gods (*lha*), and the lake, the underground region and its deities (*klu*). Whilst some legends in this way evoke the marriage connection between two local deities (sometimes two mountains), others tell of feuds and battles between two sacred mountains. Each community inhabiting a given site thus finds its identity in its own ancestor and holy place.

The warlike nature of sacred mountains and their bonds with the clan and its ancestor are also expressed in the festivals devoted to them. In the course of the Lamaist masked dances, an interlude is usually set aside for this purpose. It consists of a dance by unmasked warriors, split into two groups which sing alternately. Their songs extol the ruler's lineage, or that of the noble family and its ancestors. Another festival, the *bsangs* par excellence, consists of a gathering of the whole group on the sacred mountain. The occasion is marked by competitions: horse-racing, alternating songs, archery. Hymns extol the winners and the horses; mockery awaits the losers.

Such are the main religious aspects of the micro-world inhabited by a tribal or village group. A small group, the family, occupies a small analogous world, the house. This restricted space is all the more important and charged with religious emotion, in that it has been the source of the majority of symbols and representations of both the macrocosm and the human body. If the sacred mountain is the central pillar of the world—pillar of the sky and fixing peg of the earth— these two expressions are drawn from the house or tent, and are synonyms of the house's 'god of the soil'. The centre of the tent is occupied by the hearth, at the side of which is sometimes a post. The smoke that rises from this hearth goes out through a hole in the roof situated right over the centre. Through this hole, too, light enters. In the house, it is also used as a communicating door leading from one floor to the next. It is reached by a ladder made of a single tree-trunk, in which notches have been cut for steps. This is usually laid against the opening with very little tilt, i.e. almost vertically. It is movable: in the event of attack, it is withdrawn from floor to floor, denying access to each of them in turn, primarily of course in the high defence towers which have a great number of floors.

The world, and in part the human body, were thought of in this image. The sky and the subterranean world each have several storeys, usually nine above and nine below, on a pattern very wide-spread in ancient China, among the aborigines of the Sino-Tibetan marches and in northern Asia. Sometimes the sky has thirteen storeys. That, it seems, is a specifically Bonpo concept, but the figure is quite commonly used (like three and nine) to indicate a round total. The storeys are reached by a 'sky door' and an 'earth door', the former being the hole in the roof for light and smoke, the latter the hearth. You come down from the sky and climb back again by a 'mu ladder' or 'mu rope', which is thought of as a sort of luminous rainbow-coloured column. Sometimes it is called a 'ladder of the wind', some-times identified with the mountain that the ancestor and king grad-ually comes down from, which is a pillar of the sky.[1] It is the smoke of the *bsangs*—the fragrant offering made on an elevated spot (roof or mountain)—that forces the sky door open.

The ladder or rope connecting sky to earth—and as we shall see to the head of man—takes its name (*mu*) from that of a class of deities who live on one of the storeys of the sky. Their associates, probably on another floor, are the *phya*. Both terms are derived from a word in the Ch'iang language signifying Sky or Sky God (*mu-bya, mbya,* etc.). Hence the rope is sometimes called a '*phya* rope', and the sky god who becomes the ancestor of the first kings is sometimes a *mu*, sometimes a *phya*.

These scraps of mythology no longer contain, in the present state of the texts, anything but allusions to the architecture of the house. But the metaphors have persisted, in simplified form, in the vocabu-lary of divination and in certain rites intended to ward off evil influences and attract auspicious ones. In divination, the *mu* rope is identified with a 'rope for scaling the sky' (*gnam-gyi 'ju-thag*) and oracles are obtained with the aid of strings of the same name. In the rites, the 'sky door' is represented by a ram's skull and the 'earth

[1] 152b, III, f. 107a.

door' by a dog's. In some cases it is necessary to open the 'sky door' and drive in the 'earth peg', with the object of creating a dwelling site and gaining access to auspicious influences. In case of threats by baneful demons, or to do anyone harm, one must instead shut the 'sky door', cut the 'scaling rope' and pull out the 'fixing peg of the earth'.[1] As early as the ancient Tun-huang manuscripts, funeral rites and divination manuals promise man that 'the sky's *mu* rope having been stretched out will not be cut', or on the contrary threaten to 'cut from afar the white *mu* rope'.[2] In Bonpo terminology, to 'knot the *mu* rope' denotes an act of divination and calling upon good fortune; whilst the technical term *phya* here denotes oracles in general, that which is auspicious, and the quintessence (*phya-g.yang*) of all types of wealth.

Festivals of the year

We do not know what cycle of feast-days there was in ancient Tibet. In the modern period, and even before, the festivals we are told about in texts were nearly all Buddhist: the 'great prayer' (*smon-lam*) instituted by Tsongkha-pa, at the New Year, the anniversary of the Buddha's birth and death on the eighth and fifteenth of the fourth moon, that of Padmasambhava's birth on the tenth of the seventh moon, the Buddha's return to the world of the gods on the twenty-second of the ninth moon, Tsongkha-pa's death on the twenty-fifth of the tenth moon, and yet others. But a certain number of non-Buddhist elements have been more or less well kept up, and it is of these that I would like to give an idea here.

The ancient Chinese authors have unfortunately not told us whether the annual or triennial renewal of the oath of loyalty, accompanied by sacrifices, took place on a set day of the year and at a fixed spot. The rite presumably contained a reference to the order established in mythical times, i.e. to the origin of the ancestor and of the place where he took power. In festivals observed in modern times, the only ones we know, these evocations of the past are most often held at holy places and at two critical times of year, in winter and summer: above all at New Year.

As we have remarked, the date of the New Year has changed.

[1] 156, *WAM*, f. 280*b*.
[2] 63, Nos. 1043 and 1194.

Now, as for some centuries past, it is officially that of the Chinese New Year, probably introduced in the Mongol period. This 'King's New Year' (*rgyal-po lo-gsar*) establishes the beginning of the first moon (usually in February). But the old 'Farmer's New Year' (*so-nam lo-gsar*) has persisted beside it, and especially on the periphery (in Ladakh and Sikkim). It is more or less tied to the winter solstice, at the end of the tenth or on the first of the eleventh moon, when—we are told—the grain crop has been stored away for two months and yak-meat and mutton for six months. According to the ancient Chinese, remember, it was the harvest that fixed the beginning of the year.

The 'Farmers' New Year' is nowadays only celebrated by villagers and, in certain towns like Shigatse, by people who own fields. It is distinguished by a remarkable custom. For some days servants do no work, but are richly dressed and treated with respect by their masters, who present them with offerings and treat them to parties and carousals. As in the carnivals of ancient China, the world is turned upside down to mark the uncertain interval or crossing from the old year to the new. We are reminded of the fact that in the cycle of cosmic periods (*kalpa*), the end of our present age is also to be marked by a turning upside down of society's established structures, and in particular that servants will rule over their masters (page 156).

As in many other civilizations, of Asia and elsewhere, the New Year has an important place. It marks a time of transition. After a rite of closure and expulsion of evils and antiquated virtues, a fresh period is inaugurated, characterized by a feeling of renewal and promise for the future. A less distinct break corresponds to it at midsummer. But festivals take varying forms from one social group or district to another. The differences between countryside and capital are particularly pronounced. Here is what used to happen at Lhasa as reported by eighteenth-century Chinese works, confirmed by contemporary Italian missionaries' accounts:

'Traders leave off their business for three days, and presents of tea, alcohol and fruits are exchanged. On this day (New Year), the Dalai Lama gives a banquet at the top of the Potala. He invites the Tibetan and Chinese officials to a gathering at which drink is served and where a warrior dance is staged. Some ten young boys are chosen (for this): clothed in garments of many-coloured silk,

213

they wear white linen turbans on their heads, with small bells attached to their feet and halberds in their hands. Before them, dressed in the same manner, stand some ten drummers. The boys dance facing them, to the rhythm of the drumbeats. The next day the spectacle of "flying on the rope" takes place. This is a statute-service supplied by the Tibetans of Tsang. A leathern rope, several tens of *chang* (25–30 yards) long, is hung on the summit of the

Fig. 13. The 'five kinds of offerings' to the Buddhist Triple Gem. On the altar three shelves bearing lamps, bowls of water and grain. Top, incense sticks and flowers beneath a table bearing sacrificial cakes (*gtorma*).

Potala temple (and stretched to the foot of the hill). Those people go clambering up it like monkeys. Then, their chest protected by a wooden plank, their arms and legs outstretched, they descend like an arrow leaving the bowstring, like a swallow swooping over the water. It is undoubtedly a feat of tightrope acrobatics.

'Later, on a chosen day, the lamas of all the monasteries are assembled in the Great Jo (the Jokhang, "cathedral" of Lhasa). The Dalai Lama comes down from the Potala to salute the statue of the Buddha there, mounts the dais and preaches a sūtra of the Mahāyāna. This is what is known as "releasing (setting at liberty) the Court". Tibetan tribes from far and wide throng here. Going on their knees before the Dalai Lama, those people offer him the gold, pearls and precious stones they have brought. If he accepts them, he touches them on the head with a fly-whisk or strokes their head with his hand, which he does three times. They think that the "living buddha" (in this way) makes good luck come down (on them).

'On the fifteenth of the first month, scaffolding several storeys high is erected at the Great Jo and thousands of lamps are hung on it. Flour and butter images, of every colour, have also been made for the occasion: famous men, dragons and serpents, birds and quadrupeds. (This display) lasts all night until the dawn. Depending on whether the sky is then overcast or clear, whether it is raining or snowing, whether the lamps are bright or shining weakly, prognostications about the (next) harvest are made. On the eighteenth, an army of three thousand men, horsemen and footsoldiers, is assembled. Dressed in armour and holding weapons, they thrice make the circuit of the Jokhang and then proceed to the south of the Turquoise Bridge where they fire off cannon. This is supposed to drive away demons. During the operation a sheep is left inside a black tent pitched on the Ox-Head mountain. Everyone hopes the cannon-balls will not kill that sheep, for it is held that it would be most inauspicious for it to be hit. . . . After this display, they bring out treasure of gold, silver, silk brocades, tea and linen to reward (the soldiers) and to distribute to the monks as remuneration for the reading of sūtras. As a rule, some 360 taels of silver are spent in this way.

'Two or four days later, the ministers (*bka'-blon*), generals (*mda'-dpon*) and lamas severally choose young boys, and enter them for horse-races over a course of some thirty *li* (10 miles), from the eastern part of Sera monastery to the Potala. The winner is rewarded. Young boys are also made to race on foot, naked, over a course of some ten *li* (3 miles), starting west of the Potala and running right to the east of Lasha. The spectators pour cold water over the heads of the laggards to help them in their efforts. . . .

Fig. 14. 'Offering of good omen' for a play, the New Year or an important event. Two flasks and two bowls of beer, the froth visible. Behind, dish of wheaten flour with decorated stalks and ears of corn. Below, riches: jewels, ivory, money-bags, fabrics, hides.

'On the thirtieth, after the reading of the sūtras, they bring back the Lügong Gyelpo (King of Ransom, *glud-'gong rgyal-po*; this rite is mentioned in a certain *T'ung-chih* where it is called "beating the ox-demon king"). A lama is disguised as the Dalai Lama, whilst a man of the people plays the demon-king, his face painted half white, half black. This rôle is traditionally filled by members of a special group which has undertaken to do so regularly year by year. Some days earlier this man goes from door to door levying contributions, and so carrying off calamities that might otherwise befall the donors. Accordingly, the Tibetans make haste to give him money. (On the thirtieth,) he goes right in front of the sham Dalai Lama and disparages him by maintaining that his "five aggregates" (*skandha*, things of the phenomenal world) are not yet "empty" and that his "outflows" (*āśrava*, which bind to existence and are the cause of suffering) are not yet stopped (i.e. that he has not yet become an arhat or saint). The (false) Dalai Lama refutes him with arguments. In this way each shows off his doctrinal skill. Then they produce dice, one each, the size of a walnut. The Dalai Lama casts his three times, and each is found to be a "winning" throw. The demon-king does the same, and each time it is a "loser". The reason is that the six faces of each dice are all one colour. During this dice match several boys and girls, descendants of the elder line (that of the chief wife) of the King of Tibet (the regent, *sde-srid*), have to be in attendance. Gorgeously dressed and holding flags, they sit beside the false Dalai Lama and seem to act as witnesses. The demon-king then runs away in fright, and the crowd of laymen and monks pursues him shooting arrows and firing rifles and cannon. Previously, tents have been pitched on the mountain of the Ox-Demon, at the other side of the river (presumably the same as Ox's-Head where the sheep waited in its black tent). When the (Ox) demon-king takes refuge in it, he is fired on with big cannons and so forced to flee. He only comes back to Tibet at the end of a year.'[1]

In this way authority is preserved by means of a scapegoat, on to whom outworn virtues are discarded, and a period of interregnum during which contests are held with him. Other contests take place

---

[1] 189, *ch.* 7, f. 17*b*; 198, *ch.* 4, f. 14*a*. The rite actually occurs at the end of the second month, not the first.

elsewhere on the occasion of the New Year, in the form of alternating songs and dances, by men and women, recounting the creation of the world. The feat of sliding down the rope is also the occasion for an exchange of songs, between the acrobat and the crowd of spectators: in these the gods of the sky and underworld are referred to, with a liberal admixture of witticisms (at Shigatse). It is now that these gods of the various 'storeys' of the world (*lha*, *klu*, etc.) with whom the environment teams, make themselves incarnate in popular mediums, who go into trances and sing.

Other specialists, at New Year time, sing about subjects connected with the creation, and chant wishes of good omen, joking the while: these are the masked figures known as 'white demons' (*'dre-dkar*). Sometimes their face is half black and half white—like the scapegoat —and they wear a pointed cap resembling that of our clowns; sometimes they wear a white triangular mask with a little goatskin beard; often too they borrow the rather similar dark blue, triangular 'hunter's' mask of the plays, with its sun and moon—a mask which represents a yogin and, in the drama, is worn by the narrator and buffoon. We shall be referring again to these ambiguous figures whose character is at once sacred and hilarious. They suit the crossing from old to new year very well: that indecisive period in which jousts and jests, men and gods, living and dead, mingle and confront one another. The mask is now that of a 'hunter' or 'white demon', now a 'harlequin'; a face smeared with ashes or grey earth to represent the dead, or again the comical face of a shepherd, covered with little bells and leading a lion, two lions, or two yaks, in the dance. The yaks stand for sacred mountain gods and the lion, or rather turquoise-maned white lioness, represents the glacier: her 'milk' is glacier-water, regarded as a medicine of long life.

All kinds of performances and folklore elements are mixed up in these carnival merry-makings and rites, and it is impossible to examine them in detail here. But it is well to point out something which shows that some non-Buddhist features, which have been genuinely Tibetan since very early on, are in fact of foreign origin. The curious custom of holding races between naked boys, who are sprinkled with cold water in the depths of winter, marks the celebration of the Iranian New Year. The practice was introduced to China, via Samarkand and Chinese Turkestan, before the eighth century, along with the lion dance: its aim was to drive out the cold. Only the lion dance survived in China and Vietnam. But in Tibet and Japan it was preserved alongside the sprinkling and racing of naked boys which took place at the same time. The lion of the snows or glaciers plays a prominent part in Tibet. It is the national emblem, seen on banknotes and the Dalai Lama's crest. It is the token of the country's prosperity. The poet Mila Rêpa was already celebrating it, in songs which are certainly folk-inspired. The whole tradition of the 'religion of men' corresponded, as we have seen, to the parts of this animal's body. And as we shall find, ancient traditions seem to provide the explanation for a set of odd-looking lions carved under the porchway of the Jokhang, at Lhasa.

There are no lions in Tibet. The lion is only known there as a legendary creature. A good deal of its folklore is evidently of Indian origin but the New Year festivities show that Iran had a hand in it, too.

Most of the characteristic features of the New Year festivals are also found in feasts of rather indeterminate date spaced out, according to the district, around the middle of summer (fifth to seventh months). They too are great gatherings where gods and men mingle, where ancestral lines and the creation of the locality are extolled, where opposing groups engage in all kinds of contests (alternating songs, races, etc.) and where the sacred continually verges on fun and merriment. Warlike displays recall the character of the gods protecting man and his homeland (*dgra-lha*). And lastly, amusements, with theatrical performances at their head, delight the god of the soil and so ensure a good crop for the village that comes under his protection.

'On the thirtieth of the sixth moon', the eighteenth-century almanac quoted above tells us, 'mediums (*chos-skyong*) make the gods descend (into themselves, so as to incarnate them), whilst the layfolk, men and women, dressed in fine clothes and rich ornaments, sing songs or engage in games of hand-to-hand combat or "inverted poles" (?). On the fifteenth of the seventh moon, an officer (*sde-pa*) is instructed to inspect the agricultural work. The local chiefs follow him as he travels about. Carrying swords, bows and arrows and flags, they are led through plains and outskirts. While viewing the fields, parties are organized with drinking and archery to celebrate the crops. It is only after (these rites) that the people harvest. During the seventh and eighth moons, tents are pitched along the rivers, where men and women bathe together.'

The theatrical displays presented to the Dalai Lama at New Year are repeated at the end of the sixth moon. Elsewhere, e.g. at Batang, they take place at the end of the seventh moon, just before the harvest: the god of the soil or ground (*gzhi-bdag*) is in this way given thanks for the crop. Others[1] maintain that the plays at Batang are performed during the eighth moon, after the crop is harvested. At the same time people gather for picnics: boys and girls then compete in alternating songs and play games on the basis of which marriage forecasts are made.

The year's end, as we should expect, is marked by the driving out of evil. Although masked dances and the expulsion of the scapegoat took place in the first moon at Lhasa, other masked dances entailing the driving out of evil are performed before the New Year. In Sikkim, an interval in the Buddhist rite is occupied by a warrior dance, with accompanying hymns, in honour of the sacred mountain and the royal family's ancestors. Other, more popular rites no doubt existed and may still do so, but have not so far been described. A single exception is known, in Ladakh. At Khalatse, on the evening of the thirtieth day of the tenth moon (eve of the peasants' New Year), several persons are disguised as 'babas', smeared with soot and wearing straw hats. Three dances are dedicated to them, and the 'babas' stoke up a large fire with wood. Towards morning, they go to the altar of the country-god (*yul-lha*), a heap of stones (*lha-tho*) presumably, and there make offerings. The peasants invite them to parties. On the third day of the eleventh moon, seven races are organized, and then people go up on the roof where, with offerings, they pray for a good year and fire off rifles. On the night of the seventh, a dance is performed using three masks, two of them called the grandfather and grandmother (we do not know who the third is), which ends in their expulsion. But when everyone returns to the village to feast there, the grandfather and grandmother are escorted back (again nobody knows what becomes of the third mask). Boys and girls perform a dance of good fortune, whilst the 'babas' carry away a sacrificial cake (*gtor-ma*) amid the shouts and rifle-shots of the crowd. After this they wash and change into fine clothes: the New Year is born.[2]

The rite, poorly preserved or poorly observed, has as yet no

[1] 24; 60, vol. V, 1, p. 61.
[2] 36, pp. 28–31.

explanation, save for the usual clearing out of the old year, the period of indecision marked by contests, and the welcoming of the new season on any high spot. It is possible that the three masked figures are connected with the three stones of a Tibetan hearth—the hearth being sacred as the household's 'god of the soil'.

The status of the individual

It will be recalled that the first mythical kings were gods from one storey or another of the sky, related to the *mu* and *phya* deities. Shenrap Miwo, the patron saint of the Bonpos, had the same origin, and was related to the same line. They made their descent from the sky with the aid of the *mu* ladder or rope, sometimes thought of as a column of wind, smoke or light, sometimes identified with the sacred mountain, the 'lord of the place'. These kings, by virtue of becoming lords of the country, at the centre of the world, never parted with the *mu* rope: it remained attached to the crown of their head or helmet. 'High head', 'mighty helmet', 'pillar of the sky', they epitomized in themselves the link between sky, man and earth, and thus asserted their kingship and personal authority. As life drew to its close, their body would dissolve into light, blend with the *mu* rope, and go back up to the sky. Hence they left no body, and had no tombs on earth; or they had tombs and castles 'in the manner of the *mu*'. But one day the rope was cut. In a duel with one of his subjects, King Trigum inadvertently cut his own *mu* rope, attached to his helmet, whilst brandishing his sword. The rope shrivelled upwards, to become the 'bridge of the gods' (*lha-zam*):[1] thenceforth kings died, and needed tombs. A Bonpo chronicle, however, tells us that the cutting of the rope was not a once-for-all event in the past but a misfortune that awaits men in the evil age at the end of the world, when everything will go wrong: 'The *phya* rope, the *mu* rope will be cut from bottom to top by the gods of the sky.'[2]

King Trigum's accident is only a mythic precedent explaining why kings, despite their divine nature, leave corpses and need tombs. It does not mean that man is henceforth and for ever deprived of the *mu* rope and its benefits. Bonpo experts, heretical kings good at magic (like King Shingtri of Mon in the epic) and saints have retained

[1] 177, f. 57*b*
[2] 186, f. 135*a*.

the ability to go to the sky by way of the *mu* rope. As for common mortals, they are not excluded, but they now need divinatory and funerary rites to secure this chance of an afterlife.

In the microcosm of the environment, the sacred mountain or 'god of the country' (*yul-lha*) is equated with the *mu* ladder; and that other microcosm, the human body, is thought of along similar lines. Man has in him five, or sometimes six, 'protecting gods' ('*go-ba'i lha*). One of them is the 'god of the country (*yul-lha*) himself: he dwells, as one might expect, on the top of the head, where the *mu* rope starts from. On the shoulders live the 'warrior god' (*dgra-lha*) and the 'man's god' (*pho-lha*). That Trigum could cut his *mu* rope was his own fault for wrapping his head in a black turban and laying a dog's and fox's corpse on his shoulders, a defilement which had rendered the three corresponding protector gods (*mgur-lha*, *dgra-lha* and *pho-lha*) powerless.[1]

It is true that the late authors, our only source of information on these deities, list them variously and disagree about the parts of the body they occupy. But they are always born at the same time as the person concerned. We know of the 'man's god' (*pho-lha*) and the woman's (*mo-lha*), the maternal uncle's god (*zhang-lha*), the life-principle god (*srog-lha*), the warrior god (literally, the god [who protects against] enemies, *dgra-lha*) and the god of the country (*yul-lha*).

These gods relate man to his group in space and time: in space, because identical with those controlling the physical environment, house or country; in time, because they preside over the fortunes of the line, from ancestors to descendants. For man himself, in whom these relationships intersect, his gods guarantee—if all goes well— life-force, power, longevity and success.

On the roof of the house, two altars of heaped-up stones represent the man's god (*pho-lha*) and the woman's god (*mo-lha*). A flag set up beside them is the warrior god (*dgra-lha*). These are the 'gods of the summit' (*rtse-lha*). Their worship on the roof is identical to that of the heaps of stones on mountains or passes: the same *ki-ki so-so* victory cries, the same offering of clouds of smoke, the same ornaments of five-coloured ribbons, symbolizing the rainbow; and even the 'wind horse' (*rlung rta*).

'Through the man's god (*pho-lha*) males (*pho*) are multiplied and one has a numerous line of descendants; through the woman's god

[1] 142, *JA*, f. 7*b*.

(*mo-lha*) sisters are multiplied, and the female fortune grows; through the god of the maternal uncle, one has good relations with others and prospers; through the warrior god (*dgra-lha*) one has much wealth and few enemies; through the life-force god, one obtains long life and steady life-force.'[1] Hence the pictures of the 'wind horse' bear the names of the cyclical signs indicating a man's date of birth, and the wish 'May life-force, body and strength increase like the waxing moon', or 'May the man of such-and-such a year, with his property and household, grow upwards (like) the wind horse', or again 'May life-force, body, strength, wind horse, longevity, religious merit and reputation increase! Victory to the gods!'

The 'wind horse' thus represents all aspects of vitality in a man asserting and glorifying himself. 'Growing upwards' takes place, in fact, through our old friend the '*mu* rope'. In the cult of Gesar— the epic hero, turned warrior god (*dgra-lha*) *par excellence*—the 'wind horse' is shaped like a typical flag of the warrior gods, though bearing the same markings as ordinary 'wind horses'. To make it work, or increase its effectiveness, the following invocation is written on it, addressed to the warrior god: 'Pull the *mu* rope (up)!' (*dmu-thag drongs-shig*). This action is equivalent to a king's triumph at the centre of the world, a spatial assertion to match the confidence of temporal perpetuity: 'Master of the flag of glory of the "wind horse", great king of the warrior gods (*wer-ma*) and subduer of demons, best of men, Gesar, be venerated! Be venerated, be exalted, great and mighty one! Be our mighty god of the man (*pho-lha*). . . ! Raise the wind pillar to the sky, pull up the *mu* rope of long life! May there resound, at the summit of the three worlds, the thunder of magnificent glory unrivalled in greatness and might! May the world be subjected in slavery to us!' And another prayer shows that this increase of life is thought of as a lengthening of the rope: 'In growing, may the *mu* rope lengthen!'[2] This must be in order to reach the sky.

Soul and life

'Wind', in the expression 'wind horse', is a life principle analogous to the Chinese *ch'i* and the Indian *prāṇa*. It is both the air we breathe,

---

[1] 187, II, f. 8*b* (= 322*b*); 124, pp. 34, 70; 187, I, f. 194*b*.

[2] 173, *NA*, f. 28*b*; *ibid.*, f. 35*a–b*; anonymous short prayer on 2 leaves, entitled *Kha-'dzin*.

and a subtle fluid within the body. It can be tamed and made use of by means of meditation and breathing techniques that are found in Indian yoga as well as Chinese Taoism.

The texts relating to the 'wind horse' and a man's 'protecting gods' are all late, and it is not known whether these conceptions are ancient and indigenous or not. Even if they were, some syncretism has taken place, but the result is interesting in itself. It happens that in Tibetan Buddhism—as also in Taoism—the final process of liberation of a saint, one who leaves no body behind or goes to 'paradise' in a rainbow body, is identical with the way in which the mythical kings used to melt into the *mu* rope. The syncretism dates back at least to the eleventh century, since even Mila Rêpa speaks of 'the cutting of the scaling-rope of liberation (salvation)'.[1] We cannot settle the question whether the yoga practitioners who came to Tibet employed indigenous concepts and images, or whether Tibetans interpreted their old mythological ideas in the light of yoga techniques. But we may note that the Tibetan metaphors are known all over the Far East and in northern Asia: the hole in the roof through which the soul escapes on a rainbow which is a five-coloured thread, etc. Admittedly, many Indian Tantrists are reputed to have obtained an immortal 'rainbow body', from Nāgārjuna to the famous *mahāsiddhas* (Tilo-pa, Nāro-pa, Indrabhūti and his father, the King of Zahor). Granted, to be a *vidyādhara* (magician) in one's own body is implied in 'obtaining a rainbow body, like that the gods enjoy, without forsaking one's human body'[2] (a subtle body, called *linga-śarīra*, between physical body and psyche, but which does not involve the 'rainbow' image). However, Tibetan ideas about the *mu* rope are independent of these, or merely parallel.

The way the mythical kings returned to the sky up the *mu* rope rainbow is often referred to, but two texts in particular give a precise description of it, making the operation an exact counterpart of certain yoga procedures. The first kings, a Bonpo chronicle says, 'all had on the crown of their head a *mu* rope of light, a distant (or taut) rope, pale yellow (or brown) in colour. At the time of their death they dissolved (like a rainbow) starting from their feet, and melted into the *mu* rope at the top of their head. The *mu* rope of light, in its turn, melted into the sky.' A very close variant, of which we unfortunately

[1] 134A, f. 324*a*.
[2] 149, p. 830, under *rig- dzin*.

only have the Mongol version, states: 'When it was time to trans-migrate, they dissolved upwards, starting from the feet, and, by the road of light called Rope-of-Holiness which came out of their head, they left by becoming a rainbow in the sky. Their corpse was thus made an *onggon* (saint, ancestor and burial mound) in the country of the gods.'[1]

It is this process that the 'warrior god' or the 'Man's god' must repeat for common mortals, pulling the *mu* rope upwards by means of the 'wind horse'. But the curious thing is that the translucent apotheosis of the early kings, starting at the feet to launch out from the top of the head, corresponds to the yogic technique of the 'completion process' discussed earlier. Actually the 'droplet', 'egg' or *bodhicitta* is made to rise through the central artery, starting from the sexual organ and ending at the crown of the head, by way of the three 'bamboo joints' of the psychic centres. But at the same time the texts speak of a 'wind', 'god of the wind' or light that rises from the feet upwards, as it did with the mythical kings.[2] The result of these operations is the rainbow body and the 'transference' ('*pho-ba*) of 'the soul' (conscious principle) into a heaven. Significant images are employed to depict this alteration: 'Going to the pure field (paradise), without forsaking his body', says one text; 'Like a bird flying out of the open skylight', states Mila Rêpa's biography. Handbooks known as 'Opening the door of the sky' (*nam-mkha' sgo-'byed*) are devoted to this procedure: in them the 'soul', consisting of light, is seen going off into the distance through the 'roof hole' of the sky like a flying arrow.[3] But that technique is reserved for trained specialists. For common mortals, it is the Lama who carries out the transference by 'opening' a hole in the top of the dying man's head. In the epic it is the hero who dispatches vanquished demons in this way. And lastly, in the masked dances, it is once more the celebrant who performs this operation for the enemy summoned into the dough figurine.

Lamaism, aware of the kinship of underlying ideas, amalgamated the old images with the yogic techniques in its syncretic system. In the epic, King Shingtri of the Southern Mon—Bonpo-type heretics in the Himalayas—has power over 'the staircase of the wind' (*rlung-gi*

---

[1] 178, p. 27 and Schmidt (ed.), Saghang Setsen, *Geschichte der Ost-mongolen,* Leipzig, 1829, p. 22.
[2] 168, ff. 24–26; 155, f. 7*b*; cf. the Taoist's breathing 'from his heels' (*Chuang-tzŭ* VI, 1).
[3] 30, p. 155; 169.

them-skas) or the 'devils' *mu* rope' (*bdud-kyi dmu-thag*) which is stretched above his castle. When he is threatened by Gesar and his castle encircled, he tries to escape. 'Shingtri sent a prayer to his gods with all his strength. Then the frightening *mu* ladder of the demons was lowered from the top of the Palace of the Absolute (*chos-nyid*: *dharmatā*) in the sky. King Shingtri made the three wheels (psychic centres, *cakra*) turn in his body and thus became lovely, bright and heroic in appearance. Scaling the ladder, he went off into the sky.' But Gesar pursues him on his winged horse surrounded by a tent of rainbow light (thus availing himself of the same techniques as his adversary). King Shingtri shoots arrows at him 'from the top of the thirteenth upper step of the *mu* ladder.'[1]

Faithful to Buddhism's denial of soul and personality, the Lamaist texts take care only to talk about the element of consciousness (*rnam-shes*: *vijñāna*) when they speak of liberation or 'transference'. They accept certain other, probably semi-indigenous, notions, however, to do with one or more souls and the vital principle. They sometimes equate the 'life' or vital principle (*srog*) with the 'soul' (*bla*). Sometimes the conscious mind itself becomes a mere synonym of the soul (*bla*). But normally the word *bla* is reserved for a soul that is more or less bound up with the body, in particular with breath, whilst the vital principle (*srog*) is linked to the blood. Some authors even compare these *bla* with the higher souls, *hun*, of the Chinese, which are also related to the breath.

As in China and elsewhere in the Far East, the soul (*bla*) may leave the body and roam about (*bla 'khyams-pa*), for example in consequence of a severe fright. The person it belongs to then falls ill, and to cure him the rite of 'calling the soul' (*bla-'gug, bla-'bod*) must be performed. Magical procedures also enable the soul of an enemy to be called by force. This soul (*bla*) resides in the body, where it undergoes a regular monthly migration, if we are to believe the Buddhist authors who have systematized this notion. Oddly enough, in the system drawing its authority from the *Kālacakra* tantra, the soul resides (*bla-gnas*) in the middle of the sole of the foot (left foot for men, right for women) on the thirtieth and first of each month (at new moon). Then it rises higher each day, in the shape of a letter of the alphabet, to reside at the top of the head on the fifteenth and

[1] 152B, III, f. 107*a*; *lHo-Gling* MS, Tucci, ff. 275*b*–276*b*.

sixteenth (at full moon), and return afresh to its initial position.[1] This movement accords with the wish expressed on the 'wind horse' that the vital force may increase (like the waxing moon). It thus follows the same upward route as the translucent apotheosis, from foot to crown.

At death, the soul (*bla*) survives in the tomb or elsewhere. In the ancient Tun-huang texts a house of the soul (*thugs*) and a dais of the soul within the tomb are spoken of. In modern texts, too, there is talk of a soul house (*bla-khyim*). In one tale, the soul (*bla*) of a dead man visits his still-living lady friend.[2] In early Tibet, we recall, the dead warrior was asked questions and someone answered for him. In modern Tibet, the dead man is represented by a picture and receives offerings during the *bar-do* period. For Lamaism, which tolerates these ideas and customs, the soul (*bla*) is a kind of life principle, whilst that which is subject to karma, and goes through *bar-do*, judgment in hell and rebirth, is the consciousness (*rnam-shes*) element.

Over a whole range of ideas, the 'souls' (*bla*) are scarcely distinguished from the 'gods' (*lha*). The Tibetans often confuse these two words with their similar pronunciation (the spelling *dgra-bla* is used, as well as *dgra-lha*). Just as a man's protecting gods, particularly the warrior god (*dgra-lha*) and the man's god (*pho-lha*), residing in his body and born with it, are also represented outside it by objects such as stones, flags or trees; and, moreover, are identical with the protecting deities of the dwelling-place (house or country); so too the soul or life principle (*bla*) resides both in the body and in an external object, and such an object can be 'the outer soul' or the 'seat of life' (*bla-gnas*) of an individual as well as a group of people or a country.

In a certain family, nine sons have as many soul-horses (*bla-rta*), soul-oxen (*bla-glang*) and soul-birds (*bla-bya*), all born the same year as these sons. In addition there are nine soul-trees (*bla-shing*) and nine soul-lakes (*bla-mtsho*). As long as their lineages last they remain 'alive', but as soon as one line dies out the corresponding tree and lake dry up. One Buddhist teacher had a soul-mountain or mountain-of-life (*bla-ri*). When somebody dug the earth there, he was taken ill. Even the great 'deities' of Buddhism (the bodhisattvas, etc.) have their

---

[1] 187, II, f. 213*a*.
[2] 64; *Ro-sgrung*, tale No. 3.

227

external 'life' or 'soul'. Of Lhasa's three hills, Chakpo-ri is the soul-mountain (*bla-ri*) of Vajrapāṇi, Pongwa-ri that of Mañjuśrī, and Marpo-ri, on which the Potala stands, that of Avalokiteśvara (these are the Three Protectors of Tibet).[1] Moreover, three flags erected at Lhasa are known as 'trees of life' (*srog-shing*) because they guarantee the realm and the religion: the expression used also denotes the axis of a stūpa or a statue, which axis gives it its life, i.e. animates it.

Often one and the same person or community has several external 'souls' or 'lives'. In the epic, the 'life' of the Hor people is a piece of iron or a white stone, but they also have a soul-tree (*bla-shing*) and a soul-fish (*bla-nya*). To defeat them it is necessary to hammer the iron and cut down the tree. To conquer Ata Lhamo, Gesar dries up her black lake and cuts down her soul-tree (*bla-shing*), but she survives, for she still has her 'seat of life' or of the soul (*bla-gnas*) in a black sheep.[2] These external souls or seats of life are naturally hidden and kept secret; in the tales and the epic, the hero only vanquishes the demon or giant when the secret has been betrayed. Apart from topographical features (trees, rocks, lakes, mountains, springs), the external souls are usually precious or artistic objects, kept in receptacles which are boxed one inside another and deposited in a hiding-place. 'Turquoises-of-life' (*bla-g.yu*) are often mentioned as the family treasure, on which its life and fortune seem to depend. The soul-animals are often animal figures carved from precious stones or metals.

All these 'seats of the soul' are barely distinguishable from beings or objects which are the habitation of a deity or, rather, are deities themselves. A person's soul-trees or trees-of-life (*bla-shing*) are identical with the sacred trees or god-trees (*lha-shing*) which are worshipped and which, of course, no one may cut down: the only difference lies in the degree of sanctity. They are sometimes solitary trees,[3] and sometimes sacred groves. It is the same with lakes, rocks and mountains. The 'gods of the country' (*yul-lha*) and the warrior gods are found as much in natural environments as in the human body. They are often regarded as kings, heroes and warriors of the past whose soul, exalted by their exploits, lives on and becomes a protecting deity. Hence such deities are apt to take the same form of

[1] 181, ff. 93*a*–*b*, 98*b*; 99, p. 624; 160, ff. 18*b*–19*a*.
[2] 152C, f. 10*b*.
[3] 99, p. 980.

real, or artificial, animals as the external souls. Gesar's protecting gods, his brothers and sisters born at the same time as himself, like so many souls, are animals: a white eagle, a red tiger, a blue snake and a bird-girl, and in addition a black snake with nine heads, a white (?) crow, three iron hawks, a red copper bitch and a blue she-wolf.

THE BON RELIGION

The history and characteristics of this religion are still subject to considerable uncertainty, at least as far as the early period is concerned. As I have said already, the fact that it undoubtedly existed in Tibet before the introduction of Buddhism does not mean that it was the only religion, still less a primitive one. The documents on this subject are of two kinds. There are, on the one hand, fairly late Buddhist and Bonpo works (twelfth century onwards) which sometimes give a sketchy and incoherent historical account together with general, but not entirely unbiased, ideas about its beliefs. On the other hand, we have the Tun-huang manuscripts, which go back to the ninth and tenth centuries or a little before, but only yield fragments, not a systematic account. Although they are older, they date from the period when a syncretic system had already been worked out. The chronicles found amongst these manuscripts already contain allusions to Buddhist concepts, but—though they sometimes speak of rites—not a word about Bon. According to the chronicles of a later age—and there are reasons for thinking that the tradition has been fairly faithfully handed on—Bon was only one of the components of the religious world, the Bonpos only one of the kinds of priest, in ancient Tibet. Beside them, on the same level, featured the 'tales' and 'riddles', their narrators and singers, and the 'religion of men'. The position may have resembled that of Taoism in China which, on top of its own system, had a tendency to gather within it, or take the credit for, unorganized and disparate folk customs and religious techniques. From the earliest texts onwards we find Bon and the Bonpos tied up with legends and deities that can fairly be regarded as belonging to the indigenous religion, particularly since they can be explained in the light of Ch'iang beliefs and linguistic data. To distinguish one from the other is a tricky matter, and we shall confine ourselves here to setting out under the heading of Bon only what we are expressly told is Bonpo.

Tibetan and foreign Bonpos

The Bonpo chronicles,[1] which are late, claim that people used to refer to Tibet as *Bon*, instead of *Bod*. That is probably only a pious reconstruction aimed at presenting Bon as the national religion; but the *Bon/Bod* alternation is quite consonant with the laws of the Tibetan language, and such a form has in fact been found in early manuscripts. It might also have been this that led the Chinese to transcribe Bod, the name of Tibet, by Fan (Ancient Chinese *B'įwan*). On this hypothesis, the 'Bonpos' who welcomed the first Tibetan king down from the sky would quite simply have been 'natives'. Depending on the version of the story, these men—who were then in the act of worshipping the sacred mountain—were herdsmen, kinglets, wise men or representatives of various clans. Now the best-informed late chronicle[2] enumerates Bonpos of different districts and clans—Se, Ma, Chogla, Shangshung and Tshemi Bonpos. But one of these names, Shangshung, denotes a foreign country. Surprise increases when we learn that there were also 'shen' of the Tshemi clan who were spoken of as though identical with Bonpos. Under King Thothori, the king's personal 'shen' was a Bonpo of the Mu clan. Under King Chatri, the Bonpo of Heaven was a great 'shen'. Epithets specify either their clan or homeland, or their religious speciality. There are Bonpos of the gods, of men, of horses, of magic, of the sky, of the created world, of the paternal clan (*lha-bon, mi-bon, rta-bon, 'phrul-bon, gnam-bon, srid-bon, rus-bon*) just as there are 'shen' of divination and of the apparent world, of magic, of the created world and of tombs (*phya-gshen, snang-, 'phrul-, srid-, dur-*). So no wonder a Sino-Tibetan vocabulary from Tun-huang translates Bonpo simply as *shih-kung*, 'sorcerer'.[3] The old manuscripts confirm the nomenclature. They give us long lists in which actual countries appear, without distinction, alongside mythical lands, each of them with its 'shen' or Bonpo expert (Bonpos from *rMa, rGya, lDam,* etc., but also *dgung-bon, dmu-bon, dur-bon,* etc.: *gShen* from *sMra, rNgegs, Dags,* etc., but also *sku-gshen, dog-gshen-, snyun-, rigs-*). According to the later histories, the Bonpos of the king were civil servants who

[1] 178, p. 9.

[2] 142, *JA*, ff. 6*b*, 10*a*.

[3] Thomas, 'A Tibeto-Chinese Word and Phrase-book', *Bulletin of the School of Oriental and African Studies*, London, 1948.

received insignia of rank (*yig-tshang*) like the rest. The king's physicians were known as 'personal shens' (*sku-gshen*), his counsellors as 'shen-ministers' (*gshen-blon*), those who knew the origin of the three worlds as 'father-lords' (*pha-jo*).[1] They reigned or 'protected the realm' together with the storytellers and singers. But their unity is only apparent, and each class of specialist doubtless had its own history. We already know that the dates assigned to this history are problematical (page 50) but the fact of assorted contributions remains.

Nyatri, the first king, who was welcomed by Bonpos of various clans and districts, is already said to have 'subjugated' a Bonpo of the Sumpa nation. At that period, we are told, appeared the 'religion of the gods', i.e. Bon. The next stage is the time of King Trigum and his three sons, particularly Chatri. Under Trigum, Bonpos are said to have been invited from Tasik (Iran) and the Ashas (Turko-Mongols of Koko Nor) whose speciality was to 'worship the gods (*lha*) for the living and subdue the demons for the dead'. They were foreigners, therefore, and chiefly from the west. The second name, in fact, is probably due to a confusion. According to a more reliable source, a 'heretic' (*mu-stegs*) Bonpo was invited at that time, called Asha, who was a native of the land of Gurṇawatra situated on the borders of India and Tasik (Iran).[2] The genealogical tradition of the Che clan, moreover, included a King Asha who was descended from the kings of Tasik and from Turko-Mongols who had settled in Shangshung. The origin of an important branch of Bon would thus, if tradition is to be believed, be sited in the south-west, in countries where influences from India and Iran converged. The 'heretic' Bonpo from Gurṇawatra 'uttered from his mouth revelations (demonstrating his) prescience, whilst flying in the sky; . . . he cut up stones (as easily as) an animal's carcass; he made offerings to the demons with meat and alcohol.' The king made him his chaplain (*bla-mchod*) and as a mark of high authority gave him for his insignia of office a

[1] 186, f. 61*b*.

[2] 142, *JA*, f. 6*a*; 177, f. 57*b*; 142, *JA*, f. 7*a*; 121, p. 656. The earlier chronicle of *Ne'u Paṇḍita* (fourteenth century?) has some variations: in the days of *'O-ste sPu-rgyal* (Trigum's son), 'there arrived from the land of *Ghurna-patna*, which lies on the borders of the *Sog-po* (Mongols in India) and of *sTag-gzig* (Tasik: Iran, Arabs), one known as *gShegs-po-che*—a Bonpo in dancer's guise, stemming from the Vaiśeṣika heretics (*mu-stegs Bye-brag-pa las/ gar-pa'i snang bon-po*). He followed the practice of praying to the gods for the living and taming the demons for the dead.'

231

turquoise swastika, a tiger skin and a sword blade. This 'Bonpo' may very well have been a fakir or yogi.

A war is then said to have broken out between Tibet and Khache (Kashmir), in which Tibet was victorious, but a man of Kashmir foretold the death of Trigum, whose name means 'dead by the sword'. Now when Trigum was killed by the chief of the keepers of horses at Lo-ngam (in Tsang), in the magical fight during which the king cut his 'mu' rope, tombs had to be made on earth for the first time. Hence it is from this period that the 'Bon of the tombs' (*dur-bon*) is said to date, having been introduced to Tibet by 'shens' from Shangshung and Drusha. Others state that the Tibetan Bonpos did not know any rites for slaying by the sword (*gri-bshid*), and to remedy this defect sent invitations to foreign Bonpos: one from Khache (Kashmir), another from Drusha (Gilgit), and a third from Shangshung. The first based himself on the cult of the hearth and the god of fire: he was able to fly in the sky riding on a drum, to let blood, and to cut iron with a bird's feather. The second was an expert in divination by three methods: strings (*ju-thig*), decisions of the gods revealed through his mouth (*lha-bka'*, a speciality already ascribed to male and female Bonpos in a Tun-huang manuscript) and the scapula (*sog-dmar*). The last knew the funeral rites (*bshid*) which had been sought after, particularly the 'subjection of the sword' (*gri-'dul*) and the evocations (?) of the dead (*gshin-po 'dur-ba*).[1] It was probably a matter of exorcizing or appeasing certain souls of the dead man. After King Trigum's assassination, his 'sword soul' (*gri-bla*) went back to his home and had sexual intercourse with a woman who then conceived a son.[2] It was doubtless desirable to prevent such cases of incubus-visitation.

These innovations are regarded, still by Tibetan tradition, as the beginning of the second phase of Bon, that of 'deviant Bon' (*'khyar-bon*). The eighteenth-century historian who supplies this 'periodiza-tion' of history (or the older source that he undoubtedly used) considers that that was the beginning of Bon as a philosophical system (*lta-ba*) and that its new status was due to influence from the heretical Shivaite doctrine. That is only an opinion, but there may well be something in it. For the author concerned, the first phase was that of 'revealed Bon' (*brdol-bon*), but he makes it last until King

[1] 141, f. 11*b*; 157, ff. 165 seqq.; 63, No. 992.
[2] 186, f. 39*a*.

232

Thothori's predecessor. For a sounder sixteenth-century historian, the 'revealed Bon', characterized by demon worship, only began after Trigum, in a period to which the appearance of the great 'shens' of the 'Sky Bon' and the first Bonpo treatises are dated. The whole system is said to have originated as follows. In central Tibet (Ü) at Ön (Amshö district), a boy of twelve (or thirteen) of the Shen clan had ass's ears. Demons carried him off and took him all over Tibet for twelve (or thirteen) years. When he came back amongst men, he knew the names of numerous demons and the places where they lived. To hide his ass's ears he wore a woollen turban.[1] This turban is actually a distinctive sign of the Bonpos, and the legend is used to explain it. Once again it brings Western influences to mind since it contains the Midas theme, of which we know a version in the Burushaski language (of Gilgit, the ancient Drusha). Bonpos who claimed descent from this ass-eared ancestor are said to have been expert in the following rites: 'Below, they tamed the demons, above they worshipped the gods of the ancients (or of the old, *rgan-lha*—probably ancestors) and in the middle they purified the hearth in the event of pollution.'

From then on, we are told, all Bonpos accompanied themselves on drums and cymbals and excelled at various feats of illusion such as making a stag travel in the sky or riding on their drum. At the same time, they are divided into four types. The 'shens' of the apparent world wore woollen turbans and carried out the rites of calling on good fortune and increase of wealth; the 'shens' of magic employed woollen strings of various colours, put up thread structures intended to capture demons (*yas*, *mdos*) and dispersed the causes of error; the 'shens' of divination used threads (*ju-thig*) and foretold the good or evil future; lastly the 'shens' of the tombs had weapons (?) and practised the reckoning of the dead and living. These four kinds of specialists made up the 'Bon of causes' (*rgyu'i bon*). At the same time, and since the period of the ancient kings, the 'Bon of effects' (*'bras-bu'i bon*) is supposed to have developed, consisting of a very elaborate system whose object was salvation or paradise—a system largely derived from the known great religions. Actually its origin is attributed to an Indian pandit, clothed in a blue garment, who hid heretical writings mingled with Bon and later 'revealed' them to the Tibetans. That is again only an author's opinion, but it does perhaps

[1] 142, *JA*, f. 8*b*; 157, f. 165.

deserve to be borne in mind. Still following our eighteenth-century historian, a third phase began with the persecution of Bon under King Trhisong Detsen. It was marked by a systematic overall assimilation of Bonpo terminology to that of Buddhism. This syncretic form (*bsgyur-bon* or 'transformed Bon') has persisted down to the present day and presents the appearance of an aberrant order of Lamaism very close to the Nyingma-pas, with its own enormous literature and its monasteries. We shall refer to it again.

But let us return once more to early times. On leaving the legendary period and approaching the first historical kings, we find that foreign Bonpos continue to play a part. King Drongnyen Deru, the great-grandfather of Songtsen Gampo, sent for a physician from the country of the Asha and a Bonpo from the Sumpa country whose mother was Chinese (*rGya-mo*), to cure him of an illness. King Songtsen Gampo himself, though the patron of Buddhism, is said to have taken care to have scenes drawn from the traditions of the 'storytellers', 'riddle-singers' and Bonpos represented in his temple at Lhasa, such as, for example, 'the stag travelling in the sky'.[1] Paintings were then put together in a collection called the 'cow's udder' (*be-bum*), an expression that has remained in use to denote first Bonpo tales, then Lamaist collections of edifying legends. Elsewhere we are explicitly told that, while working for the propagation of Buddhism by adapting this religion to indigenous ideas and customs, King Songtsen Gampo did not neglect Bon. He is stated to have brought Lhadem the Bonpo from the Shangshung country and put him in the school of Awa Namsê the (probably Tibetan) Bonpo. They had to devote themselves to divination for the sick, invocations to the gods, 'Bonpo practices' and the exorcising of demons. 'Having taught one another in this way, Bon too was diffused',[2] presumably by adapting itself to forms more Tibetan than foreign. Then came the break. After a contest between Bonpos and Buddhists that ended in the defeat of the Bonpos, King Trhisong Detsen decided to prohibit Bon at Samyê, declaring it a 'heretical' (*mu-stegs-pa*, *phyi-rol*) religion and exiling the Bonpos. They had, however, the right to practise certain special skills, and held their ground in Ü and Tsang. According to a fairly early chronicle, it so happened that while performing rites for the dead in Phen-yül

[1] 141, f. 13*b*; 142, *JA*, f. 11*a*; 141, f. 27*a*; 142, *JA*, f. 44*a–b*.
[2] 167, I, f. 244*b*.

(north-east of Lhasa) they became demons themselves. This failure in their art earned them prohibition from practising necromancy in future.[1] It was decreed that the Shangshung Bonpos and those of the Tshemi clan should henceforth only perform certain Bonpo rites against demons, whenever the sovereign's body had to be relieved of 'obstacles' (caused by demons). Finally it was enacted that horses might be killed for the dead, but their meat was not actually to be eaten, and that the Bonpo books were to be cast into the water or buried under a black stūpa. It is possible that the existing manuscripts of this chronicle have left out a negative in the phrase relating to horse sacrifices. Perhaps the edict imposed the obligation to replace actual horses with figurines at these sacrifices, as is the case in the Buddhist or Bonpo rites of ransom (*glud, gto*, etc.). But we have seen that, according to some authors, actual sacrifices went on until the present day.

It is hard to know what distinguished purely Tibetan Bonpos from the foreign Bonpos whose presence tradition acknowledges in Tibet at a very early date. They have often been described as shamans, especially with reference to their hand-drum—which they ride on, horse-fashion, in the sky—and their blue apparel. Ancient Chinese texts and the Tibetan manuscripts from Tun-huang, as we shall learn, prompt us to see them more as sorcerers or priests who performed sacrifices on the occasion of funerals and oaths, and cured the sick by exorcisms. The feat of flying in the sky astride a drum is certainly typical of the shamans, but it is met with again among Indian Tantrists, who still practised ritual murder in the eleventh century. The blue robe was also worn by Tantrists,[2] and we have seen that this was the clothing of the Indian pandit who introduced one form of Bon to Tibet. According to Tibetan tradition, the executioners who tortured and beheaded prisoners in King Aśoka's gaol wore blue clothes and long hair, like Tantrists and Nyingma-pas.

Be that as it may, one cannot but be struck by the stress both

---

[1] 170, chap. LXVII, f. 114*b*; 183, p. 28.
[2] 141, f. 48*a*; 103, p. 216; 15, p. 49. Cf. Das, *Dictionary, sham-thabs sngon-po-can* = *tīrthika*; and, for Aśoka, *Divyāvadāna*, chap. XXVIII (Burnouf, *Introduction à l'histoire du Bouddhisme indien*, I, Paris, 1848, pp. 416–417).

Buddhist and Bonpo tradition lays on Bon's foreign origins, which it locates to the south-west of Tibet where India meets the fringes of Iran. Bon's founder saint, Shenrap Miwo, 'The Man of the Lineage of the Shens', is stated to have been born at Ölmo Lungring, which is always assigned a place in either Shangshung or Tasik (Iran). It is true that one good chronicle sites this country in central Tibet, but we have seen that the saint's legend is only a variant of the Midas theme. The idea of hiding ass's ears under a special hat or turban must have been devised to explain the peculiar shape of a head-dress: it may have resembled the three-pointed mitre worn nowadays by the epic bard. In the sacred books of assimilated Bon, which imitate Buddhist sūtras and their Sanskrit titles, the foreign languages they are supposed to be translations from are most often those of Shangshung and Drusha (Gilgit). These foreign-language titles are only pious reconstructions, and the few recognizable words are explained more in terms of the Ch'iang language, but the desire to connect Bon with foreign countries to the west remains. Hence Iranian, Manichaean and Gnostic influences have been considered: at least as regards Bon worked up into a system, in which the emanations of light, for instance, play a great part. But there once again, India could have given as much as Iran or Gilgit.

We have already had occasion to remark that Shangshung, embracing Kailāśa, sacred mount of the Hindus, may once have had a religion largely borrowed from Hinduism. The situation may even have lasted for quite a long time. In fact, about 950, the Hindu king of Kabul had a statue of Viṣṇu, of the Kashmiri type (with three heads), which he claimed had been given him by the king of the Bhoṭa (Tibetans) who, in turn, had obtained it from Kailāśa.[1] This means that Bon may have done more than has hitherto been supposed towards preparing the ground for the adoption of Buddhism, by assimilating Indo-Iranian elements before Lamaism did so.

Ancient rites

If we now turn to the Tun-huang manuscripts which, though dating from a period when Bon must already have confronted Buddhism, are none the less the oldest documents that we possess, we discover, first, that the Bonpos seem to have been distinct from the 'shen'.

[1] 39, p. 37.

A long narrative relates, one after another, the adventures of certain persons, each belonging to one of the principalities of Tibet or one of the lands of gods. There are marriages and hunts: usually a woman is courted by many suitors, including all sorts of gods and demons, and eventually has to marry one; generally unhappy, she sometimes employs poison to get her revenge. Often an accident happens or someone is poisoned: the hero or heroine falls ill. Then, from the white mountain (masculine in Tibetan)—the sunlit slope—there flock a hundred male 'shens' in white turbans, and from the black mountain (feminine in Tibetan)—the shaded slope—a hundred female ones wearing hats. But for all their casting of lots and reading of the (formulae of) divination, they cannot find the physical form (zo) of the illness or understand the riddle (lde: or the god?) of the illness. Then a Bonpo comes upon the scene. He washes the pollution of the mouth in ice and that of the hands in the lake. Casting lots and reading the (formulae of) divination, he finds the physical form of the illness and understands the riddle (or god?) of the swelling. He explains how the illness has come about in the course of hunting (through the sky, stars, sun, moon, clouds and rainbow). Eventually (the text is extremely obscure), the patient is cured. Each time, the Bonpo is from the country to which the narrative is devoted: sometimes a real country (like sMra), sometimes mythical (like that of the dmu deities—the sky). The illnesses are induced by the apparition of a deity of the watery underworld (klu) and possession by a demon. They are cured by the performance of certain rites. Country follows country in this way, always with the same displays of incompetence on the part of the 'shens', followed by the Bonpo's discovery of the cause and cure. Each time the method of magical cure bears the name of the country concerned, and each time the story related is brought forward as the precedent that explains, justifies, authenticates or guarantees the effectiveness of the rite.

It is hard to say what the opposition between 'shen' and Bompo in these accounts corresponds to. They clearly seek to disparage the 'shens' and praise the Bonpos. But they are followed, on the same scroll, by other sets of very short anecdotes devoted to the sacred mountains, deities and rulers of various countries: taken ill, they are cured each time by a 'shen' of the country concerned, who carries out a rite on a different bird each time, or on animals.

While this manuscript supplies legends that explain methods of cure, others[1] give us detailed rites for funerals. Bonpos and 'shens' officiate side by side at these. The 'shens' are of all kinds, as listed earlier (personal, family, etc.). They pour libations, present offerings and sometimes, in company with the Bonpos, greet certain funerary objects: the figure that represented the dead man's soul, an unidentified ritual object, horses, yaks, treasures, musical instruments and many others. But they have nothing directly to do with the corpse: a specialist (*ring-mkhan*) takes care of that. Although he is not identified, we may suppose that the Bonpos took care of everything else. For there was a ransom (*glud*) for the dead man: it was a sheep, with precious stones and precious metals making up the different parts of its body. There were sacrificial animals, particularly horses, a great number of objects placed in the tomb and magical structures designed to appease or avert the demons (*lto, nam-mkha', gtor-ma*, etc.). Most of these items, except for the blood-sacrifices, have persisted till the present day in Bonpo and Buddhist rituals.

It is remarkable that these funeral rites are thought of in a purely ritualistic manner, with a particularly strong emphasis on the order of performance and a meticulous regulation of details: not the least sign of trance is found in them on the part of any of the officiants.

About two centuries later, the picture we can form of the Bonpo from the songs and biography of Mila Rêpa, who liked to imitate their rituals, is perceptibly the same.[2] A rich man, falling ill, is tended by physicians (*sman-pa*) and Bonpos who have the significant title of 'ritual-specialists' (*cho-ga-mkhan* or *rim-gro-ba*). The Bonpo rite of curing consisted of sacrificing a hundred yaks, a hundred goats and a hundred sheep as a ransom (*glud*), of building structures designed to capture demons (*yas*) and of songs. We only know the imitation of these rites by Mila Rêpa, who makes use of them to slip in a Buddhist meaning. But the broad outlines can be reconstructed. The first task was to evoke the beginning of the world, the castle, the father and mother, the sons and daughters, the brothers and sisters, calamities, demons and various kinds of illness. Then comes the means of effecting a cure. First divination was resorted to, by this time—eleventh century—completely Chinese. The oracle was unfavourable. It revealed that a hearth had been polluted and that on that account the 'man's god' (*pho-lha*) had vanished to the sky,

---

[1] 64; 63, No. 1042.
[2] 134A, ff. 113 seqq.; 56, pp. 279 seqq.

and the 'country-god' (*yul-lha*) and 'warrior god' (*dgra-lha*) had gone away. In the absence of these protectors, all kinds of demons had been able to do harm. After such an oracle the Bonpo spread out a 'carpet of the gods' in the morning, and prepared a framework of threads (*mdos*) as a ransom, together with figurines. He intoned a chant, made an offering of first-fruits, and proffered excuses to the 'man's god', pleas to the 'country-god' and a ransom to the 'warrior god'. He drove a nail (or a sword-sickle) in the 'evil omen'. He oppressed the different demons by various rites or magical artifices (crosses of coloured threads, stag's horns, arrow decorated with ribbons, etc.). In that way the evil omens were averted and transformed into auspicious ones. The patient, once cured, gave a party in thanksgiving. He drove a yak out into the mountains as an offering to the 'man's god', a sheep to the 'warrior god' and a goat to the 'god of the life-force' (*srog-lha*). In the plain, he assembled guests and made a woman's breast out of butter, which he offered to the goddess (of the hearth?). Then he fixed arrows adorned with ribbons everywhere, tied a turban on the soothsayer's head and made the Bonpo mount a stallion. The yak, sheep and goat were then felled by a 'butcher' who opened their 'life hole' (heart), cut their life artery, skinned them and cut them up. The different Bonpos placed the pieces of meat in a container and cooked them on a hearth made of three stones. As for the invited company, the different choice morsels were each distributed to a particular category of distinguished guests (including the Bonpos and physicians) and the various lesser morsels to the ordinary folk. Beer was served to everyone and the donor, the cured invalid, broke into a song of thanksgiving.

Another episode from Mila Rêpa's biography[1] shows that Bonpos used to call the dead and guide them on their way. A rich man from a Bonpo village had faith in Mila Rêpa and made a will in his favour; he hoped that at his death Mila Rêpa would show him the road to paradise. Despite the hostility of the Bonpo villagers, the saint was sent for whilst the Bonpos were performing their funeral rites. Inside their circle the dead man could then be seen, dressed in his blue fur mantle, drinking beer; for the Bonpos boasted of being able, through their religion, to call the dead in person (*gshin-po mngon-sum-du khugs-pa*). But Mila Rêpa proved that the apparition was a demon of the Bonpos, employed in the carrying off of souls. Chased out into

---

[1] 134A, ff. 312–313.

the road in broad daylight, in its blue garment, it resumed its true appearance, that of a wolf. Mila Rêpa then said to the Bonpos: 'You people, you show the road to the "executioners" (*gshed-ma*, demons which carry off souls), but me, I show the road to the dead.' Whereupon he demonstrated that the dead man had been reborn in a dried-dung worm, which he called to him. The worm took refuge in Mila Rêpa's lap, and was taught by him the art of 'moving house' (transference, *'pho-ba* and *gnas-spo*). Then the worm died, and from its corpse there emanated a light which merged into the saint's heart, then left it, and soared into the sky thanking Mila Rêpa for having led it along the road of salvation.

We see that, despite the prohibition of Bon and expulsion of Bonpos to the frontiers under King Trhisong Detsen, they continued to exist and the task of conversion and adaptation undertaken by Buddhist monks and Lamas still went on. In a legendary story, Mila Rêpa vanquished another Bonpo from Mt. Kailāśa. Mila Rêpa had gone there to meditate, but the Bonpo claimed that the mountain belonged to the Bonpos. The contest was threefold: in magic, athletics and ingenuity. It ended with a race around the mountain with the summit as its goal; the Bonpo arrived dressed in his blue cape, riding astride his drum and sounding his hand-drum.

Assimilated Bon

Although Bon and Buddhism engage in contests of magic and illusion, they do so as kindred schools. Assimilation has long since taken place on both sides. All the Bonpo specialities listed in the early texts, structures of threads, sacrificial cakes, figurines used as a ransom and even blood sacrifices, have been taken over by Lamaism and are practised by 'sorcerers' or Tantrists (*sngags-pa*). So much so that the word Bonpo has become synonymous with 'Tantric magician' (*sngags-pa*) and is confused with *dbon-po*, 'nephew', a word also denoting the Tantrists. On this account European travellers—especially in eastern Tibet—have often thought they were dealing with Bonpos, in the old meaning of the term, when it was a question of 'magicians' or Tantrists of the unreformed (Nyingma-pa) orders of Tibetan Buddhism. Tibetan historians, for their part, continued to regard not only the true Bonpos of Tibet, but other sorcerers too, as 'Bonpo'. According to them a meeting of magicians and scholars from Iran, India, China and Tibet was held in a Bon secret cave in Tsang to compile a digest of Bonpo doctrines.[1] These authors are also in the habit of using the term Bonpo to denote the Taoists of China.

The Bonpos had adopted the policy of imitating Buddhism. They created their own collection of sacred texts (Kangyur and Tengyur) alleged to be translated from foreign languages. They have their 'nine vehicles' like the Nyingma-pa, their monasteries and their technical vocabulary of philosophy and meditation, modelled on that of Lamaism. Only instead of walking round sacred objects in a clockwise direction, as in Buddhism, they do so in the opposite direction (and their swastika is distinguished from the Buddhist one by the same reversal of direction). Instead of saying '*oṁ maṇi padme hūṁ*', they chant '*oṁ matri muye sale 'du*'. For all the growing power of the Lamaist Church, Bonpo monasteries have been founded up and down the country and to some extent kept up till our own times, especially in eastern Tibet and north Nepal. Throughout its last thousand years' history, Bon has had its holy places, its faithful, its religious writers, and even its missionaries. The latter chiefly converted various aborigines of the Sino-Tibetan marches, especially the Moso and Nakhi, amongst whom is found, not the ancient or primitive Bon, but Bon assimilated to a Lamaist school.

The beliefs of systematized and adapted Bon are consequently identical with Nyingma-pa doctrines, apart from names and technical terms. The rest of Bon merges to a large extent with the nameless religion discussed earlier. Is this because Bon by itself really represented that indigenous religion, as is often thought? Or is it because the Bonpo sorcerers necessarily had to relate to and integrate with it? It is hard to tell, in the absence of any specifically Bonpo *exposé* of their religion.

Lamaist authors remark that the Bonpos 'liked the Sky' and, in consequence, the *mu* and *phya* deities which live there. Hence they describe as Bonpo the legend of the first Tibetan king Nyatri's having come down from the Sky as a god (*lha* or *dmu*). And Bonpo works—though the only known ones are of the late, adapted Bon—do in fact

[1] 157, chap. VIII, end.

give the same legends about origins as does Lamaist tradition. The first couple, Sangpo and Chhucham, are the same as in the genealogy of the Lang family. As in the tradition of all the clans, the Bonpo teacher's line descends from 'gods of light' and especially from nine or ten *mu* whose collective name (*'then*) recalls the nine steps or storeys of the sky. This line leads to Shenrap Miwo, the patron and founder of Bon in Tibet. Another variant makes the line pass through Indra (*brGya-byin*) to culminate in King Mahāsammata (*Mang-pos-bskur*).[1]

The story of the birth and life of Shenrap Miwo forms the subject of a Bonpo sūtra (the *gZer-myig*). It is modelled on the story of the buddha Śākyamuni. The miraculous conception is effected by two rays of light, which enter the top of the father's and mother's head respectively. The first, in the form of an arrow, represents the male element (semen); the second, in the form of a distaff, the female element (blood). The remainder of the conception and formation of the embryo is in conformity with the ideas of Lamaist and Indian medicine.

But we have an older version of this miraculous conception.[2] In the beginning there is a strange couple, consisting of a King and a Grandmother, but known as the 'nine brothers and nine sisters'. The whole diversity of creation derives from them. Then, without any transition, Shenrap descends from the Akaniṣṭha palace in the form of rays of five colours (those of the rainbow). He comes down near a tree, a willow or poplar, on top of which is perched a blue cuckoo: this apparently is himself in another form. The bird alights on the top of the Queen of the Sky's head. Flapping its wings thrice, two rays come from its sexual organ, one white and one red, and penetrate the mother's body through the top of her head. As soon as he is born he speaks with the same melodious voice as did the cuckoo.

In the common tradition, as adopted by Buddhism, this Queen of the Sky (Kunggyel) is also the ancestress of the first king, Nyatri. As queen of the land of Pu, she is also connected with the mythic genealogies of the Tibetan kings, through the ancestor Pude Kunggyel, and with the sacred mountain Ode Kunggyel. This mountain, in turn, is identified with a King of the Sky.

Although several legends thus justify the assertion that the Bonpos

[1] 178, pp. 19–20, 23.
[2] 139, chap. XXII.

'liked the Sky', that may be only true insofar as Bonpos had accepted native ideas of the day. Moreover, a fairly early work, the same one that gives the legend of Shenrap descending from the Sky, states that, in Bonpo belief, the first Tibetans were descended from subterranean water-deities (*klu*, Sanskrit *nāga*).[1] Again, the most widely known Bonpo work, which has even been accepted by Lamaism in a slightly expurgated form, is entitled 'Collection of the Nāgas' (*Klu-'bum*). As the title suggests, it is chiefly concerned with the gods which haunt the environment and especially with those of the watery 'subsoil', the *klu*. A story of the same type is told in numerous versions. Upset by the labours of 'civilization', the building of houses, ploughing and so forth, which disturb the soil, the deities in question bring on illnesses. Only the Bonpos (here referred to by the old word *dbyal*) can cure them, by finding out the cause and by using their ritual thread structures and figurines. Remarkably enough, the numerous stories in this collection are largely constructed on the pattern of certain texts from the Tun-huang manuscripts which have already been analysed in this book. They have even partly kept the archaic vocabulary. As in those early texts, the experts—the Bonpo healers—only come into the narrative in that capacity and not as participants in events which would be incomprehensible without them. They insert themselves into common beliefs and justify their art by a legendary precedent. The peculiarity of the new accounts lies, however, in the dominant part played by the gods of the underworld (*klu*, the nāgas of India).

One example will suffice to illustrate the stereotype. In a certain country lives a certain king—both of these differing in each variant. Since this king is thought to be very wonderful, he is made 'the elect of the created world' (*srid-pa'i bskos-mkhan*) among all the '(gods) of the) created world' (*srid-pa*). He marries. One day, a blue snake appears, touches the water-mill and vanishes. 'The elect' asks an expert (*dbyal*) and a 'little child of the mind' the reason. It is the last-named who tells him that he must throw precious stones and medicines into the mill (as offerings to the snake: these are in fact the specific offerings for *klu* and nāgas). Later the married couple are ploughing—and the king of nāgas (*klu*) appears in the shape of a marmot. The man tries to kill it, but it disappears. The 'Bonpo' (*dbyal*) explains that it was a god. Shortly afterwards the couple are

[1] 163, chap. XII, pp. 101–102; 139, chap. X, f. 223*b*, 334*a*.

taken ill. Then the 'Bonpo' consults the oracle and performs rites (*gto* and *dpyad*, a sort of prophylactic treatment and diagnosis) but is unable to find the name of the god who is the cause. Then a physician is consulted: he prescribes medicines, but these have no effect. Finally, the man appeals to the Miraculous-Queen-of-the-World, the White-Lady-of-the-Sky (*srid-pa'i 'phrul-gyi rgyal-mo gNam-sman dkar-mo*) who in turn questions the King-of-the-Sky (*gNam-gyi Gung-rgyal*)—both of them deities whose names occur in the epic and other traditions. The King of the Sky looks in his magic mirror and discovers the cause of the illness: the ploughing, which has angered the king of the nāgas (*klu*). But he gives no remedy. The man then appeals to the 'little child of the mind' (*yid-kyi khye'u-chung*), who asks Shenrap for help. The latter, at last, identifies not only the cause, but the remedy. The king of the nāgas must be restored to health. The rites to be carried out with this object are the same as in Buddhism, and are inspired by Indian beliefs about the nāgas.

The things that make the gods of the soil angry are always of the same kind, and a general statement of the position[1] sums them up:

'Formerly, when the "god of the created world" (*srid-pa*), Prince Thingge, took possession of the country and divided it into regions, when King Yekhyen—Shenrap's teacher—chose for the country an "elect" (*skos*, the first ruler), these were the reasons for disputes and hatred. As (the elect) pulled up stones that are sacred (*gnyan-po*, haunted by deities), with levers, and used them for building castles, he earned the hatred of the lord of stones (*gtod*). As he cut down the sacred trees with the axe, in order to build houses, he earned the hatred of the lord of trees (*gnyan*). As he shaved the sacred bushes (or sacred grasses) with the sickle, in order to make huts out of them, he earned the hatred of the lord of bushes (*gzed*, deities mentioned as early as a Tun-huang manuscript[2]). As he dug the sacred soil, with the hoe, to build castles on the soil, he earned the hatred of the lord of the *tshon*, the lord of the place and of the soil. As he pulled out the hairs of the black wild yak, lord of the place, to make tents of, he earned the hatred of the "gate-keepers", lords of the place. As he applied moxas and bleedings to the soil, disputes resulted. And when I say "moxas applied to the soil", it means that through making stūpas, pagodas

---

[1] 163, chap. VIII, f. 38*b* (Peking edn., f. 62*a*).
[2] 63, No. 1060, l. 57.

(*gsas-mkhar*, small Bonpo shrines) and "oppressions" in the centre of the place, disputes resulted with the masters of the place, the deities of the subsoil (*klu*) and the land (*gnyan*). When I say "bleedings applied to the land", it means that through digging the soil starting from the earthen reservoirs (ponds) and thus drawing off water, disputes resulted. Through making use of the soil to dam up the ponds and to drain (the water along) channels, disputes resulted. Through removing the earth and opening "windows" (holes in a roof for smoke and light) in it, through sieving the earth and breaking it in fragments, disputes resulted. Disputes resulted when (the elect) built tombs on a sacred palace of the nāgas (*klu*), . . . when he drew water from the sacred springs by means of impure vessels, when he established a tomb above a nāga (*klu*), when he erected a scaffolding above a nāga and when he burnt a corpse there, when he cast grains of mustard-seed like (magic) arrows and objects of blood as magic weapons, and lastly in the three cases of (polluted?) hearth, (polluted?) fire and prohibited sexual relations (near a sacred place, presumably).'

This list of infringements is a very good summary of the multiple stories of which we have given a sample, each of them dealing with one of the possible cases. Every time, the country's first 'inhabitants' or occupants, the deities that represent or idealize the various physical features of the environment, find themselves jostled by man, the newcomer, and his activity as *homo faber*. Every time, they get their revenge through an illness sent to the man concerned, and every time the man seeks out the expert who will discover the cause of his trouble and teach him the antidote. It is for the glory of these experts that the tales are told: they prove the effectiveness of their exorcisms. And it will have been noticed that, as in the ancient manuscripts, care is taken to distinguish those who succeed from those who get nowhere.

A curious point is that the cosmogonies this Bonpo work does not fail to supply are as abstract as these stories of man's taking possession of the environment are concrete. It might be said that, as in China, the primary interest is only in the fitting out of the world, not its creation. And when Bon felt obliged to have cosmogonies like the great rival religion, it found them, all right, but they quite betray their foreign origin. The work contains a fairly large number of independent versions of these.

In a world where there was neither body nor reality, a miraculous (or magical) man appears between Being and Non-Being and calls himself 'Created, Master of Being' (*srid-pa yod-kyi bdag-po*). At that time there were neither seasons nor meteorological phenomena. Forests sprang up spontaneously, but there were no animals. Nor was there any difference between night and day. The gods above had no power; neither did the demons or the gods of the subsoil. And consequently there were no illnesses.

In this 'spontaneous creation of the Three Worlds', Bon spontaneously appears. Two lights appear, one white and one black. They become a white and a black mustard seed respectively. Then comes, created (*srid*), a black man resembling a spear. His name is 'Black Hell' (*dmyal-ba nag-po*). He makes all that is evil, divides day from night, lets fall thunder and lightning, sends illnesses, appoints the hawk for (killing) birds, the wolf for animals, men for cattle, the otter for fish, demons for man. He creates discords, feuds and wars. He is against everything and embodies Non-Being (*med-pa*).

But next there appears a white man surrounded with light. He gives himself his own name: 'Master who likes Existence'. He gives soft warmth to the sun, shares out sun and moon anew, sets the stars in order, in short makes everyone happy. But he tries to build a house. Now while fashioning the earth, he knocks against a god of the subsoil (*klu*), and there ensues a story like the one we have just examined.

The reader will note the awkward way this narrative moves from two primordial principles of good and evil to a specific case of site development. The Bonpo collection contains numerous other versions of cosmogonic narratives, in which foreign influences are evident.

From uncreated Being there emanates a white flower, and out of that comes a perfect, luminous egg. A man emerges from it. He is 'the Elect', the one who has been appointed (*bskos-mkhan*). He orders the universe and sets the course of time.

Or again, a succession of wheels of various elements—the *cakras* of Buddhist cosmogony, water, fire, wind, etc.—culminates in a golden tortoise. It produces six eggs, of six different colours, each being the source of one of the six nāga castes. Finally a queen of the nāgas, born of the void and called She-Who-Arranges-The-World, creates this world out of her own body. The top of her head becomes the sky, her right eye the moon, her left eye the sun. When she opens her eyes, it is day; when she closes them, it is night. Her voice is the thunder, her tongue the lightning, ... and so on.

Manichaean or Gnostic influences have been discerned in these accounts by some, and that is quite possible. It is well to add, however, that cosmogonies of this type (Non-Being → Being → egg → world formed from its parts) are already present in some very early Indian texts (*Brāhmaṇas* and *Upaniṣads*).

V

Art and Letters

Literary creation is rich and varied. Its different genres correspond to the principal divisions of society. Since there is a strong oral tradition as well as the written forms, a few words must be devoted to language in order to form an idea of the means of expression available.

The medium

In structure and vocabulary the Tibetan language is related to Burmese, and to other languages of the Tibeto-Burman family spoken by small population groups in the Himalayas and the Sino-Tibetan borderlands (K'iang/Ch'iang, Moso or Nakhi, Jyarung, ancient Hsi Hsia, etc.). Some of its vocabulary is also akin to that of Archaic Chinese. The language is of the monosyllabic type, and since the seventh century has been written with an alphabetic script from India. In this form of writing, the 'word' of one syllable features as an irreducible root (consonant + vowel, or consonant + vowel + consonant), often with one or more non-syllabic prefixes or suffixes added. It is not known whether every letter in a word was actually pronounced at the time the spelling was fixed, or whether some letters were only added from a wish to distinguish between two otherwise homophonous words. Even with prefixes and suffixes there are plenty of words identical in spelling and pronunciation, but differing in meaning, not to speak of the many cases where one and the same word has several different connotations. This explains the translator's doubt and perplexity, particularly when dealing with archaic texts. His only ally is the context, and the fact that the language prefers expressions made up of two or three words, clarifying one another's meaning or grammatical function.

There is a wide divergence between the orthography laid down by the inventors of the script and present-day pronunciation in the Central dialects (especially the official Lhasa tongue). In the course of time all the prefixes and suffixes have been lost, whilst tones have made their appearance, and some consonants and vowels have undergone sound-changes. Thus the word 'Ü' is written *dbus*, 'nê' is spelt *gnas*, 'chang' *byang*, 'trhi' *khri*, and so forth. In the dialects of regions nearest the periphery, such as Amdo or Ladakh, the pronunciation comes much closer to the classical orthography, but is still not identical with it. This casts some doubt on whether the spelling really represented the pronunciation of the period at which it was devised. The first authentic documents we possess, the Tun-huang manuscripts, are unquestionably one or two centuries from that time: they display baffling inconsistency in spelling; the same word is written in several different ways a few lines apart. Obviously this makes them hard to translate, especially as these texts have an archaic vocabulary, largely unknown to our dictionaries, and a very peculiar syntax that has not yet been studied. At the other end of the time scale, the living language of the modern dialects and the oral literature couched in it are equally impenetrable. Little work has been done on dialects, for the most part, and except for that of Lhasa their vocabulary is still largely unknown. Teaching of spoken Tibetan was till quite recently very uncommon, and it was almost impossible to practise the language because Tibet was so inaccessible. The oral literature has hardly been written down in any case. Having scarcely any trustworthy recordings on disc or tape, we can only get at it through rare manuscripts which, being written by rather ignorant scribes, are simply swarming with spelling mistakes.

So although most of our evidence is written, that does not mean that the literary output it represents was exclusively in written form. On the contrary it was frequently oral, and what we know of it can only be its more or less accurate reflection. Simply because education was the privilege of the clergy, it was by them alone that this literature could ever have been given permanent form. And closely as they may have tried to keep to the oral source, their intervention was bound to stiffen and distort it. With that reservation, however, we should not forget that oral composition came first in many cases, nor overlook the spoken language's important contribution to literary expression.

The validity of this observation is not restricted to the epic and to those ancient and modern documents that contain legends and songs (specialities of the *sgrung* and *lde'u*). Not only do biographies contain many passages of direct speech in the vernacular, but a whole department of literature (plays, some biographies, etc.) is written in a language which, though it *is* written, is still very close to the spoken idiom even in the narrative portions. Further, learned works on history or philosophy often seem to have been dictated by the author to a disciple. Hence their rather frequent spelling errors. Hence, too, the need for one or more 'revisers' who had to correct these errors by re-reading the written text.

Some of the conditions under which works were handed down complicate matters further. Despite the strict requirement of correct recitation and the Tibetans' amazing memory, oral transmission was bound to result in variants and differing versions. Written transmission itself was subject to certain drawbacks which we have already discussed (page 160), principally the repeated copying of texts. The use of cursive (*dbu-med*) letters, differing from the printed ones (*dbu-can*), and the practice of contracting several words into abbreviations played their part in multiplying the uncertainties of transmission when the copyist only worked mechanically, without understanding the text.

Literary forms

Tibetan literature is absolutely vast, and we are far from having a complete inventory of it. It may be roughly divided into two departments, indigenous and non-indigenous. On one side are the two great scriptural canons, the Kangyur (*bKa'-'gyur*) and Tengyur (*bsTan-'gyur*): the former containing works regarded as expressing the Word of a buddha, the latter the commentaries. These texts are nearly all translated from Sanskrit and couched in an artificial language closely modelled on the Sanskrit original, not only as regards vocabulary but even in its syntax. The subjects dealt with are obviously nearly all religious and philosophical, except for a few treatises on the traditional sciences—grammar, prosody, astrology and medicine. We need not, therefore, concern ourselves with this literature which has nothing specifically Tibetan about it. Suffice it to say that accurate catalogues were compiled very early on (eighth century) and that the works making up the canon were first assembled in the thirteenth century, then arranged once more by Putön (*Bu-ston*) and others about the middle of the fourteenth century.[1] A number of printed editions of the collection were produced at various monasteries (Narthang, Derge, Choni, Peking) from the eighteenth century onwards. The Kangyur usually takes up a hundred or a hundred and eight volumes, the Tengyur two hundred and twenty-five, and the two together contain 4,569 works.

The Bonpos, as we have pointed out, have their own voluminous Kangyur, though the number and contents of the volumes are as yet unknown. Works which had been excluded from the Kangyur and Tengyur, or which were only compiled or known of later, have been published similarly in other large collections, that of the 'old-style Tantras' (*rNying-ma rgyud-'bum*), for instance, and that of the 'revealed works' (*Rin-chen gter-mdzod*) of the Nyingma-pas. The practice of forming collections spread into other fields. All great Lamaist authors had their 'complete works' (*gsung-'bum*). Like the other great compilations, these always contain a table of contents indicating the number of pages in each of the works included.

These authors were prolific scholars. Their learning was encyclopaedic. They deal first and foremost with philosophy, religion and ethics. In the first two matters it is often only a question of commentaries on canonical works, though the Tibetans very soon produced a large number of original treatises on philosophy and new ritual handbooks, as well. But authors also devoted their labour to historical works, textbooks of grammar and prosody, dictionaries—Sanskrit-Tibetan, or vocabularies of technical terms and old words—treatises of chronological computation, astrology, divination and medicine, bibliographies, geographical descriptions and pilgrim's guides, accounts of travels—real or mystical—treatises on the art of government and on various techniques (agriculture, the making of statues, china, tea, etc.). We also find collections of letters written by high-ranking ecclesiastics to colleagues or kings, and lastly notes taken at the classes or lectures of some teachers.

This literature plainly pertains more to science than to belles-lettres, and it is impossible to go into details here. But that does not

[1] 101A.

mean that the art of writing and creative poetry are wanting. They make their appearance in numerous edifying legends. Even some books of ritual are real dramatic creations. Numerous works, on the other hand—even chronicles and biographies—are written in an ornate, flowery style, modelled on the Indian *alaṁkāra*. Although this style certainly strikes us as turgid, and its ponderous tone and lengthy sentences are the translator's despair, it possesses a stylistic refinement which is undoubtedly much appreciated by the Tibetans.

We reach literature, properly so-called, with the collections of songs or poems (*mgur*), hymns and verse prayers, the plays and some of the biographies which have a novelish manner, and, above all, the epic and the collections of tales. But it must be added at once that all these forms, including those we should take for straight secular literature, are the work of monks, steeped in a religious, even ecclesiastical atmosphere. That at least is the case with all currently known works—whose composition scarcely goes back earlier than the twelfth century. It is otherwise with the thousands of manuscripts that remained shut up in their cave at Tun-huang right from the beginning of the eleventh century, when it was sealed.

Among these manuscripts can be found canonical texts translated from the Sanskrit, a translation or adaptation of the *Rāmāyaṇa*, a yearly-dated chronicle on the Chinese pattern, other chronicles in the epic style containing numerous songs, ancestral legends, Bonpo ritual texts, works of divination, medical drawings, numerous administrative, commercial (letters, contracts, etc.) and judicial documents, moral aphorisms in stanza or proverb form, adaptations of Chinese and Indian tales, Sino-Tibetan bilingual vocabularies and lastly texts in foreign languages (Chinese, Turkish) transcribed in Tibetan characters.

Ancient poetry

The language of the Tun-huang texts is so archaic and as yet so little known that their translation is often a chancy or makeshift affair. In the case of poems, songs and a very distinctive kind of prose—marked by its brisk rhythm, great vitality and use of onomatopoeia—it becomes well-nigh impossible. The fact is that, in default of the customary devices of other poetic traditions—rhyme or alliteration—the whole beauty lies in rhythm and structure. It is almost impossible for a European language to keep this rhythm, because the meaning cannot be expressed in so few syllables. Moreover, both verse and prose writers are prone to use certain reduplicated or trebled syllables that have no lexical meaning, but serve to describe specific appearances or situations, rather like onomatopoeia but without being restricted to representing sounds. This mode of expression is similar to that of the alternating songs of ancient China (*Shih ching*). In Tibet it has survived till our own time in the epic and in prayerbooks devoted to minor deities. In each case it implies a particularly emotive or dramatic situation, and is marked by a jerky rhythm.

No systematic study has been devoted to this very engaging form of poetic expression, and we know nothing of the associations of ideas that determined the use of a given expression for various situations. They are better defined in the epic than in the old manuscripts, thanks to the context. Thus *kyi-li-li* is used for a woman's glance, the rainbow and lightning, *kyu-ru-ru* for laughing or songs, *khyi-li-li* for a squall and for heaving waves, *khra-la-la* for the sound of hooves, *tha-ra-ra* for 'clouds' of assembled warriors and the black poison, *me-re-re* for a thick crowd, the ocean, stars (the crowd of stars no doubt), and so forth.

In ancient texts—and surviving in modern *bsangs* handbooks—a quick dactylic rhythm is punctuated by the particle *ni*, a sort of caesura always repeated at the same point in each line, usually to place a strong emphasis on the logical subject. Oddly enough, this function is identical with that of the particle *hsi* in the ancient mystical songs of China (*Ch'u tz'ŭ*). The rhythm of these poems suggests songs accompanying dance steps. One is tempted to recognize them in certain latter-day Tibetan rounds, where the dancers whirl in a ring stamping their feet to the rhythm —ᴗᴗ—ᴗᴗ. On the other hand, in many cases, the parallelism between two matching lines suggests alternating songs as we already know them with the *lde'u* of old, and the marriage songs of the modern period.

The principle of parallelism is so strong that the same sentence is often uttered twice, once with a descriptive expression, once with the corresponding proper name:

'Of the enemy, he cut out the heart; of the wild yak Karwa, he cut out the heart.
For the kinsman, he achieved vengeance; for the brother Yikyi Dangcham he achieved vengeance.'

Furthermore, the process is taken as far as splitting up a name—which usually has a meaning and is formed at least partly from epithets—into two portions, including each of them in one of the two limbs of the sentence. Thus we are told of the minister Pungse Sutse, of the Khyungpo clan, 'Khyungpo Pungse offered . . ., Sutse was loyal', as though we had to do with two people. Of the minister Tsennya Dombu of the Gar clan, too, we are told: 'The minister Tsennya went to the country of the Trugus, Dombu paid a visit to the market (of lake) Trhishö (Koko Nor).'

Naturally this structure is chiefly used to associate or contrast images and ideas. Thus, two sentences formed with the caesura *ni*, which I shall translate as 'yes' or 'ah yes' depending on the number of syllables in English, read:

'With a wide mouth, yes, grass he eats; with a wide neck, yes, water drinks.'

and:

'If he lives, yes, country open; if he dies, ah yes, tomb open!'[1]
And now some examples of these poems. We have to lose the dactyl in translation, but I have tried to produce a similar rhythm and maintain the sentence structure as far as possible:

'Nearer, ah yes, ever nearer,
Yarpa, yes, is near to the Sky,
Stars of the sky, yes, *si-li-li*.

Nearer, ah yes, ever nearer,
Lakar, yes, is near to the rock,
Stars of the rock, yes, *si-li-li*.

Durwa, yes, near to the river,
Lively otter, yes, *pyo-la-la*.
Nyenkar, yes, near to the earth.

All kinds of fruit, yes, *si-li-li*.
Maltro, yes, is near to Lum,
Icy the wind, yes, *spu-ru-ru*.'[2]

[1] 6, pp. 106, 15; 118, Text I A, ll. 78, 84, 86.
[2] 6, foot of p. 116.

These songs were no doubt partly improvised, as *ad hoc* variations
on known themes and clichés, using a stock of proverbs and
metaphors. Their very style recalls the occasions at which they were
produced, great talking matches where everyone vied in praising,
glorifying and vaunting himself; when challenges, too, were exchanged, and bragging, as we are told of the gathering of ministers
at Samyê in the early ninth century, by quite an old chronicle:[1] 'Each
sang his own greatness and his pride.' Taunts and witticisms alter-
nated with hymns of submission and loyalty. In a Tun-huang manuscript we read:

> 'The chief of men, yes, mighty king,
> Lovelier, yes, than green artemisia.
> Chief of beasts, ah yes, the stallion,
> Lighter, ah yes, than is wool (?).
> The foreigners, yes, Turks-Chinese,
> Heavier, yes, than a gold bar.'[2]

Cunning, aptness, the art of telling truths or hinting at blame in a
veiled and indirect way, play a great part in these compositions.
Here, from the old Tun-huang chronicle, is how one and the same
subject can be treated successively in two different ways according
to the singer's character and position. The occasion was the king's
victory, after the rallying to him of certain vassals, as related above
(pages 133–136).

'Then the king and sovereign offered a feast of joy to his
subjects (vassals). And yet again Khyungpo Pungse broke into a
song, whose words were these:

> 'In Mon, ah yes, the lone tiger,
> It's Sutse, yes, who did it kill.
> To the king's hands, the body gave.
> With Lho Ngek, yes, was rewarded.

> Above, ah yes, the fort of Tsang,
> With belly white the vulture soared:
> It's Sutse, yes, who did it kill.
> To the king's hands, the wings offered.
> With Lho Ngek, yes, was rewarded.

[1] 183, p. 49.
[2] 63, No. 1196.

255

In days of old, yes, formerly,
From Tise, yes, the snow mount,
Wild asses, yes, and stags took flight,
Took flight, ah yes, to Mount Shampo.

In present days, yes, and henceforth,
At Shampo, yes, at the god's foot,
Wild asses and stags fear no heat,
Wild asses and stags, if they feared,
With Tise's snows would be refreshed.

In days of old, yes, formerly,
From the shore, yes, of Lake Maphang,
The ducks, ah yes, and geese took flight,
Took flight, ah yes, to Lake Danko.

In present days, yes, and henceforth,
At Danko, yes, lake of a god,
The ducks and geese heat do not fear.
The ducks and geese, if heat they feared,
In Maphang's lake would be refreshed.

By Phen was Lho Ngek made larger,
By Phen was Se Khyung established.
(The king) was feeble (phen) formerly,
Nowadays his eye sees beyond.
Who, at the start, was — — —(?),
At last by yaks was surrounded.
Sutse, upright, was rewarded.'

'Such was his song. Then the king thought to himself: "I hope someone will reply to the minister from Lho Ngek." But nobody replied. Now Shang Nang, who was in the king's personal service and charged with the secret seals, was there. (The king) said to him: "You, son of a father who was close to my heart (faithful, loyal), couldn't you sing?" And he gave the order: "Let Shang Nang make a speech!" Shang Nang sang:

'Ho! In the days of old, yes, formerly,
Beyond, ah yes, the River, the River,
Beyond, ah yes, the River Yar;

LITERATURE

The 'singpoche', the haughty lord,
Reduced to pieces right from the sinews,
Reduced to nothing right from the pieces.

From Kyi, yes, who drew out fishes?
It was, yes, Chitsap Pangtore.
At Lum, ah yes, who cut water?
It was, yes, Tsenku Möntore.
Fences, yes, and dams he builded,
The lands, yes, he distributed:
It was Pangsum, the 'drönposhik'.

Summit of Thanglha was cut off,
Tillage on Shampo was increased.
Once fallen the fort Yuna,
The castle Chhinga was increased,
Before, yes, already tall,
By now, the Sky he touches.

The crest of Ngêpo was cut off,
Yarmo, yes, as serf accepted.
Before, yes, already great,
Nowadays, he knows no bounds.

By Phen was Lho Ngek larger made,
By Phen was Dongtong established.
(The king) was feeble (phen) formerly,
Nowadays his eye sees beyond.

In days gone by, yes, formerly,
The migrant, the wild yak, got killed.
Bamboo, wood from the South, conquered.
But till iron has torn open,
Bamboo itself can never pierce. (*Allusion to the arrow*)
No eagle (feathers) trimming it,
The wild yak it could not have hit.

Of Ngêpo, yes, country of goats,
Winner is the komtse hedgehog.

257

Now until the needle has pricked,
The sinew cannot travel through.
If the sinew, one did not pull,
The komtse would not be enough.'

Such was his song. The king, preferring these words, made Shang Nang of Nyang his minister. And as minister he conferred on him the name of Ngülgyi Phukpuchung.'[1]

If the first song appears to have displeased the king, it is probably because it gave too much praise to certain vassals and their exploits. The second seems to praise the king more. The allusions are obscure for us of course, but they provide a good illustration of the genre. I must forgo other examples that would strengthen the impression. Without being able to convey the flavour of assonance and rhythm, we can at least form an idea of the way thought is expressed. A major part is played by the wisdom of the ancients, in proverb form, and above all by a stock of metaphors. Such metaphors are generally used for enigmatic allusions, and we may suppose that this art belongs to the tradition handed down by the singers of riddles (*lde'u*).

The same art of metaphor and proverb appears in the collections of maxims which are probably part of the tradition of the ancients, later known by the name 'religion of men' (*mi-chos*). Unlike the poems we have been reading, which were sung, these maxims are in prose. Here are some excerpts from a work preserved among the Tun-huang manuscripts, the 'Sumpa Mother-Book, Maxims left as an example to future generations',[2] containing one hundred and ten adages. Often one thought is expressed in two parallel statements, the second providing an illustration for the first.

'(1) A wise man's mind: even in the sky letters appear; (it is like) the running of a swift horse: even in chasms or precipices he is long-suffering.'

'(4) A wise man: by long association one obtains his friendship; (he is like) a gold bar: by lengthening it, it becomes heavy.'

[1] 6, pp. 107–108, translation (differs from mine) pp. 141–142.
[2] 63, No. 992.

'(5) To have children without making them study, is the foundation of obscurantism; their birth had no meaning, and it is a great waste of food and clothing.'

'(15) Bad words coming from a bad man's mouth end by harming him: fire is at first produced in a hole in wood, but ends by burning the wood.'

'(30) A vicious guard-dog guards a whole village; a vicious woman can divide even members of the same family and friends.'

'(34) A wise man and a swift horse make themselves famous when they are displayed outside; a woman and an antique turquoise are honoured when hidden at home.'

'(53) When the wise praise the wise: pillar of the turret of the sky; when the base disparage the base: beneath the nine storeys of the earth.'

For all their antiquity, these texts already bear the stamp of Chinese ethical and Buddhist religious ideas. But from the stylistic point of view and in their use of imagery, they retain a purely Tibetan flavour which has survived elsewhere till the present day, despite the ever-increasing assimilation of Buddhist elements.

New departures

The dactylic line of five or six syllables is not, of course, the only verse metre found in the Tun-huang manuscripts. But it is incontestably the most frequent and typically Tibetan. Others only appear sporadically and without definite rules.

Once we leave these records and turn to the classical literature, we find that a great change has taken place. Learned metres of Indian origin have replaced the dactyl. They already appear in the ancient translation of the *Rāmāyaṇa*. I shall not linger over the complex and rather boring prosody involved. Lines of seven, eight, nine, ten, eleven or seventeen syllables occur. But the commonest form, from the poet Mila Rêpa to the epic and the marriage songs, seemingly of folk origin, is the trochee, and it is of this verse form that I shall give some examples ($\stackrel{\smile}{-}\smile\stackrel{\smile}{-}\smile\stackrel{\smile}{-}\smile-$).

We can follow the transition from old to new metrical types in the hymns devoted to worship of the gods of the soil (*bsangs*), which have best preserved the atmosphere and manner of the ancient songs. It sufficed to insert a demonstrative pronoun (*de*) in the ancient texts, to effect this change. The very characteristic caesura, marked by the particle *ni*, was retained and is sometimes even inserted in the middle of a proper noun, so splitting it into two parts:

'That Yarlha, yes, Shampo; that Ode, yes, Kunggyel. . . . From Seru, yes, the poison-lake; from Tongra, yes, the black lake', says one of these modern prayer-books. In a similar ritual work from the Tun-huang manuscripts, we read: 'Of the land, yes, in the midst; sacred gods, yes, give us signs'.[1]

Henceforward, then, the trochee replaces the dactyl. Sometimes a monosyllabic word is placed in an extra-metrical position preceding the line, and does not count in the number of beats required (*kye*— something like 'ho!'—for instance; or the logical subject). This technique, too, is met with in the Tun-huang manuscripts, and we have seen a specimen of it (page 256). Here is an example from Mila Rêpa:

> 'Song! If anew I do not sing it,
> The meaning enters not the heart.'

Mila Rêpa took the pattern for his prosody and the religious subjects of his songs from Tibetan translations of the mystical songs (*doha*) of the Indian Tantrists. But what distinguishes him from many other religious poets of his order (the Kagyü-pa), making him one of the greatest poets and giving him such popularity, is the fact that he annexed and adapted this foreign model to the indigenous songs of his country. He certainly did so from personal preference, but also with the idea of popularizing Buddhist thought and making it more familiar by putting it into folk-songs. At the contests of meta-phorical songs at ploughing time, we find him composing a song for a farmer,[2] and we are already acquainted with his imitation of a Bonpo ritual song (page 238). In Mila Rêpa's songs we find, for the first time, the standard animals of each realm of nature which still characterize folk-songs of the modern period: the white lioness with her turquoise mane among the glaciers, the eagle, 'king of the birds', on the rocks, the tiger, 'the variegated one', in the forests and the 'golden eye' fish in the lakes.[3] At the same time Mila Rêpa uses

---

[1] 176, f. 13*a*; 1, p. 446.
[2] 134A, ff. 87*b*–88*a*.
[3] 134A, ff. 297, 308, 333.

all the stylistic methods (some of which already occur in the Tun-huang manuscripts, especially the descriptive trisyllables, metaphors and epithets) nowadays found in folk-songs, the epic, and plays. Mila Rêpa thus stands at the turning-point, and smooths the transition between the ancient and modern periods. Here are two excerpts from his songs to give some idea of the style, despite the impossibility of translating both meaning and poetry at once.[1]

'Above, the southern clouds wheel round (*khor-ma-khor*),
Below, a pure river ripples (*gya-ma-gyu*),
Between the two the eagle soars (*lang-ma-ling*).
Grasses of every kind are blent (*ban-ma-bun*),
Trees shake in movements of the dance (*shigs-se-shigs*).
The honey bees sing, *khor-ro-ro*,
The flowers are fragrant, *chi-li-li*,
The birds warble, and *kyur-ru-ru*.'

. . . .

'Father, who vanquished the Four Demons,
Translator Marpa, homage to you!
Of myself, I've naught to mention:
Of the white glacier-lioness, (actually) the son I am.
From my mother's womb directly, "of triple strength" complete
     and formed.
All my years of early childhood, in the den I lay a-hiding.
And in years of adolescence, the door of the den I guarded.
But since when I first was adult, on the glaciers I go walking,
In the storm I do not waver,
Chasm great does not afright me.

Of myself I've naught to mention:
Of the eagle, king of the birds, (actually) the son I am.
From inside the egg already, both my wings were quite unfolded.
All my years of early childhood, in the nest I lay a-hiding,
And in years of adolescence, the door of the nest I guarded.
Once become a full-grown eagle, summit of the sky I outflew.
In boundless sky I don't waver.
On narrow earth I have no fear.

[1] 134A, ff. 4–5.

Of myself I've naught to mention:
Of great fish, of "trembling wave", (actually) the son I am.
From my mother's womb directly, my round "golden eyes" were
 full-grown.
All my years of early childhood, in the nest I lay a-hiding.
And in years of adolescence, always at the shoal's head I swam.
Finally grown to a great fish, all around the Ocean swam I.
In the ground-swell I don't waver,
Fishing nets do not afright me.

Of myself, I've naught to mention:
Of the oral teaching's *guru*, (actually) the son I am.
From my mother's womb directly, the religious life I entered,
And the years of adolescence spent in study of the doctrine.
Grown at last, great meditator, mountain hermitages haunt I.
Faced with demons I don't waver,
Their phantasmata I fear not.'

The poem is a long one, and this excerpt will have to do. It remains
for us to survey the other modes of expression which I spoke of. Some
of them are not met with in Mila Rêpa's songs, but were used by his
teacher Marpa and later, more especially, by another great poet
saint—Drukpa Künlek (early sixteenth century).

In the epic, as in drama, the prose narration is very short and
chanted rapidly. Its only use is to link together the songs which are
the main point. These songs are usually duets. Accordingly the parties
introduce themselves at the beginning with a phrase of the type:
'If you do not know me, I'm so-and-so', and so on for the place where
the incident happens and for everything that rates a personal name—
the helmet, the sword and the horse. This phrase is nearly always
accompanied by another of the type: 'Listen to me (over here: *tshur
nyon*)', the form of both expressions calling an atmosphere of
challenges and duelling to mind. Mila Rêpa uses them too:[1]

> 'Well then, little child so handsome,
> Who would understand, hark hither!
> What man I am, do you know me?
> If what man I am, you know not,
> Kungthang's Mila Rêpa am I.'

[1] 134A, f. 72*a*.

FIG. 15. The 'six companions of Long Life' (*tshe-ring drug-'khor*): old man making an offering, crane, pine, rock, waterfall, and unicorn (*bse-ru*).

And as in the epic, the songs usually close on a stock expression of the type: 'If you understand this song, all right; if not, so much the worse for you.' Thus Mila Rêpa, at the end of one of his songs:[1]

'If you understand this song, just this once you've scored a point; If you do not understand, I can simply go away.'

And the biography adds: 'Such was his song of provocation (*rtsod-pa'i glu*).' It is impossible, unfortunately, to preserve the meaning and the metre together. To retain them both *and* give an idea of the word order might produce something like this:

'Song—this know?—then, one time got; | lu-te she-na len-chik thop
Not known, yogin elsewhere go.' | ma-she nem-jor yül-la shü

$$\acute{-}\ \cup\ \acute{-}\ \cup\ \acute{-}\ \cup\ -$$

The second characteristic common to great poets, epic and drama is the prefacing of the song with a sung imitation of its melody, without any actual words, reminiscent of our own 'fal de rol'. No instances are found in Mila Rêpa, but they occur with other poets of his order. Thus we have *a-la-la* or *shō-ni la-yi sho-o la-yi sho-o, la-yo la-mo lā-yō-ya*. And in the epic: 'The song is *tha-la tha-la la-mo la-ling*; it is *tha-la la-mo la-la*.'[2]

Although these are indeed poems, it is obvious that they are meant to be sung. So sometimes, and nearly always in the epic, some well-known tune they should be sung to is indicated. Marpa sang to the tune of 'The Great Eagle flies with wings outspread', a melody also found in the epic; or to 'The bright cascade'. The practice is an ancient one. The chonicles give us the titles of tunes to which poems improvised at the great Samyê festivals were sung, in the ninth century.[3]

To these factors, we must add, lastly, the epithets, whose use also goes back to ancient times and continues, through the poet saints, down to the epic, drama and songs of today. Certain Indian epithets, such as 'water-holder' for cloud, had gained currency quite early on, in the poems of Mila Rêpa for example. But most of them—and there are a great many—are only used in the ornate prose and poetry of erudite authors. We shall not discuss that literature here. Although certainly very popular with Tibetan men of learning it is only an

[1] 134A, f. 120.
[2] 137, f. 81*a*; 137A, f. 88*b*; 131, f. 118*a*; 152, Hor MS, Kalimpong, f. 13*a*.
[3] 137A, ff. 35*b*, 46*a*; 179, f. 91*a*; 177, chap. XI; 68, pp. 130-133.

exercise in Indian style. But the purely Tibetan epithets are very characteristic. They are probably related to the style of the sung 'riddles' (*lde'u*). They must be accounted for by the wish not to refer to things and beings by their real or ordinary names, whether out of politeness or for religious reasons. The poet saints, who were inspired both by folk poetry and the Tantric mystical songs, must have taken an interest in them. In these Tantric songs too a veiled, enigmatic language, the 'twilight speech' or 'secret language of the *ḍākiṇīs*', was used to conceal certain matters. In Tibetan poetry these epithets, expressing some emotion towards the subject, are of two kinds. Some of them can be translated; others have no known lexical meaning: they are a jargon or secret language. In the first category are found, for instance, 'the blue one' (*a-sngon*) for the sky, 'the square' (*gru-bzhi*) for the earth or a seat, 'the narrow one' (*dog-mo*) for the earth, 'white muzzle' for the kyang, 'white breast' for an eagle, 'little speckled one' for the eye, 'triple strength' for a young lion, 'sixfold smile' for the tiger or a strong man's body, and many others. These epithets do sometimes accompany the ordinary term, in apposition, but often they denote the object referred to on their own, and any one ignorant of this picturesque language is left in the dark. Of course his prospects are even blacker with the other epithets that are untranslatable, either because their meaning has been lost—words from some dialect or foreign language?—or because they never had a meaning, and have been purely descriptive words from the start. Here are a few specimens: *tshe-tshe*, the goat; *bre-se* the wild yak; *sa-le*, the female yak (*'bri-mo*); *mdo-ba* or *'do-ba*, the excellent horse (in the epic; but in the Tun-huang manuscripts, this word is applied to the yak as well as the horse); *de-bo*, the cock; *co-rong*, the ass.

The task of assimilation

What came of all this? The people evidently continued as before to cherish the tradition of songs and talking matches, especially at the great festivals where opposing groups took part in contests; but folk literature, being purely oral in its transmission, is naturally unknown to us, except in the modern period. The only ancient poetic compositions to have been written down and preserved are the work of monks, since education was limited to this class.

Now some of these monks thought that the best means of propagating Buddhism among the people was to incorporate it within the framework of popular literature, prose as well as verse. We have seen that even the ancient kings took care to preserve native traditions in order to use them as a mould, so to speak, in which to pour the concepts of the new religion. A Tun-huang manuscript (Pelliot 239) provides early evidence for this policy of assimilation. In it, a Bonpo funeral rite is interpreted and adapted in the light of Buddhist beliefs.

We have no information about the way in which the alternating songs and the riddles (*lde'u*) were transmitted. We can only observe that they have survived in marriage songs and colloquies, and it may be supposed that they have left their mark in the use of metaphors and epithets, in circumlocution, in rhythmic alternation and in formulae of introduction. The poet saints, as I have shown, may have combined the epithets with the secret parlance of Tantric songs. What is quite certain is that the authors of songs, epic and drama, all of them monks, seized the opportunity offered by the symbolic interpretation of native expressions and actions to slip Buddhist teachings into works available to the public at large. One and the same word—*brda*—means 'sign', 'gesture', 'symbol' and 'word'. It thus continually comes up, along with the word 'mark' (*rtags*) in symbolic explanations. In a Karma-pa song,[1] where the hare is introduced as a yogin, we read: 'The fact that he has two long ears: aspect of the mystic union of Method (*upāya*) and Wisdom (*prajñā*), sign (or symbol) that he has entered the path to salvation.' The same symbolic explanation, with the same use of the word 'sign', is found in the epic, where it is applied to the bard's hat, with its long ass's ears. Mila Rêpa explains his hat and staff in analogous fashion. And he applies the same technique to natural images as well:

> 'Tise, the icy mountain far renowned,
> Its head is covered up with snow; and this
> Stands for the whiteness of the Buddha's doctrine.'

Gomo-pa, another poet of the same Kagyü-pa order—in which songs and dances were especially pursued—portrays a ferry-boat on the River Tsangpo in similar style.

But it is in the literature of tales and maxims that the process of

---

[1] 132, f. 213*b*. A Bonpo example occurs in *mDzod-phug*, Commentary, p. 7.

adaptation can best be followed. Witness the collections of tales, songs and imagery under the ancient kings. These unquestionably offered a framework into which Buddhist writers were able to insert Indian stories. In the eleventh century the old tales (*sgrung*) gave birth to an edifying literature of anecdotes and moral maxims, bearing the same name as the old collections—'calf's flask', i.e. 'cow's udder' (*be'u-bum*). They were also known as 'mind exercises'

FIG. 16. Ferry-boat on the Tsangpo. Horse's head and beflagged tree-branches at the prow.

(*blo-sbyong*). This literature is still almost unexplored. But we know that Bonpo *be'u-bum* exist today and that there was once, for example, a *be'u-bum* of the god Vaiśravaṇa, which related his origin:[1] it may be that this last work has links with an epic that pitted Vaiśravaṇa against Pehar (*Pe-har ar-la gtad-pa'i lo-rgyus*), but we only know of it through a few allusions. The 'Mind exercises' (*blo-sbyong*) are more familiar. They are typical of the first great Kadam-pa authors.

[1] 162, *YA*, ff. 7*b*–8*a*.

The founder of the order, Atiśa (982–1054, in Tibet from 1042), helped spread the Indian collection of the 'Twenty-five Vetāla tales' (*ro-sgrung*). The narrative framework of this collection had first been converted—perhaps while still in India?—from a Brahmanic to a Buddhist one, by giving the main part to Nāgārjuna, whom tradition credits with the authorship of many works of literature (drama, etc.). After that, the Indian legends were progressively ousted by Tibetan legends. The indigenous tale of Masang, which nowadays forms the third tale in the Mongol and Tibetan versions, once existed in its own right.[1] Successive disciples of the Kadam-pa school continued to produce literary works. In the eleventh century Poto-pa wrote his 'Maxims' (*dpe-chos*, 'religion in parables'). This short treatise was followed by commentaries explaining the allusions to tales, which they tell in full, and claiming to belong to the 'oral tradition' (*sñan-brgyud*). Early in the twelfth century, Shang Pa-tsap Nyima-trak translated and adapted Indian śāstras, while his disciple Sheugang-pa translated tales which have become plays today. In the thirteenth century, the famous Nyingma-pa saint Guru Chhöwang (1212–1273), the great 'discoverer of concealed texts', had in his youth learnt śāstras on song and dance, royal genealogies and ancestral legends of the house of De.[2] He is supposed, too, to have written legends for strolling storytellers (*ma-ṇi-pa*) and directions for the masked dances ('*cham*).

A little later in the same period, Sakya Paṇḍita (1182–1251) wrote a collection of moral precepts in verse which has been imitated by other people and was translated into Mongol. It too is accompanied by a commentary giving, in detail, the tales and anecdotes to which the stanzas make only a brief allusion. Because its author was more of a scholar than a poet and thoroughly imbued with Indian tradition, this work, widespread and much quoted in Tibet, has a different flavour from the Karma-pa and Kagyü-pa poets, who have stayed closer to folk tradition.[3]

> '(29) He who is not made glad by praise, nor saddened by insulting words,
>   Who well abides in what he knows,
>   A holy man is, that's the sign.'

[1] 171, *KHA*, f. 397, chap. XX; 142, *JA*, ff. 8*b*–9*a*.
[2] 162, *RA*, f. 2*a–b*; 162, *ZA*, ff. 3*b*–4*a*; 142, *THA*, f. 55.
[3] 164.

'(36) A great man's counsel, carried out with effort,
Is ruined by the wicked in an instant.
A field that's cultivated for a year,
Hail lowers it to dust within an instant.'

'(37) Its own defects, the throng of evil-doers
Ascribes to others, whomsoever they be.
Its beak, which it plunges in ordure,
The crow wipes on a pure object.'

The metre is always trochaic, in lines of three-and-a-half feet, i.e.
seven syllables, and four lines to the stanza. Sakya Paṇḍita's pattern,
for both prosody and content, was a collection of quatrains by
Nāgārjuna which had been translated into Tibetan (*Shes-rab sdong-
bu: Prajñādaṇḍa*). This genre of moralistic stanzas was maintained
and developed, as for instance in the '*Water Śāstra*' (*Legs-par
bshad-pa chu-yi bstan-bcos*) by the Ninth Panchen Lama (1882–1937)
and the '*Story of the Monkeys and the Birds*' (*Bya sprel gyi gtam-
rgyud*) by the Eleventh Dalai Lama (1838–1855). In the last-named
work, however, the stanzas are put into the mouths of various inter-
locutors, and their verse dialogues are connected by a prose narrative,
as is the case in the plays. It is an allegory of the war between the
Tibetans (birds) and Gurkhas (monkeys) at the close of the eighteenth
century. The tradition of wise adages is allied to that of animal fables
(the wise or crafty hare, etc.). In other works of the same type, the
prosody is different, as in the *Kha-che pha-lu* which uses trochees in
lines of four-and-a-half feet. Lastly, in some of these śāstras the
dialogue is in prose, as in the '*Disputation between the goddesses of
Tea and Beer*' (*Ja chang lha-mo'i rtsod-gleng bstan-bcos*), in which
each boasts of the qualities of her respective beverage and accuses
the other's of every misdeed. But we only know this work from a
recent publication, and it is possible that it originally took the form
of alternating songs linked by a prose text. The same topic was
treated by one of the T'ang dynasty Chinese 'ballads' (*pien-wên*), in
the colloquial language, which were found among the Tun-huang
manuscripts.

As far as we can say in the present state of our knowledge, there
has strictly speaking been no development or innovation since the
eleventh and twelfth century period of adaptation. From that date
onwards, we find side by side one style that is nearer to the

indigenous tradition, in spite of adaptation, and another more learned or pedantic one of Indian inspiration.

Sakya Paṇḍita's *Maxims* are, indeed, in the tradition of collections of proverbial wisdom going back to the ancient period, but the style is closely modelled on that of Nāgārjuna. Alongside this type of work the ancient maxim tradition has also been maintained in more popular or indigenous surroundings. An epic-type chronicle,[1] probably written about 1400, adduces a whole series of adages, which are introduced as the teaching of the 'religion of men' (*mi-chos*). It is the elders of the group who enunciate them, in the course of one of those gatherings at which the 'easy tongues' or 'clever mouths', the good rhetoricians, indulge in talking-matches. The metre of these sayings is not the ancient dactyl, but it is not uniformly the three-and-a-half foot trochaic one, either. By contrasting a series of lines in three feet (‒◡‒◡‒◡), first, with a parallel series in two-and-a-half feet (‒◡‒◡—), the rhythm is made quicker and livelier. To add further emphasis, an interrogative form in the first series is answered by an imperative in the second. Only at the end, to round it off, does the three-and-a-half foot line make its appearance:

> khê-pa rang-yang e-yin? dün-ma e-khê tö!
> dün-ma sü-la ma-tong, mi-yi sam-tsö tö!
> ‒◡   ‒◡ ‒◡   ‒◡ ‒◡   —
>
> . . . .
> rang-la yö-na di-nam gö
> yi-la sung-tang khor-wa yong
> ‒◡ ‒◡   ‒◡   —

—of which we may venture the following translation:

'Watch how a worthy man behaves!
Is he really a wise man? See if he's wise in counsel!
Can he really talk? At the end of his speech may one be without regret!
Is he really a rich man? Having amassed, may he know how to give!'

The Nyingma-pa saint who drew up these maxims concludes:

[1] 180, f. 33*a*.

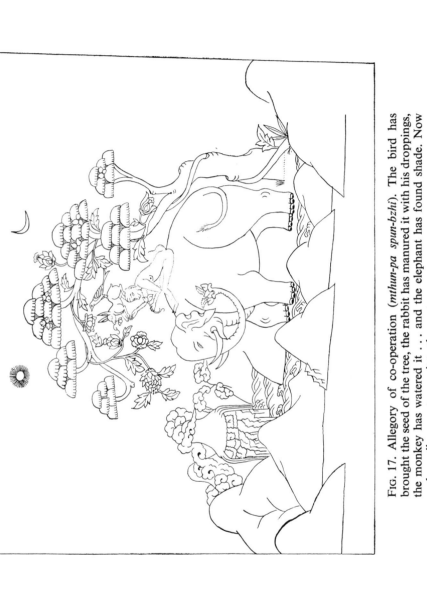

Fig. 17. Allegory of co-operation (*mthun-pa spun-bzhi*). The bird has brought the seed of the tree, the rabbit has manured it with his droppings, the monkey has watered it . . . and the elephant has found shade. Now each ascribes greater merit to the next.

'If you claim to be it, that's what you lack.
Bear it in mind! Me, I'm off a-wandering,
I'm going to move house this instant.'

Mila Rêpa, we recall, ended one of his songs on a similar note.

The three-footed line has a distinctly more popular air than that of three-and-a-half feet. We meet it again in the symbolic songs of the 'white demon' (*'dre-dkar*), a kind of jester wearing a yogin's mask who sings auspicious wishes at the New Year: 'A cowrie fastened on the nose, that's the way of *tshe-tshe* the goat.' A great author took up this metre, in love songs of undoubted folk inspiration. This was the Sixth Dalai Lama, noted for a seemingly rakish life. The Tibetans accepted his behaviour, explaining it as that of a Tantrist who knows how to make use of sexual techniques:

'A goose has fallen in love with the marsh;
She would like to stay there a while.
But on the lake, the ice has formed,
And her spirit is downcast.'[1]

It is odd, and worthy of interest, that authors who are really well known and loved in Tibet—outside the small circle of learned monks—make their appearance as saints of a very peculiar kind, their paradoxical and unconventional behaviour making it easy for them to link up with the living springs of popular tradition, which was trained to become their mouthpiece. I have already referred to a few cases, and we shall see them at work again. Such saints belong to the non-reformed orders, especially the Nyingma-pa and Kagyü-pa, and we shall shortly be seeing how they come to play such a part in poetic creativity.

Seers and poets

Mila Rêpa, Drukpa Künlek and other poet saints of the Kagyü-pa order are depicted singing, and holding their right hand to their ear. The same gesture is characteristic of the epic hero, when identified with the bard or when receiving revelations from the gods. The gesture expresses both religious and poetic inspiration in the saints' case, too, at the same time symbolizing their receipt of the oral transmission (*snyan-brgyud*). They sometimes wear a white robe and

[1] 130, pp. 60–61.

hat, and carry a staff decorated with numerous objects which they explain symbolically in their songs. The same applies to the hero when he functions as a bard or minstrel. Like the real bard nowadays, he wears a white three-pointed hat topped with feathers and adorned with various symbolic objects. Two of its points represent the long ears of the wonderful horse that takes after the kyang (wild ass) and donkey. The white hat and clothing, like the feathers on the hat, also occur among Bonpos, and Nyingma-pa saints specializing in the 'discovery of treasures' i.e. revealed texts. It will be remembered that a Bonpo master, whose distinction it was to have been abducted and initiated by demons, possessed ass's ears which he hid under a turban.

Attention is again drawn to such facts, because of the connection between the meaning of the symbolism involved and the poetic and religious inspiration of these related figures. Their peculiar kind of 'horse' is, in fact, the steed that carries both seer and poet on their mystic trips. The Bonpo's 'horse' is the drum which he bestrides, sounding his hand-drum with its little bells the while. The hero's, and the bard's, is his staff or hobby-horse. The 'hobby' is no longer adorned with a horse's head, but its ears are on the hat. Moreover, corresponding to the drum the Bonpo uses as a horse, strolling actors, singers and buffoons have a stringed instrument with its own horse's head (sometimes altered to the head of a dragon or *makara* sea-monster, because these animals are akin to the horse). And the patron of their profession is none other than the poet and singer Mila Rêpa. He and other poet saints, and the epic bard, do not accompany themselves on musical instruments. But they sing, and it is the tune to which the songs are set that is known as their 'horse'. Often we find Drukpa Künlek imitating popular songs upon the 'melodic horse' (*dbyangs-rta*) of such-and-such a region, e.g. Tsongkha or Kongpo. One day, when asked to sing an invocation to the gods 'he sang thus, with his drum, riding the *horse* of the Bonpos'.

These performances well illustrate the kinship of poetic creation and mystic inspiration, as found among the shamans of North-East Asia. We have already noted (page 188) that the bard who sings the epic goes into a trance induced and built up in the same way as the evocation or 'realizing' of a deity through meditation. A deity or a hero in the epic may speak through the mouth of a medium-bard, or else the bard may see and hear them in a world of their own where they maintain a potential existence, so to say, outside time and place.

This kind of separate world is presented in Lamaism as an inexhaustible repository from which representations of every kind can be drawn as required, some already known and classified, others, if need be, entirely new. It is called the 'granary (or store-house) of the sky' (*nam-mkha' mdzod*) or 'treasury of the mind (or of thought)' (*dgongs-gter*). That which is taken out of it—through meditation, trance or poetic ecstasy—is the actual object of mental creation, vision, or poetic composition. Though familiar images already codified in the current pantheon are often materialized from it, re-created each time on a ready-made pattern, a new representation never previously revealed may also be 'discovered' there. Thus the seventeenth-century visionary Mingyur Dorje 'draws from the treasury' unknown alphabets, such as that of Uḍḍiyāna,[1] which he subsequently reproduces in his work: he copies them down, if we may put it like that, from his vision. He also has countless dreams, visions or meditation results, and draws on these for novel ritual texts which amount to creative works of literature. The same phenomenon occurs, as we shall see, in painting. We have already encountered another, more famous, 'finder of treasures' (*gter-bton* or -*ston*), Guru Chhöwang, as the author of a masked-dance libretto and narratives for strolling storytellers. Others have done the same thing, and we know their names. The treasures they discover are only 'new' in the eyes of the profane, who were hitherto ignorant of the forms revealed. Actually, they find them ready-made in Padmasambhava's paradise, having gone there in a dream, trance or meditation, and there seen some of the athlete-dancers who populate that place.

The 'Mind treasury' is not the only source used by the 'finders of treasures', either. They also discover real treasures, hidden in caves, in the shape of manuscripts whose description as 'rolls of yellow paper' (*shog-dril ser-po*) exactly matches the appearance of ancient writings found in the Tun-huang cave. Some of these texts are supposed to have been written or revealed, earlier, by Padmasambhava or a god. Whichever it was, hid them to await 'discovery' by a pre-destined individual. The critical historian would regard them as apocrypha, composed, hidden and intentionally rediscovered by

[1] 156, *DA*, f. 55a.

authors wishing to give a religious lustre to their work. But actual ancient manuscripts may very well have been discovered in this fashion, for the 'finders' had a great predilection for the excavation of caves and other hiding places. Such texts may then have been edited to suit contemporary taste. The books of rites devoted to the gods of the soil (*bsangs*), as it happens, are regarded as having been revealed by Padmasambhava. And we have seen how they have retained genuinely ancient features which are also found in Tunhuang manuscripts. Some of the most remarkable and, in Tibet, best-known works of Tibetan literature are supposed to be discovered 'treasures' (*gter-ma*) of this kind. In some cases, notably the *bKa'-thang sde-lnga* and the *Padma thang-yig*—which celebrate Padmasambhava's life and times—they are written in verse, which is often very obscure. They certainly contain ancient material, going back far earlier than their 'discovery' in the mid-fourteenth century, though much altered and overlaid.

We thus glimpse one of the sources of classical literary authorship. The works which stand out most distinctively for their Tibetan character, and for their lack of pedantry or learned imitation of Indian patterns, are by authors who were able in one way or another to keep in touch with the living indigenous tradition. One of the *bKa'-thang sde-lnga*'s five parts, the 'Memorial of the Queens' (*bTsun-mo bka'-thang*), contains not only numerous songs and epic motifs—like the horse that weeps when he has to leave his master— but a whole Potiphar romance. The queen takes a fancy to the holy monk Vairocana, and lures him to her, but the saint rejects her advances. Vexed, the queen pretends to have been ravished and gets the king to send the saint into exile. But he revenges himself by magically sending her leprosy, and has to be recalled to cure it. Another work in the category of 'revealed treasures', the *Ma-ṇi bka'-'bum*, contains the story of King Songtsen Gampo's marriage to the two princesses, and the adventures of the minister Gar, some episodes of which are also found in the present-day epic.

The poet saints and 'finders of treasures', both Kagyü-pa and Nyingma-pa, are quite unlike the learned authors in their nonconformity to organized religion, their paradoxical attitudes and roving life. They like to call themselves 'madmen' (*smyon-pa*), and it is by this name that they are known and loved by the people. We have already glanced at their quizzical approach and their criticisms and gibes at the excesses of the great (page 153). These attitudes explain the two sources of literary creativity we have just been discussing: on the one hand, their rapture or 'madman'-like inspiration which gives access to the 'treasury of the mind'; on the other, their knowledge of the traditions, songs and poetry of the people, whose life they like to share.

The epic is said to have been composed and sung one day, at a single sitting, by a Nyingma-pa adept in a state of intoxication. The author of the play 'Norsang', in the colophon, calls himself Tshering Wangdü, the 'madman' of Dingchen, and he adds that he has merely uttered senseless words and jokes. Orgyen Lingpa, the discoverer of the *bKa'-thang sde-lnga*, if famed, according to the colophon, under the title 'madman of the treasures' (*gter-smyon*). And just as 'mad' Mila Rêpa has become the patron of strolling comedians and actors, the god and patron of the theatre is the Nyingma-pa saint Thangtong Gyelpo, also known as 'the madman of the empty land' (*lung-stong smyon-pa*).[1]

Remarkably enough, the author of the biographies of Mila Rêpa and Marpa, who usually hides behind the pseudonym 'yogin who roams in the cemeteries', is one Heruka, the 'madman' of Tsang (fourteenth century).[2] Now these two biographies, which are exceptionally famous and well-loved among Tibetans, are distinguished from many other, quite boring and pedantic, works by their near-colloquial language, their lively style, and above all the interest they take in countless details of real life. It is just this communion of the 'mad' saints with popular sources of inspiration that made them the greatest creators of Tibetan literature.

Mime, drama and epic

The masked dances have no words. They are mimes accompanied by music. Although purely ritual, they are artistic creations none the less—masterpieces of production and choreography. The steps are laid down in every last detail, and the cast is directed by a monk who acts as dancing-master ('*cham-dpon*): he stands at the centre of the ring and is distinguishable by the stick wrapped in ribbons which he holds. The order of appearance of the characters, the steps and

[1] 135, f. 36*b*.
[2] 133, Colophon.

gestures, together with the passages in ritual texts corresponding to successive phases of the mime, are laid down in dance scripts ('*cham-yig*). Some of these have been written by great spiritual leaders like the Fifth Dalai Lama and Mingyur Dorje. Besides the ritual dances properly so called, an episode from Mila Rêpa's life—the conversion of the hunter—or skits on theological disputations may be staged. In the intervals a lot of improvised clowning takes place.

Plays are purely recreational, although their subjects are nearly all edifying and religious. But, as we already know, the performance possesses a religious value in itself. It gladdens the god of the soil and thus guarantees the crops. The god of drama is worshipped at the centre of the 'stage', where an altar is erected, surrounded by trees. The god is the saint Thangtong Gyelpo, portrayed as an elderly man with a white beard. According to the legend he was born old, having spent sixty, five hundred or eight hundred years in his mother's womb. On coming into the world, his task was to overcome the 'nine united evils' and to supply the 'ten united goods'. He is said to be the originator of theatrical performances, because of the curious way he subdued a demon locked up inside a stone: he put in an appearance at the market, reproducing himself six times in 'madman's' gear, and gave a display of pranks there which drew certain old men, who arrived riding staves as hobby-horses. Accordingly, every performance of a play begins with the dance of the six 'singers of good wishes' (*bkra-shis zhol-pa*). They wear the triangular mask of the 'hunter' (*rngon-pa*) who, despite his name, represents a rollicking yogin. Another function of the 'hunter' is that of narrator, linking together the sung dialogue with an account of the framework of the story; but he also acts the clown, whilst the narrator may be a simple monk. The name of this character comes from the play 'Norsang' (an adaptation of the *Sudhana-jātaka*), where the 'hunter' or rather 'fisherman', an incarnation of Vajrapāṇi, is given a jewel by a nāgī or captures a celestial fairy. The latter is played by an actress or dancing girl, wearing a five-panelled crown, with large rosettes at her ears: she gives the drama its popular name of 'ache lhamo', 'sister goddess'. A third character, unmasked but wearing an odd yellow hat (the 'gyalu'), usually joins the other two, but his role is a mystery. Each of the three characters has his 'biography' (*rnam-thar*), a kind of recital of his origin that has to be sung before the performance. But these three actors are not part of the actual play.

They often form a team of itinerant showmen. In a real theatrical performance, their exhibition only serves as prologue.

The subjects of the plays are largely the same as those drawn upon by the strolling storytellers (*ma-ṇi-pa*), who show the episodes on a painting at the same time as they are singing their story. Some ten or so plays have been noted. Some of them are simply adaptations of famous Buddhist 'birth stories' (such as the Viśvantara and Sudhana *jātakas*) with their setting removed to Tibet. Others are a kind of Lamaic *jātaka* relating the former lives of certain great Lamas. One (the *rGya-bza' Bal-bza'*) commemorates Songtsen Gampo's marriage to the Chinese and Nepalese princesses, taking its plot from an identically named romance found in the *Ma-ṇi bka'-'bum*. Nothing whatever is known about their authors and dates of composition, apart from the name of the author of 'Norsang'— the 'madman' of Dingchen. Concerning the history of the drama, all we know is that New Year plays were already being enacted at the court of the Seventh Karma-pa hierarch (1454–1506): they included performances of *jātakas* of the Buddha, stories of great magicians (*siddha*), universal kings (*cakravartin*), rulers of great countries (such as China, Tibet, or Hor), the fight between the *devas* and *asuras*, and Indra with the guardian gods of the four directions (the *lokapālas*).[1]

The structure of the drama seems to be of Indian origin: the benediction at the beginning of the play, the narrator introducing the actors and relating in prose the circumstances into which the songs fit (*mdo-'dzin-pa*, Sanskrit *sūtradhāra*). But the style of song, the make-up, the formalized gestures and the minor parts seem much closer to Chinese opera.

The epic has some similarities, particularly in style, with the plays.[2] Its verse songs, which are usually very long, are the main point. The prose narrative, by contrast, is always brief and merely provides a setting for the songs. The two elements are distinguished by two forms of handwriting in the manuscripts. During recitation, the narrative text is chanted rapidly on a single note, whilst the songs are

[1] 142, *PA*, f. 122*b*.
[2] 78A.

set to a limited number of melodies which seem to mark situations and sentiments (anger, joy, triumph, sadness, etc.) rather than different characters in the story. Two schools of singing are known, the Kham and Hor styles; and the selfsame song may be sung in either. We have already seen what modes of stylistic expression were available: metaphors, symbolic interpretation of actions and objects, introduction by means of the 'Do you know me?' formula, and proverbs. All these techniques were common to every species of folk poetry. They allow a certain freedom to improvise on given themes. Composition by means of set phrases explains how the numerous chapters or stories making up the epic are all written in a uniform, homogeneous way, so that it would be impossible to classify or date them on stylistic criteria. And yet, to our certain knowledge new chapters were continually added, as they are to this day. The twenty-five chapters, or more, at present known represent more than ten thousand manuscript pages, of eight to twelve lines each. What the primitive nucleus is we do not know; and there is no clue to the date and author of the original composition.

For the epic does form a unity distinct from all the rest of literature. It *is* a single work, the creation of one author or compiler. But, of course, it contains all kinds of elements antedating that creation and made use of by that author. They are sometimes simply motifs, sometimes subject-matter, and sometimes whole episodes which occur in quite different contexts elsewhere. Yet the story of the hero and his country, taken as a whole, is quite unique and is found nowhere else. The basic cycle is set in Amdo and northern Kham and seems to have had an independent existence since the early fifteenth or late fourteenth century, before being incorporated in a larger work compiled by a monk. We know, indeed, that the state of Ling, where the hero Gesar was born, actually existed in Kham or Amdo as far back as the late fourteenth century, if not before. We know too that, in the modern period, the kings of that country claimed descent from Gesar's half-brother. A minor epic cycle must have been coupled with ancestral legends of the country or its nobility. The names of the present epic's principal heroes and some of the magical objects they own are mentioned in the genealogy of the Lang clan, whose final compilation may have taken place about 1400, though its contents are undoubtedly older.

But the very name of the hero and the central theme of the present epic come from another epic cycle, older and unlocalized, of which we unfortunately only know fragments. It is attested as early as the eleventh century, and notably in a song by Mila Rêpa. It was an elaboration in story form of the old Buddhist concept of the Four Sons of Heaven, i.e. rulers or representatives of the four great countries of the Asiatic world—China, India, Iran and the northern barbarians. Gesar was the King of Trhom (*Phrom*) and stood for armies and the north. Now 'Gesar' is certainly derived from the title 'kaisar' (Caesar), and Trhom from the place-name Rūm for Byzantium or Anatolia, the ancient Rome of the Near East. How this early cycle came to be tied up with the kingdom of Ling in Kham and its local cycle is a problem. But one thing that is certain is that, in the epic, the place-name Ling is taken as an abbreviation of the term denoting the whole world ('*dzam-gling*: Jambudvīpa), of which the hero is ruler. Here, then, is the gist of his story.

Everything is going badly on earth because men have no leader. They get one by compelling a sky god to send one of his sons to earth in gratitude for help given him by an elder of the country when he was fighting against a demon. The hero's conception and miraculous birth are the work of a father who is both a sky god and a sacred mountain, and a mother who is a deity of the watery subsoil. All these topics are found in various Tibetan ancestral legends, both of the kings and of great clans (e.g. the house of Lang), as well as in ancient tales like that of Masang. The primitive tribes that play a part in those legends are also the same as in the epic. In the latter the hero's life is divided into two parts; and here begins the difference. The parts are so dissimilar that the hero even bears a different name in each of them. In his youth, he is Joru, an ugly snotty-nosed lad, mischievous to the point of wickedness, unruly, but divine by nature and possessing supernatural powers. His great antagonist is his paternal uncle, cowardly, vain and pretentious, who hopes to rule the country. The hero is banished with his mother, but his exile enables him to build up hidden strength. His horse shares his fate and his foul appearance. It also assures his victory in a horse-race, whose winner is to become the country's king. That is the end of the hero's youth (at thirteen or fifteen years of age): the end too of his trials. Thereafter he is the glorious king, the warrior clothed in helmet and armour, and from that time he takes the name of Gesar, King, Great Lion of the World. And so begins the second part, devoted to the subjugation of sundry demons and kings of countries all over the world.

ART

The growing interest in Tibetan sculpture and painting nowadays is clearly due as much to their religious subject-matter as to their aesthetic value. What is known to us of those arts is almost exclusively religious, for religion pervades art even more than literature. The painters and sculptors are often monks, and their names mean 'depictors of deities' (*lha-'bri-pa*) or 'makers of deities' (*lha-bzo-pa*); they are regarded as humble craftsmen, and not as individual creators. Apart from a few monks, remembered for reasons unconnected with their art, only a few obscure names have been preserved for us, on fifteenth-century frescoes. The Tibetans tell us nothing, throughout their history, of any eminent painter, any remarkable or famous work of art, nor are their paintings and sculptures ever signed. Some of the monks painted in addition to writing. We are told that the Tenth Karma-pa (1604–1674) was already a good painter and sculptor at the age of eight. He learnt the pattern in Tsang for the painted representations of Kalāpa, capital of the mystic land of Śambhala. The famous ecclesiastic Phagmotru-pa also did some painting, around 1119.[1]

Ritual requirements

We should not conclude that the products of these craftsmen fall short of being works of art, for all their creators' humility and religious preoccupations. Tibetans are certainly capable of evaluating the quality or execution of a work aesthetically. But it is above all the religious subject they are interested in. So we miss the whole point, of some of the paintings at any rate, if we admire composition and colours that are not due to the painter's free choice but imposed on him by textbooks of ritual. The maṇḍalas, for instance, whose well-ordered symmetry would delight a town-planner, are likely to give the European beholder an impression of stylistic elegance or an aesthetic satisfaction that were not intended by the artist, and are not felt by a Tibetan audience. It is the same with the colours, gestures and attributes of various deities which are all carefully laid down in books.

[1] 132, f. 169b and 172b; 142, *NA*, f. 38b.

The reason for this dependence on ritual texts is that pictorial representation is a religious act, in the same way as mental creation when meditating. We have already met with cases where the subject depicted becomes actually present through its representation. Somewhat after the fashion of the 'Heavenly Questions' addressed, in ancient China, to pictures, we find the Eighth Karma-pa questioning a Mañjuśrī painted in fresco . . . and receiving answers which amount to revelations.[1] As in the poetic type of creation used by the bard, the deity must be conjured up in meditation before being painted, unless of course it is first seen in a dream and then painted accordingly. The great 'finder of treasures' Mingyur Dorje painted in that way, just as, also, he made notes of a deity's secret biography in a dream, or took down the text at his dictation.[2] It is this process which explains the proliferation of iconographic variants on a single subject. Meditative creation is manifold by its very nature, and is reflected in poetic or artistic creation.

The need to create the deity exactly as required by the ritual code, sprung from meditation, underlies the realism characterizing these works of art, a realism that stops at nothing. The statues are clothed and adorned with real precious stones. Where the deity's meaning or function demands, the sexual organ is deliberately emphasized, as in Yama's case and that of the ḍākinīs. The willingness to go so far with realism is probably distinctive. For whereas their Indian and Nepalese models depicted mystical union with the 'Mother' and the sexual meditation techniques (page 170) by representing the consort seated on the god's hip, thus contenting themselves with a vague allusion, the Tibetans made a very real and visible representation of his male organ penetrating the female organ. Some statues are even made in two movable parts fitting into one another. The fact that these images are often hidden behind a veil changes nothing—quite the contrary. Even when they are not meant to be seen these details must be there, in all their precision, to ensure the reality of the divine presence. This realism dominates all representations of deities and demons, whether pictures, sculptures, or masks to be worn. Even where the grotesque or terrifying may seem expressionistic to us, we only have to do with codified iconography which has settled the actual appearance of the figures of the pantheon once and for all.

[1] 142, *PA*, f. 219*a*.
[2] 156, *MĀ*, ff. 97*a*, 107*b*, 97*b* and 91*a*.

ART

Art-forms and styles

Even this iconography has its stylistic varieties, in the treatment of facial features, clothing, appurtenances and background landscapes. Yet there are very few of them. They are not created by great artists individually but represent styles from foreign countries surviving in Tibet, sometimes alone, sometimes in combination. Once we have noted the Indian style, with its variants from Nepal and Kashmir, the Khotanese style from Central Asia, and the Chinese style, we have exhausted the possibilities. The earlier a work of art is, the closer it tends to be to India, whilst Chinese influence has usually asserted itself, or at least joined with the other two styles, in work of recent centuries.

Syncretism, or simply using different styles side by side, has never shocked the Tibetans. An attempt was even made, in the beginning at least, to combine styles from the great neighbouring countries, whose cultures they were aware of borrowing, with the Tibetan style, just as the fusion of Buddhist tales with indigenous tradition had been encouraged. When Samyê temple was built, the lower part is said to have been done in the Tibetan manner, the middle with a Chinese roof and the upper part with an Indian roof. The Chinese roof was allegedly built without walls or pillars:[1] though hard to picture, the design might have been inspired by Chinese ideas about the 'Ming-t'ang'. The same tradition also claims that a castle built by King Mutik Tsenpo south-east of Samyê had nine turrets and three floors. The ground floor, it states, was Tibetan; the two-roofed first floor, in the style of Khotan, was built by Khotanese carpenters; the second, in Chinese style, by Chinese carpenters (with three roofs); and the third, in Indian style, by Indian carpenters (also with three roofs).[1] The description, from an obscurely-phrased chronicle of the 'revealed' type, seems scarcely possible, but it must be admitted that many buildings, such as the Lhasa Jokhang and the Potala, do combine a Chinese roof with purely Tibetan architecture. The combination of three styles described in the chronicle was probably more in evidence on the frescoes with which the temple was adorned representing, *inter alia*, the whole assembly at the feast of consecration, together with the principal countries.[2] In any case,

[1] 177, ff. 66*b*, 71*a*; 177, f. 72*b*.
[2] 177, ff. 69*b*–72*a*; 183, pp. 48–49.

another chronicle clearly refers to the three styles as those of the statues of deities situated on the three floors respectively.[1] The basis of these somewhat contradictory accounts was probably a relatively early source.[2] From it, we learn that at first the question was one of making statues for the shrine of Tārā or Āryāpalo. The teacher Bodhisatva, i.e. Śāntarakṣita, wished the Indian style to be adopted, but the king preferred the Tibetan style. Then a handsome man from the Khu clan was taken as the model for the statue of Āryāpalo, and two fair ladies from the Chogro clan as models for the statues of Mārīcī and Tārā. Was the style as Tibetan as the models? We do not know, but we are later told of other statues in Tibetan, Chinese or Indian style.

We hear in another connection of artists who must have been responsible for the third foreign style recognized in Tibetan art, that of Central Asia. Wishing to build a temple, King Trhitsuk Detsen invited skilled craftsmen (*bzo-ba*) from India, China, Nepal, Kashmir, Khotan and Tibet. But he was especially impressed by what he had heard of a craftsman in Khotan, who had come to be known as the 'Khotan King of Works' (*Li spyod-pa'i rgyal-po*). He asked the King of Khotan to send him, threatening an armed invasion if he refused. The craftsman accordingly came with his three sons to Tibet, where he worked alongside 'stone-workers' (*rdo-bzo, rdo-mkhan*) from Nepal.[3]

The tradition of the Khotanese school was kept going, and Tibetans remained aware of it. At Iwang, in Tsang, fifteenth-century artists themselves record, in written captions, that they followed the fashion of Khotan (*Li-lugs*);[4] the royal type with fine wavy moustache, in portraits of Songtsen Gampo and sometimes of Padmasambhava, and the peculiar way of representing architectural groupings in a sort of bird's eye view, seem to come from this source.

And so, despite the strictness of the ritual directions, even subjects of religious iconography bear the imprint of style. In the portrayal of other subjects, there is of course a good deal of freedom. The

[1] 179, f. 87.
[2] 183, pp. 31, 32, 35.
[3] 183, p. 71.
[4] 120, IV, 1, p. 33.

buffoons' masks representing Indian yogins (atsara) are treated with exceptional liveliness and variety. Tibetan humour and good-natured fun lend them a peculiar charm in which veneration, respect and warm affection for the foreign saint hide behind the laughing mockery to which his grotesque appearance gives rise. Elsewhere, in paintings, the love of nature and animals which has inspired so many songs and poems finds expression in landscapes, forming the background to the large central figure of a composition, or in the numerous scenes that often surround it. As in the pictures of our own fourteenth- or fifteenth-century masters, there are plenty of miniature scenes which bring everyday life and nature humourously and lovingly to mind. Often, even, the scenes are the reason for the paintings' existence. They are biographical illustrations. Thus we have sets of paintings illustrating the lives of great teachers and saints, the Buddha, Shenrap, Mila Rêpa, Gesar, the eighty-four *mahāsiddhas*, Tsongkha-pa and successive incarnations of high-ranking ecclesiastics, such as the Dalai Lama and Panchen Lama for example. There are also sets of tales, *jātakas* of the Buddha and Shenrap, and incidents from plays. Paintings of these types are used in conjunction with a sung or chanted narrative, the storyteller using a stick to point out the scenes on the painting as he goes along. Before circulating in Tibet, this technique of illustrated recitation had been employed by monks in India, China and Japan. As in those countries, the illustrations could be painted in fresco or on portable scrolls. In Tibet, fourteenth-century frescoes illustrating the life of Sudhana (hero of a tale that was adapted as a play), the arhats and the Sakya-pa Lamas, were noted at Gyang, near Lhatse, by Professor Tucci. Frescoes depicting episodes from the sūtra of the Wise Man and the Fool have been described by the Eighth Karma-pa (see page 282). The 'literary' or narrative character of these paintings is emphasized by the presence of captions, sometimes quite long, written under each scene, which serve to identify the figures and episodes and often reproduce the text of a corresponding manual, with a reference number.

It is in the portrayal of famous personages that inspiration has best succeeded in freeing itself from prescriptive codes. Granted, even in this field, the facial features and postures are conventional. The reason, no doubt, is that individual characteristics were thought less important than the codified type of the saint. Also, certain details were often symbolic, as for instance facial expressions—mild or wrathful—or body colour (dark blue for one type of yogin). But sometimes we come across real individual portraits, especially in sculpture. The fact that we know of so few is again because we often lack photographic documentation. Photographs taken in Tibet not many years ago revealed that unsuspected discoveries are still possible.

Intimations of antiquity

What can true Tibetan art have been like before Buddhism, or during the first period of assimilation, from the seventh to the tenth century? Practically nothing is known, but a few traditions and some handicraft products may give an idea.

During the reign of Songtsen Gampo, according to several traditional histories, the old traditions of the storytellers, singers and Bonpos were depicted in sculpture and painting on the pillar capitals, beams and wall-surfaces of the Lhasa 'cathedral' (Jokhang). We are also informed that a collection of drawings or paintings was made, known as the 'Cow's udder (i.e. Collection of tales) of the Forefather', and was deposited in the archives.[1] The Fifth Dalai Lama, too, in the description of that temple which he wrote in 1645–1646, speaks as though the frescoes and sculptures were still in existence at that time. There is doubt on this point, and the temple's restoration by the Fifth Dalai Lama himself must assuredly have entailed stylistic alterations. But photographs recently taken in Tibet showing, for the first time, details of the temple, which was till then barred to photographers, have thrown a sudden unexpected light on the question. Waddell, who visited the temple in 1904, compared the carved wooden pillars in certain niches with the style of the cavetemples of eighth- and ninth-century India. Tucci, in 1948, attributed the pillars and capitals to Nepalese craftsmen and judged them to be earlier than the rest of the temple. The Chinese authors who took the photographs[2] found, for their part, that the great round columns (a score of them) and wooden capitals were in 'Roman style' and might date from the T'ang period, whilst certain frescoes in the first floor ambulatory corridor, badly deteriorated in their colours, were

[1] 179, f. 65*b*; 141, f. 27*a*; 142, *JA*, f. 44*a–b*.
[2] 78.

of T'ang 'Chinese style'. Those impressions may have no great value, but they give an idea of the quite unusual character of these sculptures. The shock is still greater when we see a photograph of a long row of carvings in the round, the ends of beams situated under the entrance portico. They are recumbent lions with human or animal heads: they gave the Chinese photographers the impression of being 'Egyptian' (because of the Sphinx, no doubt), and they might well show the influence of ancient Iran. The tradition of the 'religion of men', it will be remembered, was correlated with the various parts of a lion's body, whilst the religious folklore of the lion unquestionably came from Iran. Future research may one day determine what lies behind these impressions.

Another recent and equally surprising discovery raises fresh problems. It is a group of three large statues (of earth and clay, apparently) representing Songtsen Gampo and his two wives, Chinese and Nepalese. It is preserved in two slightly differing exemplars, one in the 'cathedral' of Lhasa (the Jokhang), the other in the Potala palace. Both, but especially the one at the Potala, show an ethnic type more European than Far Eastern. Their style, too, is found nowhere else in Tibetan painting and sculpture. It seems neither Chinese nor Indian, but rather 'Graeco-Buddhist', and at least one of the female figures strangely resembles a sculpture from late mediaeval Europe. The impression must have been still stronger in the originals since the eyes are blue (the face being covered with a thick layer of gold). The unusualness of these statues struck the Tibetans themselves. They date them as far back as the seventh century, the work of non-human ('phrul) craftsmen. The golden face and blue eyes they explain as characteristic marks of somebody who has attained buddhahood.

There remains one very peculiar style. It is certainly of foreign inspiration in spite of being fairly well acclimatized, though dates and details of the borrowing remain unknown. The style is only known to us through objects of daily use dating from the modern period. The decoration of most handicraft products—carved boxes, vases, etc.—is Chinese (dragons, *yin-yang*, entwined flowers) or Kashmiri. But flint-and-steel pouches, stirrups and sword-scabbards, especially common amongst the Horpas and for the most part manufactured in the Hor country and Derge district, are decorated with animal motifs, reminiscent of the Ordos bronzes and what is known as the 'art of the steppes', 'animal' style or 'Scythian' art: paired animals, back to back but with heads turned rearwards, outlandish creatures that defy identification. Today, such products of this art as are obtainable are pretty sketchily executed as a rule, and the tradition is by now merely a survival. It is hard to get hold of any information about genuinely ancient objects. But what we know of the early settlement of north-eastern Tibet allows us an inkling of how this very old animal style may have been kept alive. Two things inevitably spring to mind here: the fact that 'Lesser Yüeh-chih' (remnants of the Indo-Scyths) were in the region, mingled with Ch'iang tribes; and the cultural features shared by the Tibetans, Hsiung Nu, Scyths and other northern peoples, particularly the use of skulls as drinking cups. Recent Chinese excavations of the tombs of the ancient kingdom of Tien (on the lake at Kunming, in Yünnan), of the last two centuries B.C., prove that this art was already flourishing there. Now that kingdom had close connections with the aboriginal populations spread along the Sino-Tibetan border regions, from Koko Nor to Yünnan. True, the problem of Tibetan animal art is a complex one. Some of its motifs, notably the two-headed bird (eagle?), also occur among objects found in western Tibet, regarded by Tibetans as 'fallen from the sky'. All that is still obscure, but it does go to suggest how far different factors may have contributed to the shaping of Tibetan civilization, even before the introduction of Buddhism.

Epilogue

❧

Many travellers and writers have used words like 'mediaeval' and 'feudal' when describing Tibet. Often it has been just a rather vague expression, but sometimes a pejorative one. We have not the slightest inclination to copy that. A civilization is an objective fact which the historian has no cause, and no right either, to judge, especially in relation to the supposed 'values' of the one he at present belongs to. It is also a whole like an organism whose parts all depend on one another and are not to be graded into a value hierarchy. Would we find a zoologist speaking disapprovingly of snake-venom, or a physiologist taking a prim view of defecation?

With this clear proviso, it is worth bearing in mind that many of the institutional and mental structures of Tibetan civilization resemble those of mediaeval Europe. Of course the term is vague, like feudalism, and a mediaevalist would no doubt take exception. But between the beginning and end of the Middle Ages and perhaps even of the Renaissance, between specifically feudal structures and later institutions that may be left over from them, there is a sufficient margin to allow comparison with Tibetan data, which also range over many centuries and have plainly changed during that long period. The fact remains that, reading the books of Huizinga, Marc Bloch or Lucien Febvre, the Tibetanist might continually note corresponding Tibetan data in the margins; he might insert whole passages from those books into a treatise on Tibetan 'sociology'. He would only need to alter the names, and disregard the dates of course. These are only one's impressions, and it is to be hoped that they can eventually be replaced by exact and well documented studies from both angles.

What we have just said does not mean that Tibetan civilization can be looked upon as just another specimen of institutions that are

EPILOGUE

already familiar to us. Its interest lies precisely in the fact that structures we were used to seeing in European guise now reappear among Far Eastern surroundings, thereby assuming a distinctive form. Granted that structures of this type may also be studied, as they have been, in other great civilizations of the East—like those of China, Japan or India. But I hope this brief book will draw attention to Tibet and the uncommon interest that country offers for human history as a whole.

If, therefore, I find the word 'feudalism' applicable to Tibet, it is not in the pejorative sense of exploitation which modern parlance often lends the term, but in its technical meaning. The word itself was coined in the eighteenth century to describe institutions which had survived from the Middle Ages. As for the system, it has been defined by R. Colbourn in terms of the following five criteria: the essential relationship is that between lord and vassal; political action depends on personal agreements between a limited number of individuals, with political authority treated as a private possession; distinctions of office (military, judiciary, etc.) are relatively few; there is a pronounced hierarchical structure within the aristocracy; and land, the fief, is usually given by the lord in return for certain services.

By and large these criteria do hold for Tibet, if we bear in mind the differences inevitably existing between periods as remote from one another as those of the ancient kings and the Dalai Lamas respectively. However, these feudal-type institutions were counterbalanced in Tibet by other factors which may be summed up as: a principle of cohesion and collectivity in certain groups, and a tribal or communal form of organization.

The opportunities for comparison between seventh to twentieth century Tibet and tenth to sixteenth century Europe extend to other spheres apart from the structure of power and property. It is in the cultural, intellectual and artistic field that they stand out most, and particularly in the enormous part played by organized religion. There, Tibet is the very opposite of China and, in all likelihood, India, too. The Eastern civilization that seems to come closest to Tibet's is probably that of Japan. There have been comparable periods in China but they were the exception rather than the rule. In Japan, comparisons can be made throughout the country's history —until we come to the modern period, of course, when there is a great deal of difference; for whereas Japan was able to adapt rapidly to the modern world, preserving her tradition at the same time, Tibet, unable to do likewise, was brought to a rough breach that could prove fatal for her tradition.

In the cultural field it is plain that, though the structures are alike, the forms are not exactly the same, and it is precisely here that the interest of Tibetan studies lies. Both in Europe and Tibet, a great organized religion was adopted, and it overlaid indigenous systems. But differences between Christianity and Buddhism, and between the religious substrata of East and West naturally decided the details.

I shall not attempt to draw up a list of resemblances here. The reader already familiar with the European past will have done so for himself, and I have occasionally taken the liberty of underlining them. But, in conclusion, I can try to say a word on a point not yet touched on, the most elusive of all—man and his character. This is no easy undertaking for an author who has not had the good fortune to live in Tibet and only knows Tibetans through associating with a few of them outside their country. It takes some temerity, too, to compare Tibetan man with mediaeval or Renaissance man, of whom one can only form an idea through a few works. However, the temptation is great, so strong is the impression that one is dealing with similar types of character. To be sure, there is no question of reducing the variety of individual characters to a single formula. But certain traits are striking, all the same.

What seems most remarkable is a kind of condensing or concentration, a single-minded and hence often extreme character. One might say that feeling and thought are not diluted or dispersed, but sharply focused. Man gives himself up to a feeling all the way, unwaveringly, with a sort of wilful naïvety. He may be very gentle or very violent, very faithful and very crafty or wily. He may be gay, he may like singing, talking and joking. But he can also stubbornly withdraw and turn in on himself, refusing to countenance the contingencies of a world whose reality he denies. When he believes—and believe he does—his faith is deep, whole-hearted, unqualified and engrossing.

It is hard to define character from a mass of individuals; it would be better to try to grasp it in the great saints this man venerated, who can serve to represent a kind of ideal type. Two, or three, kinds of saints may be distinguished. Some are grave and stern; others laugh. The former are thinkers, scholars and moralists, the latter mystics and magicians. The laughter, as a matter of fact, is also of two kinds: the gentle smile or mischievous laugh on the one hand, and the fearsome threatening laugh on the other. The first kind is characteristic of Mila Rêpa, the second of Padmasambhava, the two typical great saints. Thus, those of one sort seem engrossed in the 'silence of the saints' of which Buddhist literature speaks. Others show their superiority, their absolute freedom, their emancipation from every bond by a playful attitude in which goodness blends with roguery. The third and last kind keep the fierce will and tense valour they need for their steep plunges into psychic depths, expressing them in a burst of proud laughter that is likened to the neighing of a horse or the warrior's shout of victory.

There, in a few strokes, is the portrait of Tibetan man. He is no less engaging than the civilization he bears within him. As its last living specimen, still true to the old pattern, he may recall and bring closer to us the typical man of the other great civilizations of Europe and the East. It is not quite too late to listen eagerly to what he has to tell.

Proper Names:
Precise Transliterations*
(together with a few words in common use)

Aku Tömpa = *A-khu sTon-pa.*
Amdo = *A-mdo.*
Amshö = *'Am-shod.*
Asha = *'A-zha.*
Ata Lhamo = *A-stag lha-mo.*
Awa Namsê = *A-ba rnam-gsas.*
Ba = *rBa/sBa.*
Bashe = *sBa-bzhed.*
Batang = *'Ba'-thang.*
Belnön = *sBal-gnon.*
Bere = *Be-re.*
Beri = *Be-ri*
Bhata Hor = *Bha-ṭa hor.*
Bod (Pö) = *Bod.*
Bon (Pön) = *Bon.*
Chakpo-ri = *lCags-po ri.*
Chala = *lCags-la.*
Chamdo = *Chab-mdo.*
Chang = *Byang.*
Changchup Dreköl = *Byang-chub 'dre-bkol.*
Changchup Gyentsen = *Byang-chub rgyal-mtshan.*
Changchup Jungnê = *Byang-chub 'byung-gnas.*
Changchup Ö = *Byang-chub 'od.*
Changyka = *lCang-skya.*
Changthang = *Byang-thang.*
Chatri = *Bya-khri.*
Chayül = *Bya-yul.*
Che = *lCe.*

* See Preface, pp. 16–17.

Chetön = *lCe-ston.*
Chhana = *Phyag-na.*
Chhimphu = *'Chims-phu.*
Chhinga Taktse = *'Phying-ba sTag-rtse.*
Chhökyi Sherap = *Chos-kyi shes-rab.*
Chhödor = *Chos-rdor.*
Chhökyi Wangchuk = *Chos-kyi dbang-phyug.*
Chhöseng = *Chos-seng.*
Chhucham = *Chu-lcam.*
Chitsap Pangtore = *sPyi-tshab Pangs-to-re.*
chö = *gcod.*
Chödzong = *Chos-rdzong* (?).
Chogla = *Cog-la.*
Chogro = *lCog-ro.*
Chonggyê = *'Phyong-rgyas.*
Choni = *Co-ne.*
Chungye = Chonggye?
Dakpo = *Dvags-po.*
Dakpo Gomtsül = *Dvags-po sGom-tshul.*
Dakpo Lharje = *Dvags-po lha-rje.*
Dam = *'Dam.*
De = *lDe.*
Demchok = *bDe-mchog.*
Den = *'Dan.*
Denma Tsemang = *lDan-ma rTse-mang.*
Derge = *sDe-dge/bDe-dge.*
Dingchen = *sDing-chen.*
Dokham = *mDo-Khams.*
Doltog-la = *Dol-stag la.*
Dong = *lDong.*
Dongtong = *lDong-sTong.*
Drang = *'Brang.*
Draya = *Brag-gYab.*
Drêpung = *'Bras-spung.*
Drichu = *'Bri-chu.*
Drigung(-pa) = *'Bri-gung/khung.*
Drigung Rinpoche = *'Bri-gung rin-po-che.*
Drithorek Anu = *'Bri tho-regs A-nu.*
Dro = *'Bro.*

Drogmi = '*Brog-mi.*

Drokpa = '*Brog-pa.*

Dromtön = '*Brom-ston.*

Drongnyen Deru = '*Brong-gnyan lde-ru.*

Drukpa = '*Brug-pa.*

Drukpa Künlek = '*Brug-pa Kun-legs.*

Drusha = '*Bru-zha.*

Dzokchen(-pa) = *rDzogs-chen-pa.*

Dzorge (-nyingma) = *mDzo-dge (rnying-ma).*

Gampo-pa = *sGam-po-pa.*

Ganden (-pa) = *dGa'-ldan (-pa).*

Gar (Trhindring) = *mGar/'Gar Khri-'bring.*

Gara = *rGva-ra.*

Gar Günsa = *sGar dgun-sa.*

Gartok = *sGar-thog.*

Gar Yarsa = *sGar dbyar-sa.*

Gedün Gyatso = *dGe-'dun rgya-mtsho.*

Gedün-trup = *dGe-'dun-grub.*

Geluk-pa = *dGe-lugs-pa.*

Gendzo = *Ge-'dzo, Ger-dzo,* etc.

Gerap-sel = *dGe-rab-gsal.*

Gesar = *Ge-sar.*

Gö = '*Gos.*

Golok = '*Go-log/'Gu-log/mGo-log.*

Gomo = *sGo-mo.*

Gomo-pa = *sGo-mo-pa.*

Gonjo = *Go-'gyo/Gon-gyo.*

Gorum = *sGo-rum.*

Guge = *Gu-ge.*

Guru Chhöwang = *Gu-ru Chos (-kyi) dBang (-phyug).*

Gyamda = ?

Gyang = *rGyang.*

Gyangtho = *rGyang-tho/mtho.*

Gyantse = *rGyal-rtse.*

Gyatsa = *rGya-tsha.*

Gyawo-pa = *(lha-rje) rGya-bo-pa.*

Gyelsê = *rGyal-sras.*

Gyer = *dGyer.*

Hor = *Hor.*

Isho Lek = *I-sho Legs.*
Jamchen Chöje Shakya Yeshe = '*Byams-chen chos-rje Shākya ye-shes.*
Jamyang Chöje Trashi Pelden = '*Jam-dbyangs chos-rje bKra-shis dpal-ldan.*
Jang = '*Jang/lJang.*
Jangtsa Lhawön = '*Jang-tsha lha-dbon.*
Jokhang = *Jo-khang.*
Jorga = *Jo-dga'.*
Kadam-pa = *bKa'-gdams-pa.*
Kagyü-pa = *bKa'-brgyud-pa.*
Kandze = *dKar-mdzes.*
Karma (-pa) = *Karma-pa.*
Karma Lhadeng = *Karma lha-sdeng.*
Karma Pakshi = *Karma Pakṣi.*
Karong = *Ga-rong.*
Karwa = *sKar-ba.*
Kathang De-nga = *bKa'-thang sde-lnga.*
Kathok = *Kaḥ-thog.*
Kêsang Gyatso = *sKal-bzang rgya-mtsho.*
Khache = *Kha-che.*
Khalatse = ?
Kham = *Khams.*
Khê-trup = *mKhas-grub.*
Khön = '*Khon.*
Khorre = '*Khor-re.*
Khu, Khutön = *Khu, Khu-ston.*
Khyunglung (Ngülkhar) = *Khyung-lung (dNgul-mkhar).*
Khyungpo the Yogin (Neljor) = *Khyungpo rnal-'byor.*
Könchok Gyelpo = *dKon-mchog rgyal-po.*
Könchok Kyap = *dKon-mchog-skyabs.*
Kongjo = *Kong-jo.*
Kongkarnê = *Gong-dkar-nas.*
Kongpo = *Kong-/rKong-po.*
Künga Dorje = *Kun-dga' rdo-rje.*
Künga Nyingpo = *Kun-dga' snying-po.*
Kunggyel = *Gung-rgyal.*
Kingsong Kungtsen = *Gung-srong gung-btsan.*
Kungthang = *Gung-thang.*

Küntu-sangpo = *Kun-tu bzang-po.*
Kurgyi Gömpo = *Gur-gyi mGon-po.*
Kyichu = *sKyi-chu.*
Kyimshang = *Gyim-shang.*
Kyishö = *sKyi(d)-shod.*
Kyo Shakya Yeshe = *sKyo Shākya ye-shes.*
Lab-drönma = *Lab (-kyi) sGron-ma.*
Ladakh = *La-dvags.*
Lang = *Rlangs/Glang/Blang.*
La-ngak = *La-ngag.*
Lang Darma = *Glang Dar-ma.*
Lek = *Legs.*
Lhabu Gokar = *lHa-bu mGo-dkar.*
Lhadem = *lHa-ldem.*
Lha Lama Changchup Ö = *lHa-bla-ma Byang-chub 'od.*
Lha Lama Yeshe Ö = *lHa bla-ma Ye-shes-'od.*
Lhalung = *lHa-lung.*
Lhapsang Khan = *lHa-bzang khan.*
Lhari = *lHa-ri* (?)
Lhatse = *lHa-rtse.*
Lhatsün = *lHa-btsun.*
Lho Ngek = *lHo rNgegs.*
Lhotrak = *lHo-brag.*
Ling = *Gling.*
Lo (-pa) = *Glo-/Klo-pa.*
Lo-ngam = *Lo-ngam.*
Longthang = *Klong-/Glong-thang.*
Löntsen = *Slon-btsan.*
Lopsang Chhökyi Gyentsen = *Blo-bzang chos-kyi rgyal-mtshan.*
Lopsang Pelden Yeshe = *Blo-bzang dpal-ldan ye-shes.*
Lügong-gyelpo = *Glud-gong rgyal-po.*
Ma, Machu = *rMa (-chu).*
Ma Chhökyi Sherap = *rMa Chos-kyi shes-rab.*
Ma-chik = *Ma gcig.*
Makchen Rampa = *dMag-chen ram-pa.*
Mangsong Mangtsen = *Mang-srong mang-btsan.*
Mang-yül = *Mang-yul.*
Mapham, Maphang = *Ma-pham, Ma-phang.*
Mara Serpo = *sMa-ra ser-po.*

Marpa (Golek) = *Mar-pa (mGo-legs).*
Marpo-ri = *dMar-po ri.*
Maryül = *Mar-yul.*
Masang = *Ma-sang.*
Mashang Trilbukhar = *Ma-zhang Dril-bu-mkhar.*
Mashang Trompa-kye = *Ma-zhang Grom-pa-skyes.*
Me Aktsom = *Mes ag-tshom.*
Mel Kawachen = *Mal Ka-ba-can.*
Mila Rêpa = *Mi(d)-la ras-pa.*
Mingyur Dorje = *Mi-'gyur rdo-rje.*
Minyak (Gomring) = *Mi-nyag (sGom-ring).*
Mon = *Mon.*
Mön = *sMon.*
Mong = *Mong.*
Mönpa-thang = *Mon-pa thang.*
mu = *dmu/rmu/smu/mu.*
Münshang = *Mun-shang.*
Musi, Musu = *Mu-zi, Mu-zu.*
Nakshö = *Nags-shod.*
Nam = *Nam/sNam.*
Namdong = *Nam-lDong.*
Namri Löntsen = *gNam-ri Slon-btsan.*
Namri Songtsen = *gNam-ri srong-btsan.*
Namtso = *gNam-mtsho.*
Nanam = *sNa-nam.*
Narthang = *sNar-thang.*
Nêchung = *gNas-chung.*
Nel = *sNel.*
Neudong = *sNe'u-gdong.*
Ngamring = *Ngam-ring.*
Ngamshö = *Ngam-(b)shod.*
Ngari Korsum = *mNga'-ris skor-gsum.*
Ngawang Lopsang Gyatso = *Ngag-dbang blo-bzang rgya-mtsho.*
Ngemda = *dNgul-mda'.*
Ngêpo = *Ngas-po.*
Ngoktön = *rNgog-ston.*
Ngomchu = *Ngom-chu.*
Nön = *mNon.*
Norsang = *Nor-bzang.*

Nyang = *Nyang/Myang*.
Nyangchu = *Nyang-chu*.
Nyang Rel Nyima Öser = *Nyang/Myang Ral Nyi-ma 'od-zer*.
Nyatri (Tsenpo) = *Nya-khri btsan-po*.
Nyenchen Thanglha = *gNyan-chen Thang-lha*.
Nyingma-pa = *rNying-ma-pa*.
Nyö = *gNyos*.
Ode Kunggyel = *'o-lde gung-rgyal*.
Öka = *'ol-kha*.
Ölmo Lungring = *'ol-mo lung-ring*.
Ön = *'on*.
Önshing = *'on-shing*.
Orgyen Lingpa = *O-rgyan gling-pa*.
Ösung = *'od-srung*.
Othang = *'o(-ma) thang*.
Pawo Tsuk = *dPa'-bo gTsug-lag phreng-ba*.
Pehar = *Pe-har/Pe-dkar*, etc.
Pelgyi Dorje = *dPal-gyi rdo-rje*.
Pelkhortsen = *dPal-'khor-btsan*.
Pelpo = *Bal-po*.
Phagmotru-pa = *Phag-mo-gru-pa*.
Phakpa = *'Phags-pa*.
Phen (-yül) = *'Phan (-yul)*.
Phuktön = *Phug-ston*.
Phülso = *Phul-so*.
Phüntsok Namgyel = *Phun-tshogs rnam-rgyal*.
Pö = *Bod*.
Pome = *sPo-smad*.
Pongwa-ri = *Bong-ba ri*.
Powo = *sPo-bo*.
Poyül = *sPo-yul*.
Pude Kunggyel = *sPu-lde gung-rgyal*.
Pungse Sutse = *sPung-zad Zu-tse*.
Purang = *sPu-hrang(s)*.
Putön = *Bu-ston*.
Ramoche = *Ra-mo-che*.
Rêchung = *Ras-chung*.
Relpachen = *Ral-pa-can*.
Reting = *Rva-sgreng*.

Rinchen Sangpo = *Rin-chen bzang-po.*
Rinpung = *Rin-spungs.*
Riwoche = *Ri-bo-che.*
Rok Sherap ö = *Rog Shes-rab 'od.*
Rongtsa = *Rong-tsha.*
Rulak = *Ru-lag.*
Rula-kye = *Ru-la/-las skyes.*
Ruyong = *Ru-yong.*
Saka = *Sa-dga'* (?).
Sakya = *Sa-skya.*
Sakya Panchen = *Sa-skya paṇ-chen.*
Samdruptse = *bSam-'grub-rtse.*
Samten Pelpa = *bSam-gtan dpal-pa.*
Samyê = *bSam-yas.*
Sanggyê Gyatso = *Sangs-rgyas rgya-mtsho.*
Sanggyê the Nephew = *Sangs-rgyas-dbon.*
Sangpo = *bZang-po.*
Sangpo Bumtri = *Sangs-po 'bum-khri.*
Sangshi = *Sang-shi.*
Saya Pechö = *Sa-ya pe-chos.*
Se, Se khyung = *Se, Se-khyung.*
Selnang = *gSal-snang/-gnang.*
Sena Lek = *Sad-na-legs.*
Sera = *Se-ra.*
Serip = *Se-rib.*
Serkhung = *gSer-khung.*
Setsün = *Se-btsun.*
Shalu = *Zha-lu.*
Shampo (Kangtsen) = *Sham-po* (*gangs-btsan*).
Shang = *Shangs.*
Shang-nang = *Zhang-snang.*
Shang Pa-tsap Nyima-trak = *Zhang* (*s*)*Pa-tshap Nyi-ma grags.*
Shang Rinpoche = *Zhang rin-po-che.*
Shangshung = *Zhang-zhung.*
Shatön = *Sha-ston.*
Shatri = *Sha-khri.*
shen = *gshen.*
Shenrap Miwo = *gShen-rab/rabs mi-bo.*
Sherap Ö of Rok = *Rog Shes-rab 'od.*

Shigatse = *gZhis-ka-rtse.*
Shingtri = *Shing-khri.*
Shongthok = *gZhong-thog.*
Shüpu = *Shud-pu.*
Sochung-wa = *So-chung-ba.*
Sok(po) = *Sog-po.*
Sönam Gyatso = *bSod-nams rgya-mtsho.*
Sönam Lama = *bSod-nams bla-ma.*
Song-nge = *Srong-nge.*
Songtsen Gampo = *Srong-btsan sgam-po.*
Sothang = *Zo-thang/-dang.*
Sumpa (Khenpo) = *Sum-pa (mkhan-po).*
Taktsang-pa = *sTag-tshang-pa.*
Ta-kyawo = *sTag-skya-bo.*
Ta-kye = *sTag-skye.*
Talung (thangpa) = *sTag-lung (thang-pa).*
Tampa Gommön = *Dam-pa sGom-smon.*
Tampa Sanggyê = *Dam-pa Sangs-rgyas.*
Tang-re = *Dang-re.*
Tao = *lTa'o/rTa'o.*
Tara Lugong = *Ta-ra/sTag-ra Klu-gong/-khong.*
Tari Nyensik = *sTag-ri gnyan-gzigs.*
Tasik = *Ta-zig/sTag-gzigs.*
Tatsienlu = *Dar-rtse-mdo.*
Tenpê Nyima = *bsTan-pa'i nyi-ma.*
Thangtong (-Gyelpo) = *Thang-stong rgyal-po.*
Thil, Thel = *mThil, Thel.*
Thingge = *mThing-ge.*
Thoding = *mTho-lding.*
Thogar = *Tho-gar/-dkar.*
Thogje Thoktsen = *Thog-rje thog-btsan.*
Thönmi Sambhota = *Thon-/Thu-mi Sambho-ṭa.*
Thothori Nyentsen = *Tho-tho ri gnyan-btsan.*
Thupten Gyatso = *Thub-bstan rgya-mtsho.*
Tise = *Ti-se/Te-se.*
Toling = *Tho-ling/Tho-lding/mTho-lding.*
Tölung = *sTod-lung.*
Tongtsen Yülsung = *sTong-rtsan/-btsan yul-zung.*
Tra = *Gra.*

Trakpa Sengge = *Grags-pa seng-ge.*
Traksum Dingma = *Brag-gsum lding-ma.*
Trena = *sPre-sna.*
Trenka = *Bran-ka.*
Treshö = *Tre-shod.*
Trhagen of Rongtsa = *Rong-tsha Khra-rgan.*
Trhandruk = *Khra-'brug.*
Trhi = *Khri.*
Trhide Songtsen = *Khri-lde srong-btsan.*
Trhide Tsukten = *Khri-lde gtsug-brtan.*
Trhinyen Sungtsen = *Khri-gnyan gzungs-btsan.*
Trhipangsum = *Khri-pangs-sum.*
Trhishö = *Khri-bshos.*
Trhisong Detsen = *Khri-srong lde('u)-btsan.*
Trhi Songtsen = *Khri srong-btsan.*
Trhitsuk Detsen = *Khri-gtsug lde-btsan.*
Trhom = *Khrom, Phrom.*
Trigum = *Gri-gum/khum.*
Tromo Semakhar = *Grogs-mo Ze-ma-mkhar.*
Trubbe = *Grub-be.*
Truk, Trugu = *Drug, Dru/Gru-gu.*
Tsang, Tsangpo = *gTsang (-po).*
Tsangma = *gTsang-ma.*
Tsangpa Tungkhur-wa = *gTsang-pa Dung-khur-ba.*
Tsang-Pö = *rTsang-Bod.*
Tsari = *Tsa-/rTsa-ri.*
Tsen = *bTsan.*
Tsenku Möntore = *Tseng-sku sMon-to-re.*
Tsennya Dombu = *bTsan-snya lDom-bu.*
Tsenthang Goshi = *bTsan-thang sgo-bzhi.*
Tsepa, Tsenma = *rTsad-pa, (Khri) bTsan-ma.*
Tsethang = *rTse-thang.*
Tshangyang Gyatso = *Tshangs-dbyangs rgya-mtsho.*
Tsharong = *Tsha(-ba) rong.*
Tshawa (-rong) = *Tsha-ba rong.*
Tshel (pa) (Kungthang) = *Tshal (-pa) Gung-thang.*
Tshemi = *Tshe-mi.*
Tshepel Namgyel = *Tshe-dpal rnam-rgyal.*
Tshepong = *Tshe-spong.*

302

PRECISE TRANSLITERATIONS

Tshering Wangdü = *Tshe-ring dbang-'dus.*
Tshur Lhalung = *mTshur lHa-lung.*
Tshurphu = *mTshur-phu.*
Tsona = *mTsho-sna.*
Tsongkha (-pa) = *Tsong-kha (-pa).*
Tungkyong Karmo = *Dung-skyong (-khyung) dkar-mo.*
Tüsong = *Dus-srong.*
Tüsum Khyenpa = *Dus-gsum mkhyen-pa.*
Ü = *dBus.*
Urgyen = *U-rgyan.*
Wa = *dBa'.*
Yamdrok = *Yar-'brog.*
Yarlha Shampo = *Yar-lha Sham-po.*
Yarlung = *Yar-klung.*
Yarmothang = *gYar-mo/dByar-mo thang.*
Yashur = *Ya-bzhur.*
Yasi Pöntön = *Ya-zi Bon-ston.*
Yatse = *Ya-tshe.*
Yekhyen = *Ye-mkhyen.*
Yemön = *Ye-smon.*
Yeshe Gömpo = *Ye-shes mGon-po.*
Yeshe Ö = *Ye-shes 'od.*
Yeshe Wangpo = *Ye-shes dbang-po.*
Yikyi Dangcham = *Yid-kyi gdang-pyam.*
Yönten Gyatso = *Yon-tan rgya-mtsho.*
Yumbu Lagang, Lakhar = *Yum-bu bla-sgang, bla-mkhar.*
Yum Ngösung = *Yum-ngos-srung.*
Yumten = *Yum-brtan.*
Yuna = *Yu-sna.*

Bibliography

꧙

I *Works by Modern Authors*

1. ZAHIRUDDIN AHMAD, *Sino-Tibetan Relations in the Seventeenth Century*, Rome, 1970.
1A. J. BACOT (ed. and tr.), 'La table des présages signifiés par l'éclair' (*Journal Asiatique*, March–April 1913).
2. J. BACOT, *Three Tibetan mysteries*, London, 1924 (tr. from the French by H. I. Woolf).
3. J. BACOT, *Le poète tibétain Milarépa*, Paris, 1925.
4. J. BACOT, 'Le mariage chinois du roi tibétain Sron bcan sgan po' (*Mélanges chinoises et bouddhiques*, III, 1934–1935).
5. J. BACOT, *La vie de Marpa le 'traducteur'*, Paris, 1937.
6. J. BACOT, F. W. THOMAS AND CH. TOUSSAINT, *Documents de Touen-houang relatifs à l'histoire du Tibet,* Paris, 1940–1946.
7. SIR CHARLES BELL, *The People of Tibet*, Oxford, 1928.
8. SIR CHARLES BELL, *The Religion of Tibet*, Oxford, 1931.
9. R. BLEICHSTEINER, *Die gelbe Kirche*, Vienna, 1937.
9A. A. M. BLONDEAU, 'Les pélerinages' (*Sources Orientales*, III, Paris, 1960).
10. W. L. CAMPBELL (ed. and tr)., *She-Rab Dong-Bu or Prajnya Danda, by Lu-Trub (Nagarjuna)*, Calcutta, 1919.
11. W. L. CAMPBELL, 'Die Sprüche von Sakya' (*Ostasiatische Zeitschrift*, n.s., 2, 1925).
12. P. CARRASCO, *Land and Polity in Tibet*, Seattle, 1959.
12A. C. W. CASSINELLI and R. B. EKVALL, *A Tibetan Principality. The political system of Sa sKya* (Ithaca, New York, 1969).
13. G. A. COMBE, *A Tibetan on Tibet*, London, 1926.
14. S. C. DAS, *Indian Pandits in the Land of Snow*, Calcutta, 1893.
15. S. C. DAS, 'Life of Atíśa' (*Journ. As. Soc. Bengal*, LX, Pt. I, 2, 1891).

BIBLIOGRAPHY

16. S. C. DAS, 'Marriage Customs of Tibet' (*ibid.*, LXII, Pt. III, 1893).
17. S. C. DAS, *Journey to Lhasa and Central Tibet*, London, 1902.
18. S. B. DASGUPTA, *An Introduction to Tāntric Buddhism*, Calcutta, 1950.
19. A. DAVID-NEEL, *With Mystics and Magicians in Tibet*, London, 1931; as *Magic and Mystery in Tibet*, republished, London, 1967.
20. A. DAVID-NEEL, *The Superhuman Life of Gesar of Ling*, London, 1959.
21. A. DAVID-NEEL, *Textes tibétains inédits*, Paris, 1952.
21A. A. DAVID-NEEL, *Initiations and initiates in Tibet*, London, 1931.
22. J. W. DE JONG, 'Le problème de l'absolu dans l'école Mādhyamika' (*Revue Philosophique*, July–September, 1950).
23. P. DEMIÉVILLE, *Le Concile de Lhasa*, I, Paris, 1952.
24. M. H. DUNCAN (tr.), *Harvest Festival Dramas of Tibet*, Hongkong, 1955.
24A. M. H. DUNCAN, *More Harvest Festival Dramas of Tibet*, London, 1967.
24B. M. H. DUNCAN, *Love Songs and Proverbs of Tibet*, Alexandria, n.d.
25. W. EBERHARD, *Kultur und Siedlung der Randvölker Chinas*, Leiden, 1942.
26. R. B. EKVALL, *Tibetan Sky Lines*, London, 1952.
27. R. B. EKVALL, *Tents Against the Sky*, London, 1954.
28. R. B. EKVALL, 'Some differences in Tibetan land tenure and utilization' (*Sinologica*, IV, 1, 1954).
29. R. B. EKVALL, 'Mi sTong, the Tibetan custom of life indemnity' (*Sociologus*, n.s., IV, 2, Berlin, 1954).
30. W. Y. EVANS-WENTZ, *Tibet's Great Yogī Milarepa*, 2nd edn., London, 1951.
31. W. Y. EVANS-WENTZ, *The Tibetan Book of the Great Liberation*, London, 1954.
32. W. Y. EVANS-WENTZ, *The Tibetan Book of the Dead*, 3rd edn., London, 1957.
33. A. FERRARI and L. PETECH, *mK'yen brtse's Guide to the Holy Places of Central Tibet*, Rome, 1958.

BIBLIOGRAPHY

34. W. FILCHNER (and UNKRIG), *Kumbum Dschamba Ling. Das Kloster der hunderttausend Bilder Maitreyas*, Leipzig, 1933.
35. A. H. FRANCKE, *A History of Western Tibet*, London, 1907.
36. A. H. FRANCKE, *Tibetische Hochzeitslieder*, Hagen and Darmstadt, 1923 (Tibetan text, *rTags-ma-gcig gi nyo-glu*, Leh, 1904).
37. A. H. FRANCKE (ed. and tr.), 'gZer Myig, a book of the Tibetan Bonpos' (*Asia Major*, I, 1924. N.s., I, 1949).
38. A. GETTY, *The Gods of Northern Buddhism*, Oxford, 1928 (2nd edn.).
39. H. GOETZ, 'The historical background of the great temples of Khajurāho' (*Arts Asiatiques*, V, 1, 1958).
39A. M. C. GOLDSTEIN, 'Study of the *Ldab-Ldob*' (*Central Asian Journal*, IX, 1964, pp. 123–41).
40. A. K. GORDON, *Tibetan Religious Art*, New York, 1952.
41. A. K. GORDON, *The Iconography of Tibetan Lamaism*, 2nd edn., Rutland (Vermont) and Tokyo, 1959.
42. A. GOVINDA, *Foundations of Tibetan Mysticism According to the Esoteric Teachings of the Great Mantra Oṁ Maṇi Padme Hūṁ*, London, 1959.
43. F. GRENARD, *Le Tibet, le pays et les habitants*, Paris, 1904.
44. A. GRÜNWEDEL, *Mythologie des Buddhismus in Tibet und der Mongolei*, Leipzig, 1900.
45. A. GRÜNWEDEL, 'Padmasambhava und Verwandtes' (*Baessler-Archiv*, III, 1, Berlin, 1914).
46. A. GRÜNWEDEL, 'Der Weg nach Śambhala', Munich, 1915 (*Abh. Kgl. Bayer. Akad. d. Wiss.*).
47. A. GRÜNWEDEL, 'Die Geschichten der 84 Zauberer (Mahāsiddhas)' (*Baessler-Archiv*, V, 4–5, Leipzig, 1916).
48. H. V. GUENTHER (tr.), *The Jewel Ornament of Liberation*, London, 1959.
48A. H. V. GUENTHER, *The Life and Teaching of Nāropa*, London, 1963.
48B. H. V. GUENTHER, *Tibetan Buddhism without Mystification*, Leiden, 1966.
48C. H. V. GUENTHER, *The Royal Song of Saraha*, Seattle, 1968.
49. J. HACKIN, 'The mythology of Lamaism' (*Asiatic Mythology*, London, 1932, pp. 147–186).

BIBLIOGRAPHY

50. H. HADANO, 'The influence of the Buddhism of Khams on the bKaḥ-gdams-pa sect' (in Japanese, *Bunka*, XX, 4, July, 1956).
51. H. HARRER, *Meine Tibet-Bilder*, Seebruck, 1953.
52. M. HERMANNS, 'Überlieferungen der Tibeter' (*Monumenta Serica*, XIII, 1948).
53. M. HERMANNS, 'Schöpfungs- und Abstammungsmythen der Tibeter' (*Anthropos*, XLI-XLIV, 1946–1949).
54. M. HERMANNS, *Die Nomaden von Tibet*, Vienna, 1949.
54A. M. HERMANNS, *The Indo-Tibetans*, Bombay, 1954.
55. M. HERMANNS, *Die Familie der Amdo-Tibeter*, Freiburg/ Munich, 1959.
56. H. HOFFMANN, *Quellen zur Geschichte der tibetischen Bon- Religion*, Mainz, Wiesbaden, 1950.
57. H. HOFFMANN, *The Religions of Tibet*, London, 1961.
57A. H. HOFFMANN, *Märchen aus Tibet*, Cologne, 1965.
58. S. HUMMEL, *Geschichte der tibetischen Kunst*, Leipzig, 1953.
59. S. HUMMEL, Eurasiatische Traditionen in der tibetischen Bon-Religion (*Opuscula ethnologica memoriae L. Biro sacra*, 1959).
60. *K'ang-tao yüeh-k'an*, Chinese periodical published in Sikang.
61. E. KAWAGUCHI, *Three Years in Tibet*, Madras, 1909.
62. KO CH'IH FÊNG, *Tsang-pien ts'ai-fêng chi*, Chungking, 1945.
63. M. LALOU, *Inventaire des manuscrits tibétains de Touen- houang conservés à la Bibliothèque Nationale*, I–III, Paris, 1939, 1950, 1961.
64. M. LALOU, 'Rituel Bon-po des funérailles royales' (*Journal Asiatique*, 1952).
65. M. LALOU, 'Fiefs, poisons et guérisseurs' (*ibid.*, 1958).
65A. M. LALOU, *Les Religions du Tibet*, Paris, 1957.
66. B. LAUFER, 'Über ein tibetisches Geschichtswerk der Bonpo' (*T'oung Pao*, II, 1, 1901).
67. B. LAUFER, 'Die Bru-ža Sprache und die historische Stellung des Padmasambhava' (*ibid.*, IX, 1908).
68. B. LAUFER, *Der Roman einer tibetischen Königin (bTsun-mo bka'-thang)*, Leipzig, 1911.
69. B. LAUFER, *Milaraspa, Tibetische Texte*, Hagen and Darmstadt, 1922.

BIBLIOGRAPHY

70. L. DE LA VALLÉE POUSSIN, 'Madhyamaka' (*Mélanges Chinoises et Bouddhiques*, II, 1933).

71. F. LESSING, 'Aufbau und Sinn lamaistischer Kulthandlungen' (*Nachrichten d. Deut. Ges. f. Natur u. Völkerk. Ostasiens*, Tokyo, No. 40, 1936).

72. F. LESSING, 'Wesen und Sinn des lamaistischen Rituals' (*Hyllningsskrift tillägnad Sven Hedin*, Stockholm, 1935).

72A. F. LESSING, 'Yung-Ho-Kung, An Iconography of the Lamaist Cathedral in Peking, with notes on Lamaist Mythology and cult' (*Report of the Sino-Swedish Expedition*, VIII, 1, Stockholm, 1942).

72B. F. LESSING, 'The Thirteen Visions of a Yogācārya' (*Ethnos*, 3-4, Stockholm, 1950).

72C. F. LESSING, and A. WAYMAN (tr.), *mKhas grub rje's Fundamentals of the Buddhist Tantras*, The Hague, 1968.

73. S. LÉVI, *Matériaux pour l'etude du système Vijñaptimātra*, Paris, 1932.

74. LI AN-CHE, 'The Sakya sect of Lamaism' (*Journal of the West China Border Research Society*, XVI, A, 1945).

75. LI AN-CHE, 'Rñiṅ-ma-pa: the early form of Lamaism' (*Journal of the Royal Asiatic Society*, 1948).

76. LI AN-CHE, 'The Bkah-Brgyud sect of Lamaism' (*Journal of the American Oriental Society*, 69, 2, 1949).

77. LI FANG-KUEI, 'The inscription of the Sino-Tibetan treaty of 821-822' (*T'oung Pao*, XLIV, 1).

78. LIU I-SZŬ, *Hsi-tsang fo-chiao i-shu*, Peking, 1957.

78A. A. D. MACDONALD, 'Préamble à la lecture d'un rGya Bod yig chan' (*Journal Asiatique*, 1963).

78B. A. D. MACDONALD, 'Note sur la diffusion de la "Theorie des Quatre Fils du Ciel" au Tibet' (*Journal Asiatique*, 1962).

78C. A. W. MACDONALD, *Matériaux pour l'étude de la littérature populaire tibétaine*, Paris, 1967.

79. D. MACDONALD, *Moeurs et Coutumes des Tibétains*, Paris, 1930.

79A. D. MACDONALD, *The Land of the Lama*, London, 1929.

80. D. MACDONALD, 'Tibetan Tales' (*Folklore*, vol. 42, 1931).

81. O. MONOD-BRUHL, *Peintures tibétaines*, Paris, 1954.

82. G. M. NAGAO, *Mōko gakumon-ji*, Kyoto, 1937.

BIBLIOGRAPHY

83. G. M. NAGAO, *A Study of Tibetan Buddhism being a translation into Japanese of the exposition of Vipaśyanā in Tsoṅ-kha-pa's Lam-rim-chen-mo with annotation and prefatory remarks* (in Japanese, with English summary), Tokyo, 1954.

84. R. de NEBESKY-WOJKOWITZ, *Oracles and Demons of Tibet*, London/The Hague, 1956.

85. E. OBERMILLER (ed. and tr.), *History of Buddhism by Bu-ston*, 2 vols., Heidelberg, 1931-1932.

85A. P. PELLIOT, *Histoire ancienne du Tibet*, Paris, 1961.

86. L. PETECH, *A Study on the Chronicles of Ladakh*, Calcutta, 1939.

87. L. PETECH, *China and Tibet in the Early 18th Century*, Leiden, 1950.

88. L. PETECH, *I missionari italiani nel Tibet e nel Nepal*, 7 vols., Rome, 1952-1956.

89. P. RATCHNEVSKY, 'Die mongolischen Grosskhane und die Buddhistische Kirche' (*Asiatica*, Festschrift Weller).

90. H. G. RAVERTY, 'Tibbat three hundred and sixty-five years ago' (*Journ. As. Soc. Bengal*, LXIV, I, 1896).

91. S. H. RIBBACH, *Drogpa Namgyal, ein Tibeterleben*, Munich. 1940.

92. H. E. RICHARDSON, 'Three ancient inscriptions from Tibet' (*Journ. Roy. As. Soc. Bengal*, letters, XV, 1, 1949).

93. H. E. RICHARDSON, *Ancient Historical Edicts at Lhasa*, London, 1952.

94. H. E. RICHARDSON, 'Tibetan Inscriptions at Žva-ḥi Lha Khaṅ' (*Journal of the Royal Asiatic Society*, Oct. 1952, April 1953).

95. H. E. RICHARDSON, 'The Karma-pa sect' (*ibid.*, Oct. 1958, April 1959).

95A. H. E. RICHARDSON, 'Early burial grounds in Tibet and Tibetan decorative art of the VIIIth and IXth centuries' (*Central Asiatic Journal*, VIII, 2, 1963).

96. W. W. ROCKHILL, 'Tibet. A geographical, ethnographical and historical sketch, derived from Chinese sources', (*Journal of the Royal Asiatic Society*, 1891). Reprinted Peking, 1939.

97. W. W. ROCKHILL, 'The Dalai Lamas of Lhasa and their relations with the Manchu Emperors of China 1644-1908' (*T'oung Pao*, XI, 1910).

BIBLIOGRAPHY

98. G. N. ROERICH, 'The Animal Style among the nomad tribes of northern Tibet' (*Skythika*, 3, Prague, 1930).
99. G. N. ROERICH (tr.), *The Blue Annals*, 2 vols., Calcutta, 1949, 1953.
100. G. N. ROERICH, *Le Parler de l'Amdo*, Rome, 1958.
101. A. RÓNA-TAS, 'Social terms in the list of grants of the Tibetan Tun-huang Chronicle' (*Acta Orientalia Hungarica*, V, 3, 1955).
101A. D. S. RUEGG, *The Life of Bu-ston Rin-po-che*, Rome, 1966.
102. G. SANDBERG, *Tibet and the Tibetans*, London, 1906.
103. R. SÂṄKṚTYÂYANA, 'Recherches bouddhiques. I: Les Origines du Mahâyâna; II: L'Origine du Vajrayâna et les 84 siddhas' (*Journal Asiatique*, Oct.–Dec., 1934).
104. T. SCHMID, *The Cotton-clad Mila: the Tibetan Poet-saint's Life in Pictures*, Stockholm, 1952.
105. T. SCHMID, *The Eighty-five Siddhas*, Stockholm, 1958.
106. G. SCHULEMANN, *Geschichte der Dalai-Lamas*, 2nd edn., Leipzig, 1958.
106A. W. D. SHAKABPA, *Tibet—a Political History*, New Haven and London, 1967.
107. A. L. SHELTON, *Tibetan Folk-tales*, Saint-Louis, 1925.
108. T.-L. SHEN and S.-C. LIU, *Tibet and the Tibetans*, Stanford, 1953.
108A. M. SINGH, *Himalayan Art*, London, 1968 (UNESCO).
109. D. L. SNELLGROVE, *Buddhist Himālaya*, Oxford, 1957.
110. D. L. SNELLGROVE (ed. and tr.), *The Hevajra tantra*, 2 vols., London, 1959.
110A. D. L. SNELLGROVE, *Four Lamas of Dolpo*, Oxford, 1967.
110B. D. L. SNELLGROVE, *The Nine Ways of Bon*, London, 1967.
110C. D. L. SNELLGROVE and H. E. RICHARDSON, *A Cultural History of Tibet*, London and New York, 1968.
111. R. A. STEIN, *L'épopée tibétaine de Gesar dans sa version lamaïque de Ling*, Paris, 1956 (Annales du Musée Guimet, Bibl. d'Ét., LXI).
112. R. A. STEIN, 'Peintures tibétaines de la vie de Gesar' (*Arts Asiatiques*, V, 4, 1958).
113. R. A. STEIN, 'Le Linga des danses masquées lamaïques et la théorie des âmes' (*Sino-Indian Studies*, V, 3–4, 1957).
114. R. A. STEIN, *Recherches sur l'épopée et le barde au Tibet*, Paris, 1959.

BIBLIOGRAPHY

115. R. A. STEIN, 'Les tribus anciennes des marches sino-tibétaines' (*Mélanges publiés par l'Institut des Hautes Études chinoises*, Paris, 1961).

115A. R. A. STEIN, 'Une source ancienne pour l'histoire de l'épopée tibétaine', (*Journal Asiatique*, 1962).

115B. R. A. STEIN, 'Un saint poète tibétain' (*Mercure de France*, July–August, 1964).

116. H. STÜBEL, *The Mewu Fantzu, a Tibetan Tribe of Kansu*, New Haven, 1958.

117. F. W. THOMAS, *Tibetan Literary Texts and Documents concerning Chinese Turkestan*, I–IV, London, 1935–1963.

118. F. W. THOMAS, *Ancient Folk-Literature from North-Eastern Tibet*, Berlin, 1957.

119. G.-C. TOUSSAINT (tr.), *Le Dict de Padma* (*padma thang yig*), Paris, 1933.

120. G. TUCCI, *Indo-Tibetica*, 7 vols., Rome, 1932–1941.

121. G. TUCCI, *Tibetan Painted Scrolls*, 3 vols., Rome, 1949.

122. G. TUCCI, *The Tombs of the Tibetan Kings*, Rome, 1950.

123. G. TUCCI, 'On the validity of the Tibetan historical tradition' (*India Antiqua*, 1947).

124. G. TUCCI, *Tibetan Folk Songs from Gyantse and Western Tibet*, 2nd edn., with 2 appendices by Prof. Namkhai Norbu, Ascona, 1966.

125. G. TUCCI, *To Lhasa and Beyond. Diary of the expedition to Tibet in 1948*, Rome, 1956 (tr. M. Carelli).

126. G. TUCCI, *Preliminary Report on Two Scientific Expeditions in Nepal*, Rome, 1956.

126A. G. TUCCI, *Tibet: Land of Snows*, London, 1967.

126B. G. TUCCI, 'Die Religionen Tibets' (*Die Religionen Tibets und der Mongolei*, Stuttgart, 1970).

127. G. URAY, 'The Four Horns of Tibet according to the Royal Annals' (*Acta Orientalia Hungarica*, X, 1, 1960).

128. L. A. WADDELL, *The Buddhism of Tibet, or Lamaism*, London, 1895 (2nd edn., Cambridge, 1934).

129. L. A. WADDELL, *Lhasa and its Mysteries*, London, 1906.

129A. T. WYLIE, *The Geography of Tibet according to the 'Dzam-gling rgyas-bshad*, Rome, 1962.

130. YU DAWCHYUAN, *Love-songs of the Sixth Dalai Lama Tshangs-dbyangs-rgya-mtsho* (Chinese and English translations, text, notes) Academia Sinica, Peiping, 1930.

312

BIBLIOGRAPHY

II *Tibetan Sources*

(Tibetan names and words are in 'strict' transliteration, whether italicized or not)

131. *Autobiography of 'Brug-pa Kun-legs*, xylograph (xyl.) edn., 2 vols., sixteenth century.
132. *Biographies of the Karma-pas*, xyl., 236 ff. Written in 1891 at mTshur-phu.
133. *Biography of Mar-pa*, spung-thang edn., xyl., 104 ff. By gTsang-smyon He-ru-ka (late fifteenth century).
134. *Biography of Mi-la Ras-pa*, Peking edn., xyl., 342 ff. Same author as No. 133 (ed. de. Jong, The Hague, 1959).
134A. *Songs of Mi-la Ras-pa (mGur-'bum)*, Peking edn.
135. *Biography of Thang-stong rgyal-po*, xyl., 174 ff. sDe-dge edn. Written in 1609 or 1588.
135A. *Biography of the Physician gYu-thog the Elder*, xyl., 141 ff., sDe-dge edn.
136. *Biography of the IIIrd Panchen Lama*, xyl., 376 ff.
137. *bKa'-brgyud mgur-mtsho*, xyl., 96 ff., nineteenth century.
137A. *bKa'-brgyud bla-ma-rnams-kyi rdo-rje'i mgur-dbyangs*, xyl., 92 ff., eighteenth century.
138. *bKa' rDzogs-pa chen-po yang-zab dkon-mchog spyi-'dus*, xyl., 102 ff., Sikkim edn.
139. *Blon-po bka'-thang (bKa'-thang sde-lnga)*, xyl., 281 ff., sDe-dge edn., vol. *Kha*. Discovered 1347.
140. *Chronicle of Bu-ston*, xyl., 203 ff., sDe-dge edn. Written 1322.
141. *Chronicle of the Fifth Dalai Lama*, xyl., 113 ff. Written 1643.
142. *Chronicle of dPa'-bo gTsug-lag phreng-ba*, xyl., Lho-brag. Written 1545–1565.
143. *Chronicle of Padma dkar-po*, xyl., 189 ff. spungs-thang edn. sixteenth century.
144. *Dag-yig mkhas-pa'i 'byung-gnas*, by lCang-skya Rol-pa'i rdo-rje (1717–1786). Peking edn.
145. *Dag-yig Thon-mi'i dgongs-rgyan*, by Tshe-tan zhabs-drung (*Han-Tsang tz'u-hui*), 2 vols., Tsinghai, 1957.
146. *Dam-pa'i chos-kyi 'byung-tshul*, xyl., 228 ff. sDe-dge edn.: Pt. 1, ff. 1–128, sixteenth century; Pt. 2, eighteenth century.
147. *Deb-ther dkar-po*, xyl., by *dge-bshes* dGe-'dun chos-'phel (d. 1947).

313

BIBLIOGRAPHY

148. *Deb-ther sngon-po*, xyl., 486 ff. By gZhon-nu-dpal of 'Gos; written 1476–1478. Translated by Roerich, see No. 99 above.
149. *Dictionary of dge-bshes Chos-grags: brDa-dag ming-tshig gsal-ba*, Lhasa, 1949. Chinese edn. (*Tsang-wên tz'ŭ-tien*), Peking, 1957.
150. *dKar-chag of the Co-ne bsTan-'gjur*, Bla-brang edn. Written 1773.
151. *dPag-bsam ljon-bzang*, xyl., 316 ff. Ed. S. C. Das, Calcutta, 1908. Written in 1748 by Sum-pa mkhan-po Ye-shes dpal-'byor.
152. *Epic of Ge-sar* (*Ge-sar sgrung*).
152A. *Epic of Ge-sar*, Bacot MS.
152B. *Epic of Ge-sar*, Gling xyl. (ed. R. A. Stein, see No. 111).
152C. *Epic of Ge-sar*, rGyal-rtse (Gyantse) xyl.
153. *Genealogy of the Kings of sDe-dge*, xyl., 56 ff. sDe-dge edn. Written 1828.
154. *Genealogy of Hor dKar-mDzes*, xyl., 40 ff. Written 1849.
155. *gCod-dbang mdor bsdus rin-po-che'i phreng-ba*, xyl., 15 ff.
156. *gNam-chos*. Works of Mi-'gyur rdo-rje, late seventeenth century. dPal-yul edn. Vol. *Mā*: his biography.
157. *Grub-mtha' thams-cad kyi khungs . . . shel-gyi me-long*, xyl., 164 ff. sDe-dge edn. By the Third Thu'u-bkvan (1737–1802).
158. *gTam-thos* (*Yang-zab nam-mkha' mdzod-chen las/ gTam-thos rin-chen phreng-ba*), xyl., 50 ff. Bonpo work by Nyag-btsun Sa-trig.
159. *gTam-tshogs* (*gTam-gyi tshogs theg-pa'i rgya-mtsho*) xyl., 271 ff. By Rang-byung rdo-rje, eighteenth century.
160. *Guide to Lha-sa* (*lHa-ldan sprul-pa'i gtsug-lag-khang gi dkar-chag*), xyl., 21 ff. By the Fifth Dalai Lama, 1645.
161. *'Jig-rten-lugs kyi bstan-bcos*. Chap. IV ed. in S. C. Das, *Leg-Dui-Na-Na*, Calcutta, 1890.
162. *Klong-rdol bla-ma Ngag-dbang blo-bzang* (1719–1805): Works (*gsung-'bum*).
163. *Klu-'bum* (*Bon rin-po-che 'phrul-dag bden-pa gtsang-ma Klu 'bum*), Peking edn., 152 ff.; sDe-dge edn., 459 ff.
164. *Legs-par bshad-pa rin-po-che'i gter-gyi 'grel-pa*, xyl., 97 ff. By Rin-chen-dpal.
165. *lHa-'dre bka'-thang* (see No. 139).

BIBLIOGRAPHY

166. *Lo-paṇ bka'-thang* (see No. 139).
167. *Ma-ṇi bka'-'bum*, xyl., 2 vols. (*E, Waṁ*), 324 and 269 ff. sDe-dge edn. Discovered late twelfth century.
168. *Nam-mkha'i rnal-'byor Gar-gyi dbang-po yi 'khrul-snang rol-bar shar-ba'i rdzun-chos las/ rJe-btsun Seng-ldeng-nags-sGrol sgrub-pa'i thabs*, xyl., 33 ff.
169. *Nam-mkha' sgo-'byed kyi dbang gi bshad-pa'i zin-bris*, xyl., 4 ff. Peking edn. By Klong-rdol bla-ma, eighteenth century.
170. *Padma thang-yig*, xyl., 220 ff. sDe-dge edn. Discovered 1352. For translation see No. 119.
171. *Pha-chos bu-chos* (*bKa'-gdams pha-chos bu-chos*), xyl., 2 vols., 361 and 432 ff. sNar-thang edn. Tradition of 'Brom-ston, eleventh century.
172. *Phya-'phrin nor-bu-mchog-rgyal-gyi chog-'khrigs dGos-'dod kun-'byung*, xyl., 30 ff. By Padma 'Phrin-las, seventeenth century.
173. *Prayers of Mipham*, vol. *Na* of the works of Mi-pham ('Jam-dpal dgyes-pa'i rdo-rje, 1846–1912). sDe-dge edn.
174. *Prophecy of Khotan, Li'i yul lung-bstan-pa*, followed by *Li-yul gyi lo-rgyus*. bsTan-'gyur. For translation see No. 117.
175. *rGya-Bod yig-tshang*, MS copy.
176. *rGyal-brngan lha-bsangs*, xyl., 49 ff. Anonymous.
177. *rGyal-po bka'-thang* (see No. 139).
178. *rGyal-rabs Bon-gyi 'byung-gnas*, ed. S. C. Das, Calcutta, 1915. Fifteenth century.
179. *rGyal-rabs-rnams-kyi 'byung-tshul gsal-ba'i me-long*, xyl., 104 ff., sDe-dge edn. By bSod-nams rgyal-mtshan, 1508.
180. *Rlangs-kyi gdung-brgyud Po-ti bse-ru*, MS copy.
181. *rNa-ba'i bcud-len*, xyl., 110 ff. By Sangs rgyas rgya-mtsho, 1696.
182. *Sa-bdag bshags-'bum*, xyl., 17 ff. Anonymous.
183. *sBa-bzhed*, MS (ed. Stein, Institut des Hautes Études Chinoises, Sorbonne, Paris, 1961).
184. *sBas-yul Padma-bkod-pa'i gnas-yig*, MS, anonymous.
185. *sDig-bshags gser-gyi spu-gri*, xyl., 15 ff. Jo-khang edn.
186. *Srid-pa rgyud kyi(s) kha-dbyangs* (*bka'-byang*) *rnam(s)-thar chen-mo*, MS copy, Bibliotheque Nationale, No. 493, 199 ff. Bon-po chronicle.

BIBLIOGRAPHY

187. *Vaiḍūrya dkar-po*, xyl., 2 vols., 314 and 321 ff. sDe-dge edn. By Sangs-rgyas rgya-mtsho; 1669, 1683 or 1687.

III *Chinese Sources*

(The Wade-Giles romanization is used)

188. *Fo-tsu li-tai t'ung-tai* (Taishō, No. 2036). By Nien-ch'ang, 1341.
189. *K'ang-yu chi-hsing* (Chung-fu-t'ang ch'üan-chi edn.). By Yao Jung (observations made 1844–1846).
190. *Li-t'ang chih-lüeh*, MS. By Ch'ên Ch'iu-p'ing, nineteenth century.
191. *Lung-chin fêng-sui p'an* (Hsüeh-chin t'ao-yüan edn.). By Chang Tsu, *ca.* 700.
191A. *Man-shu.* By Fan Cho. *ca.* 860. Chê-hsi-ts'un shê edn.
192. *Ming-shih-lu*, excerpts concerning Tibet, ed. J. Tamura and H. Sato, *Meidai Seizō shiryō*, Kyoto, 1959.
193. *Hsi-tsang k'ao* (Huo-ts'an ts'ung-shu edn.). Anon., Ch'ing dynasty.
194. *Hsi-tsang chi* (Lung-wei pi-shu edn., *chi* 9). Anon., eighteenth century.
195. *Hsi-tsang la-ma shuo-yüan* (*Hsü Tsang-ching* edn., *pien* B, *chi 1*, *t'ao* 23). By Shou-i, soon after 1803.
196. *Hsi-tsang hsin-chih*, Shanghai, 1911. By Hsü Kuang-shih and Ts'ai Chin-ch'êng.
197A. *T'ang-shu* (*Chiu* – –), chap. CXCVI A, 941–945. T'u-shu chi-ch'êng edn.
197B. *T'ang-shu* (*Hsin* – –), chap. CCXVI A, 1045–1060. Same edn. as 197A.
198. *Chu-kuo chi-yu.* By Chou Ai-lien; preface dated 1804. 1913 edn.
199. *T'ung-chih*, chap. CXCV. *ca.* 1160. Hung-pao shu-chü edn., Shanghai.
200. *T'ung-tien*, chap. CXC, 766–801. Same edition.
201. *Tzŭ-chih t'ung-chien*, 1085. Shih-chieh shu-chü edn.
202. *Ts'ê-fu yüan-kuei*, 1013.
203. *Wei-tsang t'u-shih.* By Ma Ko and Shêng Shêng-tsu, 1792.
204. *Yu-yang tsa-tsu.* By Tuan Ch'êng-shih. *ca.* 860.

Index

317

INDEX

INDEX

INDEX